Marriage *and* Death Notices

from

Baptist Newspapers

of

South Carolina

VOLUME 2: 1866–1887

By

Brent H. Holcomb

SCMAR
1996

HERITAGE BOOKS
2021

HERITAGE BOOKS

AN IMPRINT OF HERITAGE BOOKS, INC.

Books, CDs, and more—Worldwide

For our listing of thousands of titles see our website
at
www.HeritageBooks.com

Published 2021 by
HERITAGE BOOKS, INC.
Publishing Division
5810 Ruatan Street
Berwyn Heights, Md. 20740

Copyright © 1996 Brent H. Holcomb
SCMAR
Columbia, South Carolina

Library of Congress Catalog Card Number: 96-68735

International Standard Book Number
Paperbound: 978-0-7884-1200-4

INTRODUCTION

Since compiling my first volumes of notices from the Baptist newspapers of South Carolina in 1980, I have realized the need for later notices. Indeed as we move ever nearer the twenty-first century, nineteenth century records become more important. In the difficult post-war years many persons could not afford to erect tombstones or erected only wooden stones which have long since weathered away. For some of them, the obituary notices may be the only record of their deaths. Marriage notices are especially important in South Carolina, where there was no state-wide marriage license law until July 1, 1911.

The notices included in this volume are from *The South Carolina Baptist* (1866-1868) published at Anderson, *The Working Christian* (1869-1878) published first in Yorkville and later (beginning 19 May 1870) in Charleston, and *The Baptist Courier* (1878-1887). The notices are from all over South Carolina, as we would expect. However, the lion's share at times seems to concern the Barnwell County area.

My appreciation goes to Mrs. Carolyn Lancaster of the Baptist Historical Collection at Furman University in Greenville, South Carolina, for making the microfilm copies of these newspapers available to me and for securing copies of notices from the original newspapers where the microfilm was illegible.

Brent Howard Holcomb
June 14, 1996

MARRIAGE AND DEATH NOTICES FROM BAPTIST NEWSPAPERS OF SOUTH CAROLINA 1866-1887

THE SOUTH CAROLINA BAPTIST

Issue of May 4, 1866

Died at her residence in Anderson Dist., on the 5th of March 1866, Mrs. Mary K. Mattison, wife of Capt. James Mattison dec'd, and daughter of Charles and Kizziah Stark, dec'd of Abbeville Dist. The dec'd was gathered home at a good old age, having attained her fifty-eighth year. She was the child of pious parents and at an early period of life devoted herself to the service of her Redeemer, and united with the Baptist Church of Christ, at Rocky River, of which she lived a consistent member for over thirty years... Her remains were deposited in the family grave yard, on the 6th of March. April 5th 1866.

Issue of June 8, 1866

Married on the 3rd instant, at Williamston, by Rev. W. P. Martin, Mr. James Franklin Allen to Miss Henrietta Jane Gurley, all of this District.

On the 31st ult., by Rev. W. E. Walters, at the residence of the bride's father in Greenville District, Miss Fannie L. Charles to Dr. O. R. Horton, of Abbeville District. Greenville and Abbeville papers please copy.

By the Rev. B. F. Mauldin, on 31st ultimo, Mr. B. B. Brezeale and Mrs. Rachel L. Anderson, all of this District.

Issue of July 20, 1866

Married on Tuesday morning, 17th instant, by Rev. W. E. Walters, Col. Chas. S. Mattison to Mrs. Mary J. Brown, all of this District.

Issue of August 3, 1866

Married on the 26th ult., at the residence of James Gambrell, by the Rev. W. P. Martin, Mr. David Coleman to Miss Margaret Nabors, all of Abbeville District.

On Tuesday evening, 31st ult., by the same, Mr. Richard S. Owens to Miss Emma Crymes, all of this District.

Issue of August 31, 1866

Died of Intussusception of the bowels, Mrs. Maria Kay, wife of J. B. Kay, of Little River, Abbeville Dist., S. C., on the 14th Aug. 1866. Death came suddenly and snatched her away, leaving behind a bereaved husband and eight children. Mrs. Kay had been, for many years, a consistent and devoted member of the Baptist Church.

In Memoriam. Mrs. Susie C. Hart, the beloved consort of Prof. Thomas E. Hart of Furman university, and daughter of the Rev. C. H. Lanneau, of Greenville, who breathed her last in Darlington, on Wednesday the 1st of August. Nearly six years ago, a happy young bride, rejoicing in the tender love and manly protection of him whom she had chosen as the companion of her life, she left her home in Greenville to accompany her husband to the distant land of Germany, where he was pursuing his studies in the University of Heidelberg. they then expected to return in about one year. But ere this time had rolled around, a dreadful war-cloud overhung their native land. The ports were blockaded... On the 14th of June, after a prosperous voyage, they arrived safely in Darlington, the paternal home of the male partner. Here they remained for several weeks, pleasantly visiting among his relatives.... Two sweet little girls, one only nine months old, are left without a mother's tender care.... T. H. L. Darlington, S. C., Aug. 6, 1866.

Issue of September 14, 1866

Killed, on South Mountain, Md., Sept 14, 1863, John L. Wright, aged 50 years. The subject of this brief memorial, enlisted in Co. E., Holcombe's Legion, S. C.V., at the formation of the regiment in which he served faithfully and gallantly... He left a loving and tender wife, with a large circle of relatives and friends....

Issue of October 19, 1866

Married in this vicinity, on the 17th inst., by the Rev. W. F. Walters, Mr. W. A. Fant to Miss Kittie Jackson.

On Thursday, 11th inst., by Rev. W. E. Walters, at the residence of the bride's mother, Miss J. A. McLees to Mr. B. W. Harbin, all of Anderson District.

Issue of November 2, 1866

Death of an Old Citizen. it is with sincere sorrow that we record the death, of our kind and esteemed friend, Mr. D. T. Rainwater, at his residence on last Friday night.... He has for many years been a consistent member of the Baptist Church....

Issue of November 9, 1866

Married on Thursday evening, 25th ult., by Rev. W. P. Martin, at the residence of the bride's father, Mr. John R. Harper, of this District, to Miss Laura A. Chapman, of Greenville District.

By the same, on Sunday evening the 4th instant, at the residence of Mr. J. W. Poor, Mr. William A. Shockley to Miss Clarissa Jane Poor, all of this District.

On the 7th of October, by Rev. W. H. Stratton, Mr. James M. Price to Miss Maggie E. Land.

On the 31st of October, by the same, at the residence of Robert Smith, Esq., Saml M. Crayton to Miss Sallie J. Nevitt.

Died, in Anderson District, on the 30th of September, Mrs. Esther W. Moore, in her 40th year. She was for many years a member of the Presbyterian church....

Issue of November 16, 1866

Married November 4th, at the residence of Wm. O. Alexander, by Rev. Saml. Donelly, Mr. John F. Gambrell to Miss P. Emeline McCaster.

On the 8th inst., by Rev. W. H. Stratton, Mr. James M. McFall to Miss Minnie Robinson. All of Anderson.

Issue of November 23, 1866

Married on the 6th inst., by the Rev. D. F. Hadden, Mr. James B. Burress, of Anderson District, to Miss Martha A. Tompson, of Laurens.

Issue of November 30, 1866

Married on Thursday evening, 22nd instant, at the residence of the bride's father, by Rev. W. P. Martin, Mr. Solomon D. Chapman, of Greenville, S. C., to Miss Mary Elizabeth Phillips, of this District.

Mr. Adam Stinebeck died in Savannah Ga., of congestive fever, Nov. 8, 1866, aged forty-two years, seven days. Mr. Stinebeck was born in Philadelphia, and joined a Baptist church in that city when only fourteen years old. For more than twenty years before his decease, he was a resident of the South. The greater part of this time, he spent in Charleston. He had recently gone to Savannah to seek some employment, by which to earn a support his family, and had just obtained business, when the call came to drop al toil and suffering, and enter into rest. The church in Aiken, of which he has been a deacon, and also the clerk for years past, is deeply afflicted... J. A. G. Aiken, S. C., November 15, 1866.

Issue of December 7, 1866

Married on Thursday the 19th ult., at the residence of the bride, by Rev. W. E. Walters, Mr. Robert J. McDavid, of Rusk county, Texas, to Mrs. Christiana Williams, of Anderson District, S. C. Texas Baptist Herald will please copy.

On the 29th ult., by Rev. W. P. Martin, at the residence of the bride's father, Mr. Aris Cox, of this District to Miss Margaret C. Machen, of Greenville District.

On the evening of the 22nd of November last, at the residence of the bride's mother, by Rev. A. Rice, Mr. J. M. Glenn, of Mississippi, to Miss Martha E. McGee, of this District.

On Sunday evening 2nd instant, by Wm. Buchanan, Esq., Mr. James Lawrence Orr Shaw to Miss Nannie E. Smith, all of Anderson District.

Issue of December 21, 1866

Married on Thursday, 13th instant, by Rev. A. Rice, Mr. John Allen Emerson to Miss Sallie S. Kay. All of this District.

Issue of January 4, 1867

Married on Thursday evening, 20th ult., at the residence of the bride's father, by Rev. W. E. Walters, Mr. John Eskew and Miss Amanda E. Burriss. All of this District.

On Tuesday evening, the 18th December, by Rev. William P. Martin, at the residence of the bride, Mr. Stephen J. McKee, of this District, to Mrs. Frances E. Stark, of Abbeville District.

By the same, on Thursday evening, 20th ultimo, at the residence of the bride's father, Mr. John H. Little, of this district, to Miss Martha L. Robinson, of Abbeville District.

By the same on the 23rd ultimo, at the residence of Mr. Anderson Brock, Mr. R. Sanders Smith to Mrs. Emeline Gambrell, all of this District.

Issue of January 25, 1867

Married on the 17th inst., by Rev. W. P. Martin, at the residence of the bride's father, Mr. Toliver Rogers, to Miss Margaret F. Ballentine, all of this district.

Issue of February 8, 1867

Married on the 30th ult., by Rev. W. E. Walters, at the residence of the bride's father, Mr. Alexander Sharpton, Miss Sue Sharpton, of Edgefield District, and Capt. James Pratt, of Abbeville Dist. Abbeville papers please copy.

On the 4th December last, by Rev. T. D. Gwin, at the residence of the bride's father, S. Meredith, Esq., Rev. John T. Gwin, and Miss Amelia C. Mobby, all of Laurens District.

On Tuesday evening 5th inst., by Rev. W. E. Walters, Mr. William N. White, of Pickens district, to Miss Belle McClure, of Anderson Dist. Pickens *Courier* please copy.

On Thursday 20th September last, by Rev. Willis W. Abbott, Mr. Elam Hembree to Miss Martha J. Sanders, all of Pickens District.

On Thursday, 2nd November last, by the same, at the residence of the bride's mother, Mr. Newton Mitchel, of Abbeville, to Miss Martha, daughter of Mrs. Hannah Sanders, of Pickens District.

On 5th of November last, by the same, at the residence of the bride's mother, Mr. William Davis to Miss Anna Patterson, all of Pickens Dist.

On 23rd December last, by the same, at the residence of the bride's father, Mr. J. B. Boyd to Miss Lucy Donald, all of Pickens District.

On 13th of January 1867, by the same, Mr. Balus Fredericks to Miss Harriet McKay.

Issue of March 8, 1867

Married, February 21st, at the residence of Mrs. M. H. Witherspoon, Cabarrus county, N. C., by the Rev. John E. Pressly, Miss Maggie C. Woodside and Mr. D. J. Sherard, of Anderson District, S. C.

On the 28th ult., by the Rev. W. P. Martin, at the residence of the bride's father, Mr. William Thompson and Minerva C. Cooley, all of this District.

On the 28th ult., by Rev. J. B. Hillhouse, Mr. J. W. Lewis and Miss s. A. Millwee.

Issue of March 15, 1867

Married on the 7th of February, by the Rev. Willis W. Abbott, Mr. George W. King and Miss Carrie Miller, both of Pickens

On Thursday evening, 7th instant, at the residence of the bride's father, by Rev. W. E. Walters, Mr. Milton Richardson, of Hart county, Ga., and Miss Sallie L. Smith, of Anderson District.

Issue of March 29, 1867

Married on Sunday, the 4th of November 1866, at Bethlehem Church, by Rev. H. N. Hays, Mr. Franklin Duncan and Miss Cyntha M. Hooper, both of Pickens District.

By the same, on the 28th November, at Tunnel Hill, S. C., at the residence of the bride's father, Mr. Wm. T. Rochester and Miss Elizabeth Visage.

By the same, on Sunday the 17th inst., at the residence of Mr. Jas. L. Hays, Mr. T. Dickens Frachuer and Mrs. Lucinda Walden, both of Pickens District.

Issue of April 5, 1867

Mrs. Hetty Lincoln. This lady, wife of Hon. Heman Lincoln, died in Boston on 3d February. She was known in this state, many years since, as Mrs. Hetty Gillison, having married Mr. Thos. Gillison, of Beaufort District, where she resided for twelve years. She was born in Pennsylvania. she was an active Christian.

Issue of April 26, 1867

Married, at the residence of the bride's father, on Tuesday evening, April 23d 1867, by the Rev. A. Rice, Rev. William E. Walters, editor of the *South Carolina Baptist*, and Miss Anna M. Millford, eldest daughter of Dr. W. J. Millford-- all of Anderson District, S. C.

Married on the 13th February last, by the Rev. Robert King, Mr. Jno. S. Smith to Miss Sue L. Shirley, all of Anderson District.

Issue of May 24, 1867

Died, April 24th, 1867, D. T. B. Holland, youngest son of Dr. W. T. and Mrs. J. E. Holland, aged 14 years, 2 months and 3 days. He was a Member of the Methodist Church....

Issue of May 31, 1867

Death of Col. C. J. Elford. We are pained to announce the death of this excellent and useful brother.... He died at his home in Greenville, on last Saturday morning.... The Sabbath School at Greenville was organized in 1838, and Bro. Elford was one of the teachers in the School at the time of its organization, and continue to each until 1843. [eulogy]

Married, on the morning of the 16th instant, at the residence of Z. Hall, Esq., by Rev. A. Rice, Mr. R. L. Pratt, of Abbeville District, and Miss M. F. C. Swilling, of Anderson District.

By the same on the evening of the 26th instant, at his residence, Mr. Mason Henderson of Abbeville District, and Miss Carrie Fisher, of this District.

Issue of June 7, 1867

Charles J. Elford died May 25th 1867, aged forty-seven years and fourteen days. [one and one-half column notice]

Issue of June 21, 1867

Married, on Wednesday, June 12th 1867, by Rev. W. H. Stratton, at the residence of the bride's mother in this village, Mr. Thomas M. White and Miss Nannie T. Benson, all of Anderson.

Issue of June 28, 1867

Married, on Wednesday, June 19th, 1867, by Rev. W. H. Stratton, at the residence of the bride's mother in this village, Mr. William Lee and Miss Julia V. Robinson, both of this village.

On Tuesday, 25th inst., at the residence of Mrs. Elizabeth Brazeale, by Rev. W. E. Walters, Mr. David K. Brazeale and Miss Augustus B. Malone.

On Tuesday, 25th inst., at the residence of the bride's father, by the Rev. Wm. F. Pearson, Mr. James M. Sloan, formerly of Pendleton, now of Pickens C. H., to Miss Sallie J. Lynch, of Abbeville, S. C.

Issue of July 5, 1867

Death of Mr. Van Wyck. We regret to chronicle the death of Wm. Van Wyck, Assessor of the Internal Revenue for the Third District of South carolina. He died at his residence, in this place, on Sunday morning last, after a protracted illness for weeks. He was a member of the Episcopal Church. Henry O. Herrick succeeds him in office....

Death of Mrs. Manly. Died, June 27th 1867, in Greenville, S. C., Mrs. Charlotte E. Manly, wife of Rev. B. Manly, Jr., D. D., Professor in the Southern Baptist Theological Seminary. [eulogy]

Issue of July 19, 1867

Married, at the residence of the bride's father, on Tuesday, July 2, 1867, by Rev. T. P. Gwyn, William Burriss, of Anderson District, S. C., to Miss Nannie L., youngest daughter of John Dickinson, of Calhoun County, Ala.

On Sunday evening, 30th ult., by Rev. W. P. Martin, at his residence, Mr. B. L. Crymes to Miss Mary E. Tinson, all of this District.

Issue of July 26, 1867

Married on the 18th inst., by Rev. W. D. Beverly, Mr. R. M. Clinkscales and Miss Jane E. Fant, all of this village.

Departed this life, at his own residence, in Hernando county, Florida, on the 3d of November, 1866, Col. Francis H. Edrington, in the 43d year of his age. The deceased came to Florida with his family from Fairfield District, in 1851. it was our privilege to baptize him into the fellowship of the Eden Baptist Church at Lake Lindsey, Fla., and soon after to ordain him Deacon of that church. he afterwards united in constituting the Union Baptist Church at Brooksville, Florida, of which he remained an active, devoted and useful member and deacon up to the period of his death.... J. H. H.

Issue of August 2, 1867

Departed this life on the 24th ult., in the 55th year of her age, Mrs. Elizabeth Motes, the wife of Mr. Hogan Motes, and daughter of Mr. Thos. Powell, who formerly resided at Beaverdam in this District. The subject of this notice was in early life divested, by the remorseless hand of death, of the pious teachings and examples of a fond mother. Her place was subsequently well filled by a step-mother, Mrs. Dumas. Mrs. Motes died, leaving a widowed daughter, whose husband died while on the evening of returning, as an exchanged prisoner, to a happy reunion with his wife and beloved children. Her son, Marshall, fell amid the siege of Knoxville, leaving an affectionate wife and a lovely daughter.... J. W. C.   Cross Hill, S. C. July, 1867.

Issue of September 6, 1867

Married, on the 15th of August, at the residence of the bride's father, by the Rev. Alfred Reid, Mr. John J. Baker, of this village, and Miss Lula L. Broyles, eldest daughter of A. R. Broyles, of this District.

Issue of September 13, 1867

Died, near Friar's Point, Mississippi, on the 6th of July last, Casper Sharpe, son of Marshal Sharpe, of Abbeville District, S. C. He had been for many years an exemplary and useful member of the Baptist Church... He left an affection wife and child, with kind parents and brothers and sisters....

Issue of September 27, 1867

In Memoriam. Clarence Lane, third son of M. E. and C. A. Magee, departed this life on the night of Sept. 17, 1867, at Walhalla. Born January 27th, 1867.

Died, at the residence of her son, Robt. M. Anderson, at Chappell's Depot, Newberry District, S. C., on the evening of the 14th September 1867, Mrs. Susan Martin Anderson, wife of Dr. George Thomas Anderson, in the 57th year of her age.

Issue of October 18, 1867

Married, on Tuesday evening, October 8th, at the residence of the bride's father, by Rev. W. D. Beverly, Mr. John H. Clark and Miss Annie M., second daughter of Milford Burriss, Esq., all of this District.

At the same time and place, and by the same, Mr. Thomas M. Cater and Miss S. Elizabeth, third daughter of Milford Burriss, Esq., all of this district.

In Memoriam. Fannie, eldest daughter of Mrs. A. T. and Rev. B. F. Mauldin, departed his life, October 6, 1867, on Sabbath day, at noon, at the residence of her father, at Williamston, Anderson District, S. C., aged 15 years and 11 months. [eulogy]

Issue of October 25, 1867

Married on Wednesday evening, October 16, at the Presbyterian Church, in this village, by the Rev. W. H. Stratton, Mr. Wm. F. Barr, and Miss L. A. Hubbard, all of this village.

Issue of November 15, 1867

Death of Rev. W. J. Lunn. We are pained to announce the death of this estimable brother and faithful minister of Jesus Christ.

Died, on the morning of Friday, September 20th, Fluellar Clinkscales, the only daughter of Col. William and Margaret Clinkscales, in the twelfth year of her age. She was a scholar in the Little River Sabbath School [eulogy].

Died, at Lawtonville, May 5th 1867, after a painful and protracted illness of one year and three months, Eliza Jane Rhodes, wife of George Rhodes, and daughter of John and Eveline Robert, aged 58 years, three months, and six days.

Married, on Thursday 24th ult., by Rev. W. E. Walters, at the residence of the bride's father, Mr. J. M. Carwile, Mr. James Wilson and Miss Ann Carwile, all of Abbeville District.

Issue of November 22, 1867

The Late Rev. W. J. Lunn. The Greenville Mountaineer of the 14th inst., says... He died at his residence in Timmonsville, S. C., on the 4th instant. Many of our citizens will remember Mr. lunn, the blind preacher, who sojourned among us while attending the lectures at the Theological Seminary a year or two ago....

Married on the 12th inst., at the residence of Mrs. Robert Cathcart, in the City of Columbia, by Rev. W. E. Boggs, Mr. P. K. McCully, of Anderson, S. C., and Miss Maggie J. Cathcart, of Columbia, S. C.

Issue of December 6, 1867

Married, at the residence of the bride's father in this village, on Thursday evening, Nov. 28th, 1867, by Rev. J. S. Murray, Mr. George W. Miller, of Abbeville and Miss Emmala T., eldest daughter of the Hon. J. P. Reed, of Anderson.

On Wednesday evening, 27th ult., by Rev. Hugh McLees, Mr. James A. Gray and Miss E. J. Sadler, both of Anderson District.

Issue of December 13, 1867

Married at the residence of the bride's father, in this District, on Thursday evening, December 5th 1867, by Rev. J. S. Murray, Dr. John Hopkins and Miss Sallie A., eldest daughter of Mr. Thomas Harper, all of this District.

Issue of December 20, 1867

Married, at the residence of the bride's father, on Thursday, the 12th December, by the Rev. Thomas Dawson, Mr. Melville Saunders to Miss Jane Davis, both of Pickens.

Issue of January 17, 1868

Died, of brain fever, on the 31st day of December, 1867, Kiturah Pauline, infant daughter of G. W. and E. S. Maret, aged 10 months and 22 days.

Issue of January 24, 1868

Married on the 25th December, by Rev. Fletcher Smith, at the residence of the bride's father, Mr. J. B. Carpenter, of Anderson, and Miss Fannie Mauldin of Pickens.

Married on the 5th inst., at the residence of Rev. H. Vandiver, by Rev. W. P. Martin, Mr. William Gambrell and Miss Adaline Whit, all of Anderson District.

Issue of February 14, 1868

Married at the residence of the bride's father, on 23d ult., by Rev. W. P. Martin, Mr. James S. Lawless to Miss Sarah M. Cothran, all of Anderson District.

Issue of February 28, 1868

Died, at his residence in Darlington District, S. C., on the 22d of November 1867, Josiah A. Fort, after an illness of two weeks from Bronchitis. He was born April 1, 1801, and was baptized by Rev. Wm. Cassey into the fellowship of the Welsh neck Church in May 1829. Thus he departed in the 65th year of his age and the 36th of his Christian profession. Soon after his baptism, his membership was removed to the Antioch Church, where he became a leading and influential member and an officer. After a few years, his membership was removed to the Black Creek Church, of which he was an honored and useful member and a deacon until the period of his death.... J. O. B. D.

Issue of February 28, 1868

Mrs. Sally Rice, wife of Rev. A. Rice, died after a few days illness, February 15, 1868, in the 71st year of her age.... Her seat was seldom ever vacant at Varennes Church, of which she was a consistent member to the close of life. W. F. P.

Issue of March 20, 1868

Died, on Thursday, March 5, 1868, of a disorder of the brain, Thomas Pascal Gaines, second son of Rev. W. A. and Mrs. Mary E. Gaines, aged 11 years... with an elder brother, baptized into the fellowship of the Baptist Church at Red Bank. W. A. G. Phoenix, S. C., March 10, 1868.

Married on Wednesday evening the 18th inst., at the residence of the bride's father, by Rev. W. E. Walters, Captain E. G. Roberts and Miss Ella, eldest daughter of William Perry, Esq., all of Anderson District, S. C.

Issue of March 27, 1868

Col. James F. Wyatt breathed his last on the 10th inst., at 10 o'clock and 45 minutes a. m. For nine weeks he had been painfully and unceasingly afflicted ... On Wednesday, 11th, his remains were carried into Pisgah Church, where he held membership, and at 3 o'clock p. m. a funeral sermon was delivered by Rev. T. R. Gary... the corpse was consigned to the grave in the burying ground near by. Thus passed away one of Carolina's nobles sons, in his 67th year. He was born May 1, 1801. Married in early life... he honored the old 4th Regiment by being its Colonel....

Issue of April 3, 1868

Married in the Baptist Church at Fincastle, Va., at 8 p. m., on the 17th of March, 1868, by Rev. G. Gray, Rev. T. A. Reid, of Georgia, returned African Missionary, and Miss Virgie T. Ammen, daughter of the late deacon Benjamin Ammen, of Fincastle.

Issue of April 24, 1868

Death of Rev. R. B. C. Howell. The demise of this distinguished brother imposes on us the pleasingly melancholy duty of paying a tribute to his memory. Our acquaintance with him commenced about the year 1824. We then resided in the family of Rev. Nathaniel Chambliss, of Sussex County, Va. At a Saturday meeting at Highhill meeting house, two young Baptist ministers made their appearance. They were both strangers, travelling by private conveyance, and stopped to spend the Lord';s day with a plain country congregation. These young brethren were Rev. P. W. Dowd, late of North Carolina, and Rev. R. B. C. Howell, on their way to Columbian College, in the District of Columbia.... When we next hear of Howell, he had become the pastor of the Cumberland Street Baptist church, Norfolk, Va. We next heard him preach at Peterville, Powhatan county, Va., at the anniversary of the Virginia Temperance Society. [account over two columns].

Issue of May 1, 1868

For the South Carolina Baptist. A few weeks ago we were called to mourn the death of Rev. R. Bradford, in the 68th year of his age. Bro. Bradford was well known to the denomination in South Carolina, and for the last year or two has labored as missionary for the Edisto Association. Bro. B. was a native of Maryland, but removed to this State many years ago.... Our venerable brother, Rev. Hansford Duncan, has recently been deeply afflicted in the loss of his affectionate wife. Sister Duncan was a native of Beaufort, S. C., and had been a member of the church for over forty years.... Palmetto. April, 1868.

Issue of May 15, 1868

In Memoriam. Reminiscent thoughts on the Anniversary of the death of the Rev. Peter C. Edwards, late Professor of Ancient Languages and Literature in the Furman University, at Greenville, S. C. This day (15th May) twelve months age, the beloved Edwards expired at his residence in Greenville [two columns]

Issue of June 5, 1868

For the South Carolina Baptist. Bush River Baptist Church, Newberry District, S. C. Resolution on the death of Deacon John Johnston, having survived far beyond his "three score years and ten...." 9th May 1868. B. C. Griffin, C.C.

For the South Carolina Baptist. Lines on Fannie Mauldin, who died at Williamston, October 6, 1867, aged 15 years and 11 months.

Issue of June 26, 1868

Married, on the 18th inst., by the Rev. J. I. Bonner, at the residence of the bride's father, Dr. H. T. Epting, of Williamston, S. C., and Mrs. Mary Jane Knox, daughter of William Hill, Esq., of Abbeville.

On Wednesday evening, June 17th, at the Baptist Church, by Rev. W. D. Beverly, Mr. William N. Clark, and Miss Emma E. Beverly, eldest daughter of the officiating minister-- all of Anderson C. H., S. C.

Issue of July 3, 1868

Married, on the 20th May, 1868, by Rev. W. P. Martin, Mr. Jordan G. Green to Miss Mary Ann Cooley.

On the 23rd June 1868, by Rev. W. P. Martin, James T. Holladay to Miss Martha E., eldest daughter of J. W. Poor, all of this District.

Issue of July 10, 1868

Died, at his residence in Fairfield District, on 23d May last, Col. William Smith, in the 75th year of his age. The deceased was among the oldest citizens of his District. His father was William Smith, of Spartanburg District, who emigrated from Pennsylvania at an early age, and came one of the earliest settlers of that District. He held the office of Colonel in the American Army during the Revolution, and afterwards represented his Congressional District in the United States Congress. Still later in life he held the office of district Judge. [long account]

Died, at Anderson, June 22d 1868, Mrs. Mary B. Prevost, wife of Joseph Prevost, in the 57th year of her age.

Issue of July 17, 1868

Died, at his residence in Greenville District, S. C., on the 28th of April 1868, Thomas Goldsmith, Sr., in a good old age, honored and respected by all who knew him. He was born Dec. 19, 1787, and became a member of the Baptist Church, Dec. 25, 1819. B. M., Jr.

Died, at his residence in Tippah county, Miss., June 1st 1868, Col. James Simpson Liddell, in his seventy-eighth year. The deceased was born in Anderson, S. C., and emigrated to Mississippi in 1841, where he resided up to his death. He leaves a widow, with children and grandchildren, to mourn his loss. Col. Liddell was a participant in the war of 1814. He gave three sons to the service of his country in 1861-- Samuel Baylis Alfred fell at Gettysburg, Wm. Anderson at Chicamauga, and Charles Gaillard at Jonesborough, Geo.

Issue of July 24, 1868

Died, near Rocky Mount, Fairfield District, S. c., on the 26th of June 1868, Willie D. Scott, son of Dr. Ira S. Scott, aged 11 years, 5 months, and 27 days. [account and eulogy]

Issue of July 31, 1868

Married, by Rev. W. P. Martin, on the 22d inst., at the residence of the bride's father, in Greenville County, S. C., Mr. Wm. T. Woodson, of Anderson County, to Miss Frances M.., fourth daughter of K. Vaughn.

Issue of August 21, 1868

Married, by the Rev. A. C. Stepp, on the 28th July 1868, Dr. John M. Roberts, of Nelson Co., Va., to Miss Kate M. Charles, of Greenville, S. C.

By the same, at the residence of the bride's father, on the 5th inst., Mr. J. D. Miller, of Newberry, and Miss S. C. Cromer, of Abbeville, S. C.

Issue of September 11, 1868

Married on the evening of the 1st instant, at the residence of Mrs. Elizabeth Taylor, in Abbeville District, by Rev. A. Rice, Mr. Phillip L. Hampton, of Stone Mountain, Ga., and Mrs. Joannah S. Campbell, of Abbeville District.

Issue of September 25, 1868

Married near Camden, Madison Co., Miss., August 5, 1868, at the residence of Robert W. McMurtray, Esq., by Rev. C. M. Atkinson, Mr. W. B. J. Barnett and Miss Susan A. McMurtray.

On the 20th August 1868, By Rev. W. P. Martin, at the residence of Mr. J. w. Turner, of Laurens, Mr. Absalom Morrison, of Abbeville, and Miss Mary Reed, of Laurens.

On the 12th inst., by Rev. Wilson Ashley, Mr. J. Roddy Martin, of this District, and Miss Lou McDavid, of Greenville District.

Mrs. Sarah Elizabeth Hemingway, daughter of J. M. and Lavinia Patrick, died on the 8th of September 1868, at her father's residence, near Midway, S. C. She professed religion and was baptized when about fifteen years old, and from then till her death, at the age of 24 years and 6 months, she was almost exemplary Christian....

Issue of October 9, 1868

Tribute of Respect from Citadel Square Baptist Church, Charleston, S. C., September 20, 1868, to Deacon James Tupper. Joseph Whilden, Church Clerk.

Died, on Sunday afternoon, September 27, 1868, at the residence of his father in Darlington District, Robert Lide Dargan, son of Rev. J.O. B. Dargan, aged 18 years 8 months and 18 days. [eulogy]

Departed this life on the 27th of January last, Mrs. Mary Crump, wife of M. W. Crump, and eldest daughter of W. E. Eskew. She was a member of the New Prospect Baptist Church. In October, 1867, she was married to Mr. M. W. Crump, of Georgia, and very soon after marriage moved with her husband to Arkansas. In a few weeks after her arrival in Arkansas, she was taken sick and lingered until the 27th day of January....

Issue of November 6, 1868

Departed this life on the 28th September at his residence in Abbeville District, David L. Bozeman. He was raised in Anderson District, and after the death of his father, continued to live at the old homestead for several years. In 1860, he moved near Ninety-Six in Abbeville District. He was married in 1861, and in 1862 he joined the army, in Stevens' 24th Regiment of S. C. V. At the battle of Franklin, Tenn., he was severely wounded, and was disabled from active duty, but his connection with the army was not severed until the close of the war. In August 1866, he united himself to Siloam Baptist church, and was baptized by Rev. J. A. Broadus, D. D. On the 28th, he was engaged in work at his saw-mill, and while moving a stock on a log-carriage, some part of the track gave way, he made an attempt to jump off, but fell and the log rolled over him and killed him immediately. He has left a wife and three children, with an affectionate family to mourn his loss.

Issue of November 13, 1868

Married, on Wednesday evening, Oct. 21st, 1868, by Rev. A. C. Stepp, Mr. Henry Johnson, of Richland, to Miss Mary Hutchison, of Newberry, S. C.

Issue of November 20, 1868

Died, near Allendale, in Barnwell District, South Carolina, on the 5th inst., Mr. Rufus W. Bonnette, son of the late David Bonnette, aged 36 years. On his way to visit his mother in Orangeburg District, he was thrown from his horse, while six miles on his journey, and almost instantly killed. He was baptized near Blackville, by Rev. J. P. Norris in 1857. A numerous circle of relatives and friends mourn his departure.

Issue of December 25, 1868

In Memoriam. The death of Mrs. Susan Acker... this event occurred on Wednesday, the 7th day of October 1868, at 5 o'clock p. m., at the residence of her youngest son, Capt. J. S. Acker, in Anderson county. The deceased was 88 years, 1 month and 9 days. Susannah was the daughter of William and Elizabeth Halbert; and when quite young removed from the State of Virginia with her parents, and settled in old Pendleton District, one and a half miles above Calhoun. In the early part of the year 1798, she was married to Peter Acker. In February 1821, she united with the Baptist Church of Christ at Big Creek, and was baptized by the Rev. Moses Holland. Subsequently she removed her membership to Shady Grove church, of which she continued a faithful and exemplary member to the day of her death....

Abner Cox, the fifth son of Reuben and Elizabeth Cox, who removed from the banks of the Rappahannock River, Essex County, Virginia, soon after the close of the Revolutionary war, and settled on the Saluda side of old Washington County-- in that portion now known as Anderson-- was born on the 21st day of September A. D. 1801, and was consequently, sixty-seven years and fourteen days old at the time of his death. He was happily united in marriage to Miss Catharine Stanton, on attaining his majority, and commenced the business of life in earnest. By her he was blessed with many daughters and sons; three of the later of whom surrendered their lives, a patriotic offering upon the altar of right, in the recent terrible conflict. upon the death of Catharine, he was a second time most happily married to Miss Milley Wyatt, who bore him a son and two daughters, and whom, with her survive to mourn his loss. In the prime of life he became impressed with the prime necessity of religion, under the preaching of Rev. Wm. McGee, and united with the Baptist Church of Christ at Friendship. Subsequently, on the fifth day of May 1859, he transferred his membership to this church.... tribute of respect from Shady Grove Church.

THE WORKING CHRISTIAN

Issue of July 29, 1869

Married at the residence of the bride's father, on the 20th instant, by Rev. W. D. Thomas, Mr. B. O. Mauldin and Miss E. Julia Smith, all of Greenville, S. C.

A Tribute. Cross Roads Baptist Church, Newberry District, S. C. Deacon Jas. Hill, Sr., died full of years and good works. He was about one hundred years old and had ben for more than fifty years a deacon of our church, being one of its founders. This church was the spiritual home of Deacon Graves Spearman for more than half a century, during most of which time he was a faithful deacon. He also had reached a ripe old age, being about seventy-six years old when he died. C. B. Griffin, Silas Walker, G. W. L. Spearman, committee. W. A. Gaines, Moderator.

Issue of August 5, 1869

Married on the 15th ultimo, by Rev. Tilman R. Gaines, Mr. S. Lafayette Melton of N. C., and Miss Sarah R. Atkinson, of Yorkville, S. C.

Departed this life on the 12th of July, Wm. C. Williams, son of M. W. and Adaline Williams, of Edgefield County, in the 8th year of his age. [verse]

The demise of Mrs. L. S. Reynolds, of Edgefield County, S. C., who departed this life on the 12th of July 1869. She was baptised on profession of her faith in Christ in fellowship with the Gilgal Church in Edgefield District, by that lamented man of God, N. W. Hodges, some 87 years ago. She was one of the first taken from the Sunday School nursery and planted by the grace of God in the church. [eulogy] D. D.

Issue of August 19, 1869

Departed this life, at his home, near Doko, in Fairfield County, S. C., on the morning of Sunday, the 8th instant, Mr. Buckner Hagood, aged 84 years. [verse] B. W. W.

Departed this life on the 24th ultimo, George Howell, second son of Rev. G. W. and M. J. Pickett, aged 16 years, 2 months and 29 days. [eulogy]

Issue of August 26, 1869

Died in this County on the 13th instant, Jas. Randolph, infant son of W. H. Nicholson, aged 11 months.

In this County, on the 7th instant, at the residence of his uncle Morrison Russell, M. C. Russell, son of the late Rev. R. Y. Russell.

In this County, on the 16th inst., Mr. Gideon Seahorn, aged 83 years.

Issue of September 9, 1869

Died at her father's in Newberry, on Sabbath, the 18th of July, Mrs. Mattie C. Spearman, after an illness of twelve weeks, of typhoid fever, aged 18 years, 5 months, and 29 days. Mrs. Spearman was the second daughter of Dr. R. P. Clark, of Jalappa, the price and hope of the family. She graduated in the Due West Female College just one year before her death. In December she was married to W. R. Spearman, Esq., of Newberry, and on the very day she was taken sick they were to move into their own new house.

Departed this life, August 4th, Mrs. Ann V. Edmunds, in the 73rd year of her age. She was a consistent member of the Baptist Church of Beulah for years. She left children and grandchildren [eulogy and verse].

Issue of September 16, 1869

Obituary Notices. We will publish, without charge, all obituary notices sent to us which do not exceed ten lines; but we shall charge 10 cents a line for all over ten lines.

Issue of October 14, 1869

Died in Shelby, N. C., on Friday evening, the 1st of October (instant), of typhoid fever, Mrs. Sarah Patterson, consort of J. R. Logan, aged 51 years, 7 months and 14 days. The deceased was a native of York County, S. C., and a lady of exemplary character.... A funeral discourse was delivered on the occasion of her death, at the Baptist Church (where her membership was), by her beloved pastor, Rev. M. C. Barnett. Her remains were interred in the Zoar Church Cemetery, with two of her sons, one of whom fell by disease while of young and tender age, and the other in the late struggle for Southern independence, near Petersburg, Va.

Died on the 18th of September 1869, Mrs. Kiziah J. Gaines, consort of Deacon James H. Gaines, and only daughter of Mr. and Mrs. Martin M. Arnold, of Laurens District, S. C. She was born on the 17th of August 1835 and married on the 13th of November 1853, during which year she was baptised into the fellowship of the Columbia Church. She left two daughters [eulogy]. A. C. S.

Issue of October 21, 1869

Departed this life at the residence of her husband, W. H. Bull, in Orangeburg County, South Carolina, on the 2d day of October 1869, Mrs. Harriet C. Bull, aged forty-two years, four months, and twenty-three days. Mrs. Bull was a devoted mother, consistent Christian and amiable... She has left a kind husband and three children....

Issue of October 28, 1869

Died in Chester County, on the 12th instant, of Cholera Morbus, Mr. H. M. Gwinn, aged about thirty-three years.

Issue of November 4, 1869

Married by Rev. W. A. Gaines, at Cambridge, S. C., on Thursday the 19th inst., Mr. B. W. Mason and Miss Martha C. Morbert.

Died at Santuc, S. C., on the 15th of Aug., 1869, Sarah Farr, daughter of Dr. J. P. and S. A. Thomas. She was only detained 4 months and 11 days in this vale of tears....

Issue of November 11, 1869

Married on Thursday, Oct. 28th, by Rev. Luther Broaddus, Mr. W. H. Brunson and Miss Fannie M. Penn, all of Edgefield, S. C.

Married on October 26th, by Rev. W. L. Brown, Capt. Benjamin Kennedy and Miss Eunice E., daughter of Gen. B. B. Foster, all of Spartanburg District, S. C.

Issue of November 18, 1869

Married at Anderson Court House, on the 26th ultimo, by Rev. J. Scott Murray, Mr. James H. Thornwell of Yorkville, S. C., and Miss Florence L., youngest daughter of Mr. Elias Earle, of the former place.

Issue of November 25, 1869

Married on the 14th inst., by Rev. W. D. Beverly, Pastor of the Baptist Church at Anderson, C. H., S. C., Mr. N. O. Farmer, of Greenville, S. C., and Miss G. A. Earle, eldest daughter of Rev. J. R. Earle, of Anderson Co., S. C.

Issue of December 2, 1869

Married on the 8th inst., by Rev. W. D. Beverly and Rev. A. Rice, Rev. W. H. Kipp of Anderson, to Miss P. M. Pratt of Abbeville county.

Obituaries counting ten lines will be inserted in THE WORKING CHRIS-TIAN free of charge; after that a charge of ten cents per line will be made. Persons sending obituaries must provide for the payment of the excess beyond the lines published gratis.

Died on October 12th 1860, at the residence of her father, in Barnwell Co., Miss Sophrina S. Courtney, daughter of Mr. A. S. and Mrs. S. Courtney, in the 16th year of her age. She was an affection daughter, a tender sister, and a kind friend.

Issue of December 9, 1869

Married on the 8th inst., by Rev. W. D. Beverly and Rev. A. Rice, Rev. W. H. King of Anderson, to Miss P. M. Pratt, of Abbeville county. [see apparently error in preceding issue]

Issue of December 23, 1869

Married by A. C. Stepp, at the residence of the bride's father, on Thursday evening, December 9th 1869, Mr. Wm. Robert Kay, of Anderson, and Miss Laura C. Machen, of Greenville County, S. C.

By the same, on the same afternoon, Mr. Wm. Gambrell, of Greenville, and Miss Anna Law, second daughter of Rev. J. B. Davenport, of Laurens County, S. C.

Died in York County, on the 4th inst., of consumption, Mr. J. A. Lock, son of Levi and Malinda Lock, aged 19 years and 9 days. He joined the Baptist church at Catawba in the 15th year of his age, and proved one of the most pious young men in the community.

Issue of January 6, 1870

Married at the residence of the bride's father, on the 12th of October, by Rev. A. L. Stough, Mr. Samuel Williamson and Miss Jennie Fisher, all of Mecklenburg county, N. C.

At the residence of M. A. Key, on the 2nd of December, by the same, Mr. Samuel Wilson and Miss Jane Crowell, all of York County, S. C.

At the residence of the bride's mother, on the 9th of December, by the same, Mr. Hartwell Davis and Miss Jennie Hill, all of Mecklenburg county, N. C.

At the residence of the bride's father, on the 14th of December, by the same, Mr. Anson Sizer and Miss Novella Davidson, all of Lancaster county, S. C. Biblical Recorder please copy.

On 21st instant, by Rev. Thos. Dixon, at the residence of the bride's father, Mr. Willie H. Herndon, and Miss Emma, second daughter of J. R. Logan of Shelby, N. C.

Departed this life on the 19th of December, in Edgefield, Mrs. H. Ana Turner, daughter of Henry H. and Frances W. Mayson, aged 23 years. She joined the Baptists eight years ago, and has been a devoted member ever since....

Died on the 12th of October 1869, at the residence of her father, in Barnwell District, Miss Sophronie S. Courtney, daughter of Mr. A. S. and Mrs. S. Courtney, in the 16th year of her age. [verse]

19

Died, November 2d, 1869, at her father's residence in Charleston County, little Ula E. Winter, daughter of Thomas and Caroline Winter. The subject of this notice died in the 9th year of her age.... J. L. Rollings.

Issue of January 13, 1870

Married, on Thursday, December 16th, at Edgefield, S. C., by Rev. Luther Broaddus, Mr. W. B. Sanders, of Sumter, to Miss Ella Frazier, daughter of Col. M. Frazier, of Edgefield.

On the 16th December, 1869, at the bride's residence, in Lexington county, S. C., by the Rev. Wm. G. Mack, Dr. I. D. Durham, of Orangeburg Village, S. C., to Miss Lizzie M. Knotts, of Lexington county, S. C.

On the 23d December 1869, by Rev. Dr. Williams, Mr. A. S. Townes, of Greenville, to Lillie B. White, daughter of S. P. Brooks, of Abbeville, S. C.

Issue of January 20, 1870

In Yorkville, on the 11th instant, by Rev. T. R. Gaines, Mr. F. C. Alexander, and Miss M. S. Nichols, all of York county.

Died-- Mrs. F. M. Rowland, consort of Maj. Jno. S. Rowland, late of Bartow County, deceased, died at the old homestead, on the night of the 6th ult., in the seventieth year of her age.... In early life, she joined a Baptist Church in South Carolina, subsequently she came to Georgia, and at the time of the writer's first acquaintance with her, was a member of a Church, of which her brother, the lamented Dr. Lewis, was the pastor. [eulogy]

Issue of January 27, 1870

Married, at the residence of the bride's father, on the 19th December, by the Rev. W. H. Dowling, Mr. J. A. Chasscreau to Miss Martha Rizer.

On the 26th December, by Rev. G. D. Kinard, Mr. J. L. Herndon to Miss Sallie Kinard, all of the St. John's congregation in Barnwell Co.

On Monday evening, Jan. 23, 1870, at the residence of the bride, by Rev. A. C. Stepp, Capt. Thomas A. Peden, of Greenville, and Miss Emily Meares, of Laurens County, S. C.

By the same, Tuesday evening, January 11th, 1870, at the residence of the bride's mother, Mrs. Cecilia Vance, Mr. Ira Davenport, and Mrs. Ellist Chandler, both of Greenville county, S. C.

Issue of February 3, 1870

Married, on the 15th December, by Rev. T. H. Pope, Mr. Matthew Hip and Miss Sarah Copeland.

By the same on the 22d December, Mr. Bluford Goodman and Miss Sue Spearman.

By the same, on the 20th January, Mr. John Riser and Miss Laura Metts, daughter of W. F. Metts, Esq., all of Laurens.

On the morning of the 14th December, at Mr. W. J. Tucker's, by Rev. J. T. Jeter, Mr. John C. P. Jeter, of Union County, S. C., and Miss M. Luella Coleman, of Ringgold, La.

On the 19th of December last, at the residence of the bride's father, Mr. C. T. Tribble by Elder T. Robertson, Mr. John H. P. Burns and Miss Emma P. Tribble, all of Laurens county.

Died, in Yorkville, on the 25th ult., Mrs. Sarah McLain, in the 53d year of her age. About three years ago she embraced religion and was baptized and made a member of the Yorkville Baptist Church.

Died, on the morning of the 6th of Jan. 1870, Laurens Nevil, infant son of John Cason and Eliza C. Hill, aged 8 months and 11 days. T. G. W. Newberry Herald and Laurensville Herald please copy.

Issue of February 10, 1870

Married, on Thursday, Dec. 23d, by Rev. W. A. Gaines, Mr. Strother D. Gaines, of Greenville, and Mrs. Nannie E. Henderson, of Edgefield.

On Thursday, the 27th ult., at the residence of the bride's father, by Rev. P. R. Elam, Mr. Ira Hardin, Jr., and Miss Eliza Jane Whisonant, all of York county.

Issue of February 24, 1870

Married on the 20th ultimo, at the residence of the bride's father, by Rev. G. W. Pickett, of Chester county, Mr. Wm. Weir and Miss Maggie Thompson, both of Fairfield county.

On the 27th ult., at the residence of the bride's father, by the same, Mr. T. B. Estes and Miss M. J. Anderson, daughter of Dr. A. F. Anderson, all of Chester county.

On the 10th instant, at the bride's residence, by the same, Mr. J. A. Teitz and Mrs. C. C. Rabb, both of Fairfield county.

On the 25th of November, 1869, by Rev. Geo. D. Kinard, Mr. B. F. Lynes to Miss Nancy Loadholt, all of Barnwell county.

On the 16th December, by the same, Mr. William Croft and Miss Simpson Brant, both of Barnwell county.

On December 26th, by the same, Mr. J. L. Herndon, and Miss Sarah Ann Kinard, both of Barnwell county.

Issue of March 3, 1870

Married, on the 1st of February in Laurens County, by the Rev. T. H. Pope, Mr. Pinckney Horton and Miss Mattie Hollingsworth.

On Tuesday evening, the 15th ult., by the same, Mr. Willis Jones and Miss L. E. Craddock.

On the 16th ult., by the same, Capt. James Y. McFall, of Newberry, and Mrs. Lavinia Kinard, daughter of Dr. Wm. Rook, of Laurens County.

In Yorkville, on the evening of the 24th ultimo, by Rev. Tilman R. Gaines, Mr. W. R. Murphy and Miss Annis J. Jones, both of Yorkville.

Issue of March 10, 1870

Married Mr. G. W. Collins, Miss Sallie M. Morton. At the residence of Mr. A. H. Morton, February 22. Attendants: Misses Lou Morton, Rosa Bolling, Sally Lake, Rosa Foushee, Mamie Moore and Sallie Jackson. Messrs. B. F. Miller, T. W. Davis, Henry Ware, George Wells, E. C. Gordon, and E. Stokes, Esq. Officiating minister, W. B. Jones.

On the 26th ult., by Rev. S. M. Richardson, Mr. John E. Steedman, of Barnwell county, and Miss Maggie L. China, of Sumter, S. C.

Died in Richland, February 20th, after a long and painful illness, Mrs. Emma Caroline Smith, in the 62d year of her age. For forty years a member of the Baptist Church, Beulah.... [poem]

Issue of March 17, 1870

Married by the Rev. Wm. Brooker, at the residence of the bride's mother, on Tuesday evening, February 15th 1870, Mr. Thos. G. Grimball, of John's Island, and Miss Lizzie A. Odom, of Barnwell county, S. C.

On the 3d instant, at the residence of the bride's father, by the Rev. G. W. Pickett, Mr. J. R. Wilks and Miss Regina Carter, all of Chester county.

Issue of March 24, 1870

Died, on the 26th of February, 1870, Deacon Joseph Whisonant, in the 81st year of his age. He lived this long life near King's Creek, in York County, S. C. He was for 57 years a consistent member, and for 37 years a Deacon of the Antioch Baptist church.... A. Hardin.

Issue of April 7, 1870

Mrs. Agnes Kinard of St. John's church in Barnwell County, departed this life on the 10th day of March, 1870, at the advanced age of 77 years, 6 months, and 20 days. She had been a member of the church for over 50 years... her sons and daughters, grandchildren and great-grandchildren number almost 70 souls. Her funeral services were conducted by her pastor, Rev. W. H. Dowling.... J. L. H.

Issue of April 14, 1870

About the first of March, Miss Peggy Underwood, as she was familiarly called by her friends and associates, was seized with a violent attack of pneumonia which terminated her mortal existence.... She had been a member of the Baptist church at Cedar Springs, Spartanburg county for at least thirty years. She was a daughter of William Underwood Sr., who served as a deacon in that church to the day of his death, being, I suppose, nearly eighty years of age. William Underwood and his associate in the deaconship, William Lancaster "seemed to be pillows in the church," more than half a century ago . Lancaster died in 1814 and after that time underwood was associated in his office with some younger men: David Golightly, Thomas Cooper, and Robert White.... Friend. Goudeysville, Union Co., March 31, 1870.

Issue of April 21, 1870

Departed this life on the morning of 22nd March 1870, Mrs. J. E. Jones, wife of J. H. Jones of Abbeville district, S. C., aged 28 years and 3 months. She has left a husband and five little children, one boy and four girls, one an infant born at her death....

Issue of May 12, 1870

Tribute from Little River Sabbath school to the deceased Capt. Addison Clinkscales.

Issue of May 19, 1870 [place of publication changed to Charleston]

Mrs. Fanny R. E. Garrison, wife of J. R. Garrison, died in Mecklenburg county, N. C., on the 30th of April, in her 37th year.... Pineville, N. C., May 8th 1870.

Issue of May 26, 1870

Married on the evening of the 4th inst., by Rev. T. H. Pope, Mr. N. P. Whitmire of Greenville, to Miss Clayton Reeder, of Newberry.

In Lancaster County, S. C., the 17th inst., by the Rev. A. L. Stough, Dr. Joseph Gribble, of Mecklingburg County, N. C., to Miss Delilah Ross, daughter of John Ross, of Lancaster County, S. C.

By the same on the same day, at Flint Hill Church, York County, S. C., Mr. John Harrison to Miss Lou Davis, both of York County, S. C. *Biblical Record, please copy.*

Issue of June 9, 1870

Married on the 26th of May 1870, by the Rev. J. K. Mendenhall, Dr. William Griffin, of Newberry, S. C., to Hattie Daniel, of Edgefield, daughter of Maj. William Daniel.

Issue of June 16, 1870

Rev. G. B. Bealer, D. D. Many of our readers have doubtless already heard of the unexpected death of this brother; but as he was for so many years an efficient pastor and successful preacher in our State, we cannot dismiss the announcement of his death without a more extended notice. He died on Thursday, June 2d, in the city of Atlanta, Ga., whither he had gone in search of health. He was born in Grahamville, S. C., Dec. 7th 1822. He was brought to a public profession of faith in Jesus in Charleston, during the great revival. At the time of his conversion, Brother Bealer had been admitted to the bar at Columbia, S. C., and had chosen the law as his profession. His first pastorate was at Cheraw, which was closed by a sever attack of disease, and he soon after became the pastor of our church at Darlington. Subsequently he settled in Norfolk... He then accepted a call to the church at Madison, Ga., where he remained for over a year....

N. W. Hodges. Early in 1841, the health of Brother Hodges began to decline... Mrs. Hodges lingered until September. I preached her funeral sermon, at Fairfield church.... Among the children that survived Mrs. Hodges was an infant daughter, who was taken charge of by Mrs. Ashford, and tenderly cherish, until removed by death....

[page 3] The Rev. G. B. Bealer, D. D., died in Atlanta, Ga., on the 2d inst. At his own request, his remains were conveyed to Darlington, and there interred on Sunday, the 5th inst.

Rev. Joseph S. Walthall, who was for two years an associate editor on the staff of the Biblical Recorded, died in Richmond, Va., on the 23d ult., aged 59 years.

Issue of June 23, 1870

Tribute of Respect to D. G. Burnett by order of the Church, H. H. Mayson, C. C. Ninety Six, June 1870.

From *The Index*:

Married, in the city of Madison, Ga., on Tuesday, June 7th 1870, by Rev. C. M. Irwin, pastor of the Madison Baptist church, Rev. W. T. Brantly, D. D., pastor of the Second Baptist Church, Atlanta, and Mrs. Mattie Marston, daughter of Col. John B. Walker.

Married on the 9th inst., by the Rev. J. K. Mendenhall, Mr. Douglas Burton to Miss Amelia Floyd, daughter of Mr. Barnabas Floyd, all of Newberry, S. C.

Issue of July 5, 1870 [day of publication changed to Tuesday]

Tribute of Respect to the Memory of the late George Lynes. A meeting of the Goose Creek Baptist Church was held at the church on Sunday, 5th of June, Rev. J. L. Rollings in the chair and C. J. Cain, clerk... our beloved brother George Lynes, who died 23rd April 1870. The deceased was a member with us about 36 years; baptized by the Rev. Daniel Shephard about the year 1834, and was appointed Deacon 11th Feb 1843....

Issue of July 12, 1870

Married by the Rev. P. J. Hiers, on the 12th of May, Mr. James L. Williams, to Miss Eliza Payton, all of Barnwell County.

By the same on the 1st of June, Mr. Daniel Jackson, to Miss Ellen Rosier, all of Barnwell Co.

Also, by the same on the 8th of June, Mr. Benj. Pressy, to Miss Mary Wood, all of Barnwell Co.

Departed this life on the 9th day of June, at the residence of her son-in-law, Rev. J. C. Furman, in Greenville, S. C., Mrs. Rebecca Davis, relict of Rev. J. Davis, of Fairfield. Mrs. Davis had entered upon her eighty-four year.... She was the youngest child of Captain Jas. Kincaid, a princely man, who, inheriting in Ireland (under the law of primogeniture) a valuable landed estate, chose to divide it with his mother and brothers and sisters, and sought a field for his enterprise in the new world. He purchased a large boyd of fertile land in what is now known as Fairfield county. During the Revolutionary war he served as captain under Marion and Sumter. he was in the battles of Camden, Cowpens, Guilford C. H., Rocky Mt. and Eutaw, in the last of which he was slightly wounded. After the war he erected a substantial family mansion on Mill Creek which is still in the occupancy of some of his descendants.. He also built the "Brick Church," which still stands a few hundred years from Little River.... an Irish Protestant of the Presbyterian order. On a visit to Charleston during the prevalence of yellow fever, in the year 8101 Captain K. sickened and died. His remains were interred int eh Scotch Presbyterian burial ground and a tablet to his memory placed upon the walls of the church. J. C. F.

Died at Bellevue, Lou., in the 8th day of February 1870, in the 26th year of his age, Aiken A. Mimms of Charleston District, S. C.

Departed this life June 30th 1870 at the residence of her husband, Mr. James A. Parler in Orangeburg County, S.C., Mrs. Jane Parler, in the fifty fourth year of her age. Sister Parler was a daughter of brother George Norriston of said County. She was married to brother James Parler in 1832 and became a member of the Antioch Baptist Church in 1833. At the rime of her death she was a member of the Corinth Church... J. E. H. Tri-weekly *Courier, News*, and *Christian Advocate*, please copy.

Died on James Island, at the residence of her father, on the evening of July 5th, Mrs. Robert Bee, in the thirty-sixth year of her age, leaving a husband and two children to mourn her loss.... a member of the First Baptist Church of Charleston.

Issue of July 19, 1870

Whereas our Brother Gen. C. B. Griffin departed this life at his residence in Laurens County on the 12th day of May in the 55th year of his age. Having united himself with the Bush River Church in 1842 during a series of meetings held by Elder Daniel Mangrum, he continued faithful for nearly forty years. Brother G. was ordained a deacon at the Chestnut Ridge Church in Laurens.. Some 16 years since he removed his membership to Cross Roads Church, since which time he has never failed to represent us as a delegate in the Reedy River Association.... Wm. B. Elkin, Moderator. Lafayette Spearman, Church Clerk. Cross Roads Baptist Church, Newberry, July 2d 1870.

Departed this life, 10th July 1870, George Stewart Heriot, aged 10 months and 3 days.

Died at Midway, Abbeville county, on Monday, 7th inst., Sophie Lake, only daughter of John C. and Emma L. Chiles, aged fifteen months.

Issue of July 26, 1870

Married in Cheraw, S. C., on the 17th July, at the residence of the bride-groom's father, by the Rev. J. F. Taylor, Mr. B. Campion to Miss Ellen C. McQuaig.

Issue of August 30, 1870

Married on the 11th ult., near Pineville, N. C., by the Rev. A. L. Stough, Mr. J. R. Garrison of York county, S. C., to Miss Hannah Davis, of Mecklenburg County, N. C.

Departed this life, August 5th 1870, Mary Elizabeth, infant daughter of John J. and Georgianna B. Singeltary, aged five months and four days.

Issue of September 6, 1870

Departed this life, at his residence in Orangeburg County, S. C., on the 27th day of August, 1870, Major Charles W. Richburg, in his 54th year. Brother Richburg was a member of the Corinth Baptist Church... Jas. A. Parler.

Issue of September 20, 1870

Departed this life on the morning of the 9th inst., at Anderson C. H., little Meta Adaline, infant daughter of Rev. W. D. and R. A. Beverley, aged 7 months and 22 days.

Issue of October 4, 1870

Died, September 4, 1870, William Carson, a bright and interesting little son of Rev. J. G. Williams, aged 4 years and 4 months.

Departed this life, at Myersville, on the morning of the 21st inst., little Sallie, infant daughter of Dr. S. D. M. and S. J. Byrd, aged 1 year, 4 months, and 21 days.

Issue of October 11, 1870

Died, of typhoid fever, after an illness of two weeks, little John R. Gonza, son of Mary Ann Sweatman, aged 9 years and 5 months. he was one of our Sunday School scholars... Ridgeway, S. C., September 18.

Issue of October 18, 1870

Married in the Baptist Church at Cheraw, S. C., on the evening of the 29th September, by Rev. J. O. B. Dargan, D. D., assisted by Rev. J. W. Burn, Rev. T. J. Taylor, of Charlotte, N. C., and Miss Emily B. King of Cheraw.

Died, at his residence in Yorkville, on Monday, the 10th inst., from a second attack of paralysis, Mr. John E. Grist, in the sixty-fourth year of his age. The deceased was born in Spartanburg County, in this state; became a printer, and was employed in the printing office of Mr. Landrum in Columbia. From Columbia, he, with his small family, including his son, Lewis M., the proprietor of the Enquirer, came to Yorkville, on the 20th of April 1833, to conduct and manage the printing department of the "Yorkville Patriot, under an engagement with G. W. Williams, Esq., and W. C. Beatty, proprietors and editors. In the year 1835, he commenced and published the "Journal of the Times," and from that date until 1854, continued to publish.... He leaves a wife, several sons and daughters, and numerous grandchildren.

Died, on the 6th inst., aged two years, ten months, and seven days, William J., infant son of Rev. J. J. and R. Getsinger.

Issue of October 25, 1870

Married at the residence of J. C. Evans, Cheraw, S. C., on the 16th inst., by Rev. W. H. Leavell, Mr. Rob't Y. Leavell, of Newberry, S. C., and Miss Marie Evans.

Issue of November 1, 1870

Died, on the morning of the 14th ult., at the residence of his son, at Parnassus, in Marlboro' county, S. C., James Lucas, in the 79th year of his age. Thirty-eight years ago he professed Christ, and joined the Baptist Church in North Carolina.

Issue of November 8, 1870

Married at Lexington C. H., on the 26th October, by Rev. J. F. Morrall, Mr. David B. Morgan, of Savannah, Ga., and Miss Ellen M., youngest daughter of the late Rev. George Haltiwanger.

On the 26th of October, by Rev. W. D. Thomas, Rev. Thomas P. Lide, Jr., of Darlington, S. C., and Miss Carrie M. Hawkins, of Greenville, S. C.

Died at his residence in Lancaster County, S. C., October 14, 1870, John Ross, Esq., in the 60th year of his age. At the time of his death, he was a Deacon of the Baptist Church at Pleasant Valley, of which he had long been a beloved and useful member.... He leaves a stricken family and a large circle of relatives....

Died, in Washington, Texas, on the 11th ult., Mrs. Mary Cartmell, in the 62d year of her age. She was the widow of Major h. R. Cartmell. Mrs. C. was a native of Charleston, S. C., daughter of John M. Frazier. She went to Texas about twenty years ago, and settled in Washington, where she resided until her death. She was baptized by Rev. Mr. Huckins, late of Charleston, while he was pastor in Washington. one of her sons is a judge in Texas.

Issue of November 29, 1870

Married on the 16th of November, by Rev. W. L. Brown, Mr. E. E. Smith and Miss Sallie Smith, all of Spartanburg, S. C.

By the Rev. N. Graham, on the 10th of november, in Clarendon County, Mr. N. G. Broadway to Miss M. S. Rich.

Departed this life, August 28, 1870, Mrs. Emeline Permelia Young, wife of Rev. Valentine young. The deceased was born May 17, 1818. At the early age of 14 or 15 she was baptized into the Church of Christ.... She was married to Rev. V. Young, November 18, 1836. She leaves a distressed and heart-broken husband and five children....

Departed this life, September 26, 1870, in Chester County, S. C., in the 74th year of her age, Mrs. Mary Ferguson. In 1813 she was married to Captain William Ferguson. She embraced religion and joined the Hopewell Baptist Church in 1839. She leaves a fond husband and many friends.... J. S. Croxton.

Departed this life on the 20th of September, 1870, W. J. Morris, aged 21 years.... A. M. C.

Simeon Chaney was born in Virginia, June 8, 1797. in the year 1808, he moved to Abbeville County, S. C., where he spent the remainder of his life. He united with the Siloan Baptist Church in 1845, in whose fellowship he lived until September 23, 1870.

Miss Mary Mabury died, at the residence of her widowed mother, at Old Cambridge, S. C., on the night of October 27, 1870, at the age of 23 years. She was a devoted member of the Sunday School and Church at Fellowship....

Mrs. Emma Eliza Sheppard, daughter of Brother T. J. Pinson, and worthy sister of Siloam Church, departed her life on November 1st, 1870, in the 25th year of her age.

Issue of December 6, 1870

Married on the evening of the 7th ult., by Rev. C. T. Anderson, Thomas Murphy to Miss Sarah McNeil, all of Williamsburg, S. C.

By the same, on the 24th ult., Mr. Thomas Wiggins, of Williamsburg, to Miss Mary McGee, of Marion, S. C.

By Rev. W. P. Martin, on the 2d of November 1870, at the residence of the bride's father, Mr. John E. Russell to Miss Nancy M. Ballentine, all of Anderson County, S. C.

By the same, on the 27th of November, 1870, at the residence of the bride's mother, Mr. Warren S. Fleming, of Anderson County, S. C., to Miss Mary F. Mattison, of Abbeville County, S. C.

Died, on the 15th of November 1870, at his residence, in Monticello, S. c., Adam J. Burley, who had just entered the fiftieth year of his age... A. M. C.

Died, at his residence, near Grahamville, S. C., November 26, 1870, of pneumonia, William J. Morrall, in the 47th year of his age. The deceased was, for near twenty years, an efficient Deacon of the Euhaw Baptist church.

Issue of December 13, 1870

Married, at Edgefield, S. C., on the 24th ult., by Rev. J. P. Mealing, Rev. L. Broaddus and Miss Sallie F., daughter of B. C. Bryan, all of Edgefield.

Issue of December 20, 1870

Married in this city, on the evening of the 14th inst., by the Rev. L. H. Shuck, assisted by Rev. Dr. Winkler, Mr. Josiah Axson to Miss Lizzie, daughter of the late John R. Heriot, Esq.

At the residence of the bride's mother, on the 13th inst., by Rev. Tillman R. Gaines, Mr. J. L. Gaffney, of Spartanburg, and Miss Emma C. Kerr, of Yorkville.

At the residence of the bride's mother, on the 22d ult., by Rev. A. L. Stough, Mr. B. F. Culp, of Lancaster, to Miss S. C. Faris, of York County, S. C.

On the 25th ult., in Mecklenburg County, N. C., by Rev. A. L. Stough, Mr. S. H. Epps and Miss M. J. Blankenship, of York County, S. C.

Issue of January 24, 1871

[page 1]
Our Sleeping Dead.

Rev. W. R. Sanders was a native of Barnwell District, and was one of the most useful and efficient preachers of his day. He was baptized at Barnwell C. H. in his fifteenth year. He afterwards transferred his membership to the Columbia Baptist church... Immediately after his ordination, he became a student of the Furman Institution, located at that time in Fairfield District.... Upon the secession of South Carolina, he responded to the call of his country and raised a company of volunteers for active service. While in this service he contracted a fatal disease which soon termination his earthly career.

Rev. N. W. Walker was born in Barnwell District about the year 1800. He was the grandson of the Rev. Nathaniel Walker, one of the earliest preachers in this section of the State. Brother Walker was the son of pious parents. On the fourth Sabbath in June, 1821, he was baptized into the fellowship of the Baptist Church at Healing Springs by Rev. D. Peoples. he was licensed to preach, and on May 4, 1833, he was ordained pastor of the Little Saltketcher Church, in Colleton District, by a Presbytery consisting of Rev. John Youmans, and Rev. John Brooker. He died December 20, 1858, in the fifty-ninth year of his age.

Married on the 21st ult., at the residence of D. R. Feaster, Esq., by Rev. G. W. Pickett, Mr. J. H. Lewis and Miss Anna H., daughter of the late J. T. Rawls, of Columbia.

On the 22d ult., at the residence of the bride's father by the same, Mr. Hampton Banks, of Fairfield county, and Miss Bettie McCollum, of Chester county.

On the 12th inst., at the residence of the bride's father, by the same, Mr. Green Berry Mayfield and Miss Fannie Kirkpatrick, all of Chester County.

On the same day, at the residence of the bride's father, by the same, Mr. N. G. Simpson and Miss Lucy J. Darby, both of Chester county.

On the same day, at the residence of the bride's mother, by the same, Mr. H. N. McCollum of Chester county and Miss M. E. Banks, of Fairfield county.

On the 10th inst., by Rev. J. E. Rodgers, Mr. J. W. Stucky of Darlington county, to Miss Mary E. Woodward, of Sumter county.

On the 12th inst., by Rev. J. E. Rodgers, Mr. F. F. Baker to Mrs. Julia Scarborough, both of Sumter county.

Issue of January 31, 1871

[page 1]
Our Sleeping Dead.

The following sketch was taken from the Discourse delivered by Rev. James P. Boyce, on the occasion of Dr. Manly's funeral, December 22, 1868. Basil Manly was born about three miles north of Pittsboro', in Chatham county, North Carolina, on the 29th day of January 1798. He was baptized on the 26th of August 1816.... licensed to preach April 25, 1818, granted by Rocky Spring Church, of which he still continued a member. On may 1818, he preached his first sermon in the Baptist meeting house, in the town of Beaufort, South Carolina....

Married on the 12th inst., at the residence of the bride's father, by Rev. W. J. Hatfield, Mr. S. B. Bradley to Miss Sarah Cato, all of Sumter county, S. C.

Issue of February 14, 1871

Married on the 15th ult., by Rev. A. L. Stough, Mr. John Pitman and Miss Ollevia C. Edwards, all of Chester county, S. C.

On the 20th ult., by Rev. A. L. Stough, Mr. Joe Epps and Miss G. Harris, all of York county, S. C.

On the 5th inst., by Rev. A. L. Stough, Mr. R. J. Boyd and Miss Fannie E. Smith, all of Mecklenburg county, N. C.

On the 10th inst., by Rev. A. L. Stough, Mr. S. C. Cross and Miss Patsy Bowden, all of Mecklenburg county, N. C.

On the 12th inst., by Rev. A. L. Stough, Mr. B. Cole and Miss M. A. Porter, all of York county, S. C.

On Sabbath morning, 5th inst., by Rev. M. C. Barnett, Mr. J. P. Owens and Miss Eliza Going, all of Union county, S. C.

Died, the first week of October last, Mrs. Mary R. Stanley, wife of Dempsy Stanley, aged about 25 years. She was an affectionate, devoted, and faithful daughter, wife, and mother, and a member of the Sandy Run Baptist Church. She leaves a husband and four children. Buford's Bridge, S.C. W. H. D----.

Issue of February 21, 1871

In Memoriam. The death of William Colclough Skinner, the brother of James. D. and Joseph M. Skinner, Esq. He departed on the 2d of February in the town of Bamberg, and on the 3d was committed to the grave. At the age of thirteen, he united himself with the Calvary Baptist Church of Clarendon county, then under the care of the Rev. Mr. Mahoney, by whom he was baptized. J. F. Buist. Bamberg, February 14.

Married on the 5th January, by Elder W. H. Robert, John J. Powell and Nancy Baysinger, all of Philips county, Ark.

On the 19th January, by the same, W. Harrison Gregory and Sallie E. Fitzgerald, all of Philips county, Ark.

On the 25th January, by the same, in Trenton, Philips county, Ark., Charles T. Scaife and E. Eloise Robert.

On the 11th January, by Rev. Thomas H. Pope, Joseph Purdy and Miss S. A. Jones, all of Laurens.

On the 24th January, by the same, in Newberry, J. B. Davis and Miss Betty Tribble.

On the 31st January, by the same, Pinckney Bradley and Miss Rebecca Butler.

On the 8th instant, by the same, Colonel B. F. Griffin, of Newberry, and Mrs. Eliza Gary, of Laurens.

on the 3d instant, at the residence of the groom's brother, by Rev. W. J. Hatfield, H. J. Dunlap to Miss Martha Ann Holland, all of Sumter county.

Issue of February 28, 1871

Married, in this city, on the 16th instant, by Rev. L. H. Shuck, J. W. F. DeLorme, of Sumter, S. C., to Miss Lizzie M., eldest daughter of Robert James, Esq.

Died, on the 23d of January last, at the residence of her brother, Hon. John Townsend, Edisto Island, Miss Susan M. Townsend, a beloved member of the Citadel Square Baptist Church. [eulogy]

Issue of March 7, 1871

Married on the 22d January, by Rev. T. J. Price, Mr. R. M. Josey and Miss Araminta Crosswell, all of Darlington county, S. C.

On February 16, in Richmond, Va., by the Rev. R. M. Baker, Rector of Grace (Episcopal) Church, A. Welborne Moise, Esq., of that city, to Marie C., eldest daughter of Mr. Washington Gill, late City Engineer of Richmond, Va., now of St. Louis, Mo.

Mrs. Mary Ruth, widow of the lamented Hon. A. M. Ruth, died at her residence, in Beaufort county, on the 5th of February, in the fifty-eighth year of her age. She was attended in her last illness by the much loved and successful Dr. H. W. C. Folk, and her funeral sermon was delivered by Rev. Jonas Trowel. Among her sons and sons-in-law, we will mention the well known names of Major J. J. Harrison, Captain A. M. Ruth, Rev. W. H. Dowling, Captain P. F. Buckner, Murdough, Harvey and Anderson.

Issue of March 21, 1871

Married on February 16, at the residence of the bride's father, near Black Mingo, Williamsburg county, by Rev. N. Graham, J. M. N. Wilder, of Sumter, to Miss Mary J. Brockington.

Issue of March 28, 1871

[page 1]
Our Sleeping Dead. Sketch of Rev. I. E. H. Seymour. [Sketch of Rev. Basil Manly continued.]

A Good Man Fallen. Died, on the 14th of February last, after a short illness, Mr. John O. Barry, aged twenty-three years, five months and eight days. When but twelve years old, he attached himself to the Baptist church at Fork Shoal, in which he lived a consistent member until the day of his death. [eulogy]

Married on the 22d February, by Rev. Thomas H. Pope, Mr. Rhett Milam and Miss Mattie Duckett, all of Laurens.

Issue of April 4, 1871

Married by Rev. A. C. Stepp, on Thursday evening, February 9, Mr. William F. Bagwell, of Anderson county, to Miss Louisa J. Bagwell, of Greenville, S. C.
By the same on Thursday evening, March 9, Mr. Joel Cox, of Anderson county, and Miss Emma L. M. Machen, of Greenville, S. C.

THE WORKING CHRISTIAN

Married by Rev. F. C. Jeter, the 22d of December last, Joseph Skelton to Miss Martha Peck.

By the same, on the 23d of February, Levi Smith to Miss Letty Hawkins.

By the same, on the 28th of March, M. B. Meador to Miss Lizzie Hawkins.

By the same, on the 22d of March, at Mr. J. Meador's, Joseph Pendergrass (democrat) to widow Adaline Becknell, (both colored), all of Union county, S. C.

By the same, on the 16th of March, Robert Cuming to Miss Victoria Smith, both of Newberry county, S. C.

Brother Wm. Cone, of Barnwell county, S. C., was born January 2, 1791, and died March 22, 1871, aged 80 years, 3 months, and 20 days. For nearly fifty years he had been a member of the Baptist Church.... He leaves a large family, among whom, we will mention the well known names of his son John Cone, and his son-in-law Jerry Googe.

Mrs. Elizabeth Cone, his wife, was born September 25, 1799, and died March 1, 1871, aged 71 years, 5 months, and 7 days. Although she was a member of the M. E. Church, in her companionship she was faithful as they pilgrimaged to the glorious City of God. W. H. D.

Died on the 3d of March 1871, at her father's residence, near Maysville, S. C., Mrs. Mary K. Stiles, the beloved wife of the Rev. C. A. Stiles. In early life she united with the Baptist Church at Bethany, S. C... She leaves a husband and four little children.

Died, on the 26th of March, after a short illness, the beloved little daughter, Hassie, of M. B. and S. McGee, of Abbeville county, aged 4 years and 7 months. A. Rice.

Issue of April 18, 1871

Death of Rev. Addison Hall. We are pained to announce the sudden death of this venerable minister of the gospel. He was in his usual good health up to Sunday, April 2d, but on the morning of that day complained of acute pain in the region of his heart, and by 10 o'clock p. m., he had passed away to his final rest. He was held in high esteem by the Baptists of Virginia. He had baptized about seventeen hundred persons.

Issue of April 25, 1871

Married on the 6th April, by Rev. T. H. Pope, Mr. Joseph C. Hargrove, to Miss Emma Abrams, all of Newberry county.

Died in Laurens county, at the residence of her son-in-law, R. S. Griffin, on the 31st of March last, Mrs. Emily C. Jones, aged 68 years. Mrs. Jones was the daughter of Judge Waddy Thompson, of Greenville, and wife of General Thomas F. Jones, of Laurens. She united with the Baptist Church at Chesnut Ridge in 1831, and transferred her membership to the Warrior Creek church about the year 1846, of which church she was a consistent member until her death.

Died, in Spartanburg, on the morning of the 14th April, Mrs. Mary A. J. Kennedy, of Charleston, S. C., aged 79 years and 5 months.

Issue of May 2, 1871

Tribute of Respect from the Baptist church at the Great Saltkehatchie to Samuel Boynton, who departed this life the fifth of January 1871.... J. M. Williams, C. C.

Issue of May 18, 1871 [day of publication changed to Thursday]

Married by Elder W. H. Robert, March 2, at the resident of W. H. Roberts, Esq., near Trenton, Arkansas, Mr. William Hawthorne and Miss Lillie Joyce.

By Rev. A. C. Stepp, on Sunday morning, April 16, Mr. J. F. M. Clees, of Anderson county, and Miss M. E. Jordan, of Greenville county, S. C.

Issue of May 25, 1871

In Memoriam. Died, of consumption, at her brother's near Liberty Hall, in Newberry county, on the 12th instant, Mrs. Bettie Gaines. She had been for several years a member of the Baptist church. Her husband and brother both died in the army near Stephensburg, Va., and were buried in the cemetery of the Baptist church at Stephensburg.

On Saturday, 8th April, the grave closed over the remains of Colonel David L. Donald, of Williamston, S. C. On the previous Wednesday he had been attending to his usual duties as a merchant and railroad agent. From a volunteer private of the Palmetto Regiment in the Mexican War, he was promoted to a Lieutenancy, and received a gold medal as a reward of his bravery. In our late unsuccessful war for the liberty of the south, he was twice wounded... 2nd Rifle Regiment, S. C. Volunteers.

Issue of June 1, 1871

Married by Rev. L. H. Shuck, Thursday, May 25, Mr. B. M. Fogartie to Miss Eliza G., daughter of Mr. John S. Bee, all of this city.

By Rev. E. W. Horne, on the 27th ult., Rev. R. J. Towill, of Virginia, and Miss A. M. Bell, of South Carolina.

By Rev. Thomas H. Pope, at the residence of the bride's father, on the morning of the 18th ult., Mr. George B. Johnson to Miss Kate Workman.

Issue of June 8, 1871

Married, on the 14th ultimo, in Marshall, Texas, at the residence of Mr. T. A. Bell, by Rev. W. D. Beverly, Mr. E. R. Parker and Miss Elenora Lipscomb.

Married by Rev. R. M. King, on the 16th ultimo, Mr. James A. Bigby, of Honea Path, and Miss Mollie Wilson, of Abbeville county, S. C.

Issue of June 15, 1871

Died, suddenly, in this city, on the morning of May 3, 1871, Miss Caroline Budd, daughter of Deacon T. S. Budd, of the First Baptist church. [eulogy]

Issue of June 22, 1871

Died, suddenly, at his home in Barnwell county, on the morning of the 7th instant, Captain Henry W. McMillan, in the sixty-second year of his age. He had been a member of Springtown church forty-four years, and had the confidence and love of his brethren. J. G. W.

Died at his residence, in St. Mathew's, on the 7th instant, Brother James A. Parler, aged 58 years, 11 months and 12 days. Brother Parler connected himself long years ago with the Antioch (O) Baptist Church. Some time after he was appointed clerk, and then deacon, which position he held until 168, when he, with others, received letters of dismission to constitute Corinth church. of this church he was deacon until his death. Intensified by the recent death (June 1870) of his wife. He leaves a large family.... L. G. P.

Died, in Colleton county, May 16th, Brother Thomas Caldwell, and on the day following, his wife Sister Sarah Caldwell. They have left six children, two of them interesting little twin girls....

Issue of June 29, 1871

Died, in this city, on Wednesday, June 21st 1871, Mrs. Elizabeth Mary Heriot, beloved wife of W. J. heriot, Esq. our sister was baptized into the fellowship of the First Baptist church in the year 1860.... We commend her stricken husband and only child....

Died, in Brooklyn, New York, Sunday morning, 4th June, Henry O. Whitney, in the 27th year of his age, oldest son of James H. and Charlotte W. Whitney.

Issue of July 20, 1871

Married, on Sunday morning, the 25th ultimo, by Elder W. L. Brown, Mr. Joseph Lancaster and Miss Martha Smith, all of Union county, S. C.

Died, in this city, June 29th 1871, Miss Mary Agnes Burke, daughter of A. J. Burke, Esq. She was baptized into the fellowship of the First Baptist church in May, 1854. [eulogy]

Tribute of Respect to James A. Parker from Corinth Baptist Church, Orangeburg, S. C. [this should probably be James A. Parler--see obituary notice]

Issue of July 27, 1871

Death of Rev. C. P. Gadsden. The Episcopalians of this city, and especially the congregation of St. Luke's church, have sustained a serious loss in the death of this eminent Christian minister.....

Issue of August 17, 1871

Departed this life, on Monday evening, the 31st of July, Mrs. E. Parr, consort of Major H. W. Parr. She leaves an affectionate husband and two little children. A. M. C.

Death of Rev. John W. Robertson, who died suddenly (on last Sabbath morning, July 30), leaving behind an afflicted widow, with ten children.. S. W. A. Walterboro', S. C., August 4.

Issue of August 24, 1871

Married, by Elder A. C. Stepp, on Sunday morning, June 25, 1871, Mr. W. G. Elgin, of Abbeville county, and Miss P. A. F. Wright, of Honea Path, S. C.

Issue of August 31, 1871

Tribute of Respect to our friend and teacher, S. James Tompkins... J. P. Blackwell, Secretary Plum Branch Sunday-School. July 23, 1871.

Issue of September 21, 1871

Married, by Rev. A. C. Stepp, on Thursday evening, August 31, Mr. B. R. Bagwell and Miss Mary Jane Bolt, both of Greenville county, S. C.

Thomas Furman Brodie was born in Orangeburg district, So. Ca., April 5th, 1830, and died at Walhalla, August 30th 1871.... united with the Wentworth Street Baptist Church, then under the charge of Rev. James H. Cuthbert.... Remains were transported to the family cemetery of his father-in-law, Genl. Paul Quattlebaum, in Lancaster county....

Edward L. Rigby, son of W. W. and Elizabeth Rigby, died at Reesville, S. C., on the 26th ultimo, in the twenty-eight year of his age.... C. R. Council

Issue of October 26, 1871

Married, at the residence of the bride's mother, on the 14th September, by Rev. W. R. Parler, Mr. J. S. Hat and Miss Fannie C. Felder, all of Orangeburg county.

Married, by Rev. A. C. Stepp, on Tuesday evening, September 26th 1871, Mr. Jasper A. Bagwell, of Greenville County, and Miss Ann Davenport, of Laurens County, S. C.

In Memoriam. Death of Mr. William Rice of Graham's T. O., who died on the 24th September, aged eighty years. [eulogy] J. F. Buist

Issue of November 2, 1871

In Memoriam. Died, in Charleston, S. C., October 10th, 1871, Mrs. Martha S. Silcox, aged 52 years, 3 months, and 19 days, beloved wife of Daniel H. Silcox, a worthy deacon of the First Baptist church.... Sister Silcox was baptized at the First Baptist church, by Rev. B. Manly, September 16, 1835. Pastor. "Religious Herald" please copy.

[missing issues here through February 1872]

Issue of March 7, 1872

Married on the 20th February, by the Rev. J. K. Mendenhall, Wm. R. Spearman, Esq., and Miss Sallie A. Clark, daughter of Dr. R. P. Clark, at the residence of the latter, Jalapa, Newberry Co., S. C.

Died, Eddie, son of William Ellen Hern, departed this life in Edgefield county, Nov. 14th 1871. he was only 10 years old... Eva Blanch.

At Yorkville, on Thursday, Feb. 29th, little Bessie Pendleton, youngest daughter of Rev. W. A. and Mary E. Gaines, aged two years, seven months, and five days... On Saturday, her father took the corpse to Columbia, where he waited over until Monday when accompanied by Mrs. T. R. Gaines, he carried the child to Damascus church in Edgefield county, and buried her by the side of his little Pascal who had slept there for four years....

Issue of March 14, 1872

Died, Mr. A. W. Thompson, was born in N. C., A. D., 1800, and died at his residence in Chesterfield County, S. C., February 17, 1872, after a painful illness of about one month. He had been a member of the church about fifty years....

Issue of March 21, 1872

Departed this life, January 24th 1872, at home, Darlington County, South Carolina, Mrs. Prudence Thomas, relict of Micajah Thomas. She was in her 80th year. For fifty years she had been a member of the Gum Branch Baptist Church; succeeded in raising six children, and all became members of the Baptist church, but some of them have gone to their blessed home.

Issue of March 28, 1872

Married By the Rev. J. A. Segler, at the residence of the bride's father, on the 27th of February, Mr. F. T. Rickenbaker to Miss Pauline Able, all of Orangeburg county, S. C.

By the same, at the residence of the bride's father, on the 14th inst., Mr. Wm. Cook of Lexington county to Miss Mattie Brodie, of Orangeburgh county.

By the Rev. J. K. Mendenhall, on the 21st March, Mr. J. M. Crosswell, of St. Mathews, Orangeburg county, to Miss Sue Slawson, of Newberry, daughter of Mr. Levi Slawson.

Tribute of Respect to Deacon A. W. Thompson from Macedonia Baptist Church, March 9th 1872.

Fell asleep in Jesus, at Mt. Pleasant, Charleston county, S. C., on the 26th day of February 1872, Mrs. Harriet Emma Wallace, aged 20 years, 5 months, and 24 days. Although so young, she had been 16 months a widow, and leaves two small children. O. F. G.

Issue of April 4, 1872

Married on Thursday, the 14th of March, 1872, at the residence of the bride's father, by Rev. S. Isbell, Mr. Z. L. Burris to Miss C. L. Riley, both of Anderson county, S. C.

Issue of April 11, 1872

Married, At the residence of the bride's father, on the 2d of April, by Rev. A. P. Norris, Rev. W. R. Parler to miss Mary J. Rickenbaker-- all of Orangeburg County, S. C.

Died, on the 10th of October 1871, of Yellow Fever, contracted in Charleston, Rasselas P. M. Williams, youngest son of Col. B. S. and Emily williams, in the 26th year of his age. When only 15 years old he became a soldier... He leaves an aged father and mother, wife and child, a sister and two brothers.

Issue of April 25, 1872

Died, Mrs. Antoinette S. Wallace, was born July 27th 1851; died February 14th 1872. At the age of thirteen she united herself with the Baptist Church. She was married December 23d, 1868, to J. C. Wallace... left two little boys.

Issue of May 2, 1872

Departed this life in the blessed hope of a glorious resurrection, Mrs. Mary Randal Dawson, beloved wife of the Rev. Thomas Dawson, at 2 o'clock P. M., the 22d day of April 1872, in the 70th year of her age. She was baptized by the Rev. James Welch, at Burlington, N. J., and joined the church at that place in the 12th year of her age. She afterwards joined the Sampson Street Church under the pastoral card of Dr. Staughton, was sent by the Trienniel Board an assistant missionary to the Valley Towns Mission Cherokee Nation, and was married to her husband at that station, August 10th 1822.

Departed this life in Graniteville, on the 21st of March last, Mr. T. J. Senn, aged 38 years, 5 months and 25 days. He was married to Miss Nancy E. Marchant, April 6th 1856, baptized in July following, by the Rev. A. P. Norris... ordained to the office of Deacon of the Baptist Church in Graniteville.... W. L. H.

Issue of May 9, 1872

Married on Wednesday, May 1, 1872, by the Rev. Lewis W. Rast, Rev. Geo. S. Anderson, formerly of Va., now Pastor of the Baptist Church, Madison, Fla., to Miss Belle C., daughter of Rev. D. F. Spigener, of Orangeburg, S. C.

Died, on the 26th day of April, 1872, Miss Mary S. Beatson. She made a profession of religion early in life, and united with the Home Branch Baptist Church. She leaves an aged father and mother, loving sisters and a brother. E. H. C.

Issue of May 30, 1872

Married at the residence of the bride's father, on Wednesday evening, May 22, 1872, by Rev. J. S. Murray, Mr. B. Frank Mauldin, of Columbia, and Miss Mamie E. Reed, daughter of Hon. J. P. Reed, of Anderson, S. C.

Died, on the 21st May, William Welch Mendenhall, son of Rev. J. K. and H. E. Mendenhall, aged four years, three months, and twenty-one days.

Issue of June 20, 1872

Died on Monday, June 3d, 1872, Miss Ann G. Hext, eldest daughter of Mrs. Elizabeth Hext, of Barnwell County, S. C. The deceased had been for years a useful member of Steel Creek Church.... Steel Creek, Barnwell Co., S. C., June 8.

Issue of June 27, 1872

Married on the 19th inst., at the residence of the bride's father, by Rev. F. C. Jeter, Mr. Wm. Sartor to Miss Mary McJunkin, both of Union, S. C.

[missing issues through September 1872]

Issue of October 3, 1872

Married on the 22d of August, at the residence of Mr. John O. Darby in Chester County, South Carolina, by Rev. Mr. Cilgoe, Mr. S. Logan Hover to Miss Jennie E. R. Perry, formerly of Limestone Springs, S. C.

Died in Fairfield County, on the 10th of September 1872, at the residence of her daughter, Mrs. Scynthia Trapp, Mrs. Frances Powell, consort of Aaron Powell, deceased, aged seventy-three years. She had been a member of the Baptist Church for over fifty years, and was, at the time of her death, a member of Buffalo. B. F. Corley.

Issue of October 17, 1872

Died, at Jacksonville, Florida, January 22, 1872, Elder P. R. King, aged 57 years, 8 months, and 4 days.

Issue of October 24, 1872

Married on Wednesday, 16th inst., by the Rev. E. A. Edwards, near Mayesville, Rev. C. A. Stiles to Miss Sallie C., daughter of R. Miles Wheler.

Married on the 10th inst., at the residence of the bride's mother, by Rev. S. M. Richardson, Mr. Wm. H. Fountain to Miss Adela A. Jones, both of Darlington County. Baptist Recorder, Religious Herald, and Darlington Southerner please copy.

Dead, near King Creek, South Carolina, at half past six o'clock P. M., October 11th 1872, Joseph Pelot Oesterreicher, aged about 33 years and 5 months.

Issue of October 31, 1872

Died, on Friday, the 25th of October, in the 83d year of his age, about 10 o'clock A. M., Mr. Charles Hill of Barnwell County. The subject of this obituary was the oldest member of Friendship Baptist Church, and one among the oldest Baptists in the country; for many years he filled the office of deacon... leaves children and grandchildren. Bamberg, October 1872. J. F. B.

Issue of November 14, 1872

Married, at the residence of the bride's mother, on the evening of the 31st ultimo, by Dr. I. D. Durham, Mr. Benjamin F. Holman and Miss Belle C. McGrew, all of Aiken county, S. C.

Issue of November 21, 1872

Married, on the 24th of October, in Chester County, at the residence of Mr. Walter F. M. Coleman, the bride's brother, by the Rev. T. W. Mellichamp, Dr. Thos. W. Nelson, of Fairfield, and Miss Mollie E., daughter of Mr. and Mrs. Col. J. R. Coleman, of Chester, South Carolina.

Issue of November 28, 1872

Died, November 12th 1872, Thomas Payne, of Edgefield County, S. C. Then this century was but nineteen days old, Thomas Payne was born in the same county where he has lived and died. About half a century he has been a member of Fellowship Church, of which he was for many years a deacon. W. B. J.

Died, November 21st 1872, at the residence of her husband, J. R. Tolbert, after an illness of two months, Bettie Pope Payne, the youngest daughter of the late Thomas Payne, whom she survived only nine days. She was born April 13th 1839, and at the age of 33 years and 7 months, has been taken from her husband and four children... W. B. J.

Issue of December 5, 1872

Married, in Bishopville, at the Presbyterian Church, on the evening of the 26th of November, by Rev. N. Graham, C. C. Myres, Esq., and Miss Emma L. Dinkins. All of Sumter.

Married, at the residence of Mrs. Ann Knotts, on the 17th of November, by Dr. I. D. Durham, Capt. J. E. Knotts and Miss Sallie A. E. Shingler. All of Orangeburg, South Carolina.

Married, at the residence of Mr. William Owens, on the 28th ultimo, by Rev. M. R. Suares, Mr. Darlington Lancaster and Miss Elizabeth Owens, both of Barnwell County.

Little Anna, daughter of W. H. and Anna Cuttino, and grandchild of the esteemed and beloved Rev. David W. Cuttino, is no more. The child fell asleep on the 2d of November, aged 3 years.

Died, in the city of New York, on the morning of the 1st December, Dr. William Snead Reynolds, youngest son of Dr. J. L. and Charlotte Reynolds, of Columbia, s. C. This gifted, noble young man, was born in Charleston, July 3d, 1850; he was educated in Columbia and graduated in the South Carolina

University, July 1870. The following year he received a diploma from the Medical School of the same University. [account]

Issue of December 12, 1872

Tribute of Respect from Camden Baptist Church, on the 28th ultimo, to Rev. A. K. Durham.

Tribute of Respect from Calhoun Lodge, No. 81, A. F. M. in memory of Rev. M. C. Barnett. W. J. T. Glenn, Secretary. Glenn Springs, S. C.

Married, on Sunday, the 1st of December, by the Rev. J. F. Buist, Mr. M. A. Moye and Miss Sallie Brabham, all of Barnwell County.

Married, on the 5th of December in Fairfield County, at the residence of Mrs. Harriet Honey, the bride's mother, by the Rev. W. G. Rollins, Mr. Wm. Tidwell and Miss Martha Honey. All of Fairfield, South Carolina.

Issue of December 19, 1872

Married, at the residence of the bride's father, on the evening of the 4th instant, by Rev. Mike McGee, Mr. James E. Anderson and Miss Mollie Earle, daughter of Rev. J. R. Earle-- all of Anderson County.

Married, at the residence of Mr. John M. Glover, on the 3d instant, by Rev. E. J. Sanders, W. Quitman Davis, Esq., and Miss Lizzie C. Glover, of Aiken, S. C.

Married, at the residence of the bride's father, by Rev. J. T. Sweat, on the 1st instant, Mr. Joseph DeLoach and Miss D. M. Dowling-- all of Beaufort County, and all of the Baptist Church.

Issue of January 2, 1873

Married on Tuesday, the 19th November, by the Rev. T. W. Mellichamp, Mr. John Jackson, of Fairfield, and Miss Lizzie Smith, of the same county.

Married on Tuesday, the 17th December, by the Rev. T. W. Mellichamp, Mr. T. W. Mellichamp, Jr., of Orangeburg, and Miss Louise Hay Elliott, of Barnwell.

Married on the 11th of December, by the Rev. J. E. Rodgers, Mr. J. W. Watson and Miss Rosy M. McRady, of Sumter County.

Married on the 11th of December, by the Rev. J. E. Rodgers, Mr. Wm. McManis and Miss Virginia F. McRady, of Sumter County.

Married on the 11th of December, by the Rev. J. E. Rodgers, Mr. J. W. Wacter and Miss Sarah R. Welldon, of Sumter County.

Died, in Colleton County, South Carolina, November 20th 1872, of heart disease, Mrs. Emily Williams, in the 67th year of her age. My mother was converted when quite young and was for fifty years an unflinching, pious and useful Baptist. [long eulogy] Little more than a year ago, she lost her youngest son. She leaves an aged husband, three children (by her former marriage), grandchildren and great-grandchildren. J. G. W.

Issue of January 9, 1873

Married, on Tuesday, December 12th, at the residence of Dr. Timmons, by Elder J. Trapp, Mr. John F. Brooks and Miss Mary E. Adams, both of Edgefield County, S. C.

Married, on Thursday, December 26th, by the Rev. W. B. Jones, Rev. B. F. Miller and Miss Lizzie H. Morton, both of Abbeville.

Married, on the 29th of December, by the Rev. J. J. Getsinger, Mr. Henry Silcox, of Charleston, and Miss Laura B. P. Newell, of Barnwell.

Married at the residence of Capt. H. M. Ray, Barnwell County, S. C., by the Rev. John G. Williams, Mr. J. M. Felder and Miss Sallie J. Hooten, all of Barnwell County, S. C.

Married, at the residence of the bride's father, on the 29th of November, by the Rev. A. L. Stough, Mr. Thomas Alexander and Miss Sallie Smith, all of Mecklenburg County, North Carolina.

Married, at the residence of A. M. Rey, on the 19th of December, by the Rev. A. L. Stough, Mr. J. B. Richardson and Miss M. A. Pettus, both of York County, South Carolina.

Married, at the residence of the bride's father, on the 19th of December, by the Rev. A. L. Stough, Mr. W. H. Hill and Miss A. F. Blankenship, of Mecklenburg County.

Married, at the residence of the bride's father, on the evening of the 12th of December, by the Rev. W. G. Rollins, Mr. S. W. Dunn and Miss N. E. Wells, all of Fairfield, S. C.

Married, on the 19th of December, by the Rev. W. G. Rollins, Mr. J. T. McWatters and Miss E. J. Wells, all of Fairfield, S. C.

Married on Thursday, the 26th of December, by the Rev. C. M. Porter, at the residence of the bride's father, Mr. W. W. Collins and Miss M. M. Bony, all of Fairfield County, S. C.

Died, after a brief illness, at the residence of her daughter, near Spring Hill, Sumter County, on the 15th of November, Mrs. Dorcas Boykin. She had reached the age of three score and ten years. A. S. W.

Died, on the 5th of October, at the homestead, on the Rio Pardo, Canna-viliras, Brazil, Celia Davis Leitner, relict of the late Colonel George Leitner, formerly of Florida.

Died, at the same place, on the 31st of October, Maria Eunice Leitner, youngest daughter of the above Colonel George and Celia Davis Leitner.

James Gillespie Cook, elder son of Rev. Joseph B. Cook and Mary O. G. Cook, was born in Sumter District, S. C., 19th June 1823 and died 18th September 1872, of typhoid fever, in the fiftieth year of his age. Early in life he joined the Baptist Church.... He was twice married. His first wife was Miss Laura E. Scarborough, daughter of Alfred Scarborough, Esq., of Sumter District, S. C., by whom he had several children, only one of whom Yancey--still lives. About the year 1845, he moved to Montgomery County, Alabama, where he lived for several years. His wife's health becoming very much impaired, he took her back to her father's where she soon breathed her last. In 1857, he married Miss Mary C. Caldwell, and resided for several years in Butler and Covington Counties, until he removed, in about the year 8170, to Orion, Pike county, and thence to Troy, where he died. By his second wife he had eight children, six of whom still live-- three girls and three boys. He leaves no sisters. His only brother, Col. Richard F. Cook, lives in or near the city of Jacksonville, Fla.

Departed this life, at the family homestead, in Laurens County, on the evening of the 2d January 1873, Mrs. Emily Spearman, wife of Thomas Spearman, and daughter of James and Priscilla Watts, aged sixty-eight years, nine months, and twenty days. [eulogy] T. G. W.

Issue of January 16, 1873

Died, in Charleston County, S. C., November 24, 1872, of congestion of the liver, Mr. J. J. Singletary, in the forty-eighth year of his age. Brother Singletary was converted when quite young, and was for thirty tow years an unflinching, pious and useful Baptist. He was for twenty years clerk in the Baptist Church, which position he held until his death. In the death of Brother Singletary, Briner Baptist Church sustains a heavy loss. He leaves a wife and five children. Holly Hill, S. C., January 11, 1873.

Issue of January 23, 1873

Tribute of Respect. Chester, S. C., January 21, 1873, to Robert Hayne Jordan, M.D. R. D. Alexander, church clerk.

Tribute of Respect to the memory of J. Mercer Jenkins, by the Fork Shoals Church, Sunday, January 12th 1873. Rev. C. N. Donaldson, Moderator. Wm. Harrison, Clerk.

Married at the residence of the bride's father, on the evening of January 15, 1873, by Rev. T. H. Pope, Dr. West A. Williams, formerly of Anderson

County, and Miss Georgia C., daughter of Dr. F. G. Parks, of Greenwood, S. C.

Married, in Fayetteville, Arkansas, on the 9th instant, by the Rev. James Barker, Mr. H. H. Albright, of Chester, S. C., and Miss Jennie E., daughter of Rev. John Mayes, of Fayetteville, Ark. Chester *Reporter* please copy.

Married, on the 14th inst., by Rev. J. K. Mendenhall, Mr. G. Fry to Mrs. M. J. Rawley, all of Columbia.

Died on the 19th instant, William Bailey, for thirty-nine years a member of the Baptist Church; for many years a Deacon of Huntsville. Age-- eighty-three years, one month, ten days.

Issue of January 30, 1873

Married, on Thursday, the 16th instant, by Rev. W. A. Gaines, Mr. J. L. Evans and Miss S. E. Simpson, both of Chester county.

Married, on Thursday the 23d instant, by Rev. W. A. Gaines, Mr. Obediah Roberts and Miss Emily Grant, both of Chester County.

Married, on the 24th January, by the Rev. W. G. R----, Mr. Isaiah Cameron and Miss Sarah Barnes, both of Chester.

Died in Stewart County, Georgia, on the -- instant, Mr. Joshua James Abell, in the thirty-sixth[?] year of his age.

Issue of February 6, 1873

Married on the 9th of January 1873, by the Rev. J. E. Rogers, Mr. Alex. Johnson and Miss Cornelia Holland, all of Kershaw county.

Married on the 15th of January, by the Rev. J. E. Rogers, Mr. D. L. Davis, of Sumter County, and Miss Mary E. Arrants, of Kershaw county.

Married on the 15th of January, by the Rev. J. E. Rogers, Mr. T. J. Marsh and Miss Henrietta C. Norris, all of Kershaw county.

Married on the 19th of January, by the Rev. J. E. Rogers, Mr. J. F. Rogers and Miss Elsey English, all of Kershaw county.

Married on the 23rd of January, by the Rev. J. E. Rogers, Mr. J. Cotton, of Richland County, and Miss Mary J. Wood, of Kershaw county.

Married, on the 12th of December, by the Rev. A. K. Durham, at Ridgeway, S. C., J. E. DuPre of Sumter, to Miss Duck, daughter of J. B. and Martha Walker, of Fairfield County.

Married, on the 17th of December last, at the bride's father's, in Sumter county, by Rev. N. Graham, Isaac Coples, Esq. to Miss Harriet H. Hodge.

Married, on the 19th of December last, by Rev. N. Graham, at Providence, Sumter county, J. J. Fox of Lexington County, and Ella V. Myers, eldest daughter of Mr. Joshua Myers.

Married, on the 26th of January, in the town of Sumter, by Rev. N. Graham, William A. Nettles, Esq., of Privateer, and Miss Eliza Ann Whilden, youngest daughter of the late Elias Whilden, of Mount Pleasant.

Married on the 25th of January, in the town of Sumter, by Rev. N. Graham, Abraham Ardis and Miss Justa Andrews.

Married, on the 16th of January, in the town of Sumter, by Rev. N. Graham, Mr. J. Williams and Miss E. Ballard, of Wateree.

Rev. W. L. Taylor was born on the 28th of February, 1855, and departed this life on the 27th of January 1873, at Fort Mills, S. C., after a painful illness of only one day's duration. He was left an orphan at the early age of ten years. From his tenth to his sixteenth year he lived with a half-brother, Mr. F. H. Reaves, near Lincolnton, N. C. When about sixteen years old, he went to live with his brother Rev. T. J. Taylor, where he remained until his death. Last year he became a member of Macedonia Church, Chesterfield County. One of His Brothers.

Henry H. Hill departed this life on the night of the 8th January, from rheumatic metastisis to the brain. He was raised on Edisto, and served in Company C, 4th South Carolina Cavalry, during the late war. Afterwards moved to Barnwell County, where he died at the age of thirty-six. he had been many years a Deacon of the Baptist Church. He leaves a wife and six little children. J. R. Black Sr. Near Midway, February 3, 1873.

Issue of March 1, 1873 [day of publication changed to Saturday]

Married on Thursday, the 6th ult., by Rev. W. A. Gaines, Mr. Wm. Brown, to Miss Sarah A. Hancock, both of Chester County.

Sweetly fell asleep in Jesus, on the evening of December 26, 1872, at his residence at Anderson C. H., S. C., Riley J. Harris, after a long and painful illness of many months. [long eulogy and account]

Issue of March 8, 1873

Married at the residence of N. G. Osteen, in the town of Sumter, on the 29th of January, by the Rev. N. Graham, Mr. Winfield S. Dinkins to Miss Leonora L. Osteen.

At the bride's mother's, on the 6th of February, by Rev. n. Graham, Mr. F. Moor, of Lynchburg, to Miss Ella L. Church, of Sumter, S. C.

At the bride's father's, on the 12th of February, by Rev. N. Graham, Mr. M. M. Hodge to Miss Maggie Rodgers, all of Sumter.

In the town of Sumter, at the residence of the officiating minister, on the 22d of February, by Rev. N. Graham, Mr. Prestly Tidwell to Miss Nancy Scott, all of Sumter, S. C.

Died, on the 15th of January, at his home in Newberry County, of meningitis, John Lark, oldest son of Dennis Lark, aged eighteen years. Also, on the 22d of January, of the same dreadful disease, Mrs. Lura C. Lark, wife of Dennis Lark, in the thirty-third year of her age. Mrs. Lura C. Lark was the daughter of Washington floyd, and was the only surviving member of that family. In early life she attached herself to the Bush River Baptist Church in Newberry county.

Issue of March 15, 1873

Died, at Barnwell, on the night of January 30, Fannie B. Hagood, only daughter of her mother, and she a widow. [poem] M. G. H.

Issue of March 22, 1873

Married, on Tuesday, the 4th instant, by Rev. W. A. Gaines, Mr. James P. Brunson to Miss Mary F. Crosby, both of Chester County.

Issue of March 29, 1873

On Thursday, 12th of March, about 8 o'clock A. M., departed this life, Mrs. Ellenor Hansbery, of Barnwell County, aged seventy-three years. She was a member of the Graham's Baptist Church for over twenty years. J. F. B. Bamberg, March 16, 1873.

Died, February 9, 1873, at the residence of her brother, Robert Yarborough, in the village of Monticello, Fairfield County, S. C., Mrs. Elizabeth Burley, wife of the late Adam Burley, kin the thirty-seventh year of her age. In early life joined the Baptist Church... a consistent and elevated member of the Rock Creek Church. J. D. M.

Issue of April 5, 1873

The venerable and beloved John Culpeper, who crossed "the river" on the 26th March 1873, in the seventy-third year of his age... missionary and colporteur Welch Neck Association. T. P. Lide. March 28, 1873.

Issue of April 12, 1873

Married, on March 19, at the bride's mother's, in Clarendon County, by Rev. N. Graham, Mr. S. Lacky to Miss M. Weeks.

Married, at the bride's father's, in Sumter County, on the morning of March 25, by Rev. N. Graham, M. Osben Witter, of Camden, to Miss M. C. Mellett, eldest daughter of Dr. R. S. Mellett.

Married, at the Jones House, in Sumter, on March 12, by Rev. N. Graham, Mr. Henry Suerry to Miss Sarah Lawrence, all of Sumter County.

Married, April 1, at the bride's father's, in Sumter County, by Rev. N. Graham, Mr. Benjamin R. Gorden to Miss Alice Fort, eldest daughter of J. G. Fort.

Died, at his residence, in Barnwell County, March 24, John Pinckney Hair, aged fifty-four years, leaving an affectionate family and friends to mourn their loss. Brother Hair had lived a consistent Christian thirty-seven years, and about thirty years a faithful deacon of the church. W. B.

Issue of May 3, 1873

Married, by Rev. J. K. Mendenhall, on the 30th of April, at the residence of Mr. Adolphus C. Lyles, Union County, Mr. Julius A. Bynum, of Richland county, to Miss Sallie R. Lyles, of Monticello, Fairfield county.

Died, on April 15, near Barnwell Court House, Mrs. Elvira Owens, in the forty-sixth year of her age. Sister Owens had been a consistent member of Long Branch church for nearly twenty-four years... a dutiful daughter, a kind wife, an affection mother, leaving an aged mother, husband and seven children. A. B.

Issue of May 10, 1873

Married, in this city, on the 6th instant, by Rev. Dr. Reynolds, Mr. Charles N. Brookbanks to Miss Emma C. Layne, daughter of John Y. Layne, Esq., of Columbia.

Issue of May 17, 1873

Married, near Blackville, S. C., at the residence of the bride's father, April 8, by Rev. J. G. Williams, Mr. B. F. Rice to Miss Ellen Reid, all of Barnwell county, S. C.

Married, on Thursday, May 9, at the residence of Mr. A. B. Douglass, by the Rev. W. G. Rollins, Mr. John Morison to Miss Lula N. J. McWatters, all of Chester.

Married, on the 8th instant, by Rev. A. Acker, Mr. Joel M. Harper to Miss Mary Jane, eldest daughter of William Riley, Esq., all of Anderson County.

Died, on the 9th of May, aged seventy-two years, Mrs. Rebecca Dowling, of Barnwell County... J. F. B.   Bamberg, May 12.

Died, on the 1st of May, at the residence of his brother, Mr. S. Moyers, near Silverton, S. C., Mr. Robert B. Moyers, of Kentucky, in the twenty-ninth year of his age, though far away from his native place, where a fond mother still survives him.

Issue of May 24, 1873

Married, by Rev. Edwin C. Rice, on the 16th of April, at the residence of Dr. John B. Watts (bride's brother-in-law), Laurens county, Mr. Farnk E. Waldrop, of Laurens county, to Miss J. Elizabeth Perrin, of Abbeville county.

Married, by Rev. E. C. Rice, on the 27th of April, at the residence of Mrs. Nancy Hill, Newberry County, Mr. James Kelly to Miss Susan Anna Hill, all of Newberry County.

Married, by Rev. E. C. Rice, on the 7th of May, at the residence of Mr. John B. Boazman, Newberry County, Mr. T. O. Holloway of Edgefield county, to Miss M. Corrie Boazman, of Newberry County.

Issue of May 31, 1873

Married, on Sunday morning, May 18, 1873, by Rev. W. P. Martin, at the residence of the bride's mother, Mr. Marshal B. Gaines and Miss Loutetia Emeline, eldest daughter of Mrs. E. Caroline Mattison, all of Calhoun, Anderson County, S. C. *Working Man* please copy.

Married, May 22, 1873, at the residence of the bride's father in Greenville County, S. C., Mr. Geo. W. Clement, of Anderson County, S. c., and Miss Cynthia, daughter of Rev. K. Vaughan. *Working Man* please copy.

Lines written on the death of little Robert Burkett, only son of Mrs. H. Burkett, aged two years, eight months and fourteen days.

Issue of June 7, 1873

Miss Eliza Mitchell Hobson, eldest daughte rof Deacon Abraham Hobson, formerly of Charleston, S. C., and now of San Francisco, California, killed May 10, 1873, aged forty-eight years. Sister Hobson had been to the Baptist Sunday School picnic at Alameda Cal., and was standing with many others, beside the track along which the train of cars was coming, when a resitve horse near her so startled her that she started to cross the track... She leaves loved ones in California and in South Carolina. O. F. G. Charleston, S. C.

Issue of June 14, 1873

Married, on the evening of the 29th May 1873, by Rev. A. B. Estes, at the residence of Dr. J. M. Turner, Mr. Marion Johnson, eldest son of Col. Thos. H. Johnson, to Miss Emma A. Turner, all of Barnwell County, S. C.

Mrs. Elizabeth J. Johnston, died at Elko, S. C. Railroad, on the 24th of May, after a long and painful affliction, in the forty-first year of her age. She was a native of Edgefield, S. C., and first united with the Dry Creek Baptist Church, but on removing with her husband, to Barnwell, S. C., she became a member of the Rosemary church. Barnwell, S. C., May 29, 1873.

Deacon Charles T. Wright. All who have visited our church at Georgetown will remember this venerable servant of Jesus Christ, who died on the evening of the 22d of May. He was permitted to see his children's children, but their grand-children... O. F. Gregory.

Issue of June 21, 1873

Married, on the evening of the 12th instant, at the residence of Mrs. M. M. Pughs, in Sumter county, by Rev. N. Graham, J. W. Lowry, of Lynchburg, to Miss Sue C. Allison, of Carlowville, Alabama.

Married, on the 11th instant, by Elder W. J. Brown, Elder T. W. Smith and Miss Vic Palk, all of Union County, S. C.

Issue of July 10, 1873 [day of publication changed to Thursday]

Died on the 21st of June, 1873, Mary Louisa, infant daughter of George W. and Mary A. Patrick, of Barnwell county. The earthly sojourn of this little one was brief--only three months and twenty-five days.

Issue of July 24, 1873

Died, at Williston, on Thursday, the 3d ultimo, the amiable wife of George P. Harley, Esqr. Her remains were interred in the succeeding Saturday in the family burying-ground, near the Philadelphia Baptist church, Buford's Bridge, Barnwell county... leaves a husband and children. J. F. B. Bamberg, July 14, 1873.

Issue of August 28, 1873

Died, near Fort Mill, York county, S. C., August 18, 1873, at his father's residence, Robert Wilson Kimbrell, youngest son of James and Jane Kimbrell, aged twelve years.

Issue of September 4, 1873

Departed this life, at Orangeburg, S. C., August 7, 1873, Mrs. Sophia O. Sistrunk, wife of S. Oliver Sistrunk, Esq., of colleton county, S. C., at the age of forty-one years. While away from home, on a visit to relatives at Orangeburg, in the hope of recovering her health, she became seriously ill.

Issue of September 11, 1873

On Wednesday morning, the 3d instant, about 4 o'clock, Mrs. Mary Black, aged about sixty-one years, breathed her last, at the residence of her friend, Col. Jared S. Johnson, in the lower part of Laurens county. Sister Black was baptized many years ago by Elder Daniel Mangum, at Pine Pleasant church, Edgefield County (if we are not mistaken), where she remained a member until recently. W. F. M. Martin's Depot, S. C., Sept. 6, 1873.

Died, in Barnwell County, on Friday, August 29, Mrs. Martha A. Croft, aged forty years.

Issue of September 18, 1873

Dr. Joseph Scriven Inglesby, youngest son of the late Deacon Wm. Inglesby, of the First Baptist church of Charleston, was born in Georgetown, S. c., in the year 1800, and finished his pilgrimage at Mt. Pleasant, Christ Church Parish, S. C., on the 21st August 1873, being in the seventy-third year of his age. His academic studies were pursued in his native State, after which he went to Philadelphia and graduated at the Medical college there in 1823. The following year he came to Charleston. In 1824 he married Miss Mary C. Grant of Sumter, and in the latter part of 1829 they were baptized by Dr. Basil Manly, Sr., in the First Baptist Church of Charleston. His consort fell asleep in Jesus at Clinton, S. C., in 1864. He was a chart member of the Mt. Pleasant Baptist Church.... O. F. G.

Died, on the 8th June 1873, Mrs. Mary A. Farrer, in the thirty-eighth year of her life, leaving a husband and eight children. Mrs. F. was a member of Fairview Baptist Church... her brother, George Speaks....

Issue of October 30, 1873

At a conference meeting of Bethel Baptist Church, on the 11th of October 1872, Dr. C. P. Woodruff offered resolutions... Rev. Warren Drummond... joined this church in 1832... [tribute of respect]

Died of Typhoid Fever. at Atlanta, Ga., Oct. 2d, 1873, John M. Parker, youngest son of J. A. & Jane Parker, aged 17 years and 7 months.... connected himself with Corinth Baptist Church. He leaves one brother, seven sisters and many friends. Holly Hill, S. C., Oct. 10, 1873.

THE WORKING CHRISTIAN

Issue of November 13, 1873

Died at his late residence, near Silverton, Oct. 31st, of that dread disease, cancer, Mr. Toliver C. Turner, aged 72 years.

Died at her late residence, Matlock Spring, near Silverton, Oct. 20th, in her 66th year, Mrs. Ruth Meyer. She was baptized into the fellowship of the Matlock Baptist Church in the year 1832. She has left a large family-- children, grandchildren, brothers, sister and numerous friends.

Died at Orangeburg, Nov. 2d, at the house of his son-in-law, J. A. Zeigler, our father, Saxby Chaplin. Born on Hilton Head in the year 1805, he had nearly completed his 68th year. William.

Issue of November 20, 1873

Married, Nov. 13th, at the residence of the bride's father, by Rev. S. M. Richardson, Mr. J. Bryant Lawhorn, to Miss Hannah Hatchel, both of Darlington Co., S. C.

Married, Oct. 30th, at the residence of the bride, near Timmonsville, S. C., by Rev. S. M. Richardson, Mr. Thomas Kelly to Mrs. Louisa Morris, both of Darlington, S. C.

Died, August 29th, Mrs. Catherine M. Janney, wife of the late Jas. C. Janney, aged sixty-two years.

Died, at the residence of her mother, Mrs. Elizabeth Boazman, in Laurens County, S. C., on the night of the 23d of October 1873, Dempsy Boazman, aged 16 years, 6 months and 21 days.

Issue of November 27, 1873

Married, on the evening of the 12th at the residence of Maj. J. W. Durham, by the Rev. W. G. Rollins, Mr. Lafayette Montgomery and Miss Sarah Cameron, all of Chester, S. C.

Married, at Greenville, S. C., on the 12th inst., by Rev. E. J. Meynardie, Mr. James L. Orr, Jr., of Anderson, and Miss Bettie Hammett, daughter of H. J. Hammett, Esq., of Greenville. The *Enterprise* says the weeding was a brilliant affair.

On Monday, the 17th day of November, about 7 o'clock, departed this life, Mr. George W. Moye, of Barnwell County, S. C., in the 77th year of his age. His remains were interred the succeeding Tuesday in the burying ground of the family at Buford's Bridge. [eulogy and account] He has left a numerous band of children and grandchildren. J. F. B. Bamberg, November 19th, 1873.

Issue of December 4, 1873

Married, in the town of Sumter, at the residence of the bride's parents, on the evening of the 25th Nov., by the Rev. N. Graham, Mr. E. Richardson to Miss Rhody V. Andrews.

Married, in Barnwell, S. C., by Rev. J. G. Williams, Mr. R. S. Williams, of Colleton to Miss E. V. McMillan, of Barnwell Co., S. C.

Married, Nov. 26, 1873, Mr. John williams Harrison, of Greenville Co., S. C., to Miss Lucia Widemam [sic], of Abbeville Co., S. C., at the residence of the bride's father, By Rev. B. F. Miler.

Died, of Typhoid Fever, November 19th, 1873, Mrs. George Hutson. Sister had been married forty-six years, and a member of the church forty-three. She leaves a devoted husband and children... J. S. M.

Rev. John Culpeper was born in Anson County, North Carolina, Dec. 1800. his youthful predilections led him to select the practice of the law... He died on the 26th March 1872, at his residence in Timmonsville, in the bosom of his stricken family.

Issue of December 11, 1873

Married, on the 3d inst., at the residence of the bride's father, by Rev. Mr. Strickland, Mr. Ben Winter, of Georgia, to Miss A. H., daughter of Capt. J. L. Rountree of Beach Island, S. C.

Married, on the 13th Nov., at the residence of her father, by Rev. F. J. Sanders, Dr. James Stallings to Miss Della Turner, all of Aiken County.

Married, on the 1st Sabbath in Dec., at the residence of the bride's father, by Rev. W. J. Rollins, Mr. W. Keistler, and Miss Lizzie Nichols, all of Fairfield, S. C.

Issue of December 18, 1873

Tribute of Respect to Brother J. Zimmerman Scarborough, member of Mt. Pleasant Baptist Church.

Married, on the evening of the 9th Dec., at the residence of Mr. T. S. Russell, Charleston Co., by Rev. O. F. Gregory; Mr. William Bradwell, and Miss Ellen Hurford, all of Charleston Co.

Married, on the 12th Nov., 1873, by Rev. H. A. Duncan, Mr. R. J. Hankinson, Jr., and Miss K. M. Williams, both of Ellenton, Barnwell Co., S. C.

Issue of December 25, 1873

Married, on the evening of the 17th inst., by Rev. N. Graham, at the residence of E. Mathis, Esq., in Sumter Co., Alfred S. Beasly and Miss Agnes Copeland.

Married, on the 18th inst., by Rev. N. Graham, at the residence of Messrs. Moore and wilson, Mr. John Byrnes, to Miss E. E. Ard, all of Sumter.

Married, Dec. 3d, 1873, by Rev. J. Rodgers, Mr. T. W. Barnes, to Miss Sarah A. Bradley, all of Kershaw Co.

Married, by the same, Dec. 4th, 1873, Mr. J. S. Wilson, to Miss S. E. Barnes, of Kershaw Co.

Married, by the same, Dec. 10th, 1873, Mr. D. D. Kelly, to Miss E. Folsom, of Kershaw Co.

Married, by the same, Dec. 17th, 1873, Mr. J. W. Smith, to Miss L. Goff, all of Kershaw Co.

Issue of January 8, 1874

Married, on the 24th ult., at the residence of the bride's father, in Sumter County, by Rev. N. Graham, Mr. Johnson Knox Newman and Miss Josephine Londond.

Married, on the evening of the 1st inst., at the residence of the bride's father, by the Rev. C. P. Boozer of the Lutheran Church, Mr. S. H. Carter to Miss Susan Carter, daughter of George Carter, all of Barnwell County.

Married, January 1, 1874, by Elder A. S. Williford, at the residence of the bride's father, Kershaw county, Mr. N. S. Helton to Miss M. E. Jones.

Married on the 17th Dec., at the residence of Mr. J. P. Hankinson, Silverton, by Rev. Mr. Strickland, Mr. Henry McElmurry of Beach Island, S. C., and Mrs. Mary B. Sanders, of Silverton, S. C.

Issue of January 15, 1874

Married, at the Baptist Church, at Greenville, S. C., on Thursday, the 1st inst., at 11½ o'clock, A. m. by Rev. J. C. Furman, D. D., Mr. Melville Dozier, of Santa Rosa, California, and Miss Lizzie W. Edwards, of Greenville, S. C.

Married, by Rev. W. L. Brown, Dec. 24th, 1873, Mr. John L. Barnett to Miss Julia Webber, both of Union Co., S. C.

Married, at Monck's Corner, Charleston Co., S. C., on the 5th Jan. 1874, by Rev. O. F. Gregory, at the residence of the bride, Mr. A. D. Hare and Mrs. Annice T. Carson, all of Monck's Corner.

Married, on the 1st of January, at the residence of the bride's mother, by Rev. T. H. Pope, Mr. Miller Wilson, of Abbeville Co., and Miss T. E. Andrews, of Laurens Co.

Nina Martin, daughter of Maj. Robt. Martin and Annie Erwin, died at Erwinton, S. C., 22d Dec., after a long and painful illness of six months' duration. M. G. H. Barnwell.

Died, in Barnwell County, Jan. 6th, Mrs. Eleanor, wife of Mr. L. S. Peacock, aged thirty six years. A. B. Barnwell, Jan. 9th 1874.

Issue of January 29, 1874

Married, on the evening of the 15th inst., at the residence of the bride's father, in Abbeville County, near Ninety Six, by Rev. A. Rice, Rev. Edwin C. Rice, of Dallas County, Texas, and Miss Lucy A. Pinson, youngest daughter of Mr. T. J. and Gilly Pinson, of Abbeville County.

Married, at 4 P. M., Jan. 8th, by Rev. Edwin C. Rice, Mr. Robt. F. Spearman, and Mrs. T. N. Boazman, all of Laurens County.

Married, at 7 P. M., Jan. 8th, by Rev. Edwin C. Rice, Mr. Dillan Lindsey, and Miss Martha Miller, all of Laurens County.

Married, at 9 A. M., Jan. 11th, by the same, Mr. Daniel H. Hitt, and Miss Cornelia M. Simms, all of Laurens County.

Married, 2 P. M., Jan. 15th, by the same, Mr. Henry F. Hitt, of Abbeville, and Miss Alice M. Wells, of Laurens County.

Married, on the evening of the 15th inst., at the residence, by Rev. N. Graham, Mr. W. Henry Plowden, of Clarendon County, to Miss S. Ann Nettles, of Sumter, youngest daughter of John Nettles, Esq.

Married, on the 31st of December 1873, by Rev. J. E. Rodgers, Mr. J. N. Davis, of Sumter Co., and Miss Florence A., daughter of C. J. Shiver, of Kershaw Co.

Married, by the same, on the 11th of January, 1874, Mr. Benjamin Dixon and Mrs. Elizabeth Nunnery, both of Sumter co., S. C.

Married, at 3 P. M., Dec. 18th, 1873, by Rev. Edwin C. Rice, Mr. David Golding, and Miss Fannie Hitt, all of Laurens Co., S. C.

Married, at 7 P. M., Dec. 18th, 1873, by Rev. Edwin C. Rice, Mr. Clarence Starnes, of Laurens Co., and Miss Emma Sadler, of Ninety Six, Abbeville Co., S. C.

Exchanged earth for heaven, on the 25th of Dec., 1873, little Kate, youngest child of Dr. S. W. and Cynthia Bookhart, aged three years and six months. R. R. V. Doko, S.C., Jan. 19th, 1874.

Issue of February 5, 1874

Married, on Thursday, the 22d of January, at the residence of the bride's mother, by Rev. J. G. Williams, Mr. A. C. Carter, to Miss Elizabeth Hiers, all of Barnwell Co.

Married, Feb. 3d, by Rev. J. K. Mendenhall, Mr. E. C. Hutto to Miss Florence Wright, all of Columbia.

Married, Jan. 21st, by Rev. W. C. Lindsay, Mr. E. H. Hagood and Miss Estelle Ingram, all of Barnwell.

Married, Jan. 31st, by the same, Mr. G. Corne, and Miss Ellen F. Sadler, all of Barnwell.

Married, on the 21st day of January, 1874, by Rev. J. E. Rodgers, Mr. W. J. Ammon and Miss Eliza L. Simmons, all of Kershaw Co.

Married, on the 22d of January 1874, by the same, Mr. T. J. Davis and Miss Mary J. Thompson, all of Kershaw co.

Issue of February 19, 1874

Married, at Chesterfield C. H., on Friday, Jan. 23d, by Rev. H. Craig, Dr. Edward H. McBride and Miss Lizzie, second daughter of Mr. John C. Chapman.

Issue of March 5, 1874

Married, by Rev. J. K. Mendenhall, in Columbia, on the 3d instant, Mr. Frederick J. Ludette, of Kingstree, to Miss Laura E. Barnett, of Columbia.

Died, in Bloomfield, Ky., February 17th, 1874, Thomas Hall, Jr., eldest son of Rev. Thomas Hall, aged 19 years and 17 days. This noble youth was born in Charleston, S. C.... J. L. R.

Issue of March 12, 1874

Married, by Rev. F. C. Jeter, on the 15th of January, Mr. G. C. Wilbourn and Miss Florence Mobley, both of Union.

By the same, Feb. 26th, Mr. John C. Slater, of Virginia, and Miss Hattie R. Fawcette, of Fairfield Co., S. C.

By the same, March 8th, Mr. W. Slengrove [sic, for Snelgrove?], and Miss Mattie Oxner, both of Newberry, S. C.

Issue of March 19, 1874

Married, on the evening of the 12th inst., by Rev. A. Buist, Mr. Richard Anderson and Miss Ella Killingsworth, eldest daughter of Mr. Caleb Killingsworth, all of Barnwell County.

Departed this life, on Friday, 6th March 1874, Mrs. Fanny Williams, consort of Mr. G. K. Williams, of Gadsden, S. C. Baptized into Christ by the Rev. W. D. Beverly... C. A. S.

Issue of April 2, 1874

Died, on Wednesday, the 25th of March, 1874, at the residence of Thos. C. Perrin (her brother) in Abbeville, Mrs. Elizabeth Lee Cothran, relict of John Cothran, deceased, in the 71st year of her age. Abbeville, 28th March 1874.

Issue of April 9, 1874

Married, at the residence of Elder D. B. Smith, March 17th, by Elder A. S. Williford, Mr. James T. Smith and Miss Maggie Tucker, all of Chesterfield Co., S. C.

Married, on Thursday evening, April 2d, by Rev. A. Buist, Mr. D. S. Oesterveicher and Miss America Anderson, second daughter of Mr. Howell Anderson, all of Barnwell Co.

Sympathy to the family of Capt. W. B. Peeples, of Errington, S. C., the deacon of Concord Church, the death on 5th March of their little Kate Alexander.

Issue of April 23, 1874

Married, by the Rev. B. F. Miller, on the morning of the 15th ult., at the residence of the bride's father, in Greenwood, Capt. John Hill James and Miss Bettie Crews, both of Abbeville Co., S. C.

Married, on Thursday evening, 2d inst., at the residence of the bride's mother, by the Rev. D. W. Cuttino, Mr. Amanuel Bull and Miss Amanda Felder, all of Orangeburg Co., S. C.

Married, on the 21st inst., by Rev. J. K. Mendenhall, Mr. W. B. Miller and Miss Mattie Wells, all of Columbia.

THE WORKING CHRISTIAN

Issue of April 30, 1874

Married, on Thursday evening, 23d inst., at the residence of the bride, by Rev. James M. Weeks, Mr. Jacob Judy of Colleton CO., and Mrs. Eleanor Metts, of Orangeburg Co., S. C.

Mr. Peter N. Rains was born in Greenville Co., April 15th 1843, and died in Columbia, S. C., Dec. 1st, 1873. He united with a Baptist Church in Greenville, early in life.... A widow and two children are left. J. K. M.

Issue of May 7, 1874

Died, at her home at Graham's T. O., on the 23d ult., Mrs. Maggie L., wife of J. E. Steadman, in the twenty-ninth year of her age. [poem] J. J. G.

Issue of May 14, 1874

Died, in Alachua County, East Florida, on the 20th of April, Mrs. Kate M. Moseley, beloved wife of Captain A. S. Moseley, in the forty-third year of her age.

Issue of May 21, 1874

Married, Jan. 20th, by Rev. W. A. Gaines, Rev. J. Trapp, of Edgefield, and Miss Mollie Campbell, of Abbeville.

By the same, May 16th, Mr. James Wier and Miss Elisabeth Castle, both of Fairfield.

Issue of May 28, 1874

Married, in Charleston, S. C., May 21st, 1874, by Rev. L. H. Shuck, Mr. C. H. Sloan, of New York, and Miss Kate T. Hyde, daughter of Deacon S. Hyde, of Charleston.

Issue of June 4, 1874

Married, at the residence of the bride's father, on Tuesday, May 26th, at 2 o'clock P. M., by Rev. M. McGee, Mr. William C. Jackson, of Amelia County, Va., and Miss P. Victoria McGee, daughter of G. W. McGee, Esq., of Belton, S. C.

New Bethel Church and community have been called to mourn the death of one of their most beloved and useful members, Mrs. Julia E. Smith. She was the daughter of Robert McKnight, and granddaughter of Deacon Thomas Gwin, and was born January 10, 1841. In her seventeenth year, she joined New Bethel Church. In her nineteenth year, she was married to Mr. Lawson H. Smith of Chester. Mr. Smith fell in our disastrous war, leaving a widow and two little children. On the 30th of April last, she fell asleep in Jesus. W. A. G. Chester.

Issue of June 25, 1874

Married, by Rev. A. Price, at the residence of the bride's father, on the 18th June, Mr. Robert Able, of Orangeburg, to Miss Dona Salley, of Aiken.

Died, at her residence, near Barnwell C. H., S. C., on the 11th June, Mrs. C. A. J. Hair, consort of Captain David S. Hair, in the 39th year of her age. This good and estimable woman was a native of South Carolina, and the only living child at her death, of Maj. A. J. Nix, death having removed them all form time to eternity. Mrs. Hair leaves an aged mother, a husband, and two little sons. The subject of this obituary united with the Baptist Church of rosemary, about seventeen years ago.... Barnwell, S. C.

Issue of July 9, 1874

Married, in Sumter, on the 17th instant, by Rev. N. Graham, Mr. Manning J. Hodge, to Miss T. J. Hodge, youngest daughter of the late B. Hodge.

Died, at his brother's residence, in Sumter County, on the 15th ult., William Thomas Hodges, after a painful and protracted illness of several months... He had been a good and brave soldier in our late struggle.

Issue of July 30, 1874

Wm. McGuinnis, for a long time a resident of Columbia, died on Friday last, He was an Irishman by birth, and a member of the Catholic Church.

Issue of August 6, 1874

Married, on the 2nd of August, at the residence of Mr. James Lewis, by Rev. W. G. Rollins, Mr. W. W. Lewis and Miss M. J. McKeown, all of Chester County, S. C.

Issue of August 20, 1874

Died, of consumption, on the 15th instant, at the residence of J. A. Meyer, Steel Creek, Barnwell County, Miss Ella Sanders, aged 22 years. His young lady was a member of the Baptist Church at Matlock. Her only sister and many friends mourn her early demise.

Issue of August 27, 1874

Married, at the residence of the bride's father, on the 20th inst., by the Rev. D. W. Cuttino, Mr. M. W. Proctor, of Marion, S. C., and Miss A. V. Shuler, of Orangeburg, S. C.

Married, on the 20th inst., by Rev. D. W. Cuttino, Mr. S. B. Stoutamire and Miss M. O. Wingard, all of Orangeburg, S. C.

Married, on the 13th inst., at the residence of the officiating clergyman, by Rev. W. E. Hughson, R. P. Weeks, of Sumter, to Miss Mary, second daughter of the late Charles Wells, of Clarendon County, S. C.

Issue of September 3, 1874

Died, on the 19th August, aged 73 years, Mrs. Abigail Scarborough, wife of Mr. A. J. Scarborough, of Upper Salem, Sumter County, S. C. She toiled with earnest devotion for her fond husband and children....

Issue of September 17, 1874

Addie, daughter of Brother A. J. Gill, of Beaufort County, S. C., died on Sunday, the 6th instant, at her father's residence, near Hopewell, and is buried in the family burying ground at Hopewell Church. H. C. S.

Departed this life, on Friday morning, September 4th 1874, at the residence of his brother, O. B. Riley, in Orangeburg County, S.C., in his fourteenth year, Freeman W. Riley, youngest child of Jacob Riley and his wife Frances L. Riley. G. W. G.   Greenville, S. C., Sept. 81, 874.

Issue of September 24, 1874

Died, on the 29th of August, 1874, Perry Benjamin Owens, son of C. J. and Rebecca A. Owens, aged one year and eleven days.

Died, at Greenville, S. C., August 31st, 1874, in the thirty-second year of her age, Mrs. Bettie Sloan Smith, daughter of Samuel Mauldin, deceased, and Mrs. C. A. Mauldin, and wife of Professor D. T. Smith, of Furman University. Six years ago she became the wife of Mr. D. T. Smith, Professor of Greek in Furman University. [long eulogy]

Issue of October 1, 1874

Married on Wednesday, September 9, 1874, at the residence of the bride's father (Mr. B. R. Mangum), by Rev. W. D. Rice, Miss Fanny L. Mangum to Mr. D. S. Satterwhite, all of Newberry, S. C.

On Tuesday, September 22, 1874, at the residence of Mr. John C. Stewart, by Rev. W. D. Rice, Miss Josephine S. Peterson to Mr. John S. Floyd, all of Newberry, S. C.

Issue of October 8, 1874

Mr. Isaac Sauls, Sr., of Colleton County, S. C., died on the 7th September, 1874, at the residence of his son, Mr. Isaac Sauls, Jr., at Smoke's Cross Roads.

he was aged eighty-six years, nine months and three days, and had ben for about thirty years a faithful Deacon in the Baptist Church. He has left behind him a large and highly respectable family of children and grandchildren, most of whom are Baptist. W. H. D. Kinardville, S. C.

Issue of October 15, 1874

Married on the morning of the 6th of October, at 9 o'clock, at the residence of the bride's father, by Elder A. S. Willeford, Mr. Amos Hough to Miss Mary Ann Sowell, all of Kershaw County, South Carolina.

Died, near Spring Grove, Laurens County, S. C., Sept. 1, little Emma, eldest daughter of J. B. and Anna B. Watts, aged eight years and ten months.

Died, in Barnwell County, S. C., October 7, 1874, Allen W., son of J. W. and M. E. Free, aged two years and eight months. J. F. B.

Died, in the town of Newberry, at the residence of her nephew, William Lake, Esq., on the 1st of October, 1874, Mrs. Phoebe K. Mendenhall, widow of the late Dr. M. T. Mendenhall, and daughter of isaac Kirk, Esq., formerly of Newberry, and long since deceased. The subject of this notice was born on the 23d of June 1807, and was the daughter of Quaker parents. In March, 1824, she was married to Dr. M. T. Mendenhall, also of Quaker parentage, and lived with him first in Newberry and afterwards in Charleston, until 1852, it pleased God to remove him out of this world.... Mrs. Mendenhall was baptized in September 1831, and with her husband, was one of the first members of the Newberry Baptist Church.

Issue of October 22, 1874

Married by Rev. Edwin C. Rice, August 31, 1874, Mr. H. Pinkney Riddle to Mrs. Nancy S. Pulley, all of Laurens County, S. C.

Issue of October 29, 1874

Death of Mr. B. O. Mauldin... in Charleston, S. C., on the 18th October 1874, of yellow fever. He was the son of the late Mr. Samuel Mauldin, of Greenville, where he spent his early life. He was the son-in-law of our brother T. P. Smith, of Charleston, and brother in law of the pastor of Citadel Square Baptist Church, Charleston, Rev. J. A. Chambliss. He lives a wife, widowed mother, and brothers and sisters. [verse]

Issue of November 5, 1874

Married, on the 29th ultimo, at the residence of the bride's father, by Rev. A. Buist, Claudius E. Ashley to Miss Mary S. Sanders, all of Barnwell County.

On the 29th of October, at the residence of Mrs. Ellen Cox, by Rev. James F. Buist, Mr. John J. Simmons, to Miss Carrie E. Cox, all of Barnwell County.

At the residence of the bride's father, on the evening of the 20th instant, by Rev. H. Lecroy, Mr. James Weeks to Miss Gula Segler, all of Aiken County, S. C.

At Clear Spring Church, October 25, by Rev. J. C. Hudson, Mr. J. T. Wood to Miss Nancy M. Simmons, all of Greenville.

Died, October 7th, little Charlie Bar, son of R. T. and E. J. Delk, aged two years, six months, and two days. M. A. D.

Died, of congestion of the lungs, on the 4th of October, Mrs. Sallie Catherine Wheler Stiles, daughter of R. Miles Wheler, of Salem, S. C., and wife of Rev. C. A. Stiles, in the twenty-ninth year of her age.   C. A. S.

Issue of November 12, 1874

Married, on the 29th of October 1874, at the residence of the bride's mother, Mr. John Rodgers to Miss Harriet Peagler, all of St. Stephen's.

On the 1st of November, at the residence of the bride's father, by Rev. S. T. Russell, Mr. W. M. Spires, to Miss Alice Walton, all of St. Stephen's.

On the 1st of November 1874, at St. Stephen's Depot, by Rev. S. T. Russell, Mr. Charles Goure to Miss Mary Pipkin.

On the 4th of November, 1874, at the residence of Mr. John Johnson, by Rev. A. Buist, John P. Harley, of Aiken County, to Miss Kittie C. Willis, of Barnwell County.

Departed this life on the 25th of September, 1874, Sister Laura Shelnits, beloved wife of Artemus Shelnits and affection daughter of J. P. and . A. Boswell... a member of the Baptist church about three years. S. T. F.

Issue of November 19, 1874

Married, on the 15th of October, 1874, at the residence of the bride's mother, by Rev. F. C. Jeter, Dr. Thomas B. Bates to Miss Sarah Ann Sarter, all of Union, S. C.

On the 5th November 1874, at the residence of the bride's father, Mr. Harrison Finley, by Rev. Edwin C. Rice, Mr. Marcus Watts, to Miss Della Finley, all of Laurens County, S. C. .

Issue of November 26, 1874

Married, on the 14th of November, 1874, at the residence of Mr. John Smith, in Sumter, by Rev. N. Graham, Mr. R. F. Cook to Miss Addie O. Ferrison.

On the 5th of November, 1874, at the residence of Mrs. H. S. Wade, in Rockingham, N. C., by Rev. T. W. Guthrie, Mr. John Duckett, of Newberry, S. C., Editor of the *Pee Dee Courier* to Miss J. A. Zachary, of Montgomery County, N. C.

On the 5th of November 1874, at the residence of the bride's father, by Elder A. S. Willeford, assisted by Elder W. J. Hatfield, Mr. J. Russell Horton to Miss Lizzie J. Hough, all of Chesterfield County, S. C.

On the 15th of November 1874, at the residence of the bride's father, by Elder A. S. Willeford, Mr. G. B. Jowers to Miss Mary Griffieth, all of Chesterfield County, S. C.

On the 12th of November 1874, at the residence or the bride's mother, by Rev. C. M. Porter, Mr. William W. Kennedy to Miss Mary A. Porter, all of Ridgeway, S. C.

On the 3d of November 1874, in Greenville, S. C., by Dr. J. C. Furman, Rev. E. W. Peeples to Mrs. S. D. Balfour.

On the 22d of November, at the residence of the bride's father, Dr. R. P. Clark, by Rev. W. D. Rice, Mr. W. C. Swittenberg, to Miss M. C. Clark, all of Newberry, S. C.

Died, at his residence, near Jefferson, Chesterfield County, S. C., on the night of the 14th instant, Mr. William Horton, aged about 70 years. He was a member of the Baptist Church.   A. S. W.

Died, at his residence in Laurens County, S. C., on the 12th of October, 1874, Mr. Samuel Meredith, in the 75th year of his age. The deceased was a member of Warrior's Creek Baptist Church for nearly a half century....

Issue of December 3, 1874

Died, in Baltimore, Maryland, October 25, 1874, in her 63d year, Mrs. Martha G. McIntosh, of Society Hill, S. C.

Died, near Spring Hill, N. C., October 30, 1874, Mr. John D. Smith, in his 62d year. The deceased was a member of Beulah Church, Richland County, S. c., for more than thirty years.

Issue of December 10, 1874

Married, on the 18th of October, 1874, by Rev. J. E. Rodgers, Captain John Davis to Miss Sarah L. Caraway, both of Sumter, S. C.

At Phenix, S. C., on Tuesday, the 8th instant, by Rev. W. A. Gaines, his eldest son John Milton to Miss Manie, only daughter of the late Rev. Theodore Williams, of Edgefield, S. C.

On the 20th of September, 1874, by Rev. J. E. Rodgers, Mr. W. B. Gardner, to Miss Percy A. Cooper, of Camden, S. C.

On the 6th instant, by Rev. R. R. Vann, assisted by Dr. A. K. Durham, Mr. W. W. Macon to Miss Sallie Vann, all of Fairfield.

On the 15th of October, 1874, by Rev. J. E. Rodgers, Mr. H. A. Marshal to Miss Mary S. Moseley, all of Kershaw.

On the 18th of November, 1874, by Rev. J. E. Rodgers, Mr. J. R. Robinson to Miss Emma S. English, all of Kershaw.

On the 26th of November, 1874, at the residence of the bride's father, by Rev. J. F. Buist, Captain Henry Ulmer, of Beaufort County, S. C., to Miss Janie E. Free, of Barnwell County, S. C.

On the 3d of December, 1874, at the residence of the bride's father, by Rev. J. A. Segler, Mr. F. P. Woodward, to Miss Kella Corley, all of Aiken County, S. C.

Issue of December 17, 1874

Married on the 1st of December, at Jackson, Mississippi, by Rev. Edward G. Taylor, D. D., of New Orleans, Rev. William Hayne Leavell to Miss Mary, daughter of General J. Z. George.

On the 26th of November, by Rev. N. Graham, Mr. Fred. Lynch, to Miss Josephine Brooks, all of Sumter.

Departed this life November 16, 1874, Eliza Camilla, youngest daughter of W. J. and Elizer Reynolds, of Kershaw county, aged four years, two months and twenty-seven days.

Issue of December 24, 1874

Married on the 22d of December, by Rev. R. F. Jeter, Mr. William Baldwin to Miss Sallie E. English, both of Union, S. C.

On Sunday morning, the 13th instant, at the residence of Mr. R. E. Tyler, by the Rev. Mr. Massabo, Mr. Brantley Eubanks to Miss Emily Green, all of Aiken County, S. C.

At the residence of the bride's father, on Tuesday, December 8, 1874, by Rev. W. D. Rice, Mr. B. Johnston to Miss Maggie Senn, all of Newberry, S. C.

On Thursday, December 10, 1874, at the residence of the bride's father, Mr. James Harrington, by Rev. W. D. Rice, Mr. William E. Welsh to Miss Mary A. Harrington, all of Newberry, S. C.

On the 13th of December, by Rev. F. C. Jeter, Mr. J. Brown Whitmire to Miss Sallie E. Duckett, both of Newberry County, S. C.

Died, at his residence in Barnwell County, Friday, December 10, Brother J. Edward Harley, in the seventy-second year of his age. He leaves seven children and a large circle of relatives.... I. A. B.

Mrs. Mary Sauls of Colleton County, S. C., was born July 4, 1803, and died September 26, 1874. She was the mother of our friend and brother Isaac Sauls, of Smoke's Cross Roads, and leaves besides her several other children. She was a member of the Baptist Church. W. H. D.

Issue of January 7, 1875

Married on the 24th of December 1874, by Rev. N. Graham, Gen. R. H. Anderson of Camden, S. C., to Miss Martha E., second daughter of Dr. R. S. Mellet, of Sumter County, S. C.

On the 23d of December 1874, by Rev. N. Graham, Mr. Samuel J. Bradford to Miss Jessie H. Thud, daughter of Col. William Nettles, all of Privateer, Sumter County, S. C. [see correction in issue of January 14]

On the 25th of December 1874, at the home of the bride's grandfather, by Rev. J. F. Buist, Mr. Henry L. Diefenback, to Miss Julia Kell, all of Barnwell County, S. C.

On the 23d of December 1874, by Rev. J. E. Rodgers, Mr. W. B. Dixon, of Sumter County, S. C., to Miss M. J. N. R. Deas, of Kershaw, S. C.

On the 21st of December 1874, by Rev. N. Graham, Mr. Mikel Kavamah [sic] to Mrs. Lenora A. Phillips, all of Sumter county, S. C.

On the 27th of December 1874, by Rev. J. A. Segler, Mr. Hugh Luke, of Augusta, Ga., to Miss Martha Barton, of Aiken County, S. C.

On the 10th of December 1874, by Rev. J. E. Rodgers, Mr. J. W. Myers to Miss Nannie A. Moseley, all of Kershaw, S. C.

On the 29th of December 1874, by Rev. J. E. Rodgers, Mr. W. A. Nunery to Miss Emma H., daughter of J. D. Spradley, Esq., all of kershaw, S. C.

On the 2d of December 1874, at the residence of the bride's father, by Rev. J. L. Vass, Mr. Lawrence A. Peebles, of Sumter, S. C., to Miss Jessie C. Wingo, daughter of Capt. T. W. Wingo, of Spartanburg, S. C.

On Wednesday morning, the 23d of December 1874, at the residence of the bride's father, by the Rev. J. F. Buist, Mr. J. A. J. Rice of Barnwell County, S. C., to Mrs. Rebecca Nelson, of Richland County, S. C.

On the 22d of December 1874, by the Rev. J. A. Segler, Mr. W. S. Walker, of Barnwell County, to Miss S. T. Friday, of Aiken County, S. C.

On the 16th of December 1874, by Rev. N. Graham, Mr. William A. Weldon, to Miss M. E. Weldon, all of Sumter County, S. C.

On the 17th of December 1874, by Rev. J. E. Rodgers, Mr. R. J. Yates, of Sumter County, S. C., to Miss Mary, daughter of Col. S. M. Boykin, of Kershaw, S. C.

Died, in Lancaster County, on the 20th of October 1874, of membrane croup, Hattie Emma, the only daughter of George and Marry Harriet Jones, aged two years, three months and twenty-four days. [verse] T. R. C.

Issue of January 14, 1875

Married, on the 23d of December 1874, by Rev. N. Graham, Mr. Samuel J. Bradford to Miss Jessie H., third, daughter of Col. William Nettles, all of Privateer, Sumter County, S. C. [The above marriage notice, by mistaking the word "third," was badly treated in out last issue, causing the groom to marry some one other than his fair bride. ed.]

On Thursday, the 6th of January, by Rev. W. G. Rollins, Mr. Andrew M. Coleman to Miss Annie I. Feaster, daughter of David R. and Mrs. V. E. Feaster, of Fairfield County, S. C.

On the 7th of January 1875, at 1 P. M., at the residence of the bride's father, by Rev. Edwin C. Rice, Mr. Mathew Crisp to Miss Virginia Dendy, all of Laurens County, S. C.

On the 17th of December 1874, at 12 M., at the residence of John R. Fuller, the bride's father, by Rev. Edwin C. Rice, Mr. William Watts Finley to Miss Allie E. Fuller, all of Laurens county, S. C.

On the 5th of January 1875, by Rev. W. L. Brown, Mr. J. S. Haney, of Georgia, to Miss Kate Spears, of Union County, S. C.

On the 7th of January 1875, at the residence of the bride's father, Rev. Spencer Atkinson, by Rev. S. M. Richardson, Mr. Baxter Morris to Miss Carrie Powers, both of Darlington County.

On the 7th of January 1875, at 11 A. M., at the residence of the bride's mother, by Rev. Edwin C. Rice, Mr. Earnst Noffz to Miss Bettie Whiteford, all of Laurens County, S. C.

On the 22d of December 1874, at the residence of the bride's mother, by Rev. S. M. Richardson, Mr. Thomas J. Powers to Miss Fannie Mims, both of Darlington County.

On the 7th of January 1875, at the residence of the bride's mother in Timmonsville, S. C., by Rev. S. M. Richardson, Mr. Abram Reynolds to Miss Martha Scafe, both of Darlington County.

Levi Hill was born near Timmonsville, Darlington County, S. C., on the 27th of September 1810. In 1833, in his twenty-third year, he united with the Lake Swamp Church, during the pastorate of Rev. Gregory Rollins, in which has been since known as the Dorsey revival. In 1856 he was dismissed with others to constitute the Midway Church. He remained in the fellowship of that church up to the time of his death. He died at his home, near Midway Church, on the 4th of January 1875, in the sixty-fifth year of his age. W. M. R.

Died, at her home, in Graham's Turnout, on the 23d of December 1874, Mrs. Maggie L., wife of J. E. Steadman, in the twenty-ninth year of her age. She leaves a husband, mother, one brother, several sisters and a host of friends. [poem]. J. J. G.

Issue of January 21, 1875

Married on the 19th of January 1875, by Rev. N. Graham, at his residence, in Sumter, Mr. J. J. Grooms to Mrs. Ovile Mixon, both of Sumter County.

On the 31st of December 1874, by Rev. J. M. Weeks, Mr. Lienis Harvesson to Miss Lienizzar George, both of Colleton County.

On Thursday, December 24, 1874, by Rev. W. D. Rice, Mr. H. B. Senn to Miss S. E. Rhoades, all of Newberry, S. C.

Issue of January 28, 1875

Married on the 9th of December 1874, by Rev. J. K. Mendenhall, Mr. J. P. Burnett, of Ninety-Six, to Miss Fannie K. Taylor, of Newberry.

On the 8th of January 1875, by Rev. J. K. Mendenhall, Mr. S. P. Reasoner to Miss Margaret E. Gleave.

On the evening of the 16th of December, 1874, at the residence of the Re.v S. B. Sawyer, by the Rev. S. B. Sawyer, Mr. John Allen Weathersbee, of Williston, Barnwell County, to Miss Lila A. Walker, of Orangeburgh County, South Carolina.

Issue of February 11, 1875

Married at the residence of the bride's father, on the 20th of January, by Rev. W. H. Dowling, Mr. Lewis Bishop to Miss Sinie Bishop.

On the 16th of December 1874, Mr. George Folk to Miss Rosa E. Ruth, daughter of the lamented hon. A. M. Ruth, of Beaufort County, S. C.

At the residence of the bride's mother, on the 17th of December 1874, by Rev. W. H. Dowling, Mr. O'Gilva Kearse to Miss Mary Kearse, all of Barnwell County, S. C.

Issue of February 18, 1875

Married on the 9th of February 1875, by Rev. W. L. Brown, Mr. Gist Briggs, of Unionville, to Miss Jennie Spears, of Union County, S. C.

On the 10th of February 1875, by Rev. J. E. Rodgers, Mr. W. F. Davis to Miss Julia E. McCutchen, both of Sumter County.

On the 28th of January 1875, at the residence of the bride's mother, by Rev. J. M. Weeks, Mr. David Hutto to Miss Z. L. Weeks, all of Colleton County.

On the 28th of January 1875, at the residence of the bride's father, by Re.v J. M. Weeks, Mr. Bennet Judy to Miss Elizabeth Heaton, all of Colleton County.

On the 10th of February 1875, by Rev. J. E. Rodgers, Mr. E. M. Lee, of Sumter, to Miss S. H. Moseley, of Kershaw.

On the 27th of January 1875, by Rev. N. Graham, Mr. Joseph Lewis to Miss A. G. McCants, all of Sumter County.

On the 28th of January 1875, by Rev. J. E. Rodgers, Mr. T. J. Marsh to Miss Rebecca Brown, all of Kershaw.

On the 17th of January 1875, by Rev. J. E. Rodgers, Mr. R. A. Reynolds to Miss Julia A. Stokes, all of Kershaw.

Died, of consumption, at his residence, in Sumter County, on Sunday, January 31st 1875, Mr. John Shiver, aged about seventy-five years, fifteen or more of which he was a member of the Baptist Church. He leaves a wife and seven children. B. C.

Issue of February 25, 1875

Married on the 16th of February 1875, at the residence of the bride's mother, by Rev. O. F. Gregory, Mr. James E. Thigpen to Miss Ella E. Kelly, fourth daughter of the late Henry Kelly, Esq., all of Clarendon County.

Issue of March 4, 1875

Married on the 16th of February 1875, at the residence of Mr. B. Williamson, in the village of Orangeburg, S. C, by Rev. I. D. Durham, Mr. R. P. Autley, of Orangeburg County, to Miss H. L. Baggot, of Aiken County.

On the 23d of February 1875, at the residence of the bride's mother, Mrs. Josiah Fort, by Rev. S. M. Richardson, Mr. James J. Carter to Mrs. Jane K. White, all of Darlington County, S. C.

On the 18th of February 1875, at the residence of the bride, Mr. H. J. Culp, Sr., to Miss Isabella Ferguson, both of Chester County, S. C.

On the 24th of February 1875, at the residence of the bride's mother, by the Rev. J. F. Buist, Mr. Henry Dubois of Colleton County, S. C., to Miss kate Rice, of Barnwell County, S. C.

On the 16th of February 1875, at the residence of the bride's father, by Rev. S. M. Richardson, Mr. Edward L. Gray to Miss Mildred Stuckey, all of Darlington County, S. C.

On the 23d of February 1875, at Mount Pleasant Baptist Church, by Rev. O. F. Gregory, Mr. Samuel V. Gregorie to Mrs. Ellen Knox, all of Charleston County.

On the evening of the 10th of February 1875, at 7 o'clock, at the residence of Mr. Henry Baker, by Rev. A. S. Willeford, Mr. William H. Stroud to Miss Martha A. Conald, all of Kershaw county, S. C.

On the 25th of February 1875, at the residence of the bride's mother, by Rev. O. F. Gregory, Mr. Samuel J. Taylor to Mrs. Julia M. Campbell, eldest daughter of the late Dr. H. DuBose, all of Williamsburg County.

Mrs. Mary Murdough, wife of Mr. L. B. Murdough, of Colleton County, S. C., died on the 4th day of January, 1875, aged about fifty-five years. Mrs. Murdough leaves to mourn her loss several sons and daughters.... She had been a member of the Methodist Church, but for a number of years before her death she had become a Baptist in principle.... The funeral services were conducted by the writer of this, and her body buried in the folk graveyard at Wesley Chapel. W. H. D.

Issue of March 11, 1875

Married on the 24th of February 1875, at 3 P. M., at the residence of the bride's father, by Rev. Edwin C. Rice, Mr. W. Preston Turner to Miss Lizzie Rudd, all of Laurens County, S. C.

Departed this life on the 9th of January in Winchester, Virginia, Mrs. Virginia A. Willis, wife of Rev. E. J. Willis. [eulogy] A. T. S.

Issue of March 18, 1875

The little son of Dr. and Mrs. S. R. League fell asleep in Jesus on the 23d of January, aged two years and twenty-seven days....

Departed this life, on the 22d of November, 1874, in Barnwell County, Mrs. Eliza J., consort of R. T. Delk, in the thirty-third year of her age. She leaves a husband and six children... Pastor.

Died, on Sunday morning, February 21st 1875, Mrs. L. B. Townes, wife of [sic] Rome, Georgia, and daughter of Mr. S. B. Brooks, of Abbeville County, S. C.

Mrs. Maggie Northcutt, wife of E. C. Northcutt, and daughter of Josiah and Martha Bass, was born in Darlington County March 7th 1845, and died at her father's February 4th 1875. She was converted and joined the Baptist Church in early age. She leaves a husband, one infant child and many relatives and friends....

Died, in this place, on the 8th instant, of gravel, Rev. Barnet Humphries, aged about sixty five years. He had preached the Gospel for forty years. He was pastor of the Gethsemane Baptist Church from the time it was organized until his death.... Chester, S. C., March 9, 1875.

Issue of March 25, 1875

Married on the 9th of March 1875, at the residence of the bride's mother, by Rev. W. L. Brown, Mr. Miles Smith to Miss Eliza Duncan, both of Union County, S. C.

Issue of April 1, 1875

Married on the 2d of March, 1875, at 12:30 A. M., at Lucknow Plantation, Savannah Back River, South Carolina, by Rev. L. C. Tebeau, Mr. Samuel Lynes, of Charleston County, S. C., to Miss Catherine G. Dennis, of Charleston, S. C.

Departed this life, on the 17th of March, 1875, at Elko, South Carolina, Mrs. Charity Hair, aged about seventy-six years.... A. B.

Issue of April 8, 1875

Married on the 4th of April 1875, at the residence of the bride's aunt, by Rev. E. W. Peeples, Mr. J. C. Smith to Miss S. V. Ulmer, both of Barnwell County, S. C.

John Knight died at his residence in Laurens county, S. C., on the 14th of March 1875. He was born on the 4th of March 1795. He married Mary Jones, with whom he raised nine children. About the year 1821 he was baptized by Elder Jonathan Dewees, and was received into the Columbia Baptist Church. Subsequently, he removed his membership to Poplar Spring, where he was a useful member till his death. A widow, six children, a large number of grandchildren and many friends are left to drop affection's tear... A. C. S. Laurens Herald please copy, and forward bill to Dr. W. J. Ballentine and Berry Knight, executors.

Issue of April 15, 1875

Married on the evening of the 25th of March, by Rev. N. Graham, Mr. Benjamin Joseph Pack, of Clarendon County, to Miss Jessie P. Hodge, of Sumter County, S. C.

On the evening of the 24th of March, at the residence of John Brogdon, Esq., by Rev. N. Graham, Mr. Joseph S. Tindal, to Sumter County, to Miss Anna Eliza Brogdon, of Clarendon County, S. C.

Died, at Barnwell Court House, S. C., March 1st 1875, Mrs. Clementine H. Brown, beloved wife of Colonel B. H. Brown. [eulogy] L. H. S.

Issue of April 22, 1875

Married on the 15th of April 1875, at the residence of Mr. F. A. Buyke, by the Rev. P. A. Buyke, Mr. W. W. Zeigler to Miss M. J. Carroll, all of Orangeburg County.

Died, March 26, 1875, of pneumonia, Nena Isadora Parler, infant daughter of W. R. and M. J. Parler, aged four months and twenty-two days. Orangeburg, S. C., April 23, 1875.

Mrs. Ann M. E. hill, of Colleton County, S. C., died March 20th, in the sixtieth year of her age. Her daughter Catherine (the blind girl) preceded her to the grave only a few weeks-- February 26th. J. S. Weeks.

Miss Julia Baynard died at the residence of her father, Rev. C. A. Baynard, at Allendale, S. C, on the 2d of April, aged nineteen years. J. A. L.

Died in Barnwell County, S. C., on Saturday, the 3d of April, 1875, at 9 o'clock P. M., Mrs. Helen M. Snelling, beloved wife of Brother Jeremiah Snelling. Sister Snelling was the daughter of the late Rev. John K. Johnson, an earnest and faithful minister of God, who was a tower of strength to the Baptist denomination of Barnwell County. Early in life she was converted and united with the Dry Creek Church in Edgefield County, S. C. On her removal to Barnwell, she united by letter with the Rosemary Church. After her marriage, she joined the church at Joyce's Branch, where she remained until she united with the people of God at the Seven Pines Church,which was organized near her residence.... W. H. D.

Issue of April 29, 1875

Died, on the 20th of April, 1875, at her residence in Colleton County, S. C., of typhoid fever, Mrs. Celia Hickman, wife of G. H. Hickman, in the sixtieth year of her age. [poem]. Bamberg, S. C., J. O. H.

Issue of May 13, 1875

Died, at her residence, near Flat Rock, S. C., Mrs. Rachel Copeland, wife of the late Rev. Joseph T. Copeland, aged 79 years, 5 months and 23 days. She had lived a consistent member of the Baptist Church for many years. A. S. W. The Camden Journal will please copy and oblige.

Married on the evening of the 29th ultimo, by the Rev. C. A. Stiles, Mr. W. W. Moys to Miss Mary Irving Clark, all of Richland, S. C.

On the evening of the 5th instant, by Rev. C. A. Stiles, Mr. Marion J. Seay to Miss Mary J. Stack, all of Richland County.

Issue of May 20, 1875

Married at the residence of the bride's father, on Tuesday, May 11, 1875, by Rev. W. D. Rice, Mr. H. H. Blease, to Miss Lizzie Satterwhite, all of Newberry, S. C.

Issue of June 3, 1875

Died, at his own residence, of heart disease, Clerk D. R. King, on the 21st of October, 1875. Brother King was born in Newberry County, S. C., on the 17th of October 1817; was married to Miss Lucinda Mills on the 19th of November 1840. He joined the Bethel Baptist Church, of Newberry County, S. C., May 20, 1847. Brother King was a church clerk twenty-seven years.... Tribute of Respect. A. J. Long, Church Clerk, Rev. J. M. Norris, Moderator.

Died, at her residence, in Barnwell County, South Carolina, on the 17th ult,. Mrs. Sarah Beck, aged eighty-five years. Sister Beck had been a faithful member of the Baptist Church for over fifty years. A. B.

Issue of June 10, 1875

Died, near Carmel Hill, Chester County, on the 24th of May, 1875, Mrs. Amanda C. McCallum, daughter of the late William Crosby, Esq., of Crosbyville, S. C., and wife of Dr. J. M. McCallum, formerly of Carmel Hill, aged 38 years and 26 days.

Issue of June 17, 1875

Married on the 18th of May 1875, by Rev. S. T. Russell, Mr. Augustus Eadie to Miss Olethea Eadie, all of St. Stephen's.

On the 6th instant, at the residence of the bride's brother, by Rev. W. H. Dowling, Mr. John B. Carter to Miss Ida Eaves, all of Barnwell County, and all of the Baptist Church.

Mrs. Anna C. Spearman, wife of G. W. L. Spearman and daughter of Colonel G. S. Cannon, was born April 14, 1840, and died March 4, 1875. She was a good and obedient daughter, an affectionate sister, and a faithful wife and mother. She joined the Baptist Church while at school in Anderson....

Issue of June 24, 1875

Married on the evening of the 16th of June 1875, at the residence of the bride's father, in Williamsburg County, by Rev. O. F. Gregory, Hon. W. W. Ward to Miss Frances Ella Tharp, all of Williamsburg County, South Carolina.

Died, at her residence, in Colleton County, on the 27th of May 1875, Mrs. Martha Hallman, aged seventy-two years, fifty-seven of which she had devoted to her Heavenly Father.... S. W. A. Walterboro, June 10, 1875.

Died, at Greenville, S. C., June 9, 1875, Eugene Harvey Williams, son of Dr. and Mrs. William Williams, aged 15 years, 4 months, and 9 days. F. C. M. Greenville, S. C., June 13, 1875.

Issue of July 8, 1875

Married at Buford's Bridge, Barnwell County, S. C., on the 30th of June 1875, by Rev. J. F. Buist, Mr. James Oneal to Miss F. R. Moye.

Fell asleep in Jesus on the 30th of April 1875, Dr. Charles R. Thompson, aged 49 years and 4 months. He leaves a wife and two small children to mourn his death. A. I. H.

Issue of July 15, 1875

Death of Rev. T. H. Pope... formerly Agent of State Missions in South Carolina and late pastor of the Baptist Church at Greenwood. This even took place at 12 o'clock on the night of July 8th 1875. Fred W. Eason. Newberry, July 10, 1875.

Berryman H. Withers died on Monday the 18th of June, at his residence in this county. he had nearly reached his fifty-eight year, having been born in Lincoln County, N. C., in the year 1818. He came to this state in 1836, quite a youth, uneducated, and poor.... He was married in 1846 to Miss Susan E. Meadow, the mother of his only surviving son, John S. Withers, and one other son who died in infancy. He was married a second time to Miss Elizabeth Meadow, and in 1862 he was married to Mrs. Coleman Crosby. *L. C. H. in Chester Reporter.*

Issue of July 22, 1875

Married on the 1st of July 1875, by Rev. J. E. Rodgers, Mr. A. J. McLeod, of Kershaw, to Mrs. S. E. McCutchen, of Sumter.

Died, June 14, 1875, after a short illness, near Flat Rock, Kershaw County, S. C., Miss M. E. Peach, in the thirty-eighth year of her age. She united with the Bethany Baptist Church, Kershaw District, S. C., in August 1868,and was baptized by the Rev. J. E. Rodgers....

Issue of July 29, 1875

Died, on the 10th of July, 1875, in Kershaw County, near Camden, Mrs. Martha Yates, widow of the late Willis Yates. Her maiden name was Josey, and she was raised in Sumter County, near Bishopville. She united with the Baptist Church nearly forty years ago and was baptized by the Rev. N. Graham. She connected herself with the Antioch Church, Kershaw, in 1846, by letter. Her children say she was about ninety years of age.

Issue of August 5, 1875

Married on the 27th of July, 1875, at the residence of Mr. Jasper Johns, by Rev. W. H. Dowling, Mr. Christian Rizer to Miss Delila Johns, all of Colleton County, and all of the Baptist denomination.

Tribute of Respect to Rev. Thomas H. Pope... born in Newberry, July 4, 1839. His mother, a Miss Harrington, was the most lovely and accomplished of ladies, and his father was one of the most prominent members of the Newberry bar. [account]

Issue of August 12, 1875

Died, at the residence of her son, in Orangeburg County, S. C., on the 3d of July 1875, Mrs. Barbara Shuler, in her ninetieth year. She became a Baptist in early life. She was one of the number with which the Four Holes Baptist Church was constituted. R. J. E.

Died, at Greenville, South Carolina, June 13, 1875, Mrs. Fannie Foster, daughter of Mr. Charles Merrick, and wife of Rev. L. S. Foster. She was born in Pennsylvania, August 21, 1848, and brought by her parents to Greenville in 1852. In 1863 she was baptized by the pastor, Rev. W. D. Thomas, D. D. In 1870 she married Mr. Foster who had been a student at the Southern Baptist Theological Seminary, and went with him to his native State of Mississippi, where her father also now resides.... husband and two little children. J. A. B.

Issue of August 19, 1875

Died recently, at her late residence, in Barnwell County, Mrs. Mary Cannon. Deceased united at an early age with the Union Baptist Church....

Issue of August 26, 1875

Married on the 18th inst., at the residence of C. M. McJunkin, Columbia, by Rev. W. D. Kirkland, Mr. Wills M. Rodgers of Charleston, and Miss Mamie C. Robinson of Greenville.

On Tuesday, the 17th instant, at Dean Swamp Baptist Church, by Rev. H. Lecroy, Mr. George Porter, of Orangeburg, to Miss Maggie Brodie, of Aiken County, S. C.

Died, August 10, 1875, at her residence in Aiken County, Mrs. Elizabeth Cherry, in the eighty-third year of her age. Barnwell C. H., S. C. A. B.

John Randolph China, youngest son of the late Thomas China, Esq., of Williamsburg County, S. C., was killed on the Northeastern Railroad on the night of the 10th of July 1875. he had been married for twelve years to Rebecca, daughter of Deacon John Nettles of Sumter county, and leaves a widow and five children. He united with the Mizpah Baptist Church, Sumter county, ten years ago, and removed his letter last August to Mount hope Church, Williamsburg County.... O. F. G.

Issue of September 2, 1875

Miss Janie Hicks, eldest daughter of Dr. Hicks, died at her father's residence, in Sumter County, S. C., April 1875, in the nineteenth year of her age. Sumter, August 20, 1875. G.

Issue of September 9, 1875

Died, at her residence, near Hough's Bridge, on Little Lynch's Creek, Kershaw County, on the night of the 21st of August 1875, after a long and painful illness of near six months, Mrs. Ramsey Munn, wife of Mr. Daniel Munn, deceased, aged about 40 years. She was a member for many years with her husband, of Beaver Dam Baptist Church. She raised four children, two of whom are members of the church. A. S. W. Flat Rock, S. C. August 23, 1875. Camden Journal please copy and oblige.

Issue of September 16, 1875

Married on Thursday, the 9th instant, at Long Branch Church, by Rev. A. Buist, Mr. Wiley I. Hair to Miss M. A. Blume, all of Barnwell County.

Died, on the 7th instant, at the residence of her father, near Silverton, after a brief illness, little Mary Eliza, aged two years and six months, only daughter of Mr. and Mrs. A. M. Harley.

Died, at Mount Pleasant, Charleston County, on the morning of September 9, 1875, of membraneous croup, Frederick, youngest son of G. Warren and

Marcella Thompson, aged one year, eight months, and nineteen days.... O. F. G.

Issue of September 30, 1875

Married on the 23d of September 1875, at the residence of the bride's father, Elder J. M. Herlong, by Elder W. G. Mack, Mr. William Buycke to Miss Irellia Herlong, all of Orangeburg County, S. C.

Died at Sumter, S. C., on the 19th of September, 1875, the infant son of Dr. and Mrs. S. M. Dinkins, aged six days.

Died, on the 25th of August, 1875, Mr. Isham Johns, about 65 years of age, and on the 15th instant his wife, Mrs. Isham Johns, about 60 years of age. They were members of the Antioch Baptist Church, Colleton County, S. C. E. W. P. Walterboro, S. C.

Issue of October 7, 1875

Married on the afternoon of the 29th ultimo, at the residence of the bride's father, by Rev. C. A. Stiles, Mr. John McLaughlin to Mrs. Elizabeth S. Braddy, all of Richland County, S. C.

Issue of October 14, 1875

Departed this life in Crockett, Texas, on the 14th of September last, little Beulah Marie, youngest daughter of Rev. W. D. and R. A. Beverly, aged four years, three months, and eleven days.

Died, on Wednesday, October 6, 1875, at the residence of her son, Mr. Amos Youngblood, in Augusta, Georgia, Mrs. Ann Youngblood, in the sixty-fourth year of her age. She sleeps beside her husband, who died thirty-three years ago, and a son who has died since. H. W. M. Windsor, S. C., October 1875.

Issue of October 21, 1875

Married on the 7th of October 1875, by Rev. A. M. Cartledge, at his residence, near Roswell, S. C., his daughter L. Sue to Mr. A. B. Wilson, of Greenville, Tennessee.

Sacred to the memory of our dear sister, Annie M. Carter, wife of Alexander F. Carter and daughter of R. B. and Eliza Beach, who fell asleep in Jesus on the 5th instant, aged 23 years, 5 months and 20 days. Ervin. Walterboro, S. C., October 12, 1875.

Issue of October 28, 1875

Married on the morning of the 18th instant, at the residence of Mr. Z. Boon, by Rev. A. S. Willeford, Mr. Daniel Boon to Miss Fannie Copeland, all of Kershaw County, S. C.

On the 9th of September 1875, by Rev. J. E. Rodgers, Mr. J. J. Bradley, of Sumter County, to Miss M. H. Reynolds, of Kershaw County.

On the 5th of August 1875, by Rev. J. E. Rodgers, Mr. Daniel Brown to Miss Amanda Davis, both of Sumter County.

On the 29th of September 1875, by Rev. J. E. Rodgers, Mr. J. M. Colver to Miss S. C. Moonyham, both of Sumter County.

Died, at her residence, near Florence, on the 12th instant, Mrs. Susan M. Brown, aged seventy-five years, eight months, and twenty-six days. For more than twenty-five years Sister Brown had been a devoted member of the Baptist Church. Her son, Wm. H. Brown, Esq. T. W. H. Florence, S. C., October 19, 1875.

Issue of November 4, 1875

Died, in Timmonsville, Darlington County, S. C., on Monday, the 25th instant, Bessie, infant daughter of A. F. and Mary H. Culpeper, aged nine months and twenty-five days. Timmonsville, S. C., October 27, 1875.

Issue of November 11, 1875

Married on the 4th of November 1875, at the residence of the bride's father, in Barnwell County, by Rev. A. Buist, Mr. J. Sid. Armstong to Miss Sophronia A. Lee.

At Laurensville, S. C., on the 26th of October, 1875, by Rev. J. B. Traywick, Mr. James H. Traynham to Miss Mary F. Brown, all of Laurensville, S. C.

Died, at her residence in Barnwell County, S. C., October 28, 1875, Mrs. Jerusha Beard, widow of William Beard. She was born April 16, 1788. Mrs. Beard was a devoted member of the Baptist Church for forty seven years. She leaves sons and daughters and a large circle of relatives and friends. J. F. B. Bamberg, November 2, 1875.

Issue of November 18, 1875

Mrs. Harriet Buchanan died in Mobile, Alabama, on Sunday, November 14th, aged 83. She was a daughter of Rev. Samuel Young, one of the earliest settlers of Winnsboro, and relict of Hon. John Buchanan, who for many years filled prominent positions in Fairfield County....

Died, on the 19th of October, 1875, at her home in Abbeville County, S. C., Mrs. Sallie M., wife of Mr. George W. Collins, in the twenty-seventh year of her age. She was baptized by the late Rev. William P. Hill and received into the membership of Beulah Baptist Church in the Fall of 1800. she was a graduate of the Greenville Female college.... She leaves a husband and three small children.... The funeral services were conducted by the Rev. Robert N. Pratt, former pastor of the church.

Married on the evening of November 4, 1875, by Rev. Benjamin F. Miller, at the residence of the bride's mother, Mr. Samuel Perrin, of Abbeville County, S. C., to Miss Fannie Quarles, of Edgefield County, S. C.

Issue of November 25, 1875

Married on the 24th of October 1875, at the residence of the bride's father, by Elder W. G. Mack, Mr. James D. Axson to Miss Henrietta Reed, all of Orangeburg County, S. C.

On the 21st of October 1875, by Rev. J. E. Rodgers, Mr. T. H. Davis, of Kershaw, to Miss Frances S. Sherrard, of Sumter County.

In Macon, Georgia, on the evening of the 16th of November, 1875, by Rev. A. B. Estes, at the residence of the bride's mother, Mr. Elliott Estes, late of South Carolina, but now of Atlanta, Georgia, to Miss Julia Ross, of Macon.

On the 27th of October 1875, by Rev. J. E. Rodgers, Mr. J. D. Evans, of Sumter, to Miss Mary J. McLeod, of Kershaw County.

On the 17th of October 1875, by Rev. J. E. Rodgers, Mr. G. Hancock to Miss Matilda Yates, both of Sumter County.

Died, near Chesterfield Court House, on Tuesday, November 16, 1875, Hattie Barnett McRae, infant daughter and only child of Dr. E. h. and R. E. McBride, aged ten months and two days.... F. and M.

Issue of December 2, 1875

Died, at his residence in Darlington County, S. C., October 25, 1875, Micajah Thomas, in the eighty-eighth year of his age. He held his membership with the Gumbranch church, in Darlington County, S. C....

Died, at Barnwell C. H., S. C., Tuesday, 13th instant, of hear disease, Colonel N. G. W. Walker. he was for many years a member of the Baptist church at this place... M. G. H. Barnwell, S. C.

Died, at his home in Barnwell County, S. C., November 15th, 1875, Mr. B. J. Ray, in the forty second year of his age. He was a member of the Springtown Baptist Church for fifteen years. J.F. Buist. Barnwell, S. C.

Married on the 10th of November 1875, by the Rev. J. F. Buist, Mr. W. C. Clark to Miss Lizzie Cooper, of Barnwell County.

On the 14th November 1875, by the Rev. J. F. Buist, Mr. J. Drummonds to Miss Ellen Rice, of Barnwell County.

On the 26th November, at the bride's residence, near Gadsden, by the Rev. C. A. Stiles, Mr. John G. Williams to Miss Mary J. James, all of Richland County, S. C.

Issue of December 9, 1875

Married on the 22d of November 1875, at the residence of the officiating minister, by Rev. A. S. Willeford, Mr. G. W. L. Cato to Mrs. Mary H. Caston, all of Kershaw county, S. C.

On the 25th of November 1875, at the residence of the bride's father, by Rev. A. S. Willeford, Mr. G. L. Horton to Miss Sue Hough, all of Chesterfield County, S. C.

On Thursday, November 25th 1875, at the residence of the bride's father, by Rev. W. D. Rice, Mr. J. Henry Dorroh, to Miss Dora Reeder, all of Newberry, S. C.

On November 24, 1875, by Rev. A. Buist, at the residence of the bride's mother, Mr. Willie A. Willis to Miss Anna E. Hardy, all of Aiken County, S. C.

On the 25th of November 1875, at the residence of the bride's father, by Rev. J. A. Segler, Mr. B. E. Grandy to Miss M. S. Johnson, all of Aiken County, S. C.

On the 2d of December, 1875, at the residence of the bride's mother, by Rev. L. Cuthbert, Mr. Judson Brodie to Miss Mary E. Prothro, all of Aiken County, S. C.

By Rev. J. C. Rodgers, November 23, 1875, Mr. T. C. Sessions to Miss M. E. Cook, all of Kershaw, S. C.

By Rev. J. E. Rodgers, November 27, 1875, Mr. Z. H. Bradley to Miss E. E. Reynolds, all of Kershaw, S. C.

Brother John Croft of Bethesda Baptist Church, of the Barnwell Association, died on the 30th day of August 1875, aged about seventy five years. he had been a member of Bethesda Church for fifty years. He leaves a widow and some children. W. H. D.

Sacred to the memory of our dear sister, Caroline H. Hadduck, wife of H. Taylor Hadduck, and daughter of Henry and Ann Conoly, who fell asleep in

Jesus on the 1st instant, aged thirty two years, one month and twenty three days. Jamima. Ridgeville, S. C. December 6, 1875.

Issue of December 23, 1875

Married on October 15, at the residence of the bride's mother, by Rev. W. D. Rice, Mr. Hayne Belle to Miss P. G. Workman, daughter of the late Mr. John Workman, all of Laurens County, S. C.

On Wednesday evening, December 15, in the Chester Baptist Church, by the pastor, Rev. R. W. Sanders, Mr. Eugene Stahn to Miss Victoria Nail, both of the town of Chester.

On the evening of December 16, by Rev. A. Buist, Mr. A. H. Mitchel to Miss Emma S. Wooley, both of Barnwell County.

On the 12th instant, at the residence of the bride's mother, by Rev. A. S. Willeford, Mr. Joseph G. Bruce to Miss Mary Ann Hough, all of Kershaw County.

On the 19th instant, at the residence of the bride's father, by Rev. A. S. Willeford, Mr. C. W. Brown of Cumberland County, North Carolina, to Miss Catherine West, of Kershaw County, South Carolina.

On the 19th instant, at the same place, by Rev. A. S. Willeford, Mr. Samuel West, Jr., to Miss Sallie Munn, all of Kershaw County.

On the 15th instant, at the residence of the bride's father, by Rev. Mr. Bradford, Mr. Wade Hankinson to Miss Virginia, third daughter of Captain J. D. Rountree, all of Aiken County.

Tribute of Respect to Caroline H. Hadduck, a member of Pine Grove Baptist Church, Colleton County, South Carolina, daughter of Harry and Anna Connoly... died December 1, 1875.

Died in Williston, Barnwell County, S. C., Mrs. Indiana C. Hart, aged about forty years. A. B. Barnwell, S. C.

Rev. Richard Judson Towill departed this life October 31, 1875, at Kalorama, Edgefield County, South Carolina, aged thirty-seven years. He was a native of Middlesex County, Virginia, where most of his early life was spent. he was ordained June 17, 1869... In the spring of 1871, he was united in marriage with Miss Angie Bell, daughter of Brother George Bell of Edgefield, and settled in that county, where he was pastor of Dry Creek and rocky Creek Churches... He left a wife and two little children. L B.

Issue of January 6, 1876

Married on the 14th December, at the residence of the officiating minister, Rev. J. S. Murray, Mr. John F. Wilson of Darlington County to Miss Fannie E. Murray, of Anderson, S. C.

On December 22d, at the residence of the bride's father, Mr. James Howle, by Rev. S. B. Wilkins, Mr. H. I. Coker and Miss Bettie Howle, all of Darlington County, S. C.

On the 16th ult., by Rev. N. Graham, Mr. Burges Scarborough and Miss Jane Baker, all of Sumter County, near Bishopville, S. C.

On the 22d ult., by Rev. N. Graham, Mr. J. D. Bradford and Miss C. F. Nettles.

At the same place, on the same evening, by Rev. N. Graham, Mr. F. B. Bradford and Miss Maggy Nettles, daughter of the late Col. William Nettles, of Sumter County, S. C.

On the 18th of November ult., by Rev. F. C. Jeter, Mr. David Thomas, of Union, and Miss Emma Lyles, of Newberry County, S. C.

On the 9th of December, by Rev. F. C. Jeter, Mr. Wm. Lyles, of Newberry and Miss Ellen Thomas, of Union.

On the 16th of December, by Rev. F. C. Jeter, Mr. Malachi McGraw and Miss Mollie Johns, both of Union.

On the 23d ult., by Rev. F. C. Jeter, Mr. Thomas Hancock of Newberry, and Miss Jane Taylor, of Fairfield County.

On the 15th December, by W. E. Sawyer, Esq., at the residence of the bride's mother, Mr. Abner P. Fallow and Miss Antonette L. Woodard, eldest daughter of Mr. William and Mrs. Mary Woodard, all of Aiken County, S. c.

On the 16th December, by W. E. Sawyer, Esq., Mr. Hiller Williams and Miss Ella Crouch, all of Aiken County, S. C.

On the 23d of November 1875, by the Rev. Mills, at the residence of the bride's father, Capt. T. M. Lyles, Mr. A. E. Davis and Miss Mattie P., all of Fairfield.

On the 23d December at the residence of Mr. Henry West, by Rev. A. S. Willeford, Mr. Wm. Truesdale and Miss Rebecca Peoch, all of Kershaw County.

On December 26th, at the residence of Mr. Amos Faulkinbury, by Rev. A. S. Willeford, Mr. James Barfield and Miss Ella Horton, all of Kershaw County.

On December 14, 1875, by the Rev. J. E. Rodgers, Mr. R. R. English and Miss Sallie E. E. Stokes, all of Kershaw.

On December 25, 1875, By the Rev. J. E. Rodgers, Mr. J. R. Yates and Miss Mary J. Stokes, all of Kershaw.

Tribute of Respect from Citadel Square Baptist Church, Charleston, S. C., Dec. 6, 1875, to Wm. B. Heriot, who departed this life November 2, 1875. j. L. Sheppard, Clerk C. S. B. Church.

Died, December 10, 18 -- ---, Brunson, P. R. R. R. R., S. C., Mr. M. Benjamin Prescott. He leaves a wife and little daughter. E. W. P.

Issue of January 13, 1876

Married on Dec. 23d ult., by Rev. John G. Williams, Mr. A. B. Hooten and Miss Rosa, daughter of Capt. H. M. Ray, all of Barnwell county, S. C.

At the residence of the bride's mother, on the 11th of December 1875, by Rev. J. Bouchell, Mr. J. D. Quattlebaum, of Lexington, and Miss Mary Bouknight, of Edgefield county, S. C.

On the 23d Dec., ult., at the residence of the bride's uncle, by Bishop Kennerly, Mr. S. W. Whitemon of Orangeburg, S. C., and Miss Carrie E. Bodie, of Mt. Willing, Edgefield county, S. C.

At the residence of the bride's father, on the 19th Dec., 1875, by Rev. N. N. Burton, Mr. Thos. B. Quattlebaum and Miss Sallie Kneece, both of Lexington county, S. C.

On Dec 23d, 1875, at the residence of the bride's father, by Rev. N. N. Burton, Mr. Elisha Jones, of Lexington, and Miss Josie Stevens, of Aiken county, S.C.

At "Duncannon," on the 6th inst., by Rev. John G. Williams, Mr. Owen F. McMillan and Miss Annie H. Harley. No cards.

Issue of January 20, 1876

Married at B. F. Baldwin's, on the 9th of January, by Rev. F. C. Jeter, Mr. Abraham Wicks and Miss Emma Cain, both of Union County, S. C.

At the residence of Jesse Rogers, in Union County, on the 12th of January, by Rev. F. C. Jeter, Mr. Butler Holly and Miss Aurelia McMeekins, both of Fairfield county, S. C.

Issue of January 27, 1876

Death of Mrs. John S. Hughson... the husband of Sister Hughson is a faithful deacon in the Sumter Baptist Church. C. C. Brown. Sumter, S. C., Jan. 22, 1876.

Married on the 9th of December 1875, by Rev. D. W. Cuttino, Mr. James Hungerpiller and Miss Laura E. Parler, all of Orangeburg County, S. C.

On the 4th of January, 1876, at the residence of the bride's father, by Rev. D. W. Cuttino, Mr. Charles Poland and Miss Georgiana Kemmerlin, all of Orangeburg county, S. C.

On the 18th of January, 1876, by Rev. D. W. Cuttino, Mr. David J. Clayton, Sr., and Mrs. Mary Ann Dantzler, all of Orangeburg county, S. C.

On the 20th of January 1876, at the residence of the bride's father, by Rev. D. W. Cuttino, Mr. Jefferson Zeigler and Miss S. J. Dantzler, all of Orangeburg county, S. C.

Issue of February 3, 1876

Married near Buford's Bridge, S. C., January 16th, 1876, at the residence of Mr. Angus Williams, by Rev. J. F. Buist, Mr. John Sanders, and Miss Rebecca Cave, all of Barnwell County, S. C.

On the 23d January 1876, at the residence of the bride's father, by Rev. J. F. Buist, Mr. James Hutto and Miss Gatsey Still.

On the 26th January 1876, by Rev. J. E. Rodgers, Mr. J. F. Matthews and Miss Sallie R. Corbitt, both of Sumter county, S. C.

On the 20th of January 1876, by Rev. J. E. Rodgers, Mr. Wesley Croft of Kershaw, and Miss Sarah Adkisson, of Sumter county, S. C.

On 20th January 1876, by Rev. J. E. Rodgers, Mr. John M. Davis and Miss Mary J. V. Davis, all of Kershaw county, S. C.

On 20th January 1876, at the residence of the bride's father, by Rev. A. S. Willeford, Mr. Louis Truesdale and Miss Eliza Ann Westall, of Kershaw county, S. C.

On the 21st December 1875, at the residence of the bride's brother, Doko, S. C., by Rev. T. W. Mellichamp, Mr. Melville Mellichamp and Miss Jessie Viola McNulty.

Issue of February 10, 1876

Married on February 3d 1875, at the bride's home, by Elder J. C. Hudson, Mr. T. Maxwell Clyde and Miss Mary J. Barrett, of Pickens county, S. C.

On the 2d of February, at the residence of Mr. B. O. Stansell, Elko, S. C., by Rev. A. Buist, Mr. S. L. Peacock and Miss L. E. Aaron, all of Barnwell County.

On the 3d of February, at the residence of the bride's father, by Rev. A. Buist, Mr. John W. Ussury and Miss Victoria Reddy, all of Barnwell County.

Issue of February 17, 1876

Married on the 26th of January, by Rev. W. B. Wells, at the bride's home, Mr. James C. Sullivan, of Abbeville County, and Miss Augusta E. O'Neal, of Barnwell County, S. C.

On 9th of February, by Rev. W. B. Wells, at the Bethlehem Baptist Church, of Campbellton, P. R. R. R., Mr. Albert P. Youmans of Barnwell County, and Miss Mary M. Rouse, of Beaufort County, S. C.

On the 27th of January 1876, at the residence of D. J. Pipkin, Esq., in Bloomingvale, Williamsburg county, S. C., by Rev. O. F. Gregory, Mr. John G. Pipkin and Miss Martha E. Cox, all of Williamsburg County, S. C.

At the same time and place, by the same, Mr. A. J. Cox and Mrs. Susan E. Evans, all of Williamsburg County, S. C.

On the 20th of January last, at the residence of Mr. W. Atkinson, near Sumter's Landing, by Rev. N. Graham, Mr. W. S. James and Miss S. E. Mitchel, all of Sumter County, S. C.

On the 10th inst., at the residence of the bride's mother, by Rev. N. Graham, Mr. Joseph A. Osteen and Miss Mary R. Pack, all of Sumter County, S. C.

At Varnville, P. R. R. R., S. C., February 3d, 1876, by Rev. E. W. Peeples, Mr. Elias R. McTeer and Miss Ella J. Peeples, both of Beaufort County, S. C.

On the 19th January 1876, at the residence of the bride's mother, by Rev. W. Brooker, Mr. Montgomery Eaves and Miss Eugenia Odom, all of Barnwell County, S. C.

G. W. Moore died at his residence near Brushy Creek, Greenville county, July 6, 1875, aged 49 years, after an illness of fifteen months. He was a member of the Brushy Creek Baptist Church....

Died, of diphtheria, on the 28th of September 1875, William Nathaniel, infant son of Hosea E. and Leonora B. Robison of Greenville County, S. C., aged 3 years and 7 months. [verse]

Issue of February 24, 1876

Married on the 20th January 1876, at the residence of the bride's mother, by Rev. W. D. McMillan, Mr. J. H. Odom and Miss Nellie Ray, all of Barnwell County, S. C.

On February 9th 1876, at the residence of the bride's brother, by Rev. John Inabenett, Mr. A. J. Hydrick and Miss V. U. Riley, both of Orangeburg County, S. C.

On the 10th inst., at the residence of the bride's father, by Rev. J. M. Herlong, Mr. H. H. Gardner and Miss Minerva Hydrick, both of Orangeburg County, S. C.

Death of Ida Gardner, 25th November 1875, at the age of eighteen years and four months. By her request, her remains were laid by those of her father.

Miss Hattie R. Nettles, youngest daughter of the late John Nettles, departed this life, at the residence of her brother in law, Mr. M. G. Ramsey, on the 13th ult., in the 36th year of her age.

Issue of March 2, 1876

Married on Sunday, the 20th ult., at the residence of Capt. J. Walton Hair, by Rev. F. J. Sanders, Mr. D. M. Johnston and Miss Jane Hair, all of Elko, S. C.

On the 20th of January 1876, at the residence of the bride's father, by Rev. S. T. Russell, Mr. R. T. Lyrely and Miss Julia Welch.

On February 2, 1876, by Rev. J. E. Rodgers, Mr. O. V. Metts and Miss V. H. Player, both of Camden, S. C.

Issue of March 9, 1876

The Late Deacon Heriot. Wm. B. Heriot, late Senior Deacon of the Citadel Square Baptist Church, of Charleston... was born 3d of August 1812, and died on 2d of November 1875. He was the third son of Roger and Catherine Heriot. At. St. Paul's Church, where he was christened, he was an attend upon the Sabbath service until about eleven years of age, when his parents became Baptists and united with the First Baptist Church of Charleston (May 18, 1823). Bro. Heriot was one of those who went out of First Church in 1840 to establish the Wentworth St. Church... [long account]

Died Dec. 18th, 176, Miss Mary E. Heriot, in the 66th year of her age...

Issue of March 16, 1876

Married on Sept. 30, 1875, by Rev. James Weeks, at the residence of Mr. C. R. Councils, near Reeves' Station, Mr. N. H. Williams, of Barnwell, and Miss M. A. Carter, of Colleton, S. C.

Departed this life February 6th 1876, after a long and protracted illness, our highly esteemed and much beloved brother, Wm. McQualters. For many years he had been a member of the Concord Baptist Church, Fairfield County, S. C. His children and grandchildren mourn his loss.... W. H. H. Ridgeway, S. C., March 10, 1876.

Died, at Buford's Bridge, S. C., February 26th, 1876, of pneumonia, Holly A., daughter of L. B. and S. E. Rents, aged three years and four months.

Died, in Barnwell County, S. C., March 1st, 1876, Thomas S., son of Raymond F. and Sallie J. Kearse, aged one year and seven months.

Died, Oct. 5th, 1876, Mrs. Annie M. Carter, in the 25th year of her age. Her husband, M. A. F. Carter, has sustained an irreparable loss. Colleton County, S. C.

Died, Nov. 2d, 1875, near Walterboro, S. C., John Alexander Halford, aged 3 months and 3 days.

Issue of March 23, 1876

Departed this life, on Saturday morning, March 4th 1876, in the twenty sixth year of her age, Mrs. Mary Ann M. Williams, daughter of J. B. Floyd, of Newberry County, S. C. She was married to Mr. Mont. Williams on the 25th Feb 1868, and leaves two children, a little boy and girl... Sister Williams was baptized at Mount Zion Baptist church, in the 13th year of her age, July 24, 1863... W. D. R.

Married at the residence of the bride's father, 12 miles northwest of Camden, on Wednesday evening, March 15, 1876, by Rev. L. S. Foster, Mr. W. F. Perkins of N. C., and Miss Sallie Moore, of Kershaw County, S. C.

On the 16th inst., at the residence of the bride's father, by the Rev. C. A. Stiles, Mr. Jesse H. Taylor and Miss Ann E. Scott, all of Richland County, S.C.

Issue of March 30, 1876

Decease of Dr. J. J. McCants... The first time that I saw Dr. McCants was at the house of his excellent and pious father in Fairfield District. He was best known to me during his residence in Columbia, to which he removed to serve as Treasurer of the Upper Division of the State... J. L. R. Greenville, S. C.

Married at the residence of the bride's father, on March 15, 1876, by Rev. J. F. Buist, Mr. Robert Broadwater and Miss Mattie Getsinger, all of Barnwell County, S. C.

Issue of April 6, 1876

Married at the residence of the bride's grandfather, twelve miles north of Camden, Wednesday morning, March 29th 1876, by Rev. L. S. Foster, Mr. Joseph P. Vaughn and Miss Annie Moore, both of Kershaw County.

Issue of April 13, 1876

Married on the 6th inst., by Rev. F. J. Sanders, Mr. Frank A. Dunbar and Miss Ogreta Brabham, of Hattieville, P. R. R. R.

At the residence of Capt. A. Mosely, on Thursday evening, April 6th, by Rev. W. J. Hatfield, Mr. B. G. Moris and Miss Adie Mosely, all of Sumter County, S. C.

At the residence of Mr. W. H. Brown, on the 8th of March last, by the Rev. Mr. Bissel, Mr. Jesse Dions and Miss Molly Kennedy, all of Aiken County.

Passed to the rest of heaven, on Thursday, the 30th day of March, 1876, in the seventy fifth year of her age, Mrs. Eliza Ann Hazel, wife of Deacon Joseph Hazel, of the Beaufort Baptist Church. She united with the Beaufort Baptist Church in October 1835 during the ministry of Rev. Daniel Bythewood, by whom she was baptized. F. J.

Died, Brother Lucius W. Woodward, on the 26th of March, at his father's residence in Barnwell, S. C., in the twenty-fifth year of his age. F. L. S. Barnwell, S. C.

Died, near Chesterfield C. H., S. C., on Monday the 27th of March, Mrs. Harriet McBride, wife of the late Dr. Wm. McBride, aged sixty-seven years, eleven months and twelve days.

Died, on Sabbath morning, 9th inst., at the residence of her sister, Mrs. Mary Turner, near Silverton, our aged sister, Pheraby Boyd, aged 72 years. J. J. M.

Died, recently, at her home, near Silverton, Mrs. Elizabeth Crocker, aged 44 years. She had been a member of the Methodist Church the past twelve years. Also, on the 11th inst., at the same place, little Lizzie Stephens, granddaughter of the above, aged 2 years. J. J. M.

Died, on the 3d inst., at his late residence, near Silverton, S. C., of consumption, Mr. Samuel Robeson, in his 32d year. J. J. M.

Issue of April 20, 1876

Married, April 4th, 1876, by Rev. J. E. Rodgers, Mr. Alfred Marsh and Miss Kate E. Raleigh, all of Kershaw, S. C.

April 9th, 1876, by Rev. J. E. Rodgers, Mr. G. A. Burke and Miss M. E. Richbourg, both of Bishopville, S. C.

Mrs. G. A. James. On the morning of the 25th of December 1875, this dear sister passed peacefully away. Mrs. James was the daughter of Deacon Alfred Scarborough, who, with his aged wife, still lives. In 1842, January 6th, she became the wife of W. A. James, a beloved brother and the efficient clerk of Piedmont Church....

Mrs. Joanna Smith, widow of the late Major Smith, of Colleton County, S. c., was born July 15th, 1876, aged 59 years, 8 months and 23 days. She laves 7 sons and 5 daughters, and is now gone to be with her husband and 4 children who had gone on before her.... W. H. Dowling, Folk's Store, S. C., April 9, 1876.

Died, at her residence, near Silverton, on the 14th inst., our aged sister, Mary Turner, the mother of Deacon William Turner, in her 82nd year, for many years a member of Matlock Church. J. J. M.

Died, on the morning of the 11th, at her father's residence, in Abbeville county, Miss Agnes M. Cook, aged thirty-one years and three months. The deceased was a consistent member of Horeb Baptist Church, Abbeville Association. B. F. M., Greenwood, S. C., April 17, 1876.

Issue of April 27, 1876

Married by Rev. W. D. Rice, at the residence of Mr. John C. Stewart, Thursday, April 6th, 1876, Mr. John W. Reeder and Miss Mary J. Schulz, all of Newberry, S. C.

Departed this life on the 4th day of April 1876, Sarah Alberta, youngest daughter of the late B. A. and G. A. James, of Richland County, S. C., in the 13th year of her age. [eulogy]

Issue of May 4, 1876

Tribute of Respect... on 8th inst., died Col. Alexander James Lawton. B. F. Buckner, Church Clerk. Black Swamp Baptist Church, Robertville, April 23d, 1876.

Issue of May 11, 1876

Tribute of Respect from Concord Baptist Church, Fairfield County, S. c., to Dr. J. J. McCants.

Death of Mrs. Borstel. On last Friday, after an illness of several weeks, Mrs. Cassandra H. Borstel departed this life, in the 47th year of her age. Mrs. Borstel came to this town in 1849 from Charleston, where her parents resided and entered in as a student in the Johnston Female Seminary, and in 1850 was married to Maj. F. C. V. Borstel, since which time, with the exception of one or two years during the war, she resided in Anderson. *Anderson Intelligencer.*

Married at the Hardeeville Baptist Church, on the evening of the 4th of April, 1876, by Rev. W. G. Rollins, Mr. C. B. Boyd and Miss F. E., eldest daughter of Mr. and Mrs. Capers Lowry, all of Beaufort, S. C.

Govan Williams, son of Henry and Mrs. E. Williams, of Barnwell County, died on the 30th day of March 1876, aged 16 years. He had been a member of the Coalson's Branch Sunday school for five years. Thomas Clayton. Buford's Bridge, S. C.

Died, near Alston, S. C., on the 17th April last, Major Henry W. Parr, aged sixty-four years. He had been a member of the Little River church about thirty-three years... T. W. Smith.

Issue of May 25, 1876

Married on Sunday, 14th inst., at 10 o'clock A. M., at the residence of the bride's father, by the Rev. S. B. Wilkins, Mr. James S. Coker and Miss Lou P., daughter of Simeon Coker, all of Darlington County, S. C.

At the residence of the bride's father, on the 24th of Feb., 1876, by Rev. R. N. Terry, Mr. M. E. Terry and Miss S. M. Rentz, all of Colleton, S. C.

Col. Alexander I. Lawton who died in the 86th year of his age at the residence of his eldest son, Gen. A. R. Lawton, in Savannah, Georgia... 8th April 1876. Col. L. was born near Robertville, Beaufort County, South Carolina, where he resided all his life... represented his parish in the State Legislature. [eulogy and account]. J. A. L.

Issue of June 1, 1876

Married, April 19, 1876, at the residence of the bride's father, by Rev. N. Graham, R. L. Jinkins and Miss May McKellar, eldest daughter of J. J. McKellar, all of Sumter county, S. C.

May 26th, 1876, at the residence of Mrs. J.J. Gordon, by Rev. N. Graham, R. Durant Brunson and Miss M. R. Wilder, only daughter of the late Charles Wilder, all of Sumter county, S. C.

Departed this life, on the morning of the 12th inst., in the 48th year of her age, Mrs. Sarah Eugenia, wife of Michael Mixon, Esq., of St. Peter's Parish. The deceased had been an invalid for many years.... Robertville, May 19, 1876.

Issue of June 15, 1876

Died, May 30th, 1876, in Barnwell County, S. C., Miss Lucretia A. Peacock, aged about 42 years. A. B.

Mrs. Lucinda W. Lawton died suddenly at her residence in Lawtonville, S. C., on the 2d February 1876. Born in Edgefield County, on the 4th March 1803, of parents in prosperous circumstances.... Forty-eight years ago she married Rev. W. A. Lawton. [eulogy]

Issue of June 22, 1876

Departed this life, June 17, 1876, Mrs. Mary Jane Ross, aged 23 years, 1 months and 1 day. The deceased was a daughter of Dr. D. M. Breaker. She had been a member of the Baptist Church more than ten years, having been baptized by Rev. John Culpeper at Grumesville, in the fall of 1865.

We deeply regret to announce the death of Mrs. Margaret Mariah Youmans, wife of A. M. Youmans, and daughter of W. C. and Rebecca Johnston, of Beaufort County, who with her infant son, Marion Johnston, aged 7 days, died on 21st day of May last, aged 26 years 2 months and 19 days [eulogy]. T. H. M. Charleston *News and Courier* please copy.

Issue of June 29, 1876

Married on the 14th inst., by the Rev. A. coke Smith, Mr. Milledge Crouch of Edgefield, S. C., and Miss Lula Gardner, of Columbia.

William S. Smith. Philadelphia Church (Spartanburg County) mourns the loss of her senior deacon, William S. Smith, who departed this life on the 12th of June 1876, having nearly completed his 79th year. Brother Smith was born, lived, and died in this community... W. P. S.

Issue of July 13, 1876

Married on the 29th of June by Elder James K. Fant, at the residence of Dr. Frank Coleman, Mr. H. Omer Fuller and Miss Hattie E. Barksdale, both of Laurens County, S. C.

On the evening of June 21, at the residence of Mr. Reese Ployers, the bride's step-father, three miles northeast of Camden, by Rev. A. S. Willeford, Mr. T. Louis Young and Miss Rebecca E. McDonald, all of Kershaw County, S. C.

Died at her residence, May 21st, 1876, after a long spell of typhoid fever, Mary McMillan, aged sixty years, five months and nine days. She was a member of Springtown Church... W. T. B.

Issue of August 3, 1876

Married at Matlock Church, 2d Sabbath in July, by Rev. F. J. Sanders, Mr. George Andrews and Miss Lillie, daughter of Mr. Crocker, all of Aiken County, S. C.

Mrs. Susan E. Mobley, relict of Dr. W. S. Mobley, of Edgefield, S. C., died at the residence of her son in law, Maj. W. Lee Coleman, Johnston, S. C., on Thursday morning, May 11th 1876, in the 58th year of her age. She was for many years a member of Red Bank Baptist Church.

Issue of August 10, 1876

Married at the residence of Mr. Elijah Crosby, on Sunday night, July 20, 1876, by Rev. J. f. preacher, assisted by Rev. W. G. Rollins, Mr. C. M. Box and Miss Mary J. Davis, all of Beaufort County, S. C.

Henry Mason Smith, son of Samie and Julia Smith, and grandson of Dempsy and Elizabeth Dubois, of Peniel Baptist Church, Colleton County, was born May 29th 1875 and died June 18th 1876, aged 2 years and 20 days.   Mrs. E. Dubois.

Died, in Barnwell County, S. C., Aug. 4, 1876, Leonard M., youngest son of F. T. and Fanstina Anderson, aged 11 months. A. B.

Issue of August 17, 1876

Married on the 8th inst., by the Rev. F. R. McClanahan, Rev. D. Weston Hiott, of Colleton, S. C., and Miss Ella E. Martin, of Anderson.

Issue of August 24, 1876

Tribute of Respect from Philadelphia Church to Wm. S. Smith. J. W. Stribling, Committee Chairman.

J. B. Black, infant and only son of Dr. J. B. and Hattie Black, of Colleton County, died on the 30th July, after a sickness of two weeks, aged 8 months and 11 days. W. H. D.   Aug. 15, 1876.

Married on the 13th of August, at the residence of Mrs. F. L. Weeks, by Rev. E. H. Cuttino, Rev. C. W. White to Miss M. A. Kinard, all of Barnwell County.

Issue of August 31, 1876

Married by Rev. J. K. Mendenhall, at the residence of the bride's father, Rev. G. H. Carter, of Tenn., and Miss Anna Whilden Roe, daughter of Mr. Thomas Roe, of Greenville county, S. C.

Died at her father's residence, July 25, 1876, after a short spell of slow fever, Miss Savilia O'Sheilds, in the 19th year of her age. W. P. S. Glenn Springs, S.C.

J. R. Hamilton, youngest child of J. R. H. and Rachel Hamilton, of Branchville, died on the 27th of August, after suffering six days, aged two years, one month and four days. W. D. B. R.

Issue of September 7, 1876

William R. Spearman, of Newberry County, South Carolina, died at his father's residence, on Wednesday morning, August the 10th, 1876, in the thirty third year of his age. He married Miss Mattie Clark, and in some three months after their marriage, she died July 18th 1869. He married Miss Sallie Clark in 1872 ... she died 2d day of June 1873. [long account] W. D. R. Newberry, S. C. Aug. 20, 1876

J. R. Hamilton, eldest daughter of J. R. H. and Rachel Hamilton, of Branchville, died on the 27th of August, after suffering six days, aged two years, one month and four days. W. D. B. R.

Issue of September 14, 1876

Married in the city of Augusta, Ga., at the residence of the bride's father, on the evening of the 24th of August, by Rev. F. J. Sanders, Mr. Isaac W. Foreman, of Silverton, S. C., and Miss Lucy, daughter of Mr. Samuel Bowers, of Augusta, Ga.

Died, of apoplexy, in the town of Bamberg, on the 2d of September 1876, Calvin Rice, son of Aaron Rice, in the fifty-third year of his age. He was born in Barnwell County. In early life he united himself with the Springtown Baptist Church, and was baptized by the Rev. W. R. Sanders. J. F. Buist.

Issue of September 28, 1876

Married on Tuesday night, 26th inst., at the residence of the bride's father, by Rev. A. W. Lamar, Mr. Albert Hammond and Miss Fannie Lane, all of this city.

Issue of October 5, 1876

Meta Bruce, youngest daughter of J. P. and O. M. Bruce, of Branchville, S. C., died on the 4th of September 1876, aged four years, nine months, and twenty-six days. W. D. B. R.

Married on the evening of the 24th of September, by the Rev. J. D. A. Brown, Mr. A. B. Walker and Miss Sallie R., daughter of Rev. A. P. Norris, all of Orangeburg.

Issue of October 19, 1876

Died, very suddenly, at her residence in Abbeville County, S. C., on the 16th of June last, Miss Sarah Britt, in the 77th year of her age. She was a member of the Buffalo Baptist Church for fifty years. She leaves two sisters, members of the same church....

Maj. R. W. Furman of Barnwell County, S. C., died on the 8th day of August, 1876, at his residence in Three Mile Township, aged 78 years and 2 months. he was a member of Bethesda Baptist Church. His affectionate and only living daughter, sister Martha Riley, was with him during his last sickness. Bro. Furman was a distant relative of Dr. Furman of Greenville, and was proud of his name. A few months before his death he was surprised by a visit from his brother on his mother's side, Mr. T. J. Millard, of Holly Hill, Charleston County, S. C., whom he had not seen in about forty years. His funeral was preached by Rev. J. m. hoover, and his remains interred in the cemetery at Great Salkehatchie Church... W. H. D.

Died, on the night of the 7th instant, at the residence of his son in law, Mr. Richard Furse, near Silverton, our aged friend, Mr. Thomas Williams, only two weeks of reaching his eightieth year. He leaves seven children, grandchildren, and many friends.... J. J. M.

Married on 5th October, by Rev. C. A. Bayard, Mr. C. C. Boggs of Liberty County, Ga., and Miss Martha E. Ellis, daughter of Mr. S. G. Ellis, of Barnwell County, S. C.

October 11, 1876, by Rev. Thomas Raysor, Mr. J. W. Woodward, of Williston, S. C., to Miss Mary C. Folk, of Colleton County, S. C.

Issue of November 2, 1876

Married on Thursday evening, October 19th, 1876, by the Rev. W. D. Rice, at the residence of the bride's father, Mr. Thos. P. Lane and Miss Ella Mangum, all of Newberry County, S. C.

On Thursday morning, Oct. 26, 1876, by Rev. W. D. Rice, at the residence of Col. J. R. Spearman, Sr., of Newberry County, S. C., Capt. J. C. Boyd (recently of Georgia, now of Greenville, S. C.) and Miss Etta Wearn, of Newberry, S. C.

It becomes our painful duty to record the death of our beloved Bro. James B. Singletary. He died at his home in Charleston County, Sunday evening, Oct. 22d 1876, aged 57 years, 6 months and 2 days. In the death of Bro. Singletary, Briner Church has lost its strong pillar. E. H. C.

Died, near Graham's T. O., S. C., on the night of the 18th inst., Annie M., second daughter of Robert and Mary M. Hightower, aged seven years and eleven months. E. I. C. Graham,'s, Oct. 27, 1876

W. S. Sanders died on the 16th inst., in the 65th year of his age. Bro. W. S. Sanders was a native of S. C. and resided near Barnwell C. H... left a wife and nine children. F. J. S.

Issue of November 9, 1876

Married on Tuesday evening, October 10, 1876, by Rev. W. J. Hatfield, Mr. R. L. Mathis and Miss Amanda Byrd, all of Spring Hill, Sumter County.

At the residence of the bride's mother, October 31, 1876, by Rev. J. F. Buist, Mr. J. E. Steadman and Miss Mary Hayne, all of Barnwell County, S. C.

Issue of November 16, 1876

Tribute of Respect to Anna Lancaster from the George's Creek School.

Married at the residence of the bride's father, Nov. 2d, by the Rev. W. G. Mack, Mr. Geo. Livingston and Miss Anna E. Gardner, all of Orangeburg County, S. C.

John Calvin Workman of Laurens County, S. C., departed this life, after a short but painful illness, October 6th, 1876, in the twenty sixth year of his age. He was a member of Bush River Baptist Church. W. D. R. Newberry, S. C.

Issue of November 23, 1876

Departed this life, in the city of Greenville, November 18th, 1876, Mrs. Emma D. Durham, wife of Rev. A. K. Durham. She was born April 8th 1851, baptized August 10, 1857, and married September 10 of the same year.... J. L. Reynolds

Issue of November 30, 1876

Married on the 23d Nov. 1876, in the Methodist Church, Bamberg, S. C., by the Rev. J. F. Buist, Mr. George Gennings and Miss Julia Slater, all of Bamberg, S. C.

On the 23d inst., by Rev. D. W. Hiott, Mr. P. Warren Leach, of Pickens County, and Miss Victoria Campbell, of Anderson, S. C.

Died recently at Silver Bluff, Aiken County, Mr. Angus Redd, aged about forty years, leaving a wife, daughter, parents and many friends. Deceased was a member of Matlock Church... J. J. M.

Died, near Silverton, recently of Diphtheria, little Robert, son of Mr. and Mrs. Faulkner. J. J. M.

Died, of Diphtheria, near Silverton, infant daughter of Mr. and Mrs. Williams. Soon followed, the father, a victim of negro violence.... J. J. M.

Issue of December 7, 1876

Married, October 19, 1876, by Rev. J. E. Rodgers, Mr. S. E. Brooks and Miss M. A. E. Deas, all of Kershaw, S. C.

November 13, 1876, by Rev. J. E. Rodgers, Mr. J. J. McCaskill and Miss Laura A. McKutchen, both of Sumter County, S. C.

November 19, 1876, by Rev. J. E. Rodgers, Mr. E. L. McKay and Miss E. V. Pate, all of Kershaw, S. C.

November 23, 1876, by Rev. J. E. Rodgers, Mr. W. B. Baswell and Miss J. M. A. King, Kershaw, S. C.

November 23, 1876, by Rev. J. E. Rodgers, Mr. C. J. Nunnery and Miss A. E. Tolbert, all of Kershaw, S. C.

November 29, 1876, by Rev. J. E. Rodgers, Mr. J. S. Arrants of Sumter, and Miss M. J. Rodgers, of Kershaw, S. C.

Henry McMillan of Colleton County, S. C., died October 23, 1876, aged seventy-six years, ten months, and twenty-three days. He leaves a large family of children, grandchildren, and great grandchildren, all together about 70. he was a native of Barnwell County, but in 1845 he removed to Colleton, and in 1848 he was bereaved of his wife. His church membership remained at old Springtown, in Barnwell.... Elizabeth DuBois. Nov. 26, 1876.

Died on the 20th october, of membranous croup, little Walter Gillett, infant son of Mr. and Mr. L. C. Hough, aged one year, seven months, and nine days. A. W. S. Flat Rock.

Issue of December 14, 1876

Married on Thursdsay, Dec. 7, 1876, by Rev. W. D. Rice, at the residence of the bride's father, Mr. J. McK. Smith, of Newberry county, and Miss Alice Miller, of Laurens County, S. C.

At the residence of the bride's mother, Charleston County, Thursday, Nov. 16, 1876, by Rev. E. H. Cuttino, Mr. J. H. Harvey and Mrs. D. E. Harvey, all of Charleston County, S. C.

Issue of December 21, 1876

Married on the 29th of November, at the residence of the bride's mother, by Rev. R. R. Vann, Mr. L. H. Sligh, of Richland, and Miss Claudia Abney, of Fairfield.

On the morning of the 10th inst., at the residence of Mr. Seaborn Jones, by Rev. A. S. Willeford, Mr. Jackson Outon and Miss Mary Knight, all of Kershaw County, S. C.

Nov. 22d, 1876, at Mt. Pleasant Baptist Church, by Rev. O. F. Gregory, Mr. John Wittschen and Miss Emeline Hiott, all of Mt. Pleasant, Charleston County, S. C.

Dec. 10, 1876, at the residence of the bride's father, by Rev. O. F. Gregory, Mr. George Gist and Miss Ella Allsbrooks, all of Williamsburg, S. C.

On Dec. 14, at the residence of Col. W. H. Duncan, by Rev. A. Buist ,Mr. Jeremiah Snelling and Miss Fannie Duncan, all of Barnwell County.

On 14th Dec., at the residence of the bride's mother, by Rev. A. Buist, Mr. S. A. Hair and Miss M. J. Keele, all of Barnwell County.

Issue of January 4, 1877

Married on December 15, 1876, by Rev. J. E. Rodgers, Mr. J. W. Stokes and Miss Flora Pate, all of Kershaw, S. C.

On December 21, 1876, by Rev. J. E. Rodgers, Mr. William Smith and Miss Susan Baker, all of Kershaw, S. C.

On December 21, 1876, by Rev. J. E. Rodgers, Mr. C. E. Cook and Miss Mattie English, all of Kershaw, S. C.

On December 28, 1876, by Rev. J. E. Rodgers, C. L. Shiver of Kershaw, S. C., and Miss Mary E. Eveans, of Sumter, S. C.

On December 28, 1876, by Rev. J. E. Rodgers, Mr. Berry Hancock and Miss N. J. V. Reynolds, all of Kershaw, S. C.

On November 21, 1876, at Santee Baptist Church, by Rev. D. W. Cuttino, Mr. G. W. Wells of Sumter, S. C., and Miss Mary R. Parler, of Orangeburg County, S. C.

On November 26, 1876, at Santee Baptist Church, by Rev. D. W. Cuttino, Mr. Joseph Zeigler and Miss Caroline Dantzler, all of Orangeburg County, S. C.

On December 7, 1876, at the residence of the bride's father, by Rev. D. W. Cuttino, Mr. Adam Shumaker and Miss Ella Dantzler, all of Orangeburg County, S. C.

On December 21, 1876, at the residence of the bride's mother, by Rev. A. S. Willeford, Mr. S. A. Clark and Miss Lou E. McDowell, all of Kershaw County, S. C.

On December 24, 1876, at the residence of the bride's father, by Rev. A. S. Willeford, Mr. D. R. Player and Miss Lizzie F. Spears, all of Kershaw County, S. C.

On December 19, 1876, at the residence of Mr. Alsey Coleman, by Rev. J. K. Fant, Mr. H. Eugene Fuller and Miss Lida A. Coleman, all of Laurens County, S. C.

On December 21, 1876, by Rev. J. K. Fant, at the residence of Dr. G. Coleman, Mr. D. Baker Dendy and Miss Sallie H. Barksdale, all of Laurens County, S. C.

At the residence of the bride's father, by Rev. G. H. Carter, Dr. James P. Johnson and Miss Rachel Davis, all of Newberry County, S. C.

On December 21, 1876, at the residence of the bride's mother, by Rev. J. J. Getsinger, Mr. W. K. May and Miss Julia Patterson, all of Barnwell County, S. C.

Mrs. Elizabeth C. Segler, daughter of John W. and Sarah Brodie, and companion of Rev. J. A. Segler, was born September 29, 1821; baptized into the fellowship of Tabernacle Baptist church by Rev. Wm. Booker, November 1, 1840; married to J. A. Segler, May 9, 1844; and departed this life in Aiken County, S. C., on the morning of the 20th of December 1876. her funeral was preached by Rev. H. Lecroy and her remains deposited in Tabernacle church yard on 21st December 1876. She laves an aged mother, a devoted husband, four affection children, brothers and sisters, and many kindred and friends. [eulogy]

James McCrorey, son of Jas. A. McCrorey, Jr., died at his father's, of dropsy of the chest, on the 29th of Nov. 1876, in the 23d year of his age, leaving weeping but not disconsolate parents to mourn his loss.... T. W. M.

Mrs. Mary Gates, relict of Christian Gates, died in Orangeburg county, S. C., Oct. 16, 1876, aged about 93 years. Mother Gates was a faithful and worthy member of St. Matthew's Evangelical Lutheran Church, having been connected with said church 64 years, 6 months and 17 days. We learn through Mrs. Mary Stoudenmire that the subject of this notice was the mother of 9 children, 40 grandchildren, 78 great grandchildren and 15 great-great-grandchildren. 2 children, 22 grandchildren, 62 great grandchildren, and 13 great-great-grandchildren are still living. S. T. H.

Died on the 16th Dec of cholera infantum, Claude Alfred, the infant son of Mr. and Mrs. H. H. Easterling, aged 1 year and six months. A. B. Barnwell, Dec. 18, 1876.

Died recently, near Silverton, infant son of Mr. and Mrs. A. M. Harley.... J. J. M.

THE WORKING CHRISTIAN

Issue of January 11, 1877

Married on the evening of 20th ult., 1876, at the residence of the bride's father, by the Rev. F. J. Sanders, Mr. Stephen Miller, of Burke County, Ga., and Miss Sallie H. Meyer, of Silverton, S. C.

On January 3, 1876, in the city of Augusta, Ga., at the residence of J. Cuthbert Shecut, by the Rev. D. Shaver, D. D., Mr. James Heath and Miss Sallie Stallings, all of Aiken County, S. C.

On December 20, 1876, at the residence of Deacon J. w. Hunter, by Rev. W. D. McMillan, Mr. G. M. Hunter and Miss Florence E. Reeves, all of Barnwell County, S. C.

On December 27, 1876, at the residence of Deacon A. Boylston, by Rev. W. D. McMillan, Mr. J. C. Wise and Miss Anna L. Wilson, all of Barnwell County, S. C.

On Wednesday, the 20th of December 1876, about 1 o'clock P. M., at his residence in Barnwell County, S. C., departed this life, Mr. John Angus Williams, son of the Hon. Jones M. Williams and Mrs. Rebecca T. Williams... in the thirty-fifth year of his age... left wife, children, father, mother, relatives and friends. J. F. Buist. Bamberg, Dec. 28, 1876.

The following unpublished obituary was written some time after the late war, and it will be gratifying to Mrs. E. H. Richardson, of Brunson, S. C., an widowed mother.... W. H. Dowling, Salkehathchie C. & S. R. R., Dec. 30, 1876:

Serg't A. R. Richardson, Co. B., 5th Regt. S. C. Cavalry. He was the son of Mr. James C. Richardson, of Beaufort District, S. C., and was a member of Beech Branch Baptist Church. On the afternoon of the 27th of February last, a reconnoitering party of Butler's Brigade, numbering about 80, met a similar party of Yankees, in Darlington District, about deep dark. A severe fight ensured. Col. Aiken, of Fairfield, and Sergt. A. R. Richardson were instantly killed.... W. H. D. Beaufort District, St. Peter's Parish, Jan. 1866.

Little Lotta E. Price was an only daughter, child of E. B. Price and Telie Price. God gave her to them on July 20, and she died November 9th. J. F. Buist. Bamberg, Nov. 16, 1876.

Died, on the first day of January, Lillian Viola, daughter of Richard and Kittie Young, of Fort Mills, aged 8 years, 7 months and 21 days....

Issue of January 18, 1877

Married on July 13th 1876, by Rev. J. M. Weeks, Mr. James Patrick and Miss Ella Wannamaker, all of Colleton, S. C.

On January 3d 1877, by Rev. J. M. Weeks, Mr. Silas Patrick and Miss Francis Hutto, all of Colleton, S. C.

West Allen Williams, D. D. S. It is a sad duty to record the death of a favorite pupil. He breathed his last at his father's at Piercetown, Anderson County, S. C., January 3, 1877. He leaves a fond and loving family.... J. W. C.

Died, recently, at his home in Aiken county, Mr. John Boyd, aged about 40 years. J. J. M.

Issue of January 25, 1877

Married on the 5th Dec., 1876, by Rev. F. J. Sanders, Mr. W. C. Rountree and Miss Sallie Weathersbee, all of Barnwell, S. C.

Issue of February 1, 1877

Married on the evening of the 31st ult., at the residence of Mr. B. F. Rhame, by Rev. N. Graham, Mr. Wiley Dunlap and Miss Emma Hatfield, all of Sumter.

On the evening of January 17, by Rev. A. Buist, Mr. James S. Rountree and Mrs. Lizzie Dyches, all of Barnwell county.

On the evening of Jan. 25, at the residence of the bride's father, by Rev. A. Buist, Mr. Jno. L. Johnson and Miss J. Alice Cave, all of Barnwell county.

Died, at his residence in Barnwell county, on the 10th of January 1877, after a protracted illness, Lucius B. Kearse, in his 42nd year. He was a man of generous and patriotic impulses. In 1861 he responded to the first call for volunteers. He leaves a devoted wife and four children, besides other relatives....

Issue of February 8, 1877

Tribute of Respect from the Greenwood Baptist church, Jan. 28, to Dr. W. H. williams, who died on Jan. 3d, at age of 30. In early manhood, Dr. W. connected himself with the Williamston Baptist church. In 1871, he located in Greenwood....

Married Feb. 4, 1877, at the residence of the bride's mother, Mrs. S. Stroman, by Rev. A. P. Norris, Mr. J. R. Stoudemire and Miss Lena Stroman, all of Orangeburg county, S. C.

On Dec. 21, 1876, by the Rev. R. J. Edwards, Mr. W. J. Strock and Miss E. F. Thomas, all of Orangeburg county, S. C.

On Dec. 21, 1876, by the Rev. R. J. Edwards, Mr. J. F. Bochette, of Clarendon county, S. C., and Miss G. F. Bochette, of Orangeburg county, S. C.

On December 26, 1876, by the Rev. R. J. Edwards, Mr. Y. P. Shuler and Miss Lizzie Bair, all of Orangeburg county, S. C.

January 4th, 1877, by Rev. J. E. Rodgers, Mr. S. D. Hurst of Darlington, and Miss Nancy McLeod, of Kershaw.

On the 10th of January 1877, by Rev. J. E. Rodgers, Mr. W. S. Smith and Miss Mattie Osteen, both of Camden, S. C.

On the 15th of January 1877, by Rev. J. E. Rodgers, Mr. W. F. Hawkins and Miss E. J. Shiver, both of Sumter county.

On the 18th of January 1877, by Rev. J. E. Rodgers, Mr. W. R. Kenington and Miss C. E. Watson, both of Sumter county.

Issue of February 15, 1877

Married at the residence of the bride's father, at Lawtonville, S. C., on the evening of Jan. 30, by the Rev. W. A. Lawton, Mr. S. F. Blount and Miss M. E. Thomas.

On the 3d of January last, at the residence of the bride's father, in the city of Augusta, Ga., by the Rev. Mr. Jarrold, Mr. Luther Rountree of Aiken county, and Miss Florence L. Peel, of Augusta, Ga.

On the evening of the 24th January last, at the residence of the bride's mother, near Silverton, by the Rev. C. G. Bradford, Mr. J. Jefferson Williams and Miss Callie Bates, all of Aiken County, S. C.

On the evening of the 8th inst., at the residence of the bride's mother, by the Rev. C. G. Bradford, Mr. W. H. Brigham, of Augusta, Ga., and Miss Lizzie Cochran, of Aiken County, S. C.

Died at her home in Fairfield County, on the 16th of January 1877, Mrs. Catharine Mobley... Attaching herself to the Baptist church more than forty-four years ago... She laves a husband in the eighty-third year of his age, and an unusually large number of children, grandchildren, and great-grandchildren. J. D. M. The weekly *Fairfield News and Herald* will please copy and send bill to Mrs. N. W. Jones, Blackstock, S. C.

Died, near Millett's, Port Royal Railroad, on the 4th of February 1877, of congestion of the brain, George Washington, elder son of Dr. and Mrs. G. W. Morrall, aged 6 years, 4 months and 14 days....

Died, in Nov. 1876, at her residence on Beach Island, S. C., Mrs. Harriet Howard, consort of Mr. Henry Howard, aged about 60 years... leaving an aged husband, three children and many friends... J. J. M.

Died in Jan. last on Beach Island, S. c., Mrs. W. C. Page, wife of Mr. Willie Page, and daughter of Mr. Henry Howard, aged 25 years. She has left a husband, four lovely children, father, one sister and brother.. J. J. M.

Issue of March 1, 1877

Tribute of Respect to Rev. William Williams, D. D., from Students of the Seminary, Feb. 22, 1877... Professor in the Southern Baptist Theological Seminary.

Tribute of Respect from Zoar Baptist Church, February 18, 1877, to Rev. Noah Graham. Willie W. Fort, Church Clerk. Sumter, S. C.

Married on the 7th ult., at the residence of the bride's mother, by Elder J. R. Earle, Dr. James P. Duckett, of Newberry County, and Miss Eugenia Watson, of Anderson County.

On Sunday morning, Feb. 25, at the residence of the bride's father, by the Rev. J. F. Buist, Mr. Wesley Collins and Miss Mary Still, all of Barnwell County.

On the 18th ult., at Wesley Chapel, Orangeburg County, by Rev. M. L. Banks, Mr. Jerome B. Cooper, of Barnwell County and Miss Emma J. Clark of Orangeburg county.

Died in December 1876, at his plantation residence, near the Savannah, Aiken County, S. C., Mr. O.D. Prentiss, aged near forty years, leaving a wife and several helpless little children. J. J. M.

Died in January last, at the residence of his son, J. Wiley Broom, in Burke County, Ga., Mr. G. L. Broom, in his 68th year, leaving a son, daughter, and numerous relatives in Georgia and Carolina. J. J. M.

Issue of March 8, 1877

Married on Sabbath morning, Feb. 25, at the residence of the bride's father, near Silverton, by the Rev. F. J. Sanders, Mr. Franklin Archibald and Miss Mary Sanders, all of Aiken County, S. C.

On Thursday evening, February 22d, 1877, at the residence of the bride's brother, by Rev. W. J. Hatfield, Mr. W. Pinckney Mathis and Miss Mattie Weldon, all of Sumter county.

Mrs. Augusta Smith. The sad news of the death of this estimable lady ,of Barnwell has just reach me... T. W. M. Doko

Died recently, near the Savannah, Aiken County, S. C., Mrs. Susan Grubs, the dear aged mother preceding her only a little while. J. J. M.

THE WORKING CHRISTIAN

Issue of March 15, 1877

Married on Wednesday morning, 7th inst., at the residence of the bride's step-father, Mr. W. A. Duncan, by the Rev. Mr. Hiers, Mr. W. M. Meyer and Miss Mary Ann Boyles, all of Barnwell County, S. C.

Issue of March 22, 1877

Married on the 14th inst., at the residence of the bride's father (Mr. Jesse DuBois), by Rev. W. H. Dowling, Mr. J. L. Buckner and Miss Carrie DuBois, all of Colleton County, S. C.

On Sunday afternoon, 18th inst., at the residence of the bride's father, by Rev. A. Buist, Mr. N. W. Peacock and Miss Nancy Stansell, all of Barnwell County.

On Thursday evening, 15th inst., at the residence of the bride's sister, Mrs. Mary A. Cochran, by the Rev. C. G. Bradford, Mr. Joseph Stallings, only son of the late Captain George W. Stallings, and Miss Laura Williams, all of Aiken County.

Died, on March, March 4th 1877, in Orangeburg County, S. C., Mrs. Mary Snider, wife of Mr. Jacob Snider, in the seventy-ninth year of her age. in early life she professed faith in Christ, and was baptized by Rev. Jacob Bair. She united with the Santee Baptist Church in its constitution... D. W. C.

Issue of March 29, 1877

Rev. Samuel Furman. This aged soldier of the cross, the brother of Dr. Jas. C. Furman, and the father of Dr. Richard Furman, passed away to his reward at 8 o'clock on Monday morning, March 19. had he lived until yesterday, his age would have been four-score years and five. C. C. Brown. Sumter, March 22.

Issue of April 5, 1877

Married at the residence of the bride's father, on the 14th of February 1877, by Rev. J. T. Sweat, Mr. Riley Cope and Miss Phoebe D. Sweat, all of Beaufort County.

At the residence of the bride's mother, on the 14th of February 1877, by Rev. J. T. Sweat, Mr. Frank Mixon and Miss Ellen Tuten, all of Beaufort County.

On Sabbath, Feb. 25, 1877, Elder Jonas Ancrum filled his pulpit at the usual hour at Gadsden Red Hill Baptist Church, where he has been pastor for more than twelve years... died that day. His age was between 60 and 75 years. he was the first pastor of Zion Pilgrim Baptist Church, Hopkins' T. O... J. B. Goodwin, Hopkins T. O., S. C., March 6, 1877.

THE WORKING CHRISTIAN

Issue of April 12, 1877

Married at the residence of the bride's mother, on the 29th of March 1877, by Rev. J. A. Segler, Mr. Luther Shellhouse and Miss L. R. Scott, all of Aiken county, S. C.

At the residence of the bride's father, on Sunday morning, 8th inst., by Rev. J. A. Segler, Mr. H. D. Hogg, of Barnwell County, and Miss Mary P. Brodie, of Aiken County, S. C.

We are called upon to record the death of Thomas Hicks. The deceased was born in Williamsburg County, S. C., in the year 1804. He came to this state in 1856, where he since lived up to the time of his death, March 14th 1877... The Eliam Baptist church, of which Brother Hicks was a member, sustains a great loss... A. E. S.   Banana, Fla. April 5, 1877.

Issue of April 19, 1877

Married Thursday evening, April 5, 1877, by the Rev. B. F. Price, Mr. Philip H. Price, of Walterboro, S. C., and Miss Emma Witherspoon, of Columbia, S. C.

On Sunday morning, March 25, at the residence of the bride's mother, by Rev. Wm. Raysor, Mr. G. B. McMillan and Miss Rebecca Bloom, all of Barnwell County.

Died in Williston, March 29th 1877, Henry Smith, in the 62d year of his age. [eulogy]

Died, on the 22d of March 1877, after a short illness, youngest child and only daughter of S. S. and E. J. Walters, of Branchville.... W. D. B. R.

Issue of May 3, 1877

Departed this life, on Sunday, April 1st, 1877, after a short but painful illness, Mrs. Mary A. Burch, consort of J. B. Burch, and daughter of Isaac R. and M. A. Timmons, aged 29 years. At the age of 11 years, Mrs. Burch united with the Hebron Baptist Church, at Friendfield, in Marion county, S. C., then under the pastoral care of Rev. John Weaver... Mrs. Burch leaves an aged mother and father, a devoted husband, affectionate brothers and sisters, and a little infant... P. M. T.

Miss Roda Baker departed this life April 18th, 1877, in the 17th year of her age. At the age of 14 she united with the White Plain Baptist church, from which she removed her membership to the Monroe Baptist Church.

Died, recently, at Hoover's, S. C., Mr. J. Burnett Walling, aged 44 years, leaving a wife and several small children. Deceased was a member of the Methodist Church... W. R. D.

Issue of May 17, 1877

Died, at Brighton, S. C., on the 3d day of March last, Thomas Jefferson Riley, in the fifty-second year of his age....

S. L. E. Steedly, mother of W. L. and A. M. Reeves and F. E. Hunter, departed this life on the 19th of april 1877. She was a member of Hunter Chapel Church....

Departed this life at Pinopolis, S. C., April 22d, 1877, Mary F. Winter, wife of D. McCants Winter, in the 39th year of her age. The deceased was baptized by Rev. W. B. Whilden, at Wassamasaw church, November 4, 1864. She leaves a husband and eight children.... D. M. B.

Issue of May 24, 1877

Died in Anderson County, S. C., little Sallie, daughter of J. M. and Lucinda Webb... D. W. Hiott.

Died, in Augusta, Ga., April 28, Hon. James J. Wilson, formerly of Barnwell County, S. C., in the seventy-first year of his age. Barnwell, May 1st, 1877.

Departed this life, on the evening of the 2d of May, at the residence of one of her sons, in Lexington County, S. C., Mrs. Christian Able, who was born June 29, 1797, married February 21st 1811; herself and husband joined the Baptist church at Old Cloud's Creek and was baptized in February, 1820. She soon after moved with her husband to Edisto, in Lexington County, where they became chiefly instrumental in organizing and building up the Convent church... She died aged nearly eighty... She was the mother of thirteen children, eight of whom have gone to the spirit-land before her, leaving three sons and two daughters....

Issue of June 7, 1877

Ann Starr Garrison, wife of Rev. J. Milton Garrison, died at her home in York County, S. C., on the night of Sunday, the 20th of May, about midnight, aged sixty eight years and twenty days. She had been a member of the Baptist church at Flint Hill nearly 40 years and had brought up her children, five sons and one daughter.... *Yorkville Enquirer* will please copy.

Issue of June 14, 1877

Captain P. F. Buckner, of Beaufort County, S. C., was born December 29th 1829, and died January 19th 1877. He married Miss Adie E., daughter of the lamented Hon. A. M. Ruth, and in 1873 was converted and united with the M. E. Church. During the war he served as an officer in local service, and also in the 5th South Carolina Cavalry, under Hampton in Virginia and elsewhere. He leaves a widow and six children... May 28th 1877.

Rev. George Walker, of Colleton County, S. C., was born February 9, 1809, and died April 24th 1877. In 1831 he was married to a Miss Carter, near Carter's Ford church, where he settled a home and resided until his death... He leaves a widow and ten children.... W. H. D.

Issue of June 21, 1877

Died, in the morning of life, on Friday, June 8th, at the house of Mr. Hampton Weathersbee, near Rouse's Bridge, Aiken County, Mr. Willie Ransey, in his 22d year. J. J. N.

Died of congestion, on the morning of the 21st of May, Miss Lizzie E. Inabnet of Reevesville, S. C.... a consistent member of the Baptist church at St. George's for six years... R. S. W. St. George's, S. C.

Died, on the 7th May 1877, at the residence of his son-in-law, Mr. Washington N. Mason, in Fairfield County, S. C., Capt. Edward A. Andrews, in the 73d year of his age. [eulogy] Winnsboro, May 14, 1877. M. S.

Issue of June 28, 1877

Tribute of Respect from Bethel Baptist Church, June 17, 1877, to Rev. W. E. Hughson.

Married at the residence of the bride's father, on the 10th inst., by Rev. J. F. Preacher, Mr. Silas Willis, of North Carolina, and Miss Susie Terry, daughter of David and Cynthia Terry, of Beaufort County.

At the residence of the bride's mother, on the 20th inst., by Rev. J. F. Preacher, Mr. Jacob M. Gray, of Beaufort County, and Miss Ursula Young, of Barnwell County.

On the 3d inst., at the residence of the bride's father, by Elder A. T. Latta, Mr. Wm. R. Fletcher and Miss Annie L. Blackwell.

Died, at Erwinton, Barnwell County, S. C., on the 14th of June 1877, Mrs. Mary Griffith Carson, wife of W. B. Carson, daughter of Stephen and Martha M. Griffith. W. B. Carson, Allendale, S. C., June 21, 1877.

Died, in Anderson County, on the 18th inst., Mrs. Elizabeth Long, in the 75th year of her age. She had been a consistent member of the Baptist church at Mt. Pisgah about 30 years. She leaves a husband who is about 83 years of age and many children. D. Weston Hiott.

Issue of July 5, 1877

Married on Tuesday, May 8th, by Rev. W. J. Hatfield, Mr. G. B. Cato and Miss Unice Wilson, all of Sumter county.

Died of cholera infantum, on Tuesday evening, June 19, near Bradford Springs, Sumter county, S. C., little Eva, younger daughter of Rev. W. J.a nd Sarah Virginia Hatfield... W. J. M.

Issue of July 19, 1877

Married on Thursday, July 5th 1877, at the residence of Col. Geo. S. Cannon, by the Rev. W. D. Rice, Mr. G. W. L. Spearman and Miss Mollie J. Cannon, all of Newberry County, S. C.

In Barnwell, S. C., June 20th, by Rev. W. A. Pearson, Mr. John O'Halloran, of Rochester, N. Y., and Miss Alice D. Shepherd, of Barnwell, S. C.

Died on the 5th July at the residence of Mr. Peacock, Jackson Station, P. R. R. R., after a long and painful illness, Miss Avretts, of Georgia. Deceased was a member of the Methodist church. J. J. M.

Issue of July 26, 1877

Married on the 17th of July 1877, by Rev. E. J. Forrester, at the Hardeeville Baptist church, Mr. John H. Ulmer and Miss Lilla Pelot, both of Hardeeville, S. C.

Died, in the morning of her life, on Thursday, July 13th, Miss M. E. Hill, daughter of J. R. and Margaret Hill, of colleton.. 17 years of age. Walterboro, S. C., July 17, 1877.

Memorial of Wm. T. Hill... born near Timmonsville, in Darlington county, on March 21st 1829, and died on February 9th 1877. His father, Rev. Amos Hill, was a member and preacher of the Primitive Baptist church... William united himself with the Lake Swamp church in his 23d year and continued a member of the same until the organization of the Timmonsville church in the fall of 1872... S. M. Richardson, May 23, 1877.

Issue of August 2, 1877

Departed this life June 29th ult., at the residence of her daughter, Mrs. Claudius Ashley, in Barnwell County, S. C., Mrs. W. S. Sanders....

Issue of August 9, 1877

Died, on 15th April last, at his residence at Effingham, Darlington county, Theodore G. Cannon, in the 48th year of his age. In May 1857, he was married to Miss Hester M. Timmons, daughter of the late esteemed Rev. J.

M. Timmons. Soon after he united himself with the Elim Baptist Church, of which Rev. Timmons was and had been for over forty years its beloved pastor.... His funeral services were held at Elim church; sermon preached by Rev. R. R. Brooks...

Mrs. Mary Pelham, widow of George Pelham, of Colleton county, S. C., died on 12th day of May 1877, aged 64 years, 5 months and ten days. She had been a member of the Peniel Baptist church for 26 years. She leaves 6 sons and daughters, and 24 living grandchildren. Saltkehatchie, S. C., July, 1877.

A. D. Dowling, of Orangeburg county, S. C., died on 23d day of May, 1877, aged about 43 years. he was the elder brother of those eminent and yet unassuming gentlemen, Drs. W. P., E. H., C.T. and John C. Dowling, and the son of the lamented Col. D. Dowling, of Barnwell, who was a descendant of a royal Irish family. The name was originally O'Dowling. Prior to the revolutionary war, three brothers of the name (with the O dropped) came to America. One stopped at New York, one at Charleston, from whom as descended this family (including the family of Rev. W. H. Dowling) and the other went further South. A. D. Dowling leaves a widow (who was a Miss Tyler or Orangeburg) and also several children... his remains were interred in the family graveyard, near Graham's, S. C.

Died, at Woodruff, S. C., July 27th, 1877, infant son of Rev. L. C. and M. S. Ezell.

Issue of August 16, 1877

Died recently, near Brown Hill, in Aiken county, Mr. William Taval, aged 27... leaving a distress wife and two dear little ones. J. J. M.

Issue of August 30, 1877

Married on the 9th instant, at Mrs. McCartey's, by W. E. Sawyer, Esq., Mr. Pickens New, of Edgefield county, and Miss Frances Inabinet, of Orangeburg county. Edgefield and Orangeburg papers please copy.

Died, after a short illness, on Monday, June 18th, 1877, Erastus V. Shuler. The deceased was born June 24th 1832, and was married to Miss E. A. Bookhart in 1851, from which marriage there were born nine children, eight of whom still live. He became a member of the Santee Baptist Church in 1856; subsequently he transferred his membership to the Antioch Baptist Church, connected with, formerly, the Charleston Baptist Association... R. J. E.

<u>Issue of January 3, 1878</u>

Married at the residence of the bride's parents, December 19, 1877, by M. E. Broaddus, Mr. Butler Pinson and Miss Vicky Franklin, all of Abbeville.

At Mr. Will Duke's, December 19, 1877, by M. E. Broaddus, Mr. Frank Elimburg and Miss Carrie Day, all of Abbeville County.

At the residence of Mrs. Higgins, Newbery County, S. C., December 23, 1877, by M. E. Broaddus, Mr. Richard Watts and Miss Lizzie Rook.

On December 26, 1877, by M. E. Broaddus, Mr. Henry Earnest and Miss Minnie Watkins, both of Newberry County.

At the residence of the bride's mother, Mrs. Elizabeth McLaughlin, December 12, 1877, by Rev. C. A. Stiles, Mr. Morgan Davis, of Clarendon County, S. C., and Miss Sallie E. Brady, of Richland County, S. C.

At the residence of Mr. Moses Bunch, November 22, 1877, by Rev. S. T. Russell, Mr. R. J. Bishop and Miss Sarah A. Garick.

On the 13th inst., at the residence of the bride's father, by Rev. F. J. Sanders, Mr. C. M. Edenfield, of Allendale, and Miss Joe Kennedy.

Near Statesville, N. C., on the 26th December 1877, at the house of the bride's father, Dr. John Robertson, by Rev. J. B. Boone, Rev. John J. McLendon, Principal of the Carolina Central Academy, Ansonville, N. C., and Miss Nellie M. Robertson.

At the residence of Dr. W. H. Timmerman, the bride's father, on the evening of December 20th, 1877, by Rev. N. N. Burton, Mr. G. Preston Seigler of Aiken County, and Miss Lydia E. Timmerman, of Edgefield.

Died, at the residence of Mr. Silas Eaves, in Barnwell County, S. C., Dec. 23, Mrs. Henrietta Baldwin, aged 76 years.... A. B.

Died, Nov. 24, Freddie, eldest son of Mr. and Mrs. Columbus B. Anderson, aged 8 years. A. B.

Miss Laura Watts died recently at the home of her mother, near Jackson Station, Port Royal Railroad, leaving a kind mother, sisters and brother. J.J.M.

Mrs. Mary Archibal died quite recently at the residence of her father, Mr. Sanders, near Silverton, after an illness of 30 days, leaving a young husband, parents, sisters and numerous friends... J.J.M.

<u>Issue of January 10, 1878</u>

Married on Thursday evening, 20th Dec. 1877, by Rev. C. A. Stiles, Mr. Charles M. Douglas and Miss Joanna Carter, Kingville, Richland County, S. C.

At Mr. P. P. Hamilton's, by Rev. F. C. Jeter, on the 3d of January, Mr. L. B. Jeter and Miss Janie Hamilton, both of Union, S. C.

At the residence of the bride's father, Jan. 3, 1878, by Rev. A. Buist, Mr. Leyton McDonald and Miss Fannie Owens, all of Barnwell County, S. C.

On December 26th, at the residence of Mr. T. J. Harper, by the Rev. W. C. Lindsay, Robert B. Keene, of Newberry, and Miss Mamie E. Webb, of Columbia.

Died, at her residence in Chester County, on the 20th Dec., Mrs. Elizabeth Nunnery, consort of Amos Nunnery, in the 78th year of her age. She had been married 54 years, and the greater part of her life an exemplary member of the Baptist church. She had lived to see all her children and many of her grandchildren settled in life.... L. C. H.

Issue of January 17, 1878

Married at the residence of Mr. J. Nevit, Dec. 20th, by Rev. J. D. Mahon, Mr. L. M. Fee and Miss L. A. Withers, all of Fairfield.

At the residence of the bride's mother, Jan 6, by Rev. J. D. Mahon, Mr. L. R. Guthrie, of North Carolina, and Miss Sallie Stone, of Fairfield.

Married at the residence of the brides' father, on the 19th December, by Rev. W. H. Dowling, under the same ceremony, Mr. Elijah O'Quinn and Miss Rebecca Beard, and Mr. Brooks All and Miss Ursula Beard.

Died, at the residence of her son-in-law ,Mr. John D. D. Fairy, in Branchville, S. C., Mrs. Elizabeth Rigby. Our departed sister was born in Colleton County, S. C., on the 27th September A. D. 1807. Her maiden name was Hussey. of her mother's children, only one survives, Mr. John Hussey, who resides in Mississippi. She was married twice-- first, to Mr. John Grimes, of Orangeburg County, S. C., and secondly to Mr. William Rigby, of Colleton, S. C. By the first marriage she was the mother of three children-- all girls, two of whom are still living: Mrs. Howell and Mrs. Fairy. By the second, she had five children, one daughter and four sons. Two of the boys preceded their father and mother to the spirit word. The other children, Emeline, Charles and John, are still alive, and are married also. R. J. e. Orangeburgh C. H., S. C.

Issue of January 24, 1878

Married at the residence of the bride's father, December 23d, 1877, by Rev. S. T. Russell, Mr. C. T. Shuler and Miss E. V. Welch.

On January 3, 1878, by Rev. J. E. Rodgers, Mr. Bradford Scarborough and Miss A. L. Smith, daughter of Henry Smith, Esq., of Sumter County.

On January 17, 1878, by Rev. J. E. Rodgers, Mr. F. B. McCaskill, of Sumter county, and Miss C. S. M. Boykin, youngest daughter of Col. S. M. Boykin, of Kershaw County.

Issue of January 31, 1878

Little James Edgar Cochran, son of Richard and Helen Furse, died recently, near Silverton, aged 2 years and 2 months. J. J. M.

Mr. and Mrs. Peacock, husband and wife, died quite recently at Jackson Station, P. R. R., the formerly preceding the latter only a few days... They leave children and many friends. J. J. M.

Died, of cancer, January 15, 1878, Mrs. Esther Walker, aged 58 years... A.. B.

Issue of February 7, 1878

Married on Tuesday, the 29th ult., at the residence of the bride's father, by Rev. A. Buist, Mr. J. L. Buist and Miss L. C. Cave, all of Barnwell County.

Issue of February 14, 1878

Married on Sabbath evening, 27th January, by the Rev. Mr. Tiller, Mr. Cornelius Tobin, aged nearly fourscore years, and Miss Robison, both of Aiken County, S. C.

On the evening of the 2d of January last, at the residence of Mr. Hampton Weathersbee, on the Upper Three Runs, Aiken County, by Rev. F. J. Sanders, Mr. W. T. Ransey and Miss L. S. Weathersbee, all of Aiken county.

At the residence of the bride's father, on the 9th of January, by Rev. Moses Boynton, Mr. W. O. Beard and Miss Sallie All, all of Barnwell County.

On the 28th of January, by Rev. F. J. Sanders, Mr. Samuel Seele and Miss Josephine Long, all of Barnwell, S. C.

On the 31st of January, by Rev. F. J. Sanders, Mr. L. F. Cave and Miss Fannie Owens, all of Barnwell, S. C.

On the 3rd of February, by Rev. F. J. Sanders, Mr. Thomas Coward, Esq., of Aiken, and Miss Josephine Owens, of Barnwell, S. C.

On 24th ult., by Rev. R. R. Brooks, at the residence of bride's father, Mr. Paul I. Bostick and Miss Saline J., daughter of Geo. J. Myers, Esq., all of Marion County, S. C.

Issue of February 21, 1878

Married on Wednesday, the 6th of February, at the residence of the bride's father, by Rev. W. H. Prentiss, Mr. James S. DeWitt and Miss Anna R. Terry, all of Beaufort County, S. C.

On the 7th inst., by Rev. R. R. Vann, Mr. T. F. Vann and Miss Ella Trapp, all of Fairfield.

On the 10th inst., by Rev. R. R. Vann, Mr. J. W. Mull and Miss Fannie Wooten, all of Fairfield.

Died, in Columbia, November 21st, 1877, Mrs. Harriet English, in the 90th year of her age.

Died, in Barnwell County, S. C., February 5, 1878, Mrs. Elizabeth Ray, aged seventy-three years. J. F. Buist. Bamberg, Feb. 15th, 1878.

Issue of February 28, 1878

Married on Thursday, February 21, 1878, at the residence of the bride's mother, Greenwood, S. C., by Rev. Jas. K. Fant, Mr. E. F. Waldrop and Miss Lou Rochester.

Died, on the 3d of February, 1878, Mrs. Sarah R. Langley, wife of Mr. C. H. Langley, Sr., of Barnwell County, in the 65th year of her age.

Issue of March 7, 1878

Margie P. Young, consort of L. L. Young, and daughter of Col. B. F. Griffin, of Newberry County, departed this life, Dec. 2d, 1877. Age 39 years. [eulogy] E. C. M.

Died, at Columbia, S. C., at the residence of her father, Rev. Edwin A. Bolles, Chaplain of the South Carolina Lunatic Asylum, February 11th 1878, after an illness of fifteen months of consumption, Mrs. Felicia Perry Bergman Holcombe. The deceased, youngest daughter of Rev. Edwin A. and Harriot A. Bolles, was born in Charleston, S. C., June 12th 1846; baptized when an infant by Rev. Dr. Bachman, pastor of St. John's Lutheran Church; confirmed while attending the Orangeburg Female College by Bishop Davis, of the Episcopal, and married by Rev. Stiles Mellichamp during the year 1865. of her three children, one preceded her to the spirit land, and two remain.... *Lutheran Visitor.*

Departed this life at Lawtonville, S. C., on the 28th February 1878, after a painful illness, Rev. W. A. Lawton, pastor of the Lawtonville Church; he was born 23d June 1793; ordained 1823; aged eighty four years and eight months and five days, and an active pastor for fifty-five years. James E. Morrison.

Issue of March 14, 1878

Married on the evening of the 7th inst., by Rev. F. J. Sanders, Mr. Alexander Harden and Miss ellen Cave, all of Barnwell, S. C.

On the evening of the 7th, by Rev. B. F. Miller, at the residence of the bride's father, 3 miles east of Greenwood, Mr. James A. Crawford and Miss S. Ella Arnold, both of Abbeville County.

At the residence of Mr. William Newton, by Rev. S. T. Russell, Feb. 17, 1878, Mr. Samuel A. Russell and Miss M. F. Lyerly.

On the 5th inst., by Rev. R. R. Vann, Mr. B. Hogan and Miss Fannie Smith, all of Fairfield.

On the 9th inst., by Rev. R. R. Vann, Mr. Samuel Dixon and Miss Fannie Gilmore, of Columbia.

Issue of March 21, 1878

Married by Rev. A. C. Stepp, February 7, 1878, Mr. J. Stobo Bolt and Miss Mary E. Baldwin, both of Laurens County, S. C.

By the same, February 21, 1878, Mr. Samuel P. Campbell and Miss Anna T. Davenport, both of Greenville County, S. C.

Died, on the 6th March, at his home in Fairfield County, Mr. Robert McBride, in the 70th year of his age. He leaves an aged wife and many relatives and friends....

Issue of March 28, 1878

Died, February 10, 1878, near Looxahoma, Miss., Mrs. J. D. Montgomery, in the 62d year of her age; she was the daughter of Elder Thomas Ray, a useful Baptist minister of Union County S. C.; she was a good wife, a devoted mother.... leaves a large family and many friends. E. E. King.

Issue of April 4, 1878

Married on the evening of March 7th, 1878, by Rev. W. D. McMillan, at the residence of the bride's father, in Blackville, S. C., Mr. S. L. Redmond, of Lexington County, and Miss M. Lucia Johnson.

Died, March 29, 1878, in Hardeeville, S. C., Mrs. F. P. Hardee, in the 56th year of her age.

Issue of April 18, 1878

Married on Wednesday, March 6, at the residence of the bride's father, by Rev. S. B. Sawyer, Mr. Charles R. Fickling, of Barnwell County, and Miss Carrie L. Gardner, of Orangeburg County, S. C.

At the residence of the bride's father, by Rev. E. H. Cuttino, February 24th, Mr. Adam Grooms and Miss Rachel Jeffers, all of Charleston.

By the same, at his residence, February 27th, Mr. H. G. Rudd and Miss R. B. Whaley, all of Charleston County.

Issue of April 25, 1878

Married on the evening of April 18, 1878, by Rev. A. Buist, at the residence of the bride's father, Mr. W. D. Dicks and Miss Carrie S. Anderson, all of Barnwell County.

Died, April 13th, 1878, Madison Baxley, youngest son of Mr. and Mrs. Barney Baxley, aged 16 years....

Died, April 21, 1878, Earnest Morrall Anderson, youngest child of Mr. and Mrs. R. H. Anderson, aged 5 months.

Issue of May 2, 1878

Died, at his home in Barnwell County, S. C., near Blackville, on the morning of the 9th April, Mr. C. M. DeWitt, in the 51st year of his age. Bro. DeWitt had been a member of the Blackville church for more than twenty years... He leaves a fond wife and eight children to mourn his loss.

Issue of May 9, 1878

Married on the evening of the 1st instant, at the residence of the bride's mother, by Rev. A. S. Willeford, Mr. John Munn and Miss Nannie Gardner, all of Kershaw co.

Died, at her residence at Packsville, S. C., on the morning of the 12th April 1878, in the 62d year of her age, Miss Mary M. Kelly, after an illness of only 24 hours... an exemplary member of the Baptist church for 40 years... F. P. C. Foreston, S. C., April 26, 1878.

Issue of May 23, 1878

Married on the 16th of May, at the residence of the bride's father, by Rev. J. K. Fant, Mr. Edwin E. Weathers, of Taladega, Ala., and Miss M. Lizzie Harrison, of Greenwood, S. C.

Issue of June 13, 1878

Married on Friday, May 24th 1878, at the residence of the bride's mother, Mrs. Sarah Reddick, by Rev. Geo. T. Gresham, Mr. William S. Bullock and Miss Willie A. Reddick, both of Ocala, Fla.

By the same, on Sunday, May 26, 1878, at the bride's residence, Mr. Charles D. Royall, of Savannah, Ga., and Mrs. Emma C. Goin, of Ocala, Fla.

On the 23d of May, at Green Savannah, S. c., by Rev. F. J. Sanders, Mr. W. B. Connelly, and Miss Josephine Cave.

In Memoriam. Maggie Lindsay. For seven days she suffered with Diphtheria, but early Monday morning, she died. M. G. H. Barnwell, S. C.

Died, of consumption, May 20th, 1878, Mrs. Martha Cave, wife of Mr. Sam. C. Cave, of Barnwell County, aged 48 years. She leaves a husband and six children to mourn her loss. A. B. Barnwell, S. C.

Issue of June 20, 1878

Married on Tuesday, June 12th 1878, at the residence of the bride's parents, by Rev. J. Adolphus French, Rev. Edwin C. Dargan, of Botetourt Springs, Virginia, and Miss Lou A. Graves, of Orange County, Virginia.

At the residence of Mr. W. A. Blunt, near Appleton, S. C., June 9, 1878, by Rev. W. A. Pearson, Mr. Marshall Hill and Miss Mariah Blunt, all of Barnwell county, S. C.

Died in Mecklenburg County, N. C., on the morning of the 26th of May, at the advanced age of 84 years, Deacon Blankinship of the Sugar Creek Church in York County, S. C. B. C. G.

Died, at Fort Mill, S. C., on Sunday night, the 25th of May 1878, Mrs. Ann E. Anderson, in the 70th year of her age.... B. C. G.

Died recently, in the city of Augusta, Ga., James Cochran, only son of Mr. Wm. H. Brigham, of that city. This loved boy is gone to join the sainted mother who preceded him only a little while. J. J. M.

Issue of June 27, 1878

Died at the residence of her father, in Richland County, on the morning of Tuesday, 25th day of December 1877, Jeannette, daughter of Mr. and Mrs. Joseph Abbot, aged 28 years, 3 months and 22 days. [poem]. Columbia, Dec. 31st, 1877.

Issue of July 11, 1878

Died at her residence in Barnwell County, S. C., on the morning of the 25th of June 1878, Mrs. Elizabeth J. Kearse, aged 68 years... J. F. Buist, her Pastor.

Died, in Darlington County, S. C., on the 3d day of April 1878, Mr. John Kirvin, in the eighty-sixth year of his age. He was forty-seven years a member of the Black Creek Church... J. O. B. D.

Died, recently, at her home near Lake Hope, Aiken County, S. C., Mrs. Mary Ridgdell, aged fifty-five years. Deceased for many years was a consistent member of Matlock Baptist Church. She leaves children and many friends. J. J. M.

Jefferson Preston, infant son of Mr. and Mrs. A. M. Harley, died, recently, near Silverton. J. J. M.

Issue of July 18, 1878

Died, at Williston, May 16th 1878, in the 26th year of her age, Laura Phillips Hankinson. In October 1870, she professed conversion under the ministry of Rev. Mr. Sawyer. She leaves a little babe, a loving husband, an affectionate family....

Issue of July 25, 1878

Died, at her residence in Barnwell County, S. C., June 4th 1878, Mrs. Minnie Williams, wife of Mr. Robert Williams, and daughter of the Rev. John M. Hoover. A faithful wife, devoted daughter, an affectionate sister... J. F. Buist, her Pastor. July 24, 1878.

Died, at her father's residence near Donaldsville, S. C., June 23, 1878, Miss Mary E. Agnew, aged 19 years. Her funeral was preached on the 24th by Rev. R. N. Pratt. For nearly five years she was an earnest member of Turkey Creek Baptist church... J. K. P.

Issue of August 15, 1878

Thomas William Pegues, son of James and Sarah G. Pegues, was born in Marlboro District, S. C., on 22d October 1808. he settled in Camden in 1829, and removed to Alabama in 1836, but after a brief stay he returned to Camden, and there dwelt to the end of his life. He married Miss Sarah J. Roberts on the 28th of December 1834, and after her death in 1857, married Miss Louisa S. Bronson, on the 27th of June 1858. During the life of his first wife, ten children were born to him, seven of whom are still living. He was, in various capacities, connected with the *Camden Journal*... During the Indian war in Alabama, he served for a short time. He fell on sleep June 11, 1878. J. O. W.

Little Annie, daughter of Mr. and Mrs. Bush Howard, died recently at Silver Hill, near Silverton. J. J. M.

Issue of August 22, 1878

Married at the residence of Mr. Adam DeHay, Aug. 1st 1878, by Rev. S. T. Russell, Capt. T. L. C. Vail and Miss Sarah R. E. DeHay.

Bro. D. McCants Winter departed this life at his home in Charleston County, S. C., after an illness of 10 days, on the 27th of May 1787, aged 46 years, 6 months and 7 days. He was baptized by Rev. W. B. Whilden into the fellowship of the Wassamasaw Baptist Church on 4th November 1864.... E. H. C.

Died, in Williamston, on the morning of the 7th inst., Miss Nannie D. Crymes, after a long and painful illness. She had been a consistent member of the Baptist church in this town for about twenty years.

Issue of September 26, 1878

Died, on the 8th September 1878, after a few hours' illness, Mrs. Elizabeth D. Lide, wife of T. P. Lide, of Darlington, in the 66th year of her age, and the 26th of her Christian profession. She was the last survived of a large family reared by the late Alexander Sparks, of Society Hill.

The Cyprus Creek Church has recently lost a most useful and beloved member in the person of R. F. Rountree. He was a useful citizen, an affection and faithful friend.

Died, near Barnwell, S. C., September 4, 1878, Mattie Harden, a member of the Graham's Sunday school.

Issue of October 3, 1878

Rev. H. T. Haddick. This noble servant of God has fallen at his post in Grenada, Miss. [long account] C. C. Brown.

Issue of October 10, 1878

Died, of putrid sore throat, September 26, 1878, little Joseph, son of Rev. Jas. M. Weeks, of St. George's, S. C., aged 13 months and 3 days.

Married in Columbia, S. C., October 2, 1878, by Rev. W. C. Lindsay, Rev. H. A. Whitman, of Georgia, and Miss Hattie L. McCants, daughter of the late Dr. J. J. McCants, of this city.

At the residence of the bride's father, in Greenville county, S. C., by Elder E. R. Carswell, Jr., Mr. Lawrence A. Dean, of Anderson county, and Miss Janie C. Ramsey, of Greenville county.

Issue of October 17, 1878

Sweetly fell asleep in Jesus, on the morning of the 3d of October, at Barnwell, little Lizzie Manville, aged three years and six months, second daughter of Albert and Alice Manville. Columbia. M. C. H.

Issue of October 24, 1878

Married on the 9th October 1878, at the residence of the bride's father, by Rev. A. Buist, Mr. Peyton R. Hay, of Barnwell county, and Miss Minnie Stroman, of Orangeburg county.

On Monday afternoon, October 14, 1878, at the residence of the bride's mother, by Rev. B. F. Miller, Mr. James Lewis Porter and Miss Janie B. Bellot, both of Abbeville county, S. C.

Departed this life, September 24, 1878, Joseph D. Zeigler, an esteemed member of the Four Holes Baptist church, Orangeburg County, S. C., from consumption and dropsy of the heart. He was a devoted husband, kind father... He leaves a widow and five children. R. j. E.

Little Fannie, infant daughter of A. M. and Sarah J. Manning, died in Chester, S. C., October 11, 1878.

Issue of October 31, 1878

Married on the 10th instant, by Rev. H. C. Smart, at the house of the bride's father, Mr. Samuel S. Paul and Miss Mary Francesca Connors, all of Hampton county, S. C.

In Greenville, S. C., at the residence of the bride's father, Rev. J. K. Mendenhall, October 23, 1878, by Dr. J. C. Hiden, Mr. Thos. N. Berry and Miss J. Pauline Mendenhall.

By Rev. S. M. Richardson, at the Timmonsville Baptist church, October 23, 1878, R. Q. Powell, Esq., of Fair Bluff, N. C., and Miss Alitha Rollins, daughter of the late Rev. Louis Rollins, of Timmonsville, S. C.

On the 24th of October 1878, at the residence of the bride, by Rev. Edwin C. Steele, Rev. C. T. Scaife, of Union County, S. C., and Miss Bettie Madge Mobley, of Chester county, S. C.

Died, at her residence in Spartanburg county, on the 13th of September 1878, Mrs. Sarah Frey, wife of J. R. Frey, in the 52d year of her age. The subject of this notice was a native of Orangeburg county, S. C., where she resided until her marriage and removal to Spartanburg. Mrs. Frey had been a member of the Baptist church for more than thirty years....

Lines on the death of Annie Vass, aged 3 years and 6 months.

Issue of November 7, 1878

Married on the evening of 23d October 1878, at the residence of the bride's mother, by Rev. A. Buist, Mr. Willie S. Mims and Miss Cornelia A. Walker, all of Barnwell county, S. C.

On the evening of the 24th October 1878, at the residence of the bride's father, by Rev. A. S. Willeford, Mr. H. P. Mobley and Miss Lizzie Croxton, eldest daughter of Rev. J. S. Croxton, all of Lancaster county, S. C.

Died with hooping cough, at Hoover's, S. C., September 17th 1878, Wm. R. DeWitt, Jr., aged 19 months and 5 days, son of Wm. and Minerva DeWitt.

Issue of November 14, 1878

Married on Wednesday evening, October 16, 1878, at the residence of the bride's father, by Rev. Dr. J. C. Furman, Mr. E. A. Tindal, of Sumter county, S. C., and Miss Fannie E., eldest daughter of Dr. A. K. Durham, of Greenville, S. C.

Issue of November 21, 1878

Married on Tuesday the 12th inst., by Rev. C. A. Stiles, Mr. Jesse D. Reese and Miss Lizzie Kennedy, all of Richland County.

Bazil Hartley was born November the 7th 1809 and died at his home in Lexington County, S. C., July the 18th 1878. The subject of this notice had been a member of the Mt. Ebal Baptist church about fifty years...

Issue of November 28, 1878

Married on Thursday morning, October 21, 1878, at the residence of Mr. H. C. Paulling, of Orangeburg county, S. C., by Rev. J. J. H. Stoudenmire, Mr. M. E. Carroll, of Orangeburg County, S. C., and Miss Sallie A. Paulling, of Fairfield county, S. C.

On October 17, 1878, by Rev. J. E. Rodgers, Capt. W. A. James and Miss E. J. Barret, both of Bishopville, Sumter county, S. C.

On November 13, 1878, by Rev. J. E. Rodgers, Mr. C. M. Myers and Miss E. R. McLeod, all of Kershaw, S. C.

Issue of December 5, 1878

Married on the 21st ult., by Rev. J. S. Croxton, at the residence of the bride's father, Mr. S. V. Stover and Miss Emma, eldest daughter of J. C. Hillard, all of Lancaster county, S. C.

On the 28th Nov., 1878, by Rev. A. Buist, Mr. Wm. C. Baxley and Miss Carrie Cave, all of Barnwell county, S. C.

Elder B. S. Sweat, who was born at Barnwell C. H., S. C., Nov. 15, 1808, died at his residence in Natchitoches Parish, La., Oct. 28, 1878. He was a member of Saline Baptist Church.

Issue of December 12, 1878

Married on the evening of 4th December 1878, at the residence of the bride's father, by Rev. A. Buist, Mr. Winton T. Walker and Miss Lessie N. Mims, all of Barnwell County.

At the residence of the bride's mother, Union county, S. C., December 5, 1878, by Rev. T. J. Taylor, Mr. J. E. Fault and Miss Ellen Duncan, all of Union county, S. C.

November 17, 1878, at the residence of the bride's father, by Rev. John D. Mahon, Mr. Rufus Lumpkin and Miss Lizzie Cockerell, all of Fairfield C. H.

Died at Bamberg, S. C., on Tuesday, the 26th of November 1878, about 5 o'clock P. M., Miss Sallie M. Nelson, daughter of Samuel T. and Rebecca R. Nelson, aged 21 years and 6 months. Her remains were interred on the succeeding Wednesday in the burying ground of the Springtown Baptist church, Barnwell County, S. C., and her funeral sermon was delivered by Rev. J. F. Buist.... J. F. Buist. Bamberg, December, 2, 1878.

Died, at his home near Danville, Kentucky, on the last day of summer, the last day of the month, the last day of the week, and at the setting of the sun, Maj. A. D. Meyer, having attained nearly his eightieth year. Major Meyer was a Carolinian by birth, born and reared near Silverton, S. C. At an early age he made Kentucky his home, married in one of the first families of his adopted State, reared a family, two sons and three daughters, all of whom survive him, and a wife of his second marriage, having lost by death the wife of his first marriage soon after the close of the late war... in early manhood united with the Presbyterian church. Silverton, S. C. Kentucky papers friendly please copy.

Issue of December 19, 1878

Married on the 22d October 1878, at the residence of the bride's mother, by Rev. D. W. Cuttino, Mr. W. L. Felder and Miss V. D. Dantzler, both of Orangeburg county, S. C.

Issue of December 26, 1878

Married on the 28th of November, by Rev. F. J. Sanders, Mr. Barney Jeffcoat and Miss Rosa Swann, of Barnwell village, S. C.

On the 5th instant, by Rev. F. J. Sanders, Mr. William Henry Langley and Miss Armedia Smith, all of Barnwell, S. C.

On the 15th instant, by Rev. F. J. Sanders, Mr. Robinson Morris and Miss Jane Hardin, all of Barnwell, S. C.

At the residence of the bride's mother, near Williston, S. C., on Tuesday evening, December 10, 1878, by Rev. W. D. Rice, Mr. M. C. Willis and Miss Mattie Matthews, all of Barnwell county, S. C.

Died, in Barnwell County, November 20th 1878, W. K. Weekley, in the 73d year of his age. J. F. Buist. December 17, 1878.

Issue of January 9, 1879

Married at the residence of the parson, on Friday, December 13, 1878, by Rev. W. J. Hatfield, Mr. D. P. Scott, of Sumter county, and Miss Eliza Jane Baker, of Kershaw County, S. C.

On Wednesday, Dec. 18, 1878, at the residence of the bride's father, by Rev. W. J. Hatfield, Mr. D. Owen McLeod and Miss Martha Rebecca McEachern, all of Sumter County, S. C.

On Sunday, December 22, 1878, by Rev. W. J. Hatfield, Mr. S. B. Hatfield and Miss Mary Trimnal, all of Sumter County, S. C.

On the evening of December 18, 1878, at the residence of the bride's father, in Anderson, S. C., by Rev. W. H. Strickland, Mr. Jas. E. Barton, of Easley's, and Miss Victoria S. Catlett, of Anderson, S. C.

.At the residence of Mrs. Catharine Fant, on the night of the 18th ult., by Rev. W. H. Strickland, Mr. James J. Anderson and Miss Ella Massey, all of Anderson, S. C.

On the evening of the 23d ult., at Orangeburg C. H., by Rev. A. W. Lamar, Mr. Henry Davis, Jr., and Miss Sue M. Sistrunk, all of Orangeburg county, S.C.

By Rev. G. S. Anderson, on the 10th ult., at the residence of the bride's brother, Maj. Roddy Sansford and Miss Susan Alexander, all of Spartanburg county.

By Rev. G. S. Anderson, on the 12th ult., at the residence of Mr. Larkin Lancaster, Mr. Christopher Lancaster and Miss Ida Smith, all of Union county.

On the 24th of December 1878, at the residence of the bride's father, by Rev. J. J. H. Stoudenmire, Mr. R. D. Kittrell and Miss M. M. Hoffman, both of Orangeburg county, S. C.

On the evening of Wednesday, December 18, 1878, at the residence of the bride's aunt, Mrs. D. J. Walker, on Beach Island, S. C., by Rev. C. G. Bradford, Mr. Charlie C. Meyer, of Silverton, and Miss Ida, second daughter of Mrs. Adaline Stallings and the late Maj. S. H. Stallings, all of Aiken county, S. C. Aiken and Barnwell papers please copy.

On the 12th ult., at the residence of the bride's father, by Rev. D. W. Cuttino, Mr. Adam Rourk and Miss Sallie Fogler, all of Orangeburg county, S. C.

December 22, 1878, at the residence of the bride's stepfather, Mr. Jesse Hart, by Elder W. A. McCrackan, Mr. H. B. Cogburn and Miss Fannie Gibbes, all of Edgefield county.

Died, near Darlington C. H., S. C., on the 23d inst., Theodora Lydia, wife of Rev. R. W. Lide. Just before her own death her little boy two and a half years old died... W. J. A. Darlington, Dec. 26, 1878.

Died, January 2, 1879, near Barnwell C. H., Mrs. Isabella Halford, aged 77 years. A. B.

Died, suddenly, at her home near Silverton, December 23, Mrs. Ann Talula Wilson, aged 28 years, wife of mr. P. T. Wilson,a nd daughter of Capt. H. P. Brown, of Aiken, S. C.... left husband, little ones. J. J. M. Aiken and Barnwell papers please copy.

Died, at his residence near Silverton, December 26, Mr. Jesse Foreman, aged near 70 years. Deceased leaves five brothers and many friends. J. J. M.

Issue of January 16, 1879

Married on December 24, 1878, by the Rev. J. E. Rodgers, Samuel Yates and Nancy C. Croft, all of Kershaw.

On the same date and by the same, Mr. J. Bradley and Mrs. F. Campbell, all of Kershaw.

On December 25, 1878, by the Rev. J. E. Rodgers, Mr. J. F. Moseley and Miss C. M. Thompson, all of Kershaw.

On the 9th of January, 1879, at the residence of Capt. Thomas M. Lyles, of Fairfield county, S. C., by Rev. A.P. Pugh, Maj. Thomas W. Woodward and Miss Rebecca V. Lyles.

Died suddenly in Lewisville, S. C., December 30, 1878, Mrs. Margaret Smoke, aged 80 or 81 years. J. J. H. S.

Died, in Sumter, S. C., on the 10th inst., in the 27th year of her age, Cornelia Elizabeth, wife of Rev. C. C. Brown... W. C. Lindsay.

Issue of January 23, 1879

Married in Sumter, at the residence of the bride's father, on December 24, 1878, by Rev. C. A. Stiles, assisted by the bride's pastor, Rev. C. C. Brown, Mr. Warren Fort and Miss Mamie W. Burch, both of Sumter county, S. C.

Near Kingsville, at the residence of the bride's father, on the 15th inst., by Rev. C. A. Stiles, Mr. Robert Clarkson and Miss Lizzy Starling, all of Richland county, S. C.

Issue of January 30, 1879

Married on the evening of the 19th inst., at the residence of Mr. J. J. Ballentine, by Rev. E. H. Cuttino, Mr. David A. Taylor and Miss Amanda Ballentine, all of Charleston County.

January 14, 1879, at the residence of the bride's mother, by Rev. J. J. Mahon, Mr. John Lindsey and Miss Melvina Mobley, all of Fairfield.

January 26, 1879, at the residence of the bride's mother, Mr. James G. McAlily and Miss Fanny P. Stone, all of Chester.

December 15, 1879, at the residence of the bride's father, in Chester County, by Rev. J. D. Mahon, Mr. Henry Taylor, of Fairfield, and Miss Alice Wicks.

Issue of February 6, 1879

Married on the 28th of January, at the residence of Capt. Thomas P.Lyles, Fairfield county, S. C., by Rev. A. P. Pugh, Mr. J. Feaster Lyles and Miss Carrie Lyles.

January 29th, at 7 P. M., by Rev. R. W. Sanders, Mr. T. J. Irwin and Miss Cattie Culp, all of Chester.

Issue of February 20, 1879

Married in Barnwell, S. C., at the Baptist church, by Rev. A. Buist, February 13th, 1879, Mr. John B. McNab and Miss Sallie Lancaster.

In the Baptist church at Bamberg, S. C., February 13th 1879, by Rev. J. F. Buist, Mr. T. J. Counts, Jr., to Miss S. H. Johnson, both of Bamberg, S. C.

Died, at his residence in Barnwell county, S. C., on the 10th inst., Mr. Silas Eaves, in his 69th year. He was a consistent member of the Baptist church for many years... February 14th, 1879.

Died on the 13th inst., at his residence in the town of St. Matthews, of pneumonia,Mr. E. J. Buyck, in the 35th year of his age. He united himself with the Baptist church several years ago. Mr. Buyck leaves a wife and five children... St. Matthews, S. C., Feb. 17, 1879.

Issue of February 27, 1879

Married on the morning of the 16th of February, 1879, at Branchville, by Rev. J. J. H. Stoudenmire, Mr. L. A. Judy and Miss Julia A. Patrick, both of Branchville, S. C.

By Rev. B. C. Lampley, at the residence of the bride's father, January 20th 1879, Mr. Q. B. Bagnal, of Clarendon, and Miss C. J. Nettles, of Williamsburg.

By Rev. B. C. Lampley, at Bethel Church, Sumter County, February 12th 1879, Mr. Frean Mellett and Miss M. A. Ramsey.

On the 2d of December, at the residence of the bride's father, Union County, S. C., by Rev. John Gibbs, Mr. W. C. Bennitte and Miss Julia Spillers.

On the 26th of December 1878, at the residence of the bride's father, by the same, Mr. Henry Burch and Miss Leana Lee.

January 29th 1879, by the same, at the residence of Mrs. O'Sheals, Mr. John Lawson and Miss Mariah O'Sheals.

On the 6th of February, 1879, at the residence of Mr. William S. Lee, Mr. joe Turner and Miss Rachel Lee, all of Union.

By Rev. R. W. Sanders, at the residence of the bride's father, in Chester County, S. C., February 20, 1879 at 7:30 P. M., Mr. Carson Warren and Miss Maggie Shannon.

Died, at his residence, in Barnwell, S. C., Mr. Thomas Beard, in the 70th year of his age. he was for many years a consistent member of the Baptist Church. J. F. Buist. Bamberg, February 20th, 1879.

Died, on the 17th instant, near Monticello, Fairfield County, S. C., Mrs. Caroline Rabb, wife of Thomas W. Rabb, in the 53d year of her age. The deceased had been a member of the Baptist Church at Little River more than 23 years... T. W. Smith. February 22, 1879.

Issue of March 6, 1879

Married on February 27, 1879, by Rev. W. C. Lindsay, Mr. Jacob Golnich and Miss Sarah Singelton, both of Lexington, S. C.

Thursday, January 30, by Rev. J. D. Mahon, at the residence of the bride's father, Mr. Willie Banks and Miss Vic Weir, all of Fairfield, S. C.

On February 11, at the residence of the bride's mother, by Rev. J. D. Mahon, Mr. F. Weber of Spartanburg and Miss Ida Newbill, of Fairfield, S. C.

By Rev. W. A. Therell, at the residence of the bride's father, in Camden, S. C., on the 22d ult., Mr. Wiley Sheorne and Miss Sallie E. Love.

On Thursday, February 20, 18798, in St. Andrews Church, at Jackson, Miss., by Rev. J. L. Tucker, D. D., Rev. George B. Eager of Knoxville, Tenn., and Miss Annie Coor Pender, of Jackson, Miss.

At the residence of the bride's mother, February 27, 1879, by Rev. T. J. Taylor, Mr. Giles G. Hill and Miss R. T. M. Dawson, all of Union County.

Died, at Darlington, S. C., January 17, 1879, Dr. Robert L. Hart, in about the 65th year of his age. He joined the Baptist church in early manhood.

Issue of March 13, 1879

Died, of pneumonia, at his mother's residence in Newberry County, S. C., February 10, 1879, Dick Lee Burton, in the sixteenth year of his age....

Issue of March 20, 1879

Married on the 23rd of February, 1879, by Rev. B. C. Lampley, at Providence Church, Sumter County, Mr. J. E. Hodge and Miss M. A. Richardson.

March 13, 1879, by Rev. A. Buist, Mr. Isaac W. Rountree and Miss Anna Baughman, all of Barnwell County.

At the residence of the bride's father, on the 6th of March 1879, by Rev. D. W. Cuttino, Mr. J. B. Cuttino and Miss Mamie E. Jenkins, all of Orangeburg County, S. C.

The 1st day of March 1879, closed the early career of Mrs. Elizabeth Vam, of Barnwell County, S. C., in the 63rd year of her age. She leaves behind two sons. J. F. Buist, Bamberg, S. C.

Issue of March 27, 1879

Tribute of Respect to Aleczandria Acker, who departed this life September 18, 1878, in the seventy-fifth year of his age. He united himself with our Church in 1833; three years afterwards he was ordained, and became the Pastor of our Church...

Departed this life February 21st 1879, at the residence of her son-in-law, Dr. W. J. Milford, in Anderson County, Mrs. Annie Shumate, in the ninety-third year of her age. She united with the Columbia Baptist Church in Greenville county early in life....

Issue of April 3, 1879

Married on the 20th of March 1879, by the Rev. J. T. Buist, Mr. N. Y. Felder, of Barnwell County, S. C., to Miss Bessie C. Johnson, of Hampton County, S.C.

Departed this life, March 1st 1879, Mrs. E. Beard, at her home in Barnwell County, S. C., in the 35th year of her age.... husband and children. J. T. Buist.

Issue of April 10, 1879

Married, April 3rd, in the Presbyterian Church, Greenville, S. C., by Rev. R. H. Nall, Mr. J. L. Killian to Miss M. Joella Moseley, only daughter of Col. G. F. Moseley, all of Greenville.

Married, April 2d, in the Presbyterian Church, Greenville, S. C., by Rev. A. Coke Smith, of the Methodist Episcopal Church, assister by Rev. R. H. Nall, of the Presbyterian Church, Mr. Herman G. Gilreath to Miss Mattie L. Cauble, all of Greenville.

Issue of April 17, 1879

Married, on Thursday evening, April 10, 1879, by Rev. J. J. H. Stoudenmire, Mr. John A. Wolfe and Miss Fannie R. Hartzog, all of Orangeburg County, S. C.

Little Jennie May, youngest child of Mr. and Mrs. W. A. Sanders, departed this life at Chester, S. C., April 10, 1879.

Departed this life on the 4th day of February last, Rev. Jacob Burress, of Anderson County. Aged 80 years. In early life he made a profession of religion and united with the old Mount Tabor Church, near Anderson village. He had a large family and connection [eulogy]

Issue of April 24, 1879

Mrs. Elizabeth M. DeWitt, wife of S. W. DeWitt, died January 13th 1879, in Hampton, S. C., in the 65th year of her age. For nearly fifty years she had been a consistent member of Springtown Church, of Barnwell County. Two years ago, she joined the Church at Hampton, C. H. H. C. S.

Issue of May 1, 1879

Married on Wednesday evening, April 23rd, 1879, at the residence of Mr. M. M. Arnold, by Rev. A. C. Stepp, Mr. J. T. Ellison, of Laurens, to Miss Abbie Gaines, of Greenville County, S. C.

Issue of May 8, 1879

Died, suddenly in York County, S. C., April 12, 1879, Angus R. Nicholson, aged about 86 years. For many years he had been a good member of the Baptist Church at Chester C. H. R. W. S.

Issue of May 29, 1879

Married on the 6th of May, at the home of the bride, by Rev. E. W. Horn, Dr. W. H. Timmerman to Miss Henrietta, daughter of Rev. G. Bell, all of Edgefield County, S. C.

Issue of June 5, 1879

Died at home, May 22d, Sister Permelia Rasor-- near 80. She lived many of these years a consistent member of Turkey Creek Church. She was the wife of Deacon Ezekiel Rasor, who went home a few years before her. Both sleep in the old grave yard at Turkey Creek. Her Pastor, Donaldsville, May 29, 1879.

Died, on the 21st day of May 1879, in Fairfield Co., S. C,. Mr. John Mobley, in the 79th year of his age. [eulogy] J. D. Mahon. Crosbyville, S. C.

Issue of June 12, 1879

Tribute of Respect to Permelia Rasor, born in Abbeville county, December 17, 1799, and died May 22nd 1879... from Turkey Creek Church.

Issue of June 19, 1879

Married on the 22d of May, at the home of the bride, by Rev. T. W. Mellichamp, Dr. J. S. Hughson, of Sumter, to Miss Lessie E. Quattlebaum, of Fairfield County, S. C.

In Memoriam. Elder B. Bonner. from Gaucher Creek Baptist Church, Spartanburg County, S. C., June 4, 1879.

Issue of June 26, 1879

Married on the 12th inst., at the residence of the bride's father, by Rev. G. W. Rollins, Mr. A. J. Allen, and Miss S. A. Allen, daughter of R. P. Allen. All of Anson County, N. C.

On the 5th inst., at the residence of Mr. John Ross, by Rev. J. D. Mahon, Mr. Thos Robertson and Miss Cora Ross. All of Chester County.

On the 8th inst., at the residence of Mr. John Chapman, by Rev. J. D. Mahon, Mr. John Weir and Miss Laura Castles. All of Fairfield County.

On the 19th inst., at the residence of the bride's mother, by the Rev. J. D. Mahon, Mr. A. J. Clark and Miss Cynthia McNiel. All of Chester County.

Death of Sallie Preston Myers, second daughter of Alfred and Ella L. Thomas, was born in Charleston, S. C., on 2nd October 1858. She was born again in 1872, and in November of that year was baptized by Rev. Dr. Dixon and admitted to the fellowship of the First Baptist Church of Augusta. She was married to G. Harrell Myers, Esq., on 5th February 1879, and died on 13th May... S. M. R.

Issue of July 3, 1879

Married in Beaufort, June 13, 1879, at the residence of Mr. Joseph Hazel, by Rev. F. Jones, Mr. George Holmes, Esq., to Miss Julia Hazel.

Issue of July 24, 1879

Died, near Williston, South Carolina, on Monday, the 7th of July, 1879, Mrs. Mary E. Lee, aged 23 years... A. B. Barnwell, C. H.

Issue of August 21, 1879

Died at her residence in Greenville county, July 5th, Mrs. Elizabeth Cox, in the 44th year of her age. At the age of 19 years she united with the Standing Springs Baptist Church, of which she remained a member until her death. [eulogy]

Departed this life at his home in Allendale, Barnwell county, South Carolina, August 5th, 1879, Dr. B. W. Lawton, aged 56 years and 10 months. [eulogy] A. B. E.

Departed this life in Orangeburg county, on the 6th inst., Rev. Peter A. Buyck, in the seventy-fifth year of his age, leaving a wife and eight children. D. F. S.

Departed this life on the 13th of May 1879, at his residence in Chester County, South Carolina, after more than one year's illness, N. G. B. Calvin, in the 44th year of his age. He leaves an affectionate mother, wife, and four children John D. Mahon.

Issue of August 28, 1879

Married at the residence of Mr. William Austin, by Rev. S. T. Russell, July 20th 1879, Mr. David Austin and Miss Ann Ulmer.

Issue of September 4, 1879

Died, at his residence in Fairfield county, S. C., August 10th 1879, Wm. J. Shelton, in the 65th year of his age. The deceased was a consistent member of the Baptist Church about 47 years. T. W. Smith.

Issue of September 11, 1879

Married, on Tuesday afternoon, August 26th 1879, in the Greenwood Baptist Church, by Rev. J. S. Jordan, Prof. A. S. Townes, of the Greenville Female College, and Miss Ella, daughter of Maj. Peter McKellar, of Greenwood, S. C.

Issue of September 18, 1879

Tribute of Respect from Greenville Baptist Sunday-School, to Rev. W. Merriwether, who died 15th August 1879.

Married on Sunday, September 10, 1879, at the Baptist Church, Pendleton, by Rev. Thomas Dawson, Mr. Johnw. Cochran to Miss Alice Boggs. All of Pickens County.

Issue of September 25, 1879

Our dear little Maggie, died at 15 minutes to 12 Friday night, 5th inst, aged 5 months and 23 days.. L. C. Ezell. Woodruff, S. C.

Died, recently, at his home near Silverton, S. C., Mr. Alfred Turner, in the seventy-fifth year of his age... united with Matlock Baptist Church, and later carried his membership to Old Hollow Creek Baptist Church, hard by where he died. he leaves wife, sons and daughters. A son and son-in-law are ministers of the Gospel. J. J. M.

Departed this life in Chester, S. C., September 10th, 1876, Mrs. Kate N. Smith, wife of Mr. J. Harvey Smith. Mrs. Smith was born December 5th 1845, in the town of Chester, and was baptized in the year 1864 into the membership of the Flint River Baptist Church, and was afterwards transferred by letter to the Baptist Church at Chester C. H... [eulogy] R. W. S.

Issue of October 2, 1879

Tribute of Respect from Wake Forest College, N. C., September 15, 1879, to Brother J. B. Silcox, a native of Charleston.

Married September 4th, at the house of the bride's mother, by Rev. G. W. Bussey, Mr. Robert Cheatham, Jr., and Miss Sallie Spikes, all of Edgefield County.

By the same on September 17th, at the house of the bride's mother, Mr. Willie Seigler and Miss Mamie Seigler, both of Edgefield County.

At the home of the bride, September 25th, 1879, by Rev. J. C. Hudson, Mr. Francis Marion Morris and Miss N. Alice E. Smith, all of Anderson County, S. C.

Death of Mrs. Sarah Thompson, wife of E. Thomson, who died at this place on the 25th inst. Her maiden name was Miss Sarah Guntharp, and she was born on the 3d day of July 1801 in Chester county, in this State, near Rocky Mount. She was in her 79th year and was married to her husband, who survives her, in 1848, as his second wife. Black's, S. C., Sept. 27th, 1879.

Issue of October 9, 1879

Married on the evening of the 25th ult., at the residence of the bride's mother, by Rev. A. S. Willeford, Mr. W. O. Mahaffey and Miss Christian Johnson, all of Kershaw Co., S. C.

On the 29th ult., at the residence of Mr. -- Lang, by Rev. A. S. Willeford, Mr. D. B. Brown and Miss C. E. Mahaffey, all of Kershaw Co., S. C.

On Wednesday evening, October 1st 1879, at the residence of the bride's mother, by Rev. W. H. Strickland, Mr. James M. Cathcart and Miss Anna, eldest daughter of Mrs. W. C. Bewley, all of Anderson.

Issue of October 23, 1879

Departed this life at Rossville, S. C., Oct. 14th, 1879, Mrs. Louisa Caroline Cartledge, wife of Rev. A. M. Cartledge. She was daughter of Buckner Haigood, and was born and brought up in Fairfield County, fifteen miles above Columbia. She became the mother of eight children, four of whom, with her bereaved husband, survived her... R. W. S.

Issue of October 30, 1879

Married, at the residence of the bride's father, by Rev. W. A. Therrell, on the morning of the 16th inst., Mr. Milton L. Gilbert, of Asheville, N. C., and Miss Sallie E. Morrell, of Camden.

Married, at the residence of the bride's father, on the 16th of October, by Rev. T. J. Taylor, Mr. W. H. Davis, of Toccoa City, Ga., and Miss M. Hemans Alexander, of Union County, S. C.

Married, at Allendale, S. C., Oct. 21st 1879, by Rev. A. B. Estes, Mr. C. W. Hickman, Jr., of Hampton, Va., to Miss Phoebe S. Estes, of the former place.

Issue of November 6, 1879

Married by Rev. R. N. Pratt, October 14th 1879, at the residence of J. M. Pruitt, Mr. David A. Carter, of Americus, Ga., to Miss S. L. Pratt, of Due West.

By Rev. R. N. Pratt, October 30th 1879, at the residence of the bride's father, Miss M. L. Cox and Mr. Walter A. Cheatham.

In Memory of Benjamin Franklin Lawrence Orr, by order of Siloam Baptist Church, October 1879. Died, at Brushy Creek, Anderson County, S. C., October 22nd, 1879, of Typhoid Fever, Benjamin Franklin Lawrence Orr, second son of Mr. and Mrs. John W. B. and Martha Orr, in the 17th year of his age. He was born June the 6th 1863 and joined the Baptist Church and was baptized 26th September 1878....

Died, October 27th, at his residence in Chester County, Hiram Shannon, Sr., aged about 80 years. Bro. Shannon had been a member of the Baptist Church nearly fifty years. He was for some five years, a member of the Blackstocks Church... R. W. S.

Issue of November 13, 1879

Tribute of Respect from Philosphian Society, Furman University,Greenville, S. C., to Ware Merriweather.

Tribute of Respect from Philosphian Society, Furman University,Greenville, S. C., to Martin L. Wilkins.

Issue of November 20, 1879

Married by the Rev. J. F. Buist, November 6th, 1879, Dr. Henry W. Kearse to Miss Lizzie Priester, all of Barnwell County, S. C.

Married, in Laurens County, November 13, 1879, at the residence of W. H. Shell, by Rev. G. H. Carter, Dr. M. W. Drummond and Miss A. G. Shell. G. R. C.

Died, at the residence of her parents, near Walhalla, S. C., November 7th, 1879, Laura Nevill, second daughter of Wm. J. and Sarah Nevill, aged sixteen years and four months... G. T. G.

Issue of November 27, 1879

Died, at his residence, Newberry County, S. C., October 6th, 1879, in the 89th year of his age, deacon Chesley Davis. He was a faithful and consistent member of Bush River Church, of which he was a deacon and licentiate, and for many years the Superintendent of the Sabbath-school. M. E. Broaddus, Pastor.

Issue of December 11, 1879

Married, at the residence of the bride's brother, Gilmer Grier, Nov. 11th 1879, by Rev. C. T. Scaife, Mr. H. V. Blankenship, of Mecklenburg County, N. C., and Miss Emma T. Grier, of Union County, S. C.

Married, November 12th, by Rev. W. B. Carson, Mr. Joseph Brunson to Miss Mary Forester, all of Barnwell County, S. C.

Mrs. Margaret Spears, of Union County, departed this life on the first inst., at an advanced age. From early youth to the day of her death she was a faithful, consistent, highly prized member of Pacolet Church...

After an illness of many months, Franklin Douglass, died 15th November, aged 67 years. Blythewood, S. C.

Issue of December 18, 1879

Married, Sunday morning, December 7th, 1879, by Rev. Olin Durant, Mr. W. T. McFall and Miss Vesta Mauldin, both of Pickens.

At Pendleton, S. C., Wednesday, December 10th, 1879, by Rev. I. W. Wingo, Rev. G. T. Gresham, pastor of the Baptist Church at Walhalla, and Miss Septima Sloan, of Pendleton.

At M. B. McGee's, on the evening of December 4th 1879, by Rev. R. W. Burts, Mr. J. Milton Ellis and Miss Laura L. McGee. All of Abbeville County, S. C.

At the residence of the bride's father, December 3d, 1879, by the Rev. R. W. Pratt, Mr. Walter K. Ellis and Miss Clara H. Barmore. All of Abbeville.

At the residence of the bride's mother, by the Rev. R. W. Pratt, December 4th, 1879, Mr. George Wardlaw and Miss Callie Cheatham. All of Abbeville.

At the residence of the bride's mother, November 20th, 1879, by G. H. Carter, Mr. --- Crawford and Miss Ida Barksdale. Both of Laurens County.

On Wednesday, Nov. 12th, 1879, by Rev. C. A. Stiles, Charles Sloan and Miss Dora Dawson. All of Richland County, S. C.

On Thursday, Nov. 27th, 1879, by Rev. C. A. Stiles, Mr. Robert L. Smyrl and Miss Lottie Love. All of Richland County.

Issue of December 25, 1879

Married, Dec. 7th, 1879, by Rev. T. W. Reid, Mr. Jackson Tate and Miss Lizzie Reid.

By the same, Dec. 14th, at the residence of the bride's father, Mr. John B. Bull and Miss Juliet Berry. All of Greenville County.

December 18th, by Rev. G. H. Carter, Mr. W. H. Drummond, of Laurens County, to Miss Mamie Rogers, of Spartanburg County.

Died, Mrs. Julia Caroline, wife of Rev. J. B. Hartwell, in San Francisco, Cal., December 3, 1879, aged 45 years, 2 months, 18 days.

Issue of January 8, 1880

Died, at Summerton, Clarendon County, S. C., December 13, 1879, Miss Ann Letitia Richardson, aged 21 years and 20 days.

Died, Sophina Florence Mack, wife of W. B. Mack, of Lewisville, S. C., Dec. 31st, 1879, aged 47 years, 1 month and 10 days.

In Memory of A. M. Heaton, who was killed by cars on the South Carolina Railroad, near Reevesville, Colleton County, S. C., November 1st, 1879. Mr. Heaton was a member of the Hope Baptist Sunday School. W. L. R. Branchville, Jan. 1, 1880.

Died, at her home in Abbeville County, S. C., Dec. 23, 1879, Mrs. Nancy O. Agnew, wife of Andrew Agnew, in the 51st year of her age.... a consistent member of the Turkey Creek Baptist Church. She leaves a kind husband and six affectionate children to mourn their loss. W.

Fell asleep in Jesus, in Midway, Barnwell County, S. C., Dec. 16th 1879, after a lingering sickness, Mrs. Rebecca Getsinger, wife of Rev. J. J. Getsinger. J. F. Buist. Bamberg, Dec. 20, 1879.

Issue of January 22, 1880

Died, on the 24th November last, Miss Adella A. Metts, daughter of Mr. and Mrs. William B. Metts, of Newberry, in the 33d year of her age. She was educated at Limestone Springs under Dr. Curtis; joined the church at Fairview under the pastorate of Elder W. D. Mayfield, and was baptized by Elder J. K. Mendenhall on the 29th September 1866, the pastor being sick on that day. W. A. G.

Married, December 7th, 1879, Mr. John H. Vermillion and Miss Laura L. Shockley. Both of Laurens County, S. C.

December 18th, 1879, John Armstrong and Miss Clara Gray. Both of Laurens County, S. C.

December 23rd, 1879, Mr. James L. Moore and Miss Lucinda Clayton Henderson. Both of Laurens County, S. C.

December 30th 1879, Mr. Robert Stone and Miss Emma C. Smith. Both of Greenville County, S. C.

At Davisboro, Ga., November 26th, 1879, by Rev. Dr. Hinton, pastor at Columbus, Ga., Rev. C. C. Brown, of Sumter, S. C., and Miss Sallie Wright, daughter of Col. H. G. Wright.

January 1st, 1880, by Rev. W. A. Gaines, Mr. C. Buford and Miss Ella Davis. Both of Newberry County, S. C.

At the residence of the bride's father in Gowensville, S. C., Dec. 23rd, 1879, by Rev. T. J. Earle, Mr. E. C. Briggs, of Laurens, and Miss Laura S. Calmes.

On the 30th December, 1879, by Rev. J. K. Mendenhall, Mr. Thomas Young, of Belton, and Miss G. Louise Stone, of Greenville.

On the 1st of January 1880, by Rev. T. W. Mellichamp, Mr. E. N. Heins and Mrs. E. B. Cloud. All of Fairfield County.

Married, December 18th 1879, By Rev. A. Buist, Mr. Wm. H. Garvin, and Miss Sue Harley. Both of Barnwell County, S. C.

At the residence of Col. I. L. Davis, Aiken, S. C., Dec. 17th, 1897, by Rev. A. Buist, Mr. Owen Alderman and Miss Mamie A. Davis, of Aiken, S. C.

At the residence of the bride's brother-in-law, on Sunday evening, Dec. 21st 1879, by Elder R. J. Edwards, Mr. J. S. C. Hoffman, Jr., and Miss Joella Jones. All of Orangeburg county, S. C.

On the evening of Dec. 17th, 1879, by the Rev. C. A. Stiles, Mr. Hugh Love and Miss Mattie Gaydon. all of Richland County, S. C.

By D. C. Hardin, Dec. 25th, 1879, near Greer's Station, Mr. Thomas Ross and Miss Mattie Peace. Both of Greenville County.

At Hollins Institute, Va., Dec. 31st, 1879, by Rev. E. C. Dargan, Rev. W. R. L. Smith, pastor of the First Baptist Church of Lynchburg, Va., and Miss Rosa P. Cocke, daughter of Prof. Charles L. Cocke, of Hollins Institute.

At Hartsville, S. C., Dec. 24th 1879, by Elder J. W. Burn, Mr. John W. Moore and Miss Julia C. Huggins. All of Darlington County, S. C.

At Lawtonville, S. C., December 30, 1879, by Rev. A. B. Estes, Mr. Charlie L. Peeples and Miss Cattie S. Johnston. All of Hampton county.

December 3rd, by Rev. J. S. Jordan, Mr. M. L. Coleman and Miss Ella Brooks. Both of New Market.

Dec. 18th, by Rev. J. S. Jordan, Mr. J. C. Timmerman, and Miss Hannah Kemp. both of Edgefield County.

Dec. 21st, by Rev. J. S. Jordan, Mr. Christie Stalnaker and Miss Carrie Aiton. Both of Edgefield County.

Dec. 23rd, by Rev. J. S. Jordan, Mr. J. P. Polattie and Miss Maria Bullock. Both of Edgefield County.

Dec. 25th, by Rev. J. S. Jordan, Mr. Marcus Luquise and Miss Ann Duncan, and Mr. J. H. Luquise and Miss Cordelia Duncan. All of Edgefield County.

Dec. 28th, by Rev. J. S. Jordan, Mr. W. M. Ward and Miss Fannie Burnett. Both of Edgefield County.

Issue of January 29, 1880

Married in Sumter County, S. C., January 7th 1880, by Rev. A. Coke Smith, Rev. J. W. Kogn, of the South Carolina Conference, and Miss Fannie S. Smith.

By A. C. Stepp, November 23rd, 1879, Mr. Wm. H. Bagwell and Margaret Jane McClary. Both of Greenville County.

December 7th, 1879, Wm. M. Boyd and Miss Eliza Hellams. Both of Laurens County, S. C.

At the residence of the bride's mother, January 22d, 1880, by Rev. A. Buist, Mr. Judson M. Birts, and Miss Maggie Templeton, both of Barnwell County, S. C.

In Blackville, S. C., January 21st, 1880, by Rev. A. Buist, Mr. Wm. T. Cave, Jr., and Miss Maggie McMillan, eldest daughter of Rev. W. D. McMillan.

January 14th 1880, by G. H. Carter, Mr. C. E. Marshall, of Georgia, to Miss Fannie Metts, of Laurens County, S. C.

Issue of February 12, 1880

Died, at his home, at Townville, S. C., December 29th, 1879, of Paralysis, Jesse Franklin Woolbright, aged 51 years, 2 months and 26 days. Many years ago he joined the Baptist Church.... W. A. D.

Died, in Sumter County, December 26th, 1878, Mr. Henry H. Wells, in the seventy-sixth year of his age... left wife and children. D. W. C.

Died, at his residence in Barnwell County, S. C., January 27th 1880, Alexander H. Johnson, M. D., in the fifty-second year of his age. Dr. Johnson was a graduate of the Medical College of South Carolina. J. F. Buist. Bamberg, S. C., Feb. 2nd, 1880.

Another Has Gone. The lamented subject of this brief notice, Miss A. M. Vogt, died of Typhoid fever, 30th December 1879. She was a native of South Carolina, received her early training under Dr. Curtis, of Limestone Springs, and her graduating course under the auspices of Dr. Reynolds, "et al." of Doko... J. B.

Issue of February 19, 1880

Died, at his residence in Anderson County, on the 27th day of January 1880, in the 81st year of his age, Noah R. Reeve. Bro. Reeve had been a member of the Baptist Church about 50 years and 6 months, and a Deacon most of the time. his Church, Mt. Pisgah, where his body was interred after funeral services by the writer. D. W. Hiott.

Married on the 28th of January 1880, by Rev. J. H. Edwards, at the residence of the bride's father, in Keyser, N. C., Mr. James S. Mims and Miss Edith C. Spear. Both of that place.

By Rev. W. L. Brown, Jan. 28th, Charles R. Meng and Miss Alice, youngest daughter of Rev. John Tolleson, both of Union Co., S. C.

At the residence of Mr. G. C. Greer, Jan. 20th 1880, by Elder C. T. Scaife, Mr. Jasper Wilburn and Miss Mattie Greer, all of Union County.

At the residence of Mr. Richard Mobley, Jan. 29th 1880, by Elder C. T. Scaife, Mr. Robert Willard to Miss Ora Mobley, all of Union County.

On December 17th, 1879, by the Rev. J. E. Rodgers, Mr. J. B. Hall and Miss V. L. Reynolds, all of Kershaw.

By the same, on the 17th of December, 1879, Mr. A. S. Woodward and Miss Mattie J. James, of Bishopville, Sumter County, S. C.

By the same, on the 23d of December, '79, Mr. W. J. Ammond and Miss Sallie M. Simmons, all of Kershaw.

By the same, on January 8th, 1880, Mr. J. R. Norris and Miss Ellen Dean, all of Kershaw.

By the same, on January 8th 1880, Mr. H. L. Boykin and Miss Adaran E. Corbitt, all of Sumter County.

By the same, on January 11th, 1880, Mr. W. L. Stokes and Miss Ellen R. Kelley, all of Kershaw.

By the same, on January 11th, 1880, Mr. Thomas Roller and Miss Priscilla Ogburn Kelley, all of Kershaw.

By the same, on January 22d, 1880, Mr. A. J. Boykin and Miss Sallie E. Bridges, both of Sumter, S. C.

On the 14th January, 1880, at the residence of the bride's mother, by Rev. J. W. Burn, John Chapman and Miss Madora Powe, both of Chesterfield County.

By Rev. A. C. Stepp, on the 15th of Jan. 1880, Mr. John Wesley Page, of Greenville, and Miss Nancy Alice Franks, of Laurens County, S. C.

By Rev. A. C. Stepp, on the 19th January, 1880, Mr. W. M. P. Hall, of Anderson, and Miss Elizabeth Alice Murff, of Laurens County, S. C.

At the residence of the bride's father, by Rev. S. T. Russell, on February 12th 1880, Mr. W. R. Cooper and Miss E. R. Hanner, all of Williamsburg County.

On the 27th of January, by Rev. F. C. Jeter, at the residence of the bride's father, near Goshen Hill, Mr. Middleton Lake to Miss Laura Smith, both of Union County, S. C.

At Timmonsville, S. C., February 10th 1880, by Rev. W. J. Alexander, Rev. S. M. Richardson, of Timmonsville, S. C., and Miss Celia D., daughter of John C. Hatcher, of Bedford County, Va.

At the residence of Mr. Jesse W. Parrott, of Darlington County, S. C., February 11th, 1880, by Rev. W. J. Alexander, Mr. T. K. Cunningham, of Lancaster, and Miss Caledonia V. Peeples, of Darlington County, S. C.

Issue of February 26, 1880

George W. Neely was born at Barnwell C. H., June 20, 1834, and died at Graham's, January 18, 1880. [eulogy]

Married at the residence of the bride's father, on the 29th of January 1880, by the Rev. C. T. Scaife, Mr. Robert Williard and Miss Ora Mobley, all of Union, S. C.

At the residence of Mr. John McKissick, on the 12th of February 1880, by the Rev. C. T. Scaife, assisted by the Rev. R. D. Smart, Mr. A. Jennings Douglas, of Bennettsville, S. C., and Miss Nannie Harlan, of Union, S. C.

At Smyrna Church, November 12th 1879, by Rev. W. B. Carson, Mr. Joseph Brunson and Miss Mary Forrester; all of Barnwell County, S. C.

At the residence of the bride's father, January 21st, 1880, by Rev. W. B. Carson, Mr. E. H. Bennett and Miss Indiana Rountree; all of Barnwell County, S. C.

At the residence of the bride's father, January 27th, 1880, Mr. F. H. Fogler and Miss Florence C. Strange; all of Barnwell County, S. C.

February 10th 1880, by Rev. W. A. Gaines, Mr. Wm. H. Baughman and Miss Isabella Talbert; all of Abbeville County, S. C.

Issue of March 4, 1880

Married by Rev. T. W. Reid, February 10, 1880, Mr. Milus McCarter and Miss Annice Green.

By the same, February 24, 1880, Mr. Frank Duncan and Miss Howard.

By the same, February 26, 1880, Mr. A. W. Adams and Miss Ella Taylor. All of Greenville.

James B. Brunson, of Concord Township, Sumter County, S. C., died at his residence after a short illness, on 30th December 1879, in the 62nd year of his age. He joined the Sumter Baptist Church about 28 years ago.. Sumter, S. C., February 27, 1880.

Issue of March 11, 1880

Married at the residence of the bride's mother, near Elko, S. C., March 4, 1880, by Rev. A. Buist, Mr. W. A. Templeton and Miss Ella H. Hair--both of Barnwell County, S. C.

By Rev. C. H. Carter, at his own residence in Laurensville, S. C., March 2, 1880, Mr. Clanchis Entrekin and Miss Eugenia Burns-- all of Laurens County.

By Rev. Lucius Cuthbert, on Wednesday, March 3, 1880, at the residence of the bride's mother, Prof. D. T. Smith, of Greenville, to Miss M. Lula Tyler, of Grahams, S. C.

Issue of March 18, 1880

Tribute of Respect to John Cox, who died 13th January last, from Lima Baptist Church.

Issue of March 25, 1880

Married on Wednesday the 11th inst., at the residence of the bride's father, by Rev. W. A. Therrell, Mr. A. R. Walker to Miss Annie L. Rickenbacker. All of Orangeburg.

At the residence of the bride's father, March 14th, 1880, by Rev. A. Buist, Mr. B. M. Darlington and Miss Ina M. Killingsworth, both of Barnwell County.

In the Baptist Church, Bamberg, S. C., March 17th, 1880, eight o'clock, p. m., by the Rev. J. F. Buist, J. P. Ott, M. D., and Miss Theodosia A. Tyler, all of Barnwell County, S. C.

Died, at the residence of her aunt, Mrs. Weyman, in Greenville, S. C., March 13, 1880, Miss Hannah Earle, aged twenty-five years. J. C. H.

Issue of April 1, 1880

Married by Rev. T. W. Mellichamp, on the 18th inst., at the residence of the bride's father, Mr. J. R. Howell, J. DuBose Huggins, M. D., of Sumter, to Miss Jessie L. Howell, of Richland, S. C.

By the same, on the 21st inst., Rev. W. A. Gaines, of Edgefield, S. C., to Miss E. M. Bookhart, daughter of Mr. James Bookhart, of Blythewood, Fairfield County, S. C.

By Rev. A. C. Stepp, March 9, 1880, Mr. Joseph A. Allen, of Anderson, and Miss Cassie Caroline Cothran, of Greenville County, S. C.

Issue of April 8, 1880

Married on Sabbath, 27th March, 1880, at the residence of the bride's father, by Rev. D. W. Hiott, Mr. W. R. Davis and Miss C. E. King, all of Pickens County.

Died, at Batesburg, S. C., March 17, 1880, Aleck Fred, only child of A. J. s. and Isabella R. Thomas, aged one year and eight months.

Tribute of Respect from Clear Spring Baptist Church, Greenville co., SC, to Deacon Thomas Goldsmith.

Issue of April 15, 1880

Married at the residence of the bride's father, Wednesday, the 31st of March 1880, by Rev. J. D. McCullough, Mr. James Geddes, of Spartanburg, and Miss Hattie Monk, of Reidville.

On 31st March 1880, by Rev. Geo. T. Gresham, at the residence of the bride's father, Mr. T. Wayland Scruggs, of Fairfield County, to Miss Anna Rebecca Beard, of Oconee County.

Departed this life, March 25th, 1880, Mrs. Elizabeth Lynes, at her residence, Fox Bank Plantation, Charleston County, S. C. She was born January 6, 1814, and became a member of the Goose Creek Baptist Church, December 20th 1829. [eulogy]

In Memoriam, Mrs. J. Pauline Berry... From her baptism, administered in early life by her own dear father, Rev. J. K. Mendenhall... E. P. S.

Issue of April 22, 1880

In memory of Lillie Andrews, of Richland County, S. C., who died on the morning of March 17, in the -- year of her age. T. W. S. Winnsboro, S. C., March 18, 1880.

Died, on the 11th April, 1881 [sic], at her residence in Richland County, Mrs. Dorcas Abbot, in the 64th year of her age... left husband and children. R. R. V. Blythewood, April 12, 1880.

Mrs. Martha Sarah Lawton, consort of Rev. Joseph A. Lawton, of Allendale, S. C., departed this life on Monday evening, April 12, 1880, in the 73rd year of her age.

Died, in Walhalla, S. C., April 11, 1880, Mrs. Annie Maxwell Sloan. She leaves a husband, one daughter and many other relatives.

Died, April 8, 1880, at his residence near Fairview Church, James Nash, in his 83rd year.

Married, by Rev. D. N. Gore, at Gourdin's, N. E. R. R. S. C., on Thursday, 8th inst., at 8 o'clock p. m., W. T. Pittman, Esq., of Charleston city, to Miss Emma B. Rich, of Gourdin's.

Issue of April 29, 1880

Married at the residence of the bride's mother, near Grassy Pond, Spartanburg County, S. C., April 18, 1880, by Rev. T. J. Taylor, J. R. Ellis, Esq., and Miss A. L. Bonner, eldest daughter of Rev. B. Bonner.

Woodward Allen, a highly respected citizen of Spartanburg County, and a leading member of the Clear Springs Baptist Church, died on the 5th of April 1880, in the 60th year of his age. He served his church as clerk for more than twenty years....

Issue of May 6, 1880

Married at the residence of the bride's father, on Thursday evening, April 22nd, 1880, by Rev. A. C. Stepp, Rev. George W. Gardner, of Lancaster, and Miss Dora L. West, second daughter of Mr. J. T. West, of Greenville County, S. C.

On the 27th of April 1880, at the residence of the bride's father, by Rev. E. H. Cuttino, Rev. Dr. A. K. Durham, of Greenville, S. C., and Miss Minnie V. Easterling ("Myrtle"), of St. John's, Charleston County, S. C.

On the morning of the 28th of April 1880, at the residence of the bride's father, by Rev. A. Buist, Mr. George Dunbar and Miss Jennie L. Peeples, all of Barnwell County.

On the 29th of April 1880, by Rev. D. W. Hiott, at the residence of the bride's mother, Mr. E. M. Mauldin to Miss S. E. Rogers. All of Anderson County, S. C.

Issue of May 13, 1880

Married at the residence of the bride's father, April 8, 1880, by Rev. C. T. Scaife, Mr. Philip Davis and Miss Mary McDaniel. All of Union County, S. C.

At the residence of the bride's father, April 15, 1880, by Rev. C. T. Scaife, Mr. J. E. Jeter and Miss Clara Tucker. All of Union County, S. C.

Issue of May 20, 1880

Married at the Baptist Church, Williston, S. C., May 12, 1880, by Rev. A. Buist, Mr. T. W. Reed and Miss Katie Thompson. Both of Barnwell County.

Issue of May 27, 1880

Married in the Baptist Church, at Gaffney, by Rev. W. L. Brown, May 5, 1880, Mr. Noah J. Miller and Miss Belle Wright, of Gaffney's, and Mr. A. b. Shuttle, of Shelby, N. C., and Miss Lou Miller, of Gaffney's.

On the 13th of May, 1880, by Rev. J. C. Furman, D. D., Rev. J. Q. Adams of Edgefield, and Miss Mamie Davis, of Greenville, S. C.

At the residence of the bride's father, at Cold Spring, Pickens County, S. C., on the evening of May 12th, 1880, by Rev. Charles Bradford, of Beech Island, Mr. Nelson C. Poe, of Greenville, S. C., and Miss Nannie Crawford, daughter of Mr. James W. Crawford.

Died, of consumption, February 10, 1880, after a protracted illness, Mrs. Mary A. Weeks, wife of Rev. J. M. Weeks, of St. George's S. C., leaving numerous friends, an affectionate husband and six children, the youngest since (an infant) has followed its mother. B. B. B.

Died, suddenly, May 5, 18808, at Silver Hill, near Silverton, S. C., Little Cecil, only child of Mr. and Mrs. C. C. Meyer, aged 5 months and 9 days. B. W. W.

Died, at Society Hill, S. C., Albert S. Parker, youngest son of Samuel and Rosa A. Parker; aged 15 months and 14 days.

Issue of June 3, 1880

Married on the 22nd April 1880, by Rev. T. W. Mellichamp, Mr. John Muse to Miss Sarah Ann Right. All of Fairfield County.

On the 24rd [sic] of May, 1880, at the residence of the bride's father, by Rev. W. F. Chaplin, Rev. J. J. Getsinger to Miss Maggie Smoak.

By Rev. T. W. Hart, on Thursday, May 20th, Mr. George Pettigrew, of Darlington County and Miss Alice P. Bostick, of Marion County, S. C.

Died, in this city, May 23, 1880, after a protracted illness, Mrs. E. F. Cunningham, having just completed her 53rd year. Her maiden name was Holman, and her early life was spent at Newberry, where she was first married to Edward Y. McMorris, Esq. Left a widow at his death in 1855, she removed to Winston County,, Miss., where her father was then living. here she was married to Dr. J. M. Cunningham, who died in 1875....

THE BAPTIST COURIER

Married at the residence of the bride's father, Mr. W. Crowder, by Rev. J. D. Mahon, Mr. W. Y. Young and Miss Isabella Crowder. All of Fairfield.

At the residence of Mr. W. T. Roberts, of Chester County, by Rev. J. D. Mahon, Mr. W. G. Orr, of Fairfield County, and Miss Abi S. Roberts.

Died, at his residence in Abbeville County, S. C., on Sunday morning, June 13, 1880, Mr. Stephen Latimer, in the seventy-sixth year of his age. Brother Latimer was an affectionate husband and father... a consistent member of the Baptist Church.

Married by Rev. W. A. Gaines, May 17th, Mr. Jesse Blackburn Reagan and Miss Francis J. Nicholls, both of Abbeville County.

Married at the residence of the bride's father, May 27, 1880, by Rev. S. T. Russell, Mr. Taylor McKnight and Miss Martha A. Kirton, all of Williamsburg County.

At the residence of the bride's father, June 20, 1880, by Rev. S. T. Russell, Mr. C. D. Howard and Miss S. A. Baylor, all of Williamsburg County.

Caroline Sarah, wife of R. J. Edwards and daughter of Emanuel and Francis H. Pooser of Orangeburg, S. C., died May 31st 1880. When quite young, perhaps in her fourteen year, she joined the M. E. Church, and worshipped at Limestone about twelve miles above Orangeburg C. H. In 1864, soon after her daughter Mary Frances, became a Baptist, she united with the Branchville Baptist Church, and was immersed by her husband, the pastor of said church. R. J. Edwards.

Mrs. Sarah Packer died, aged 73 years. T. H. W.

Died, on the 14th of June 1880, Miss H. C. Russell, in the 25th year of her age.

Tahpenes Lipscomb Brooks, daughter of Thomas and Elizabeth Lipscomb, and wife of Stanmore Books, was born December 9th 1809, and died June 27th, 1880. Married at eighteen, it was the lot of Mrs. B. to have the care of younger brothers and sisters. In 1831 Mrs. B. united with Mt. Moriah Baptist Church... Eight of her own children and a long list of grandchildren.... J. S. Jordan.

W. T. Ross, an exemplary Christian, a member of Pleasant Valley Church, was killed at his home in Lancaster county on the 29th of June 1880, by the falling of a tree during the great storm that passed over this country on that day.

Issue of July 22, 1880

Married at Darlington, S. C., July 8th 1880, by Rev. W. J. Alexander, Mr. Charles B. Edwards, of Darlington, S. C., and Miss Alice E. Baird, of Murfreesboro, Tenn.

By Rev. D. F. Spigner, July 13th 1880, at the Lewisville Baptist Church, Rev. J. J. H. Stoudenmire, of Orangeburg County, S.C., and Miss Mamie E. Rowe of Barnwell County, S. C.

Died, at his residence in Aiken County, S. C., on the 8th inst., Captain Phillip Kitching, in the 76th year of his age.

Issue of July 29, 1880

Married on Wednesday evening, July 14, 1880, by Rev. G. W. Gardner, Mr. J. H. Alexander, of Chester, and Miss Josephine Brunson, of Lancaster, S. C.

Mary Sumter Shumate died in Greenville, S. C., June 22nd, 1880. She was the eldest daughter of Wm. T. and Helen J. Shumate.... [eulogy]

Issue of August 5, 1880

Tribute of Respect from Mt. Moriah Baptist Church, Abbeville county to Mrs. Tahpenes L. Brooks.

Married July 15th, 1880, by Rev. S. T. Russell, Mr. Gilbert Freeman and Miss Mary Jane Taylor, all of Williamsburg County, S. C.

Died, at her residence in Anderson County, S. C., 24th July 1880, Mrs. Nellie A., widow of Redmond G. Wyatt, in the 72nd year of her age. She had been a consistent member of the Baptist Church for nearly a half century. Her remains were interred at Mt. Pisgah Church. D. W. Hiott.

Issue of August 19, 1880

Died, on the 9th of July last, Edwin Etheredge, youngest son of Dr. G. M. and Elizabeth Etheredge, of Aiken County, in the 17th year of his age. He was a student at Greenville this year until vacation, during which time the mother and her two sons availed themselves of the opportunity of going North on a visit to their relations in Connecticut. On their arrival at Southington, Edwin was taken with fever, which terminated in death. W. L. H.

Issue of August 26, 1880

Tribute of Respect from Catawba Church, to their pastor, Rev. J. C. Burge.

Anna M. McNulty, beloved wife of Deacon E. R. Lesesne, died near Gourdin's, Williamsburg Co., S. C., on 31st July 1880. Little Marvin, her youngest... [eulogy] O. F. Gregory.

Issue of September 2, 1880

Married on the 12th of August, 1880, by the Rev. A. K. Durham, Capt. Henry Stroud to Mrs. M. M. Green, all of Greenville County, S. C.

Died, on the 16th July 1880, in Colleton County, S. C., Mr. H. W. Cannon, in the 69th year of his age. he had been a member of Black Creek Baptist Church forty years... J. G. W.

Issue of September 9, 1880

Married August 12, 1880, by Rev. T. W. Reid, Mr. Spartan James and Miss Phebia Shockley, all of Greenville County.

August 26th, 1880, by Rev. T. W. Reid, Mr. John Hawkins and Miss Drucilla Brookshire, all of Greenville County.

Issue of September 23, 1880

Died, of Diphtheria, August 16, 1880, little Alma, youngest daughter of J. W. and Sallie Mattison, of Donnaldsville, S. C., aged 2 years, 11 months, and 14 days.

Died, on the 7th and 9th of September, 1880, of Diphtheria, Melvin D. and James W., sons of Mr. J. and Emiline Dupree, aged respectively four and six years.

Passed peacefully away on the night of the 26th of August, 1880, Mrs. Nancy Delk, in the fifty-eighth year of her age, at her home in Barnwell County, S. C. She joined the Baptist Church of Christ at Springtown, Barnwell County, in 1845.... J. F. Buist.

Issue of September 30, 1880

Tribute of Respect from Hartsville Baptist Church to Rev. James W. Burn, who rested for his labors August 1st 1880... laid away in our church cemetery... J. L. Coker, Chairman.

Tribute of Respect from Woodruff Lodge, No. 89, I. O. G. T., to Seaborn L. Griffith. J. J. Ezell, W. C. T.

Married on Tuesday evening, 21st September 1880, at the residence of N. O. Farmer, by the Rev. J. R. Earle, Mr. William P. Snelgrove, to Miss Annie Kilgore, all of Anderson County, S. C.

Died, near Reidville, S. C., on the 6th of September, Mrs. J. D. Burnett, a consistent member of the Baptist Church. She left a husband and eight children to mourn her loss.

Issue of October 14, 1880

Married September 28th, 1880, by Rev. W. N. Pratt, at the residence of the bride's father, Mr. W. H. Mays, of Edgefield County, to Miss Nola L. Barmore, of Abbeville.

On Sunday morning, October 10th 1880, at the residence of the bride's sister, Mrs. Alfred Tate, by John J. Watson, Esq., Mr. Moses Goodlet and Miss Elvira Benson, all of Greenville County, S. C.

At Blackville, S. C., October 9th, 1880, Samuel Arthur, only child of J. L. and Linna C. Buist, aged one year and nine months.

At Blackville, S. C., September 20th, 1880, Lula Buist, daughter of Rev. A. and Mrs. A. A. Buist, aged nine years, ten months and twenty days.

Died, at Blackville, S. C., September 22nd 1880, Harry Eugene, only child of W. B. and Lizzie Harley, aged nine months and fifteen days.

Died, at her home, Oct. 2nd, 1880, Miss Ella Allen, daughter of Col. E. S. Allen, of Woodruff, Spartanburg county, S. C. Miss Ella was, for two years, a pupil of the Greenville Female College. [eulogy]

Issue of October 21, 1880

Married August 8, 1880, at the residence of the bride's sister, Florence, S. C., by Rev. O. F. Gregory, Mr. Jefferson Hill of Florida, and Miss Minnie Munn, of Darlington County, S. C.

In the Baptist Church, Florence, S. C., by Rev. O. F. Gregory, Pastor, on 13th october, 1880, Mr. W. M. Marcus, formerly of Talladega, Ala., and Miss Urah J. Cox, youngest daughter of J. J. Cox, Esq., of Florence, S. C.

At 7:30 P. M., October 7th 1880, by Rev. R. W. Sanders, at Cotton Hotel, Chester, S. C., Miss Nina Jordan and Mr. E. F. Hamilton.

At 12 M., October 13th, 1880, by Rev. R. W. Sanders, at the residence of the bride's father, in Chester, S. C., Miss Susie Albright and Mr. D. P. Jarrett of Newton, N. C.

Issue of October 28, 1880

Married on the 20th October, 1880, at the bride's father's, by Rev. T. W. Mellichamp, Mr. Turner Stuart to Miss Ella Oliver, all of Fairfield County, S. C.

Sunday morning, October 24th 1880, at the residence of Scott Young, by Rev. J. R. Earle, Mr. Mike O'Neal, to Miss Othello Burriss, all of Anderson Co., S. C.

Issue of November 4, 1880

Died, at the residence of her daughter, near Rock Hill, S. C., July 14, 1880, Mrs. Charlotte R. Heath, in the fifty-ninth year of her age. Mrs. Heath was born January 12, 1822, near Rocky Creek in Chester county, grew up there, and in 1845, immediately after marriage removed to Deanville, Ky. Five years later she united herself with the Baptist church at that place. Returning to South Carolina in 1868, she connected herself with Harmony Baptist Church, and ten years later become one of the constituent members of the new Baptist church at Rock Hill. J. Hartwell Edwards.

Died, at her home, October 10, 1880, in the County of Fairfield, Mrs. E. R. Meador, in the sixty-first year of her age. [eulogy] M. T. M. Crosbyville

Mrs. Isabel Snider, daughter of Dr. John h. and Mrs. E. H. Harley, was born in Barnwell County, S. C., near Allendale, January 23, 1854, and died near the home of her childhood, October 10, 1880. ...connected herself with Mount Arnon Baptist Church. J. L. H.

Issue of November 11, 1880

Married, in the Presbyterian Church, at Port Jervis, N. Y., on the 14th of October, 1880, by Rev. A. P. Botsford, Mr. John E. Wilkes, of Greenville, S. C., and Miss Carrie B. Wells, only daughter of Peter Wells, Esq., of Port Jervis, N. Y.

At Boiling Springs, S. C., November 3rd, 1880, by Rev. A. Buist, Mr. B. F. Peeples and Miss Leila Hay. All of Barnwell County, S. C.

Issue of November 18, 1880

Died, at Beech Island, on the first Sunday in October, Deacon Anselm Irvin Miller, son of Jonathan M. Miler, aged thirty-one years. [eulogy]

Mrs. Isabella Walker had passed away... Some three of four years ago I met Miss belle and Miss Jennie Hickson, and seldom in life have I seen two sisters of such beauty... Miss Belle came, as Mrs. Walker, to live near me. She left a husband and infant daughter, two weeks old. W. B. Carson. Allendale, S. C.

Issue of November 25, 1880

Married at Edgefield C. H., on the morning of November 17, 1880, by Rev. A. J. S. Thomas, J. Curran Hartley of Batesburg, S. C., to Miss Mary Eloise Bates.

In the afternoon of the same day, and by the same, at the residence of the bride's father, B. C. Bryan, Esq., of Edgefield C. H., Eppes J. Norris, of Batesburg, S. C., to Miss Annie Laurie Bryan.

At the residence of the bride's father, in Rome, Ga., on the 16th of November 1880, Mr. S. G. Lawton, of Allendale, S. C., and Miss Hattie A. Brooks, daughter of Col. W. I. Brooks.

By Rev. A. C. Stepp, on 11th November 1880, Mr. W. Edward Gray and Miss E. A. Babb, of Laurens County, S. C.

By the same, on 16th November 1880, Mr. Vinson Austin and Miss Elizabeth Gaines. Both of Greenville County, S. C.

In this city, the 23rd inst., by Rev. Charles Manly, at the residence of S. P. Wells, the bride's father, Mr. F. M. Owens, of Spartanburg, to Miss Georgia A. Wells, formerly of Atlanta, Ga.

Issue of December 9, 1880

Died, in Edgefield County, S. C., on the 30th day of October 1880, J. T. Johnson, in the fifty-second year of his age. He was the son of Rev. Jonathan Johnson, dec'd, and brother of Mrs. John H. Jones, of Centreville, Laurens County. he leaves a wife and many friends to mourn his death.

Departed this life, at Packsville, S. C., on October 5th 1880, Thomas P. Cuttino, aged twenty years. The deceased was a son of Rev. D. W. Cuttino, by a former marriage. During the pastorate of Bro. Gregory at Foreston, he was elected to the office of deacon. C. C. B.

Married, November 25th, 1880, by Rev. A. C. Stepp, B. L. Lipford of Laurens County, and Miss M. E. Simmons, of Abbeville County.

December 2nd, 1880, by Rev. A. C. Stepp, John P. Thompson and Miss M. Adeline Owens, of Greenville County.

At the residence of the bride's father, in Blackville, S. C., on the 24th day of November, 1880, Mr. J. F. Risher, of Orangeburg, S. C., and Miss Josephine W. Gyles, daughter of W. A. Gyles.

November 24th, 1880, at the residence of the bride's father, Capt. Perrin Odell, by Rev. D. Weston Hiott, Mr. J. E. Robinson to Miss Mattie Odell, all of Easley, S. C.

November 24th, 1880, by Rev. A. Buist, Mr. S. H. Keele and Miss Mattie A. Birt, both of Barnwell County.

November 23rd, 1880, at the residence of the bride's father, J. W. Fewell, by the Rev. J. H. Edwards, Mr. Jas. S. Sturgis and Miss Maggie J. Fewell, all of York County.

On the 24th of November, 1880, by the Rev. T. W. Hart, at the residence of the bride's father, Mr. E. M. Self to Miss Josephine E. Husbands.

At the residence of the bride's father, near Carter's Ford, in Colleton County, December 5th 1880, by Rev. D. Weston Hiott, Mr. Hugh S. Smith and Miss C. M. Carter, all of Colleton, S. C.

Issue of December 16, 1880

Tribute of Respect to Hon. J. P. Reed from Anderson Baptist Church.

Tribute of Respect from the Oconee Singing Convention, December 4th, 1880, to Joseph H. Kay.

Married on the 24th ult., by the Rev. Charles Manly, D. D., at the residence of Capt. Wm. Goldsmith, the bride's father, Beattie Rowland and Miss Sadie N. Goldsmith, both of this city.

On November 3d, 1880, at the residence of Mr. J. S. Joy, the bride's brother-in-law, by Rev. T. A. Reid, Mr. A. T. Pressley and Miss K. R. Sullivan, daughter of the late Duncan Sullivan, all of Abbeville County, S. C.

By the same, on December 8th 1880, at the residence of the bride's aunt, Mrs. Fannie Perrin, Mr. T. N. Parks and Miss Emma Quarles, all of Abbeville County, S. C.

On the 8th inst., at the residence of the bride's father, Talladega, Alabama, by Rev. Dr. J. J. D. Renfroe, Rev. T. P. Bell, of Anderson, S. C., to Ada C., youngest daughter of Samuel Clabaugh, Esq.

On December 1st, by Rev. T. W. Reid, Mr. John Taylor and Miss Fannie Miller, all of Greenville County, S. C.

Issue of December 23, 1880

Died at Mount Lebanon, Louisiana, November 19th, 1880, in the seventy-fifth year of her age, Mrs. Margaret F. Hartwell, relict of Rev. Jesse Hartwell, D. D. Born and reared in the City of Charleston, S. C., she was married when you to Rev. Jesse Hartwell, then Professor in the Furman Theological institute, whom she survived by twenty-one years. [eulogy] J. B. H. San Francisco, California, Dec., 1880.

Married on September 28, 1880, in Timmonsville, S. C., by Rev. S. M. Richardson, Cooley Hill and Carrie, daughter of Rev. Elias Phillips, both of Darlington County, S. C.

On November 10th, 1880, at the residence of the bride's father, by Rev. S. M. Richardson, Jos. C. Hill and Ina, third daughter of Giles Carter, Esq., both of Darlington County, S. C.

On December 9th, 1880, at the residence of the bride's father, by the Rev. J. H. Edwards, Robert Robertson and Miss Hattie Glasscock, all of York County, S. C.

On the 9th December 1880, at the residence of the bride's mother, Mrs. R. A. Owens, by Rev. T. J. Taylor, G. A. Byars and Miss Annie Mullinax, both of Union County, S. C.

Also, at the residence of the bride's father, Mr. Joseph Byars, by Rev. T. J. Taylor, Goodman Pridmore and Miss Amanda Byars, both of Union County, S. C.

On December 7th, at the residence of the bride's aunt, Miss Caroline Hawkins, by Rev. D. C. Hardin, John Shockley and Miss A. E. Hawkins.

By the same, and at the same time and place, John Vaughan and Miss Francis E. Hawkins, all of Greenville County, S. C.

On December 9th 1880, by Rev. D. C. Hardin, at the residence of the bride's mother, at Piedmont, John Summy and Miss E. J. Keller, both of Greenville County, S. C.

On December 16th 1880, by Rev. T. W. Reid, Beauregard Smith and Ella Holtzclaw, all of Greenville County, S. C.

On the 14th inst., by the Rev. John Stout, assisted by the Rev. T. P. Lide, Jr., at the residence of Dr. F. E. Wilson, the bride's father, the Rev. R. W. Lide and Miss Annie E. Wilson, both of Darlington County, S. C.

In the Greenville Baptist Church, on Wednesday evening, December 15th 1880, by Rev. Charles Manly, D. D., Mr. George Westmoreland and Miss Elvira T. Smith, eldest daughter of Julius C. Smith, Esq., all of Greenville.

December 8th, by the Rev. H. C. Smart, Mr. James Duckett and Miss Katie Parks, all of Greenwood.

Issue of January 6, 1881

Married on the 8th of December 1870 [sic], at the residence of Dr. S. W. Bookhart, the bride's father, by Rev. R. R. Vann, the Rev. W. T. Derieux, of Manchester, Va., and Miss Lotta F. Bookhart, of Blythewood, S. C.

On the 26th December 1880, at Mr. J. W. Hodge's, by Rev. J. L. Rollins, Mr. Henry Geddings to Miss Francis Hodge.

December 22nd 1880, by Rev. A. J. S. Thomas, Rev. James A. Carson to Miss Josephine DeLoach, daughter of Allison DeLoach, Esq.

By the Rev. J. L. Rollins, at the residence of the bride's father, on the 16th of December 1880, Mr. B. O. Brockington of Williamsburg County, to Miss Jane Lockhart, of Timmonsville, Darlington County.

By Rev. A. C. Stepp, on the 23rd of December 1880, Mr. Edwin B. Bolt and Miss Mattie I. Daniel, both of Laurens.

At Grove Station, on the evening of the 23rd of December 1880, by Rev. M. M. McGee, at the residence of the bride's father, Mr. J. Preston Beam and Miss Emma Eskew, daughter of Simeon Eskew, Esq.

By the Rev. W. B. Carson, on the 18th of November 1880, at the house of the bride's mother, Mr. O'Bannon Lafitte to Miss Julia Best, all of Barnwell County.

By the same, on the 23rd of December, 1880, at the house of the bride's mother, Mr. J. W. Clary to Miss Josephine Bennett, all of Barnwell County.

November 18th 1880, by Rev. S. t. Russell, Mr. Henry Long and Miss Mary Kirton.

December 2nd 1880, Mr. J. K. Smith of Williamsburg, and Miss M. J. Long, of Georgetown.

December 9th 1880, by Rev. S. T. Russell, Mr. B. M. Britt and Miss E. A. Howard.

December 26th, 1880, by Rev. S. T. Russell, Mr. Thomas Smith of Williamsburg, and Miss Jane Richardson, of Sumter.

Died, of diptheria, September 7th, 9th and 15th, Melville Dozier, James Walker, and Lynas Ball DuPre, aged respectfully, four years, six years and ten months, and one year and six months, children of J. E. and E. W. DuPre.... Father.

Issue of January 13, 1881

Married by Rev. F. J. Sanders, on 8th December, Mr. W. J. Hightower and Miss Savannah Rountree.

On 23d December, by Rev. F. J. Sanders, Mr. J. J. Kennedy and Miss Maggie Hair.

On 30th December, by Rev. F. J. Sanders, Mr. B. Mithell [sic] and Miss Lizzie Armstrong. All of Barnwell County, S. C.

In Lancaster village, January 3rd 1881, aged 1 year, 2 month and 2 days, Paul Moore, son of Bro. M. J. and sister E. A. Hough....

Issue of January 20, 1881

Died, at Bamberg, S. C., 31st of December, 1880, after a long illness, Mrs. Margaret Zorn, wife of Levi Zorn, and daughter of Mr. J. F. Hartzog and A. E. Hartzog, of Orangeburgh County, S. C. She was a member of the

Springtown Baptist Church, and always maintained a consistent Christian character. J. F. Buist.

Married at the residence of the bride's mother, on Wednesday evening, January 12th 1881, by Rev. R. H. Nall, Mr. James O. Saxon and Miss Jennie Taylor, daughter of the late Col. A. A. N. M. Taylor, of Greenville.

In Memoriam. On the death of James, Mell Dozier, and Lynas Ball Dupre. W. E. J.

Issue of January 27, 1881

Married in Lancaster village, on the evening of the 13th inst., at the residence of the bride, by Rev. G. W. Gardner, John P. Hunter, Sheriff of Lancaster County, and Mrs. Laura Hickson.

By the Rev. L. Cuthbert, on the evening of Wednesday, December 22d, 1880, at the Methodist Church, Mr. C. E. Tyler and Miss S. Lafitte. All of Graham's.

At the residence of the bride's mother in Branchville, S. C., on January 16th, 1881, by Rev. W. D. McMillan, Mr. G. W. Hightower and Miss J. M. Carr.

Died, of diptheria, on the 26th ult., Birdie, aged eleven years, and on the 9th inst., Leila, aged five years and eight months, children of Rev. J. C. Browne, Aiken, S. C.

At his residence, Friday morning, January 14th at about 4 o'clock, Mr. Lewis Minn, for many years a useful and consistent member and deacon of the Bold Springs Baptist Church, Edgefield Association. The deceased leaves a large family and many friends. B. F. M.

Issue of February 3, 1881

Married at the residence of the bride's mother, January 20th 1881, by Rev. J. H. Edwards, Mr. Rufus Collins and Miss Mary E. McCants, all of York County.

In the Baptist Church, Florence, S. C., January 12th 1881, by Rev. O. F. Gregory, Mr. Lafayette W. Hodges and Miss Lula E. Brown, all of Florence.

By Rev. James H. Saye, on January 20, 1881, near Rossville, Chester County, S. C., Rev. A. M. Cartledge and Miss Almina M. Crockett.

Near Santuc, Union County, S. C., January 26, 1881, by Rev. C. T. Scaife, the Rev. A. McA. Pittman, originally from North Carolina, and Miss Maggie E., daughter of ex-Gov. T. B. Jeter of South Carolina.

Died, in this City, on the 14th January, Col. R. P. Goodlett, aged 70 years and 18 days. Converted in mature manhood, indeed baptized along with his eldest son, he became an ardent student of the Bible....

Issue of February 10, 1881

Married at the house of the bride's mother, in Union County, S. C., Feb. 2nd, 1881, by Rev. A. McA. Pittman, Mr. D. M. Cudd to Miss Lizzie M. Palmer.

Near Blackville, S. C., Feb. 3rd, 1881, by Rev. A. Buist, Mr. W. R. Copeland and Miss Ira Reed, both of Barnwell County.

Issue of February 17, 1881

Married on the 9th January, by Rev. F. J. Sanders, Mr. W. Snider and Miss Lizzie Richardson.

On the 13th January, by Rev. F. J. Sanders, Mr. McDuffie Kennedy and Miss Lizzie Burgess.

On the 23d January, by Rev. F. J. Sanders, Mr. E. L. Sanders and Miss Ida M. Sanders.

On the 1st February, at the residence of Col. J. Jameson, the bride's father, by Rev. D. Weston Hiott, Mr. O. Wingo, of Gowensville, Greenville, S. C., and Miss Bettie E. Jameson, of Piercetown, Anderson County.

Issue of March 3, 1881

Married on the 13th February 1881, by Rev. D. C. Hardin, Mr. Lawrence Turner and Miss Anna Harris.

On the 17th February 1881, by Rev. D. C. Hardin, Mr. William Pruitt and Miss Susan Rogers.

On the 17th inst., at the residence of the bride's father, by Rev. J. K. Mendenhall, Dr. Viroma D. Hopkins of Greenville County, to Miss Lula A. Hopkins, daughter of Dr. John Hopkins of Seneca City.

Died, at Whilden Hall, Greenville County, on February 9th 1881, Screven Hart Whilden, in the sixteenth year of his age, eldest son of Rev. R. Furman Whilden....

Issue of March 10, 1881

Married on the 27th February 1881, at the residence of the bride's father in Colleton Co., S. C., by Elder R. J. Edwards, Mr. Adam Kinard, of Barnwell Co., and Miss Lizzie Smith.

February 22d, 1881, by Rev. J. B. Wilson, Mr. S. J. Wilson, of Greenville County, to Miss Julia F. Alverson, of Union County.

February 14th 1881, by Rev. A. Buist, Mr. Preston Pendar and Miss A. Givens, both of Barnwell County.

February 15th 1881, by the same, Mr. William Jones, of Aiken County, and Miss Julia Mims, of Barnwell County.

February 27th 1881, by the same, Mr. Floyd Walker and Miss Luella Minus, of Barnwell County.

February 27th 1881, at the residence of the bride's uncle, Mr. John Wham, by Rev. D. C. Hardin, Mr. P. J. Hudson and Miss A. E. Burnett, both of Spartanburg, S. C.

February 54th[sic], 1881, at the residence of the bride's father, by Rev. J. M. Sanders, Mr. J. A. Moore to Miss Mary A. Jemison, of Oconee.

In Memoriam. Mrs. E. R. Meador, of Fairfield County, S. C., departed this life October 10th A. D. 1880, aged 67 years. [eulogy] M. E. R. Spartanburg, S. C.

Issue of March 17, 1881

March 3rd, 1881, at the residence of the bride's father, Lem. Hall, Esq., Dr. Dr. J. K. Kneece, Miss Catharine Hall and Mr. Elliott Hallman, all of Lexington County, S. C.

Issue of March 24, 1881

Married by the Rev. A. C. Stepp, on the 17th of March, 1881, at the residence of F. M. Davenport, Esq., Mr. James Hardy Epps, of Laurens County, and Miss Emma O. Davenport, of Greenville County, S. C.
At Batesburg, S. C., March 17th 1881, by Rev. A. J. S. Thomas, Mr. M. Q. Norris to Miss M. Estelle Meyer, both of Batesburg.

On January 12, 1881, at the residence of the bride's father, by Rev. J. C. Hudson, Mr. C. Earle Hamilton and Miss Annie Boggs, both of Pickens, S. C.

Died, in York County, S. C., March 8th, 1881, Miss Mary Ann Locke, aged 22 years. She joined the Catawba Baptist Church early in life... A. J. McC.

Died, November 20, 1880, Mrs. Susan J. Werts, wife of J. Belton Werts, Newberry County... L.B.

Issue of March 31, 1881

Died, at her home in Edgefield County, S. C., Jan. 10th 1881, Mrs. Frances A. Burkhalter. Another day would have completed her 32nd year... her husband Charles M. Burkhalter. [eulogy] Hugh F. Oliver.

Issue of April 7, 1881

Married in Barnwell County, S. C., on Thursday, March 24th 1881, by Rev. John G. Williams, Mr. J. W. Ray to Miss Mary V., daughter of Mr. D. H. Hutto.

By the Rev. J. C. Crouch, on the 13th of March 1881, at the residence of Joseph Sandifer, Dr. L. Smoak to Miss Mary Sandifer, of Barnwell County, S.C.

February 2nd 1881, at the residence of the bride's father, Rev. D. W. Brant, by the Rev. B. G. Price, Miss Emma Frances Grant and Mr. Edward D. Hyrne, all of Colleton County.

With sadness we announce the death of our beloved brother J. Bunyan Cuttino, son of Rev. D. W. Cuttino, who fell a victim to typhoid pneumonia on the 13th of March 1881. He joined the Baptist Church at Manning, S. C., in 1869, and subsequently united with Santee Baptist Church, in which he was ordained junior Deacon in 1879. J. B. Oakland, S. C.

Issue of April 21, 1881

Married, at the residence of the bride's mother, March 23d, by Rev. E. H. Cuttino, Mr. Bethel DeBoice and Miss Laura Smith. All of Charleston County.

At the same time and place, by the same, Mr. Benjamin Mitchum and Miss Amarintha Hood. All of Charleston County.

On the evening of the 6th inst., at the residence of the bride's father, by the Rev. J. L. Rollins, Mr. John F. McLena, of Clarendon County, to Miss Cornelia B. Rollins, of Williamsburg county, S. C.

Issue of April 28, 1881

Married on Tuesday, April 26th, 1881, in the Greenville Baptist Church, by Rev. Charles Manly, D. D., Mr. George L. Dantzler and Miss Lizzie M. Smith,

On the 20th of April, 1881, at the residence of Mr. Samuel Mauldin, by Rev. J. C. Furman, D. D., Mr. J. L. Wideman, of Abbeville, and Miss Anna M. Harrison, of Greenville.

Died, at his residence in Greenville County, S. C., April 8th 1881, J. b. Rosamond, in the 72nd year of his age. Bro. Rosamond had been a member of the Baptist church for nearly fifty years. He first united with the Greenville Church. About forty years ago he transferred his membership to the Mountain Creek Church, where he was a deacon for thirty-five years. T. W. Reid

Julia H., wife of John N. Laramore and daughter of Jordan and Elizabeth A. Williams, was born March 13th 1862, and died December 1st 1880. She was baptized into the fellowship of the Pee Dee Church by Rev. Alfred nobles in her twelfth year. S. M. R.

Died at the home of her son, Mr. T. W. Hawkins, in Sumter County, S. C., March 27th, 1881, Mrs. Elizabeth Hawkins, aged about one hundred years. For seventy years she has been a member of the Baptist Church. her son, Bro. T. W. Hawkins... F. C. H.

Departed this life, near Branchville, S. C., on December 20th 1880, Isabel M., beloved wife of Dr. Marian M. Grissett, aged 50 years, 8 months and 17 days. Pastor.

In Memoriam. Black's Station, S. C., April 18, '81. Cyrus P. Ramseur, late a merchant of this place, died of pneumonia on Thursday, 13th inst., aged 31 years and 5 months.

Issue of May 5, 1881

Married at the residence of the bride's father, in Yorkville, April 12, 1881, 7. A. M., Miss Alice Owen and Mr. S. B. Nail, by Rev. R. W. Sanders.

April 27th 1881, 7:30 P. M., by Rev. R. W. Sanders, at the residence of the bride's father, Rev. John D. Mahon, Miss Minnie T. Mahon and Mr. Lemuel B. Meador, all of Fairfield County.

April 28th 1881, at the residence of the bride's father, by Rev. A. Buist, Mr. J. B. Hartley, of Batesburg, S. C., and Miss Fannie B. Mims, of Barnwell County.

At the residence of the bride's mother, April 28th 1881, by Rev. J. O. Willson (assisted by Rev. E. H. Cuttino), Mr. W. W. Williams and Miss Annie E. Willson, all of Charleston County.

Died, April 22nd 1881, at the residence of his father in Springville, S. C., Timothy George Dargan, son of Rev. and Mrs. J. O. B. Dargan. The deceased was born March 14, 1840. At the age of sixteen he entered the Arsenal at Charleston as a student, and after spending two years there, he became a cadet at the Citadel, where he was graduated with honor. Immediately upon the completion of his school days ,he entered the Confederate service with the Boykin Rangers, and began his soldier life in Virginia. He was not long in service before he was appointed a lieutenant of the 1st S. C. Artillery, then stationed at Fort Sumter, where he served sill the close of the war. After the war he studied law and was admitted to the Bar i 1866. He pursued his calling with attention at Darlington and Florence, having his home at the latter place until a few months before his death.... leaves wife and children. R. W. L. Darlington, S. C.

Brother Jas. Ellis, a consistent member of Hartville Baptist Church died about the middle of last February. He was about 83 years old....

Mrs. A. J. Goodson, aged 38 years, died on pneumonia, on the 23d of January 1881.

Mrs. H. J. McIntosh, aged 27 years, died 3d of April 1881. She left a babe three or four days old... T. H. Burruss.

Died, March 8th 1881, at her late residence in Union County, in the 74th year of her age, Mrs. Miriam Long, mother of Mrs. U. W. Winn, of Greenville, and relict of Wm. Long, Esq., who died April 8th 1865... She laves two sons, five daughters and twelve grandchildren-- three of her sons having died during the war.

Tribute of Respect to Cyrus P. Ramseur, from the Sabbath School at Black's Station, S. C.

Tribute of Respect from Vaucluse Baptist Sunday School to Miss Hannah Jennings, who died 11th day of April 1881.

Issue of May 19, 1881

Died at her home in Aiken County, S. C., March 4, 1881, Mrs. Lizzie Shaw, the wife of James L. Shaw, and daughter of Mrs. Susan Walker. She was born on March 18, 1856... Hugh F. Oliver.

John Curran Hartley, son of Deacon Lodwick Hartley, died at Batesburg, April 17th, 1881. He was a most promising young man, just 22 years old.... He was married only last November. A. J. S. Thomas.

Rev. Elijah Hicks died, after a short sickness, on Sunday May 1st 1881, at his home near Bethel Church, in Clarendon County, S. C. He was a preacher of the gospel for more than forty years, and pastor of Bethel Church more than thirty. He was received as a beneficiary of the Welsh Neck Association in 1839... Bro. Hicks was about sixty-five years old and leaves a widow behind . S. M. Richardson.

Departed this life, near Steel Creek, Barnwell County, S. C., on the 14th day of January, 1881, Mrs. Elizabeth Baughman, aged forty-five years. Mrs. Baughman had been a consistent member of the Baptist Church for a number of years. She leaves a large family, a husband and many children... A. B. E.

O the 21st of April 1881, in the 74th year of his age, passed away, William Getsinger, father of the Rev. J. J. Getsinger... J. F. Buist.

Tribute of Respect to William Getsinger from the Midway Baptist Church.

Married in Greenville, May 3rd, 1881, at the residence of Mr. J. W. Thornberg, by Rev. J. K. Mendenhall, Mr. R. H. Russell, of Seneca City, to Miss Jessie Florence McCrary, of Greenville, S. C.

On the 20th of January, 1881, at the residence of Mr. Blackman, by Rev. Thos. H. Burruss, Mr. A. F .Miller and Miss A. E. Doughety.

On same date, by the same, at the home of Mr. Jas. Hawkins, Mr. Willis Rogers and Miss Lula Kervin.

On the 27th January 1881, by the same, at the residence of the bride's father, Mr. L. A. Witherspoon and Miss Fannie C. McInvaile.

Issue of May 26, 1881

In Memoriam. Died, at her home in Friendfield, Marion County, S. C., on the 13th of April 1881, Mrs. Margaret S. Brooks, in the 59th year of her age. Sister Brooks was the daughter of Deacon S. S. Anderson, who, wither her mother, M. H. Anderson, dispense a bountiful hospitality.... At the age of about fifteen she was baptized into the fellowship of Elim Church, by the pastor Elder J. Morgan Timmons. On the 22d of January 1841, she was married to Elder R. R. Brooks. [eulogy] S. M. R. May 18, 1881

Joseph L. Fickling was born in Barnwell County, S. C., Dec. 20, 1842, and died at his home in Aiken County, May 1, 1881, aged 38 years, 4 months and on day. He was converted at the age of 16, and baptized into the fellowship of the Willow Swamp Baptist Church. In 1875 he was ordained to the office of deacon in the Rocky Grove Baptist Church. He was a son of Rev. Wm. J. Fickling. Brother Fickling was twice married. he leaves two children by the first and three by the last marriage....

Issue of June 2, 1881

Married on Wednesday afternoon, May 25th, at the residence of Mr. B. H. Miller, the bride's uncle, by Rev. N. N. Burton, Mr. J. Clarence Glover, of Batesburg, to Miss Imogen Hord, of Edgefield.

On the 19th of May, by Rev. A. C. Stepp, Mr. F. J. Owings and Miss S. D. Barksdale; both of Laurens.

On the 26th of May, by Rev. C. A. Stiles, Mr. Moses Moak and Miss Grace Campbell, all of Richland County.

Died, May 4th, 1881, aged 59, Mrs. Susan M. Bell, widow of the late deacon Bell, of Mt. Elon Church, Darlington County, S. C. T. J. P.

Issue of June 9, 1881

In Memoriam. Bettie M. Davis, wife of William M. Davis, and daughter of Jonathan M. and Margaret S. Miller, died April 8th 1881, aged 29 years... Augusta, May 23, 1881.

Issue of June 16, 1881

Married at the residence of the bride's father, June 2nd, 1887 [sic], by Rev. E. H. Cuttino, Mr. P. P. McKelvey and Mrs. G. M. Harvey. All of Charleston County.

At the residence of the bride's mother, Sunday, June 5th,1881, by Rev. M. McGee, Mr. John F. Fagg and Miss Ellen Cheatham, daughter of Mrs. Sallie Cheatham and grand-daughter of Rev. A. Rice, deceased. All of Anderson County.

Tribute of Respect from Rocky Grove Baptist Church, Aiken county, May 71, 1881, to Joseph L. Fickling.

Died, at his residence, near Graham's, S. C., W. R. Copeland, on the 22nd of March 1881, in the 62nd year of his age. Early in life he united with the Springtown Baptist Church, having been baptized by Rev. H. D. Duncan. In the year 1843 he together with others combined in forming the church known as Cedar Springs-- now Graham Baptist Church....

Died, on the 3rd inst., in Barnwell, S. C., Bro. John E. Birt, in the fifty-first year of his age... for thirty-four years a member of Long Branch Baptist Church. He leaves a wife, seven children, and many relatives. Barnwell S. C., June 8, 1881.

John E. Russell was born November 24, 1852, and fell asleep in Jesus, March 20, 1881, at the residence of his parents, Deacon Theo. S. and Mrs. Kate Russell.... he died near St. Stephens, Charleston County, S. C. O. F. Gregory. Cheraw, S. C., May 16, 1881.

W. T. Pittman, Esq., senior partner of the firm of Messrs. Pittman Bros. of Charleston, S. C., died at the Pavillion Hotel in that city, on Saturday morning at 6 o'clock, 28th ult. He leaves a pious and devoted wife and one infant son. D. W. Gore.

Issue of June 30, 1881

Married, in the Washington Street Methodist Church, at Columbia, on the 15th of June 1881, by the Rev. R. N. Wells, Mr. Robert C. Goodlett, of Greenville, and Mrs. Emma A. Geiger, of Lexington.

Issue of July 14, 1881

Died, on the 16th of June 1881, aged two years, two months and 27 days, Charles Maxwell, youngest son of Capt. J. B. Patrick, of Greenville, S. C.

Issue of July 21, 1881

Married, by Rev. A. C. Stepp, on the 30th June 1881, Mr. John L. Reddin and Miss Leah E. Bolt, both of Laurens County, S. C.

At the residence of the bride's father, Edgefield C. H., S. C., on the 28th June, 1881, by Rev. T. W. Mellichamp, Mr. Louis S. Mellichamp to Miss Laura I. Parker, all of Edgefield County, S. C.

Near Williston, S. C., June 8th 1881, by Rev. A. Buist, Mr. M. N. Anderson and Mrs. A. M. Lee, both of Barnwell County.

Died, on the night of Wednesday, 6th inst., Jesse Wells Ball, youngest child of Rev. M. L. and Mrs. Lizzie McKay Ball, of Mayesville, S. C. W. F. R.

Died, on Saturday morning, June 11th 1881, of consumption, Miss Samuella Nelson, aged 19 years. [eulogy] James F. Buist. Bamberg, S. C.

Issue of July 28, 1881

James Madison Moore was born in York County, S. C., October 3rd, 1847, and died in Cleveland County, N. C., June 6th 1881. He joined the Baptist church at about the age of fifteen... W. M. Duncan, Black's Sta., S. C., July 15, 1881.

Died, of typhoid dysentery, at the residence of her son, Chesley Crosby, Esq., in Fairfield County, S. C., Mrs. Charlotte Crosby, in the 82nd year of her age.. He only two surviving daughters abandoned their homes to watch by her bedside.... J. D. M.

Issue of August 4, 1881

Married at the residence of the bride's father, Florence, S. C., July 24th 1881, by Rev. O. F. Gregory, Mr. W. E. Herring and Miss Ella C. Bristow, all of Florence.

At the residence of the bride's father, near Marion C. H., S. C., on the 21st June 1881, by Rev. J. F. McMillan, Miss Lizzie, daughter of James Watson, Esq., to Mr. W. H. Daniels, of Mullin's, S. C.

Died, on the 10th of June 1881, at his residence, near Red Bank Church, Edgefield County, S. C., Rev. J. F. Peterson, in the 85th year of his age. [long account]

Died, in Hardeeville, S. C., on the 18th July, 1881, Henry R. Williams, in the fifty-seventh year of his age.

Died, on Tuesday night, 26th ult., at Pacolet Depot, Spartanburg County, S. C., William Thomas James, son of A. D. and Mattie E. James, aged one year, three months and nineteen days. Grand Pa.

Died, July 2nd, 1881, in Spartanburg County, S. C., Mrs. Elizabeth Brockman, in her sixtieth year. She left a devoted husband and a number of children and grandchildren.

In Memoriam. Departed this life on the evening of the 23d ult., in the 27th year of his age, Mrs. Elizabeth Jane, wife of Mr. C. L. Evans, and daughter of Maj. John S. and Mrs. Elizabeth Miller of Chesterfield County, S. C.... baptized into the fellowship of the White Plain Church by Rev. S. J. Fincher in the summer of 1874.... leaves a fond husband, a lovely little daughter, a father and mother, brothers and sisters.

In Memoriam. Our dearly beloved pastor Elijah Hicks.

Tribute of Respect to J. E. Birt.

Issue of August 11, 1881

Married at the residence of D. B. Talley, on the 2nd inst., Mr. Richard H. Vaughn to Mrs. Lizzie Newman, by Rev. D. B. Talley. The former 70 years, and the latter, 55 years old. Both of Laurens county.

Tribute of Respect from Red Bank Baptist Church, Edgefield County, July 16, 1881, to Rev. J. F. Peterson.

Issue of September 8, 1881

Married in Baltimore on August 30th 1881, by Rev. A. B. Woodfin, D. D., Rev. J. B. Hartwell, D. D., of San Francisco, Cal., to Miss Charlotte E., daughter of G. W. Norris, Esq., of Baltimore.

On Thursday evening, August 25th, 1881, at the residence of the bride's father, by Rev. B. F. Miller, Mr. Louis Obadiah Henderson to Miss Mary Alice Whatley, all of Edgefield County, S. C.

Issue of September 15, 1881

Married at the residence of the bride's mother, Mrs. Mary Deloach, by the Rev. J. A. Carson, Mr. Joseph Cromley to Miss Ida Walton, on the 23rd of August 1881, all of Edgefield County.

In Memory of Mrs. Carrie M. Mosley. The subject of this sketch departed this life on the 13th of June 1881, at her residence, nine miles east of Camden, S. C. Sister Mosley was only twenty-six years old, and laves a husband and loving child. A. S. W.

Issue of September 22, 1881

Died, Sept. 6th, Mrs. Elizabeth Caully, wife of Alfred Caully, and the oldest daughter of Rev. E. J. and Rebecca Mullinax. Born August 14th, 1864, married December 9, 1880.... leaves her husband, parents, relatives...

Died, near Eastover, Richland County, S. C., August 24, 1881, Mrs. L. F. Rhame. Her maiden name was Graden. She was a member of the Baptist church for a number of years... leaves devoted husband and three affectionate children. Minnie C. Scott.

Died, in York County, S. C., August 24, 1881, Julius C., infant son of Lewis and Martha A. Parks, aged 8 months.

Died, in York County, S. C., September 11, 1881, Lewis Parks, aged 31 years.... united with the Catawba Baptist Church.. leaves wife, two little children, and an aged mother. A. J. McCoy

Died, near Ridgeway, Fairfield County, S. C., on the 6th inst., Mrs. Lucy Harrison, aged 88 years. She was a consistent member of the Concord Baptist Church for more than 60 years....

Died, July last, near Mt. Lebanon, La., Rev. Henry Z. Ardis, aged near 70 years. Deceased was a native Carolinian--born and reared on Beech Island. Silverton, S. C. J. J. M.

Issue of September 29, 1881

Married at Cheraw Baptist Church, September 8th, by Rev. O. F. Gregory, assisted by Rev. John Stout, Mr. Edward T. Coker, of Society Hill, and miss Mary E. Wilson, third daughter of Dr. J. J.Wilson, of Cheraw.

Death of Mr. Mike Perry. Ridge Spring, Sept. 12, 1881. our friend, E. A. perry, of this place has information by telegram of the death of his brother, M. W. Perry, on the evening of Sept. 8th... he had removed from Louisville, Ky., to a place on the Shelbyville Railroad, about thirty miles from the city.... leaves wife and two children. E. W. Horne.

Mrs. Mary Simpson Gary died in the city of Greenville, at the residence of her daughter, Mrs. Mary C. Pope, on the 7th day of September 1881. she lived to be seventy-one years old....

Died, at Lowndesville, S. C., Aug. 27th, 1881, James Judson Cooper, son of K. R. and D. A. Cooper, aged 13 years, 6 months and 5 days. J. Q. Adams.

Died, May 31st, 1881, Mrs. Nancy Riley, wife of J. M. Riley, of Edgefield County. She was born in 1832; baptized in 1854, by Rev. H. T. Bartley, into the fellowship of Salem Baptist Church.... N. G. C.

Issue of October 6, 1881

Married, on Wednesday evening, September 28, 1881, by Rev. C. A. Stiles, Mr. Henry C. Miller, of Mayesville, S. C., and Miss Nettie, daughter of Samuel A. McQuatters, Esq., of Richland County.

Died, on the 16th of May, at Bishopville, Sister Cornelia C. James, in the 31st year of her age. She united with the Piedmont Baptist Church in 1872. M.L.B.

Died, of diptheria, September 9, 1881, Aiken County, John Michael, third child of H. R. and Sallie M. Sawyer. Aged two years and thirteen days.

Issue of October 13, 1881

Rev. William Ransom Parler departed this life at his home in Orangeburg County, S. C., Aug. 13, 1881, in the thirty-second year of is age, and was buried on the 14th at Four Holes Baptist Church. Bro. Parler became a member of that church in July 1864. He leaves a wife and two little children.... T. M. G., Orangeburg C. H., S. C., Oct. 1st, 1881.

Departed this life in Greenville, S. C., on Wednesday, october 5th, 1881, Mrs. Mary Susan Whitmire, relict of the late Joseph Whitmire. [eulogy] Funeral services were performed at the Baptist church on Friday afternoon, Oct. 7th, and her remains were interred in the Episcopal burial ground. J. C. F.

Departed this life in Chester County, S. C., September 29th, 1871, Maj. John W. Durham, in the 44th year of his age. Maj. Durham was born in Fairfield County, S. C., and can claim an honorable ancestry, being a descendant of Capt. Charnel Hightower Durham, who was a brave soldier and an efficient officer during the Revolutionary war. He united with Woodward Baptist church about ten years ago. J. D. Mahon. Halselville, S. C.

Issue of October 20, 1881

Death of Mrs. Eppes Norris. This was sweet Annie Laurie Bryan... *Edgefield Advertiser*. [eulogy and poem]

Issue of October 27, 1881

Married, on Wednesday evening, October 12th 1881, at the residence of the bride's mother, by Rev. Ellison Capers, Mr. David B. Comer, of Atlanta, Ga., and Miss Metta M. Whitmire, of Greenville, S. C.

Married, by Rev. D. C. Hardin, on October 2nd, 1881, Mr. John Hollingsworth and Miss Leonora Nix.

Married, by the same, October 5th, 1881, at the residence of Mr. Willis Taylor, step-father of the bride, Mr. Frederick James and Miss Florence Hudson, all of Greenville County, S. C.

Married by the Rev. J. L. Rollins, on the 10th of October 1881, at the residence of Mrs. Elizabeth Hodge, Mr. J. W. Hodge to Miss Henrietta Hodge, all of Clarendon County, S. C.

Married, near Blackville, S. C., October 13th, 1881, by Rev. A. Buist, Mr. W. T. Ray and Miss Emma M. Barr, both of Barnwell County.

Married, on the 12th inst., by Rev. T. J. Earle, at the residence of Mr. J. F. Goodlett, Mr. J. Allender Mooney and Miss Maggie A. Montgomery, all of Gowensville.

Issue of November 3, 1881

Married at the residence of the bride's father, Mr. J. E. Meng, of Union County, S. C., on Thursday evening, October 20th, 1881, by Rev. A. McA. Pittman, Mr. G. Barnett and miss Fannie E. Meng.

Issue of November 10, 1881

Married at the residence of the bride's mother, Oct. 20th, 1881, by Rev. J. J. H. Stoudenmire, Mr. S. C. Kennedy, of Walterboro, Colleton County, S. C., and Miss Ida S. Funches, of Orangeburg County, S. C.

Departed this life May 6th, 1881, at Blythewood, S. C., J. Wesley Starnes, aged 45 years. The subject of this notice was a native of North Carolina. he came to Fairfield Co., in this state, while quite a youth... left wife and five small children.

Isaac R. Timmons died at his residence in Marion County, S. C., October 17th, 1881, after a protracted illness of heart disease in his 74th year. He leaves an aged wife and four sons and daughters of mature age. He was baptized August, 1832, by the Rev. J. Morgan Timmons, and received in the fellowship of Elim Church. he was one of the constituent members of Hebron Church at its organization in 1840. J. G. J.

Died, in Apex, near Raleigh, N. C., Oct. 24th, 1881, of consumption, Mrs. J. A. Duckett, wife of Prof. John Duckett.

Issue of November 17, 1881

Married at Rowesville, S. C., Nov. 10, 1881, by Rev. J. J. H. Stoudenmire, Mr. T. C. Metts, of Colleton County, S. C., and Miss A. E. Blackmon, of Orangeburg County, S. C.

At Clifton, S. C., Oct. 10, 1881, by Rev. T. J. Taylor, Mr. Jas. Lingley and Miss Lena Carr.

On the same day, at Mr. Noah Webster's, in Union County, S. C., by Rev. T. J. Taylor, Mr. John W. Wilkins and Miss Maggie Webster.

Died, at Chester, Nov. 8th 1881, little Girard, eldest son of Mr. and Mrs. Brainerd McLure, and grand-son of Rev. L. C. Hinton; aged 3 years and 2 months.

Issue of November 24, 1881

Died, on the 24th of October, Dr. B. F. Buckner, for years a worthy deacon and a consistent member of the Baptist Swamp Baptist Church, Hampton County.

On the 25th day of September 1881, at the residence of her father, Mr. B. C. Bryan, in Edgefield village, S. C., the spirit of Annie Laurie, wife of E. J. Norris, Esq., winged its upward flight.... Mrs. Norris was born March 1st, 1858, baptized Oct. 1st 1872, by Rev. Luther Gwaltney, and married November 19th 1880. [eulogy]

Issue of December 1, 1881

In Anderson County, S. C., Nov. 2nd, 1881, little J. B., youngest child of Mr. and Mrs. John Eskew, who was filled by falling from a wagon. His age was six years and two months....

THE BAPTIST COURIER

Issue of December 8, 1881

Married at the residence of the bride's father, Nov. 24th, by Rev. H. L. Henderson, Mr. S. W. Gould, of Greenville, to Miss M. Lavinia Bramlett, daughter of Elias Bramlett, Esq. of this County.

November 9th, 1881, at the residence of the bride's father, Timmonsville, S. C., by Rev. O. F. Gregory, Mr. Robert A. White, of Chesterfield, S. C., and Miss Florence B. Cole, only daughter of S. F. Cole, Esq., of Timmonsville, S. C.

September 20th, by Rev. J. H. Edwards, at the residence of the bride's mother, Miss Minnie Shurley and Mr. Lucien Gill-- all of York County.

November 3d, by the same, Miss Mattie Wherry and Mr. William Garrison, all of York County.

November 6th, by the same, at the residence of Maj. C. W. McFadden, Mrs. Ida McFadden and Mr. John McCollough-- all of Chester County.

November 23rd, by the same, at the residence of the bride's father, Miss Lula Fewell and Mr. Andrew Sturgis-- all of York.

Died, October 26th, 1881, infant son of Rev. and Mrs. H. L. Baggott, of Aiken County, age two months. R. M.

Having written you before of the death of little Girard McLure, I now perform the sad duty of making mention of the death of his little brother, Tommie. R. W. S.

Departed this life in Orangeburg County, S. C., November 17th, 1881, Mrs. Elizabeth Esther Snider, beloved wife of Rev. W. J. Snider, in the 53d year of her age. When quite young she united with Bethel Baptist Church, Sumter county, S. C. After her marriage she removed her membership to Santee Baptist Church, Orangeburg County, S. C.... D. W. C.

In Kentucky, October 24th, 1881, Mr. Jacob Snider, in the 88th year of his age. A few weeks before his death, he went to Kentucky to visit his daughter, and while there he died. His mortal remains were brought to this state and buried in Santee church-yard. he was one of the number that constituted Santee church, Orangeburg County, in 1827. He has left five children and a number of grand-children. D. W. C.

Departed this life on the 13th day of November 1881, near Tampa Bay, Florida, Mrs. Damaris Miriam Mays, relict of Mr. J. B. Mays. Mrs. M. was a daughter of Mr. Samuel Earle, a Revolutionary patriot, who was for years on one of the head branches of the Saluda, on lands now the property of his grandson, Jas. B. Mays, M. D., and afterwards on his Beaverdam plantation in what is now Oconee County. At one of these places Mrs. Mays was born November 13th, 1808. Herself and her sisters, Mrs. Eliza Earle of Anderson, Mrs. John Maxwell of Pendleton, and Mrs. Robert Maxwell of the same place, were long known to a large circle of cultivated people as ladies of uncommon worth of character. Their brother, the Hon. Baylis Earle (in whose office ex Governor Perry studied law), was a man of shining gifts.... Mrs. Mays was baptized by Rev. A. M. Spalding, father of Rev. Dr. Spalding of Galveston. J. C. Furman.

Issue of December 15, 1881

Married by Rev. D. C. Hardin, Dec. 8th, 1881, at the residence or the bride's father, Mr. Davis Moore to Miss Willie Miller, daughter of Mr. E. B. Miller.

Married, by Rev. N. N. Burton, at the residence of Capt. John G. Able, the bride's father, at 6 o'clock P. M., Dec. 7, 1881, Mr. Preston B. Quattlebaum to Miss Lou A. Able, both of Lexington County.

Died, at Aiken, S. C., Dec. 6, 1881, of cholera infantum, little George Felder, second son of D. W. an D. L. Segler, aged sixteen months.

Died, at Aiken, Nov. 13th, Mrs. J. C. Browne, wife of Rev. J. c. Browne. The funeral services were conducted by the Rev. Lucious Cuthbert, the former beloved pastor of the Aiken Baptist Church. [eulogy]

Issue of December 22, 1881

A Mother in Israel. Mrs. Eliza Ingraham Cuttino died in Charleston, Nov. 14th, at the residence of her son-in-law, Mr. Theo. A. Wilbur, in the midst of loving children, grandchildren and friends. She was seventy-eight year of age... a member of the Citadel Square Baptist Church. She was baptised at Providence, R. I., the place of her birth, by Rev. Stephen Gano. Her husband, the late Benj. Cuttino, was a deacon of our church in Georgetown. Her children now living are Mrs. John G. Milnor, Mr. David S. Cuttino, of Charleston, and Mr. Peter F. Cuttino, of Newnan, Georgia. Another child, who passed on before to have about six years ago, was the wife of Mr. T. A. Wilbur, of Charleston.

Married in Anderson, on the 15th inst., at the residence of the bride's mother, by Rev. Wm. Henry Strickland, Miss Teresa H. Reed, of Anderson, and Mr. Charlton H. Strickland, Jr., of Jacksboro, Texas.

December 14th, 11 A. M., at the residence of Capt. W. B. Woodward, Fairfield County, by R. W. Sanders, Mr. Thomas M. Boulware and Miss Minnie M. Woodward.

December 14th, 11 A. m., at the residence of Capt. W. B. Woodward, Fairfield County, by R. W. Sanders, Mr. Angus R. Nicholson and Miss Nannie B. Woodward.

At Greenwood, S. C., Dec. 15th, 1881, by Rev. M. McGee, Mr. W. J. McGee and Miss Theodosia E. Sproles.

At Bethany Baptist Church, Edgefield, S. C., by the pastor, assisted by Rev. Mr. Meadors, of the M. E. Church, Mr. J. Silvester Chipley, Jr., of Ninety Six, S. C., to Miss Anna C., only daughter of Dr. J. C. Lanier and lady, of Liberty Hill, Edgefield County, S. C.

At the residence of the bride's brother, on Wednesday P. M., Dec. 7th, 1881, by Rev. B. F. Miller, Mr. M. Leroy Wiley to Miss Marietta Atkins, both of Abbeville County, S. C.

Died, in York County, S. C., November 23rd, 1881, Mrs. Nannie Deese, aged 37 years. She was a member of the Catawba Baptist Church. A. J. McCoy.

In Memoriam. William P. Taylor, Sunday School Superintendent of Greer's Sunday School.

Issue of January 5, 1882

Married in Marion, S. C., on Tuesday night, the 29th ult., Miss Irene E. Davis to Mr. Jas F. Edwards, Rev. J. F. Millan officiating.

By Rev. J. J. H. Stoudmire, December 15th, 1881, at the residence of Mr. William Byrd in Branchville, S. C., Mr. A. G. Myers to Miss A. J. Judy, both of Orangeburg County.

On December 25th, 1881, at the residence of Mr. J. S. Adams, in Greenville, by Rev. Charles Manly, Miss Luvinia Cureton, of Greenville to Mr. R. M. Morgan, of Pickens County.

On December 20th, 1881, at the residence of the bride's father, Col. J. Jameson, by Rev. D. Weston Hiott, Mr. Z. D. Bramlett, of Greenville County, S. C., to Miss Mattie A. Jameson, of Anderson County, S. C.

At the residence of the bride's father, Cash's Station, S. C., December 22nd, 1881, by Rev. O. F. Gregory, Mr. Samuel B. Gandy, of Darlington County, and Miss N. Lena Odum, of Chesterfield County, S. C.

On December 21st, 1881, 11 A. M., at the residence of the bride's father, by the Rev. F. J. Sanders, Mr. Jas. A. Bates and Miss Ella Maud, youngest daughter of Mr. J. J. Myer, all of Silverton, S. C.

Mr. C. J. Woodruff and Miss Anna Edwards, eldest daughter of Col. B. W. Edwards, were married in the Baptist Church of Darlington on the evening of December 20th. Revs. John Stout and W. J. Alexander officiating.

On December 13th, by Rev. J. H. Edwards, at the residence of Mr. Kohath Smith, Mr. Absalom Locke and Miss Lizzie Campbell; all of York County.

On December 15th, by Rev. R. W. Boyd, assisted by Rev. J. H. Edwards, at the residence of the bride's father, Capt. John Backstrom, Mr. Wm. J. Waters and Miss Fannie M. Backstrom.

On December 22nd, by Rev. J. H. Edwards, at the residence of the bride's father, Mr. William Woods and Miss Minnie Crook; all of York County.

Died, in Orangeburg County, November 27th, 1881, infant son of W. M. and E. Z. Wolfe, aged two months.

Departed this life on the 10th inst., in the 15th year of his age, Robert n., son of John S. and Eliza J. Croxton.... member of Fork Hill Baptist Church. Pleasant Hill, S. C., Dec. 12, 1881.

Issue of January 12, 1882

Married at the Concord Baptist Church, November 30th, 1881, by the pastor, Rev. A. B. Estes, assisted by Rev. Jos. A. Lawton, Mr. E. G. Willingham and Miss Mamie Peeples, eldest daughter of Capt. W. B. Peeples, all of Barnwell County, S. C.

On December 14, 1881, at the residence of Rev. C. T. Anderson, by Rev. S. M. Richardson, Miss Lula Anderson and Mr. James A. Anderson, both of Marion County, S. C.

By Rev. A. C. Stepp, on the 22nd December, 1881, Mr. Willis R. Cheek and Miss Mary J. Riddle, both of Laurens County, S. C.

On Sunday morning, Dec. 11th, 1881, by Rev. T. W. Reid, Mr. Collins and Miss Harriet Dill.

By the same, the same day, in Chick Springs Church, Mr. A. Sizemore and Miss Florence Smith.

On the evening of December 25, 1881, by the same, at the residence of the bride's father, Mr. Marcus Freeman and Miss Lizzie, eldest daughter of R. B. Gibson, Esq.

On Sunday morning, January 1st, 1882, by the same, at the residence of the bride's father, Mr. Henry Brown and Miss Susan, second daughter of Mr. Irvan Hudson, all of Greenville County, S. C.

Nathan Thomson was born at Aberdeen, Scotland, in 1824. In 1836 his parents left their fatherland and came to Charleston, S. C. In early manhood brother Thompson entered business as a painter. During the late war, he refugeed to the city of Columbia, and after the war settled in Camden, S. C.... He died very suddenly on the 24th of November and leaves a sorrowing family.... A. W. L.

Mrs. Louvicy W. Kirkland, relict of Robert Kirkland, departed this life at her home near Buford's Bridge, Barnwell Co., S. C., on Tuesday morning, the 22nd of November 1881. She was a member of Philadelphia Baptist Church (near her home) for fifty-five years. W. D. R. Graham's, S. C., Dec. 26th, 1881.

Issue of January 19, 1882

Married, in Darlington County, by Rev. J. Q. Adams, Mr. Stephen Carter and Miss Sallie Meggs.

In Hartsville Baptist Church, January 4th, 1882, Mr. Jas. W. Blackwell and Miss Lottie S. McIntosh, by Rev. Thomas H. Burruss.

At the residence of the bride's mother, near Natchitoches, La., Dec. 11, 1881, by Rev. Mr. Cunningham, Miss Annie Rayborn to Mr. W. H. Phillips, of Williston, S. C.

Benjamin Lawton Estes died of typhoid pneumonia, at Rome, Georgia, the 5th instant, scarcely 20 years of age. He was the fourth son of Rev. A. B. and Cornelia Estes (whose maiden name was Willingham) of South Carolina. AT the age of 12 he united with the Allendale Baptist Church... buried at Concord Church. J. A. L.

Tribute of Respect from Clifton Union Sunday School, in memory of Mr. W. E. Gregory, son of Mr. and Mrs. Wm. Gregory, who died at his home West Springs, Union Co., S. C., December 11th 1881.

Issue of January 26, 1882

Tribute of Respect from Long Town Church to Mrs. E. M. Peay.

Married, January 17th, by Rev. J. H. Edwards, at the residence of Mr. John Steele, near Rock Hill, Mr. J. V. McFadden and Miss Sallie Atkinson.

January 17th, by Rev. J. H. Edwards, at the residence of the bride's father, Maj. Frank Rawlinson, near Rock Hill, Mr. I. R. McFadden, of Cedar Shoals and Miss Cora Rawlinson.

Died, in Augusta, January 8th, while visiting her aunt, Mrs. Milledge Rountree, after a short illness, Georgia, eldest child of Mr. and Mrs. Charlie Black, of Barnwell, S. C.

Issue of February 2, 1882

Married by Rev. D. Weston Hiott, on 22d January, Mr. Samuel A. Barr, of Easley, and Mrs. Isabella C. Webb of Anderson County, S. C.,

At the residence of Mr. D. D. Suttle, on Wednesday, January 25th, at 10 o'clock, A. M., by Rev. W. A. Nelson, Mr. E. H. Wright, of Gaffney City, S. C., to Miss Danie Suttle, of Shelby, N. C.

By Rev. T. W. Mellichamp, at the residence of the bride's mother, at 7 o'clock, P. M., December 12th, 1881, Mr. T. Duren of Columbia, to Miss Lilla Dunlap, of Fairfield County, S. C.

Died, in Laurens County, S. C., January 18th 1882, at the residence of its father, brother Frank Bailey, little Agatha Bailey, aged 1 year and 2 months. M. E. Broaddus.

At her home in Pickens County, S. C., on the 13th January 1882, Mrs. P. E. Willard, in her sixty-third year. Sister W. was born in Union County, S. C.,; her maiden name was Whiten; after her marriage settle in Pickens where she united with the Baptist Church at Liberty.... leaves an aged husband, several children... D. Weston Hiott.

On the 27th of November 1881, of Typhoid fever, Florence, daughter of Barham and Elizabeth Sparks, and wife of Wm. Nix, in her 25th year.

Departed this life, at the residence of Hon. C. G. White, in Tyler, Texas, on November 29th 1881, brother Jesse H. Chambers, in the seventy-seventh year of his age. Brother Chambers was born in Haywood County, North Carolina, March 13, 1805. When a young man he removed to Georgia, and was married in Columbia County, Georgia, to Miss Catharine D. Steed, January 5, 1837. He removed from Georgia to Texas in 1854 and soon after united with Ebenezer Church, Smith County....

Issue of February 9, 1882

Married on Wednesday, 25th ult., in the Baptist Church at Bennettsville, S. C., by Rev. J. A. W. Thomas, William W. Williams, Esq., of Greenville, and Miss Willie C. Hudson, daughter of Hon. J. H. Hudson, of Bennettsville.

On the 26th January 1882, at the residence of Mark Paden, in Woodstock, Cherokee County, Georgia, by Rev. L. C. Ezell, Miss Alice Paden to Dr. S. D. Parsons, of Martin's Depot, S. C.

Deacon John W. Nettles, after a very brief illness, at his residence near Greeleyville, Williamsburg County, S. C., passed from earth's sorrows on December 13, 1881, after forty-four years. He was born in Sumter County, S. C., and was baptized at Bethel Church by Rev. Isaac Nichols when fifteen years of age. He was united in marriage to Miss Bettie Garner, by Rev. N. Graham, and this estimable lady and seven children survive him. He was ordained as Deacon at Mt. Hope, Williamsburg county, in 1872, by Rev. J. L. Rollings. O. F. Gregory. Cheraw, Jan. 24, 1881. [sic]

Issue of February 16, 1882

Death of Mrs. Mary G. Harley... of Barnwell, S. c., about 4 o'clock Thursday afternoon. She had but the night before ministered at the bedside of a dear friend (Mrs. Aldrich) and saw her close her eyes in death. *Palmetto Yeoman, 11th instant.*

Issue of February 23, 1882

Sister Catherine Boynton fell asleep in Jesus on the 7th of December 1881, aged 72 years. She was baptized at Smyrna Baptist Church about fifty-five years ago, but at the time of her death was a member of Black Creek Church. Two sons and three daughters mourn her loss. F. O. S. C.

Married, by Rev. C. T. Anderson, on the 15th inst., at the residence of W. M. McGee, in Marion County, Miss L. H. Brown to C. F. Fry.

By the same at St. Stephens, on the 16th inst., S. F. Gore, daughter of Elder D. N. Gore, to Mr. W. J. Hughes, of North Carolina.

At the residence of the bride's mother, February 9th 1882, by Rev. J. J. H. Stoudenmire, Mr. N. Hilton and Miss Shuler Smith--both of Charleston County.

Issue of March 2, 1882

Married by Rev. T. A. Reid, assisted by Dr. Sloan, at the residence of Mrs. Dr. A. C. Hearst, on Feb. 21st, 1882, Hon. J. K. Vance, of Greenville, and Mrs. A. C. Hearst, of Abbeville, S. C.

On the 22nd of February 1882, at the residence of the bride's mother, near Pickens C. H., by Rev. D. Weston Hiott, Mr. Wm. P. Gaines, of Central, S. C., and Miss M. E., eldest daughter of Mrs. Abraham Hester.

At the residence of the bride's father, near Marion, S. C., on the 22d inst., by Rev. J. F. McMillan, Mr. Jas. R. Biggs, of North Carolina, to Miss Cornelia E. Spencer, daughter of Mr. J. F. Spencer, Sr.

On the 19th of February 1882, after six weeks of suffering from typhoid fever, little Maggie, daughter of Bro. and sister D. W. Dowtin, passed from earth to Heaven.... T. A. Reid.

Died, at Cedar Grove, S. C., on the 24th of February, 1882, Mrs. Nancy Phillips, in her 25th year. She was baptized into the fellowship of Cedar Grove Baptist Church by Rev. J. C. Hudson in 1873. J. H. A.

Issue of March 9, 1882

Married at the residence of the bride's father, by Rev. W. D. McMilan, on Feb. 12th, 1882, Mr. W. N. Dicks, Jr., to Miss P. E. Anderson. All of Barnwell County.

On January 17th, by W. B. Carson, Mr. Arnold Wilson to Miss Bettie Brant. All of Barnwell Co., S. C.

On February 2nd, by the same, Mr. R. H. Johnson, Jr., of Hampton, to Miss M. E. Bradley, of Barnwell.

On February 21st, by the same, Col. Geo. F. Crawley, of Charleston, to Miss Lou Davant, of Barnwell.

On Tuesday morning, February 28, 1882, in Lancaster village at the residence of the bride's father, Mr. J. B. Boyd, by Rev. G. W. Gardner, Mr. G. F. Payseur, of Cheraw, to Miss Mattie J. Boyd.

On Wednesday morning, March 1st, 1882, in Lancaster County, at the residence of the bride's father, Mr. W. R. Clanton, by Rev. G. W. Gardner, Mr. J. T. Sims and Miss Ross M. Clanton.

On February 28th, by Rev. A. C. Stepp, Mr. Charles Chapman and Miss Nannie E. Chandler, all of Greenville County.

Issue of March 16, 1882

Married, March 2nd, 1881, by W. J. Snider, at the residence of the bride's mother, W. B. Riley to Miss Barbary Utsey, all of Orangeburg County, S. C.

Departed this life on the 11th January 1882, Sister E. S. Munch. For the past forty-six years she was a member of the Baptist Church at Black Creek. An aged husband, two sons and three daughters mourn her loss. F. O. S. C.

Issue of March 23, 1882

Married at Mt. Arnon church, by Rev. Geo. N. Askew, on March 9th 1882, Mr. John Woodward to Miss Anna Bradley, all of Barnwell Co., S. C.

Died, in Greenville, S. C., March 10th, 1882, Miss Lucia M. Addison, in the eighteenth year of her age. [eulogy] C. M.

Died, on the 5th March, in Gaffney City, Neddie, aged 1 year, 7 months, and 3 days, little son of Mr. and Mrs. Nathan Lipscomb.

Issue of March 30, 1882

Memorial. Mr. Leroy Duncan was born in Spartanburg County, S. C., the 14th day of September A. D. 1836, and died at his home at Duncan's Station, on the Atlanta and Charlotte Air-Line Railway, November 20th, 1881. He joined the Abner's Creek Baptist Church about the year 1862, at which place he held his membership until a few years ago when he changed it to Middle Tiger, a new Baptist Church that he assisted in erecting near his residence, and beneath the shadows of which his remains are now reposing. W.

Issue of April 6, 1882

Married, March 28th, 1882, at 8:30 p. m., in Chester, S. C., Mr. Thomas N. Berry and Miss E. J. Kennedy, by Rev. R. W. Sanders.

March 30th, 1882, by Rev. J. H. Edwards, at the residence of the bride's father, near Rock Hill, Mr. Amaziah Hopper and Miss Mary Kidd, all of York County, S. C.

Died at his residence in Edgefield County, S. C., on the 16th August 1881, George Bell, in the 80th year of his age. when about 25 years old he united with the Rocky Creek Baptist Church. He was for several years a member of Dry Creek Church, by which he was licensed to preach the gospel. his latest years were spent as a member of the Batesburg Baptist Church.

Fell asleep in Jesus, at his residence in Sumter County, S. C., on Sunday evening, the 14th of August, 1881, Deacon Nelson Kerby, in the 78th year of his age. Bro. Kerby was baptized by Rev. W. H. Mahoney and received into the fellowship of Bethel Baptist Church, Welsh Neck Association in the year 1836. He has left a disconsolate widow and but one son and daughter.

Issue of April 13, 1882

Tribute of Respect to J. Toliver West, who departed this life on 9th March 1882 from Sabbath School at Sandy Spring, April 2, 1882.

Tribute of Respect to Lawrence O. Cochran, who died 28th March 1882, from church in conference at Lewisville.

Married, on the 22d March, 1882, at the residence of T. C. Martin, by Rev. H. M. Allen, Mr. A. D. Bellotte to Miss Kate Rowland, all of Central, S. C.

On the 4th of April 1882, at 7 p. m., at the house of the bride's father, by Rev. G. H. Carter, Mr. Robert Kay and Miss Lula Roe.

By Rev. N. N. Burton, on Thursday afternoon, April 6th, 1882, at the residence of Mr. B. C. Bryan, the bride's father, Miss Lulie J. Bryan, of Edgefield village, to Mr. L. D. Cullum, of Batesburg, S. C.

Died on the 19th of March 1882, Maggie McLemore, daughter of L. L. and C. A. McLemore, 11 months and 23 days old. A. McA. P.

Issue of April 20, 1882

Married at the residence of the bride's father, by R. M. Kirkley, Esq., on March 30th, 1882, Mr. J. L. Potter Simpson of Union County, N. C., to Miss Millie J. Blackwell, of Chesterfield County, S. C.

At the residence of the bride's father, March 30th, 1882, by Rev. J. J. H. Stoudenmire, Mr. M. Mims and Miss Mary Bilton, both of Charleston County, S. C.

Issue of April 27, 1882

Married by Rev. A. C. Stepp, April 9, 1882, at the residence of Dr. J. F. Coleman, Mr. P. H. E. Fuller and Miss Alla Barksdale. Both of Laurens County, S. C.

By Rev. A. C. Stepp, April 16, 1882, at the residence of Mrs. Jane Martin, Mr. James W. Thornton, of Knoxville, Tenn., and Miss Sallie E. Cooper, of Laurens county, S. C.

By Rev. B. S. Gaines, April 16, 1882, at the residence of the bride's father, Rev. H. M. Allen, of Spartanburg, to Miss Hewitt, of Central, S. C.

Issue of May 4, 1882

Married, on the 16th of April 1882, by Rev. B. S. Gaines, Rev. H. Milton Allen, of Spartanburg, and Miss Fannie Hewin, of Central, Pickens County, S. C.

On the 6th ult., at the residence of the bride's father, by Rev. D. West Hiott, Mr. Fred. Williams, of Anderson County, S. C., and Miss Mary, eldest daughter of James Lee, Esq., of Oconee County, S. C.

At Ridge Spring, S. C., April 20th, 1882, by Rev. G. F. Williams, Mr. James M. McGee, of Greenville, and Miss Mattie A. Merrit, daughter of W. A. Merrit, Esq.

At Piedmont, S. C., April 25th 1882, by Rev. M. McGee, Mr. J. B. Luquise, of Edgefield, to Miss Ella E. Calaham, daughter of W. M. Calaham of Piedmont.

Died, at the residence of Mrs. Newton Scott, in Anderson, on the 25th ult., little Weston Gary, son of W. C. and Ida Scott, in the third year of his age. His body was interred in the grave-yard at Mt. Pisgah Church on the 26th. D. Weston Hiott.

Died, on the 28th April, in Greenville County, little Selma, aged 1 year, 8 months and 18 days, only daughter of E. P. and Corrie A. Hudson. L. c. M.

Daniel H. Cork died at the old homestead in Fairfield County, S. C., March 20th 1882, in the 55th year of his age.... R. G. M.

Tribute of Respect. Walkersville, S. C., April 29, from Oak Grove Academy to James H. Carlisle Jr., who departed this life 21st April 1882.

Issue of May 11, 1882

Married by Rev. E. H. Cuttino, at the residence of the bride's father, March 28th 1882, Mr. James Winter and Miss Julia Fultz-- all of Charleston County.

By Rev. E. H. Cuttino, at the residence of the bride's father, April 23rd, 1882, Mr. George B. Davis and Miss Laura I. Bishop-- all of Charleston County, S.C.

Arville Legare Stiles, son of Rev. C. A. Stiles, perished at the explosion of the Steamer *Marion*, near Red Bluff, on the Wateree River, S. C., 28th April 1882, aged 15 years and 9 months. Misses Minnie, Nannie, Mattie Emma, and

Lizzie, four lovely young ladies, daughters of Capt. S. G. Henry, perished in the same catastrophe. C. A. Stiles.

Issue of May 25, 1882

Married by Rev. J. W. Perry, at the residence of the bride's father, April 27th, 1882, Mr. George Ridgill and Miss Rosa Bradham, all of Clarendon County, S. C.

By Rev. J. W. Perry, at the residence of the bride's father, May 11th, 1882, Mr. E. R. Lesesne, of Williamsburg County, S. C., and Miss Bettie M. Daniels, of Clarendon County, S. C.

On the 11th of May 1882, by the Rev. W. H. Ray, Mr. Samuel R. Tims and Miss Carrie McAlister, all of Anderson, S. C.

At the residence of the bride's father, on the 11th of May 1882, by D. Weston Hiott, Mr. John W. Carson and Miss S. C., second daughter of Capt. J. B. King, all of Anderson County, S. C.

By D. C. Hardin, May 24th 1882, at the residence of the bride's father, Rev. G. M. Rogers-- Mr. A. M. Rogers to Miss Ella J. Rogers, all of Anderson Co.

Died, on the 13th inst., Mary B., daughter of W. F. and M. T. Vaughan, born January 7, 1878.

Maj. John Sanders died in Chester County, the 10th of May, in the 73rd year of his age. It occurred in the family of his son-in-law, Maj. John W. Wilkes, where he had so pleasantly passed the last years of his life. L. C. H.

Issue of June 1, 1882

Died, recently, at his home in Abbeville County, S. C., Mr. George Galphin, his 68th year. Deceased was born and reared on Beech Island, S. C. Mr. Galphin has two sons who have entered the ministry. He leaves a devoted wife and several children. J. J. M.

Mrs. Rosannah F. Walker fell asleep in Jesus, May 20th 1882. She was a daughter of Mr. London Miles of Cross Anchor. Having been baptized by Rev. Thos. Ray in 1832, and married to John H. Walker the same year... J.C. H.

Died, at her residence near Greer's Station, in Greenville County, S. C., on the 25th of March 1882, Sister Martha J. Mattox, in the 30th year of her age. Two years ago she united with Pleasant Grove Baptist Church. She has left a loving husband and six little children....

Issue of June 8, 1882

Married by Rev. C. C. Fishburne, on Thursday, 27th April 1882, at Silverton, S. C., the residence of the bride's father, Maj. M. P. Howell, of Walterboro, S. C., and Miss Mittie H., second daughter of Dr. and Mrs. Isaac Foreman.

Charles Cullens was born March 23rd, 1806 and died at Piedmont, S. C., May 18th, 1882, in the 77th year of his age. He united with the Baptist Church at Turkey Creek in 1857... M. McGee

Issue of June 22, 1882

Married at the residence of Mr. John Lawton, near Lawtonville, S. C., on the evening of the 11th of June 1882, by Rev. A. B. Estes, Mr. B. W. Peeples and Miss Janette Caruthers, all of Hampton County, South Carolina.

Died, April 22d, 1882, in Charleston, S. C., in the eighty-fifth year of her age, Mrs. Susan North Thayer. She was the sister of the late Robert Brodie, Esq., for many years a deacon of the First, then of the Wentworth St., and then of the Citadel Square Baptist Church of Charleston; a sister of Mrs. Hartwell, whose son, the Rev. Dr. Boardman Hartwell, has been for many years a missionary to the Chinese; and the mother of Wm. Thayer, Esq., now a deacon of the Citadel Square Church....

Issue of July 13, 1882

Died, near White Pond, S. C., July 5th, 1882, Arthur Buist Harley, son of Mr. and Mrs. Preston Harley, aged 10 years.

Died, at his home in York County, S. C., on the 9th of June 1882, of paralysis, after an illness of four weeks, C. C. Gwin, in the 68th year of his age. He left a wife and seven children... member and officer of New Bethel Baptist Church. L. C. H.

Died, of consumption, at his residence in Barnwell, S. C., on the 19th June 1882, B. O. Sanders, in the 39th year of his age.... leaves wife and five children. Brother.

Issue of July 20, 1882

Double Funeral and Burial. John C. Willingham.. a few days ago, three of his children were stricken down with fever, and on Monday afternoon 4½ o'clock, July 20, 1882, his son Joseph L. Willingham, aged eight years, three months and eleven days, breathed his life. On the following morning, July 11th 1882, at 8½ o'clock, about sixteen hours after the first death, his son, Benjamin W. Willingham, aged eleven years, six months and twenty-five days, expired. A. B. Estes.

THE BAPTIST COURIER

Issue of July 27, 1882

Death of Rev. Wm. H. Lunn... at his home in Darlington County ,of fever, on Sunday, night, the 16th instant, aged twenty-one years. his friends in Greenville will remember him as a student of Furman University.... J. Q. Adams, Florence, S. C.

Issue of August 3, 1882

Died, at her home in Anderson County, the 25th ult., Mrs. Mary M., wife of Rev. W. H. Ray, in the 34th year of her age. She leaves a husband and eight little children, besides a mother and other relatives... member of the Easley Baptist Church. D. Weston Hiott.

Died, in Greenville, July 23d, ult., Lidie Estelle, infant daughter of Bro. W. K. and Sister H. E. Griffin, aged 8 months and 13 days.

Issue of August 10, 1882

Mary Mobley Mockbee, daughter of Bro. R. T. and sister Kate M. Mockbee, died in Chester County, July 17th 1882, at the residence of Dr. Thomas Douglass. She was seven years of age... R. W. S.

Issue of August 17, 1882

Davnor Elmore Chisholm, infant son of F. M. and S. E. Chisholm, died in Chester, S. C., july 12th, 1882, after long sickness... only 19 months of age.

On the morning of July 30th, the people of this community were saddened by the very sudden death of Rev. C. M. Porter... age of seventy-five years. W. H. Hartin. Ridgeway, S. C.

Issue of August 24, 1882

W. Rhett Kelsey, who was in his thirty-first year, died at his home in Chester Co., S. C., August 28th, 1882. He was a member of Hopewell Baptist Church... his wife, little babe, and brothers and sisters. G. W. Gardner.

Issue of August 31, 1882

Tribute of Respect from Blackville Baptist Church to John Jowers, who died at his residence, August 15th, 1882.

Died, in the town of Abbeville, on the evening of August 9th, after closing the day's work, Deacon Jacob Miller, in the sixty-sixth year of his age. He joined Mt. Moriah Baptist Church in the summer of 1842. He removed to Abbeville soon after the organization of our church here in 1871, and was made deacon. R. N. P.

Died, at the residence of her son-in-law, T. R. Potts, on the 20th of August 1882, Mrs. Larrett Osborn, of Greenville County, in the 67th year of her age.

She was the widow of Champion Osburn, and the daughter of Wm. Cox, and had lived a widow for nearly twenty years.

Issue of September 7, 1882

Died, in Charleston, S. C., September 1st, 1882, after a long and painful illness, Mrs. Kate R., wife of Mr. C. M. Patrick, in the 43rd year of her age. H. W. M.   White Pond, S. C.

Died, suddenly, of congestion, the 26th August, Ora Allein, daughter of her young parents, Mr. and Mrs. W. A. Harden, aged four years and six months. L. C. H.

Died, September 2nd, at the residence of Dr. Rembert, near Mayesville, S. C., little Clytie, only child of Rev. R. A. and Mrs. L. A. Sublett.... thirteen months and four days old. M. L. Ball

Mamie Eagerton fell asleep in Jesus at her father's residence near Lynchburg, S. C., on the 20th of August 1882. She was twelve years and nine months old... M. L. Ball.

Issue of September 21, 1882

Married by Rev. G. W. Gardner, Thursday afternoon, September 7, 1882, at the residence of the bride's father, Mr. William Knight, Mr. J. R. Williams and Miss Mary Knight, all of Lancaster.

Sept. 4th, by Rev. W. P. Smith, Mr. Willie Wofford, of Laurens County, and Miss Bonham West, of Spartanburg Co.

Departed this life, August 20th 1882, Mamie Eagerton, in Sumter County, at the aged of 13 years.

Died quite suddenly, on the 7th inst., at her home near Silverton, S. C., Mrs. Lucy Harley, wife of Deacon A. M. Harley, and member of Matlock Baptist Church. J. J. M.

Died recently at his home in Barnwell County, Mr. John Pettus, aged 83 years. J. J. M.

At Harrisburg, Abbeville County, S. C., on the night of the 31st of August 1882, Mrs. Mary L. Harris passed from earth to heaven. She was born October 18, 1827. Was baptized into the fellowship of the Horeb Baptist Church on 9th September 1852, by the late Rev. James Chiles. She was the relict of the late Capt. Harris, who himself was a consistent member of the horeb Church. Three sons and two daughters mourn her departure. T. A. R.

Died, near Blackville, S. C., August 27, 1882, Mr. John M. Zorn, aged 27 years....

Died, at the residence of her husband in Clinton, S. C., August 28th 1882, Mrs. Clara Duckett, aged 36 years. She leaves a devoted husband and five motherless daughters....

Issue of September 28, 1882

Departed this life on the 15th of September, 1882, Miss Ida C. Freeland, eldest daughter of Mr. S. E. and Mary P. Freeland, in the 22d year of her age. [eulogy] ... member of Plum Branch Baptist Church in Edgefield County. R. W. Seymour, Jr.

Issue of October 5, 1882

Married on September 20, at the residence of the bride's mother, by Rev. J. D. Mahon, Mr. T. E. Dye and Miss L. Y. D. Mobley, all of Fairfield.

On Thursday evening, Sept. 28,1882, at the residence of John C. Strother, Esq., the bride's father, by Rev. N. N. Barton, Dr. Chas. B. Cowan, of Due West, S. C., and Miss Popie B. Strother, of Edgefield.

Died, September 21st 1882, at his home in Wedgefield, S. C., Mr. James Harvin, in the 65th year of his age. The deceased was born in Clarendon County, S. C., where he lived until he was grown... united with Calvary Baptist Church.... F. C. H.

Issue of October 12, 1882

Married on Sunday, 24th of September, at the residence of the bride's father, by Rev. D. W. Hiott, Mr. J. H. Brown and Miss Mamie McCord, all of Liberty, Pickens County.

In Wadesboro, N. C., on the 4th inst., by Rev. B. G. Covington, Mr. Oscar L. Bass, of Marion County, S. C., and Miss Cornelia E. Covington.

On Wednesday, October 4th, 1882, at the residence of the bride's mother, by Rev. J. Q. Adams, Mr. F. K. Brand and Miss Rebecca E. Johnson, all of Marion.

At Allendale, S. C., on the morning of October 4, 1882, by Rev. A. B. Estes, assisted by Rev. Joseph A. Lawton, Mr. A. G. Chewning, of Washington, D. C., and Miss E. Annie Estes, of Allendale, S. C.

By Rev. D. Weston Hiott, on the 7th ult., at the residence of Mrs. C. Orr, Mr. W. C. Wyatt and Mrs. S. A. Clements, all of Anderson County, S. C.

Died, at his home in Chester County, S. C., September 15, 1882, Mr. Tyre Lee, aged 56 years... member of the Baptist Church, holding his membership first at Woodward, but for seven years at Blackstock. He leaves a wife, ten children, and many friends.

Died, at Ridge Spring, S. C., October 3, 1882, after an illness of 52 days, Albert Woodfin, son of Rev. G. F. and E. V. Williams, aged 4 years, 5 months and 21 days.

Issue of October 19, 1882

Married at the residence of Mr. William Jeffers, October 1st, 1882, by Rev. J. J. H. Stoudenmire, Mr. O. D. Balentine and Miss Vic. Chubb, both of Berkeley Co., S. C.

On the 12th inst., at the residence of the bride's father, Mr. Allan Clements, by Rev. J. K. Mendenhall, Mr. Jesse T. French and Miss Alene Clements.

On the 4th inst., at the residence of the bride in Barnwell, S. C., by Rev. John G. Williams, Rev. J. C. Browne, of Aiken, to Mrs. M. A. Ray.

October 5th, at the residence of the bride's mother, by Rev. Wm. Henry Strickland, Capt. Edgar T. Kemp, of Greenville, and Miss Mollie A. Johnson, of Abbeville County.

Died, in Greenville, S. C., Oct. 2d, 1882, Mrs. Lillie G. Reilly, in the 33d year of her age. She was a daughter of Wm. Goldsmith, a deacon of the Greenville Baptist Church, and became the wife of P. H. Reilly, October 21st 1874. [eulogy] C. M.

Died, at his residence in Barnwell County, S. C., on the 22d September last, Mr. G. F. Priester, in the 60th year of his age. He was a member of the Great Salkehatchie church.... J. F. B.

Died, in Hunt County, Texas, September 27th, 1882, Dr. O. G. Chapman. He was a native of Spartanburg County, S. C., where many relatives and friends now mourn.... He left a widow and five children. I. W. W.

Issue of October 26, 1882

Died, at his residence in Laurens County, S. C., August 16, 1882 W. A. Fuller, aged 70 years. The deceased was a member of Beaverdam church. He leaves two sons, a daughter and wife....

Died, at his residence in Laurens County, S. C., October 13th, 1882, Harrison Fuller, aged 65. He too was a member of Beaverdam church... his children recently lost their mother, Mrs. Lizzie Fuller...

Died at his home in Chester County, June 19th, 1882, Mr. James Sweat, aged about 80 years. He had long been a member of the Baptist church, first a Woodward, and afterwards at Mount Zion.

Died, at Chester, Oct. 14, 1882, little Katie, daughter of mr. and Mrs. A. M. Manning, aged 2 years and 9 months.

Also, at Chester, Oct. 15, 1882, little Katie McFadden, infant daughter of Mr. and Mrs. John C. McFadden, aged 18 months. R. W. S.

Died, at his home in Darlington County, S. C., October 2, 1882, Isaiah Lunn, aged 67 years and 21 days.... membership first at Swift Creek, and after at Ebenezer. He leaves an aged wife and five children... J. Q. A.

Issue of November 2, 1882

Married, in this city, at the residence of Col. A. S. Duncan, Tuesday evening, October 25, 1882, by Rev. W. H. Strickland, Mr. Charles T. Watkins, of Richmond, Va., and Miss Emma C. Hill, of Greenville.

Died, near McCormick, S. C., on Oct. 9, 1882, Mrs. M. V., wife of Deacon Robert Henderson, aged 22. She was baptized into the fellowship of the Bethany Church by Elder Trapp when about ten years old. She left two children, one two years old and an infant three weeks old... T. A. Reid.

After an illness of nearly three weeks with typhoid fever, Walter S. Brice, eldest son of Mr. and Mrs. R. W. Brice, died in Fairfield County, S. c., Oct. 22, 1882, aged 18 years, 8 months and 5 days. The deceased was a member of Blackstock Baptist Church... his remains were laid in the cemetery at the Concord Presbyterian Church. R. W. S.

Issue of November 9, 1882

Married on Thursday, Oct. 26, 1882, at the residence of the bride's father, by Rev. J. Q. Adams, Mr. Charles W. Wilson and Miss Annie Sanders, all of Marion.

October 25, 1882, by Rev. D. W. Thomasson, Mr. Robert G. Wallace and Miss Lucy C. Spearman, both of Newberry County.

On the 1st inst., at the residence of the bride's father, by Rev. D. Weston Hiott, Mr. Zack Gober, of Charleston, S. C., and Miss Ella Y. Willard, of Liberty, S. C.

At Mt. Willing, Edgefield County, S. C., Oct. 26, 1882, by Rev. A. J. S. Thomas, Mr. Joseph A. West to Miss Betty Aycock.

Died at his home in Richland County, S. C., Sept. 25, 1882, Dr. M. R. Clark, in the 64th year of his age. He was a patriot who had served his country in the Florida, Mexican, and Confederate wars, and was permanently injured by wounds received at the taking of the City of Mexico. He joined the church in 1860,while residing in Mississippi,and removed his membership to the Good hope Church, in his native county, subsequent to the war. He leaves a wife and children.

On the 5th of October, Dr. T. S. Lafitte, died at his home in Barnwell County, S. C. He was a consistent and useful member of Smyrna Baptist Church, and had long been our clerk. W. B. Carson.

Died, at the residence of his father, Sept. 11, 1882, Willie Milam, in the 22d year of his age. Willie had been a member of Huntsville Church eight years. He leaves a devoted father and mother....

Issue of November 16, 1882

Departed this life, Sept. 29th, 1882, at his residence in Kershaw county, S. C., Bro. John Higgins, aged 83 years, 11 months and 3 days. Bro. Higgins was married in June 1828 to Miss Jane Scott, daughter of the Rev. Mr. Scott, of South Carolina. He united with the Colonel's Creek Baptist Church in 1850, and was soon after chosen as deacon.... left wife and daughters.

Died, at her home near Batesburg, Nov. 10th, 1882, Mrs. Mary Norris, wife of Rev. J. M. Norris. A. J. S. T. Batesburg, Nov. 11, 1882.

Issue of November 23, 1882

Married by Rev. J. W. Hutchins, at his residence, Easley, S. C., October 8th, 1882, Mr. Robert Smith of Gainesville, Ga., and Miss Carrie Whitmire, of Greenville, S. C.

November 9th 1882, at the residence of the bride's mother, in Greenville County, S. C., by Rev. J. Walter Daniel, Mr. William H. Cantrell, of Spartanburg County, S. C., and Miss Missouri Terry.

At the residence of the bride's father, Mr. A. E. Rice, on Thursday evening, the 16th instant, by the Rev. J. S. Murry, Mr. W. Andrew King and Miss S. Theodosia Rice-- all of Anderson County.

By Rev. John D. Wilson, at his residence in Pickens County, on the 10th instant, Mr. Balus Banks and Miss Matilda Kay, daughter of Pleasant Kay, Esq., all of Pickens county.

By the same, on Sunday, 12th inst., at the residence of Rufus Meek, Mr. R. M. Alexander and Miss S. J. O'Bryant, daughter of Mr. Carr O'Bryan, all of Pickens County.

Died, at the residence of his father, Harrison Earle, Esq., at 7 P. M., October 31st, Richard I. Earle, in the 16th year of his age.

Died, at Campbellton, Barnwell County, S. C., October 10th 1882, Ellan, the first born of William J. and Sallie Leland Sanders, aged eight months and fifteen days.

Died, near Mar's Bluff, Marion County, S. C., Sept. 8th ,1882, Samuel Richard Richardson, aged 12 years, 6 months and 18 days. This dear child was born in Sumter, Feb. 21st 1870.... let a grandmother, step-mother, a sister and cousin.

Did at his home in Newberry County, S. C., October 18th, 1882, W. Hillery Suber, aged 43 years. he had been Deacon of Enoree Baptist Church for many years.

Deacon Mason C. Henderson, born February 7th 1807; married, first to Miss Elizabeth Dodson, May 1829, by Rev. James Wilson, by whom he was also baptized on the 22nd of October 1831, into the fellowship of the Walnut Grove Church, Saluda Association. On the 22nd of October 1853, he was ordained deacon by the fellow brethren, who constituted the Presbytery: Rev. V. Young, Rev. James Kay, H. Clark, L. Barmore, and A. H. McGee. Bro. Henderson was married the second time on the 26th of May 1867, by Rev. Amaziah Rice, to Miss Carrie Fisher, of Anderson County, S. C., whom he laves to mourn his death, for on the 27th of October, he fell asleep in Jesus. He had a family of eight children by the first marriage, none by the second, three of whom survive him. B. F. Miller.

Issue of November 30, 1882

Married at the residence of Mr. Wm. Merchant, the bride's father, on Thursday evening, November 16th, 1882, by Rev. N. N. Burton, Mr. Henry W. Farr, of Pickens, to Miss Mattie E. Merchant, of Edgefield County, S. C.

Issue of December 7, 1882

Married Nov. 23, 1882, at the residence of the bride's father, Mr. Alfred Dunn, by Rev. R. R. Vann, Mr. F. S. Hook, of Lexington, and Miss Sallie Dunn.

At the residence of Mr. A. Mauldin, Easley, Oct. 19, by Rev. J. W. Hutchins, Mr. Absalom Roper and Miss Nancy Mauldin.

At the residence of the bride's father, in Chester, Nov. 28, 1882, by Rev. R. W. Sanders, Mr. M. A. Carpenter and Miss Mamie Curtis, all of Chester.

Sunday morning, Nov. 26, 1882, by Rev. A. Buist, Mr. W. W. Limerick and Miss Mamie E. Matthis, both of Barnwell County.

On Wednesday, Nov. 25th, 1882, by the Rev. C. A. Stiles, Mr. W. D. Clark and Miss Belle Radcliffe, all of Richland County, S. C.

On Nov. 14, 1882, near Townville, by Rev. D. Weston Hiott, Mr. G. Newton Williams and Miss Mary V., youngest daughter of Mr. W. B. Compton, all of Anderson County, S. C.

On Nov. 15, 1882, by Rev. D. D. Dantzler, Mr. Pinckney A. King and Miss Eva P. Howle, both of Darlington County, S. C.

At the residence of bride's father, Mr. Paul Sharp, Thursday, Nov.30, 1882, by Rev. D. W. Key, Mr. Fletcher Joiner and Miss Nola Sharp, all of Lewisville, S. C.

Died at Batesburg, S. C., Nov. 22, 1882, Bessie, daughter of Captain Uriah X. and Minerva N. Gunter, aged three years and seven days. A. J. S. T.

Issue of December 14, 1882

Married at the residence of the bride's mother, Mrs. L. C. Bolling, by Rev. Wm. Henry Strickland, on the morning of the 30th ult., Mr. D. H. Irvine, of Florida, to Miss Rosa Bolling, of Greenville.

At the residence of Mr. Joe Chambers, the bride's father, in Union County, S. C., on Wednesday evening, Nov. 29th, 1882, by Rev. A. McA. Pittman, Mr. John Spears to Miss Annie Chambers.

On Sunday afternoon, Nov. 12th, 1882, at the residence of the bride's father, by Rev. A. Buist, Mr. T. P. Scott to Miss Maggie Owens--all of Aiken County.

November 20th, 1882, by Rev. W. P. Smith, Mr. John Jennings, to Miss Laura Reeves, both of Spartanburg County.

On Thursday, Nov. 23d, 1882, at the residence of the bride's father, Rev. W. D. Rice, of Graham's, S. C., by Rev. J. F. Buist, Mr. H. A. Hoyt, of Sumter, S. C., to Miss Jaunita [sic] Rice, of Graham's, S. C.

Issue of December 21, 1882

Deacon Stanmore Butler Brooks, of Mt. Moriah Church, Abbeville Association, after fifty years' cheerful Christian life, in which he served his generation, his children's and his grandchildren's, rests from his labors. J. S. J.

Died, near Pineville, N. C., on the 28th ult., at the age of 32 years, Mrs. M. M. E. Jennings, wife of Mr. L. Jennings, leaving a husband, six children and many friends. She was a member of Flint Hill Church. B. G. Covington.

Issue of January 4, 1883

Married on Dec. 24, 1882, by D. Weston Hiott, Mr. James M. Moseley and Miss Nannie Thompson, all of Anderson County.

By the same, Dec. 21, 1882, Mr. Lawrence Thompson and Miss Essie A., eldest daughter of Peter R. Brown, Esq., all of Anderson County.

By the same, Dec. 17, 1882, Mr. Ellis Tripp and Miss Mary J., daughter of Mr. John B. Orr, all of Anderson County.

By Rev. W. D. McMillan, on the afternoon of Dec. 24, 1882, at the residence of the bride's father, L. M. Ott, Esq., near Branchville, Mr. W. T. Connelly of Barnwell County, and Miss Mary E. Ott, of Orangeburg County.

At the residence of the bride's mother, on the evening of Dec. 21, 1882, by Rev. E. H. Cuttino, Mr. William Gelzer and Miss Cornelia Singletary, all of Berkeley County, S. C.

On the evening of Dec. 20, 1882, at the residence of the bride's mother, by Rev. F. O. S. Curtis, Mr. Joseph Ike and Miss Rosa O'Bryan, all of Colleton County.

On Tuesday, Dec. 19, 1882, at Blackshear, Ga., by Rev. A. B. Estes, of Allendale, S. C., Mr. Andrew B. Estes, Jr., and Miss M. L. Branlley, both of Blackshear.

On the 15th of November 1882, in the Marion Baptist Church, by Rev. T. P. Lide, Mr. Evan P. Lide, of Darlington, and Miss Annie E. Reaves, of Marion.

On Wednesday, Dec. 20, 1882, at Tomassee, Oconee County, S. C., at the residence of Mrs. Cornelia Jones, the bride's mother, by Rev. Francis P. Mullaly, D. D., W. J. Beard, Esq., of Sumter, S. C. and Miss Hannah G. Jones.

On the 19th ult., by Rev. Wm. Henry Strickland, at the residence of the bride's mother, Mr. A. C. McMahan and Miss Alma M. Whitmire, all of Greenville.

On the 26th ult., by Rev. Wm. Henry Strickland, at the Hon. W. R. Berry's, Mr. Z. Frank Foster, of Greenville, and Miss M. J. Berry, of Pickens County.

At Mr. Allen's, the bride's father, by Rev. W. H. Hartin, on the evening of December 7th, Mr. Henry Haynes and Miss Allen, all of Fairfield, S. C.

On the 20th of December, in Barnwell County, S. C., by Rev. W. B. Carson, Mr. J. C. Keel and Mrs. R. S. Killingsworth.

On December 6th 1882, at the residence of the bride's mother, by Rev. J. Q. Adams, Mr. Geo. Lewis of Darlington, and Miss Martha Reddick, of Marion.

On Thursday, December 28th 1882, at the home of the bride's father, by Rev. J. Q. Adams, Mr. Dan'l S. Yates, of Marion, and Miss Martha Rose, of Darlington.

On the 20th of December 1882, by Rev. T. V. Gowan, Mr. James H. Simmons and Miss Barbara Cook, all of Spartanburg County, S. C.

On the 21st of December 1882, by Rev. T. V. Gowan, Mr. Joseph K. Hall and Miss Mary E. Ramseur, all of Spartanburg County, S. C.

On the 24th of December 1882, by Rev. T. V. Gowan, Mr. B. F. Staggs, and Miss M. E. Collins, all of Spartanburg County, S. C.

On the evening of the 20th December by Rev. John Stout, at the residence of the bride's father, Mr. C. H. Race, Mr. R. D. Womack and Miss Bessie Race, all of Society Hill, S. C.

At noon of the 27th December, in the Baptist church of Cheraw, S. C., by the Rev. John Stout, Mr. J. T. White of norfolk, Va., and Miss Hattie L. Evans, of Cheraw.

At 9 a. m., of the 28th December, by the Rev. John Stout, at the residence of the bride's father, Mr. Theodore Sompayrac, Society Hill, S. C., Mr. H. P. Ingham of Jacksonvlile, Fla., and Miss Meta Sompayrac.

Mrs. Lizzie Wright, wife of Mr. J. P. Wright, fell asleep in Jesus, October 18th, 1882. She was born January 1st, 1834, united with Little Stevens' Creek Church in the great revival of 1852.... Just one month after the daughter was called to her eternal home, the mother, Mrs. Sarah Bolton, relict of the late Mr. Joseph Bolton, who after her widowhood went to dwell with her daughter and her son-in-law, Mr. J. P., Wright, followed her child... She was born July 31st, 1805, and died Nov. 18th, 1882. She was baptized by Dr. Basil Manly at Stephen's Creek Church in early life....

Died at her home in Marion County, S. C., on the 6th day of October 1882, Mrs. Elizabeth Jones, in the 87th year of her age. She subject of this notice was born in Marino County on the 26th of November 1795. She was received into the fellowship of the Antioch Church by letter in February 1847....

Issue of January 11, 1883

Married on the 11th of November, 1882,by Rev. J. L. Rollins, at the residence of Mrs. G. A. Williams, Mr. Francis H. Fenters and Miss Elizabeth Williams-- all of Georgetown County, S. C.

On the 20th of December, 1882, by Rev. J. L. Rollins, at the residence of Col. Sam. Cooper, Mr. B. J. Byrd and Miss M. B. Cooper.

On the 20th of December 1882, by Rev. J. L. Rollins, at the residence of Col. Sam. Cooper, Mr. John B. Wooten, of North Carolina, and Miss Ida B. Cooper, of Williamsburg County.

On the 28th of December, 1882, by Rev. J. L. Rollins, at the residence of Mrs. G. A. Williams, Mr. John T. Fenters, and Miss E. Williams-- all of Georgetown County.

On the 7th of December 1882, by Rev. S. T. Russell, at the residence of Mrs. R. H. Lee, Mr. A. H. McCullough and Miss Florence I. Lee.

On the 28th of December, by Rev. S. T. Russell, at the residence of Mr. W. A. Lowndes, Mr. D. N. Kellehan and Miss A. B. Hodge.

On the 2d of January 1882, by Rev. S. T. Russell, at the residence of R. H. Kellehan, Mr. W. J. Brockington and Miss L. D. Brown.

On the 31st of December, 1882, by N. N. Hughes, Esq., at the residence of the officiating magistrate, Mr. John Q. Gibson and Miss Laura A. Clark--both of Greenville County.

On the 25th of December, 1882, by Rev. G. W. Gardner, in Lancaster Village, at the residence of the officiating minister, Mr. Reese Caskey and Miss Jennie Vanlandingham.

On the 28th of December 1882, by Rev. E. H. Cuttino, at the residence of Mr. A. D. Hare, Mr. Adington Jones and Miss Mary Hyrne-- all of Berkeley Co., S. C.

On the 2d of January 1883, by Rev. D. Weston Hiott, at his residence, Mr. W. A. Simpson, and Miss Sallie J. Long, all of Anderson County, S. C.

On the 28th of December 1882, by Rev. W. D. McMillan, at the residence of the bride's father, Jno. C. Reeves, Esq., in Branchville, Mr. U. G. Bryant, of Colleton County, and Miss Mary Julia Reeves, of Orangeburg County.

On the 14th of December 1882, by Rev. A. C. Stepp, Mr. Albert B. Kay and Miss Laura Clardy, all of Laurens Co., S. C.

On the 16th of December 1882, by Rev. A. C. Stepp, Mr. John Allen Arnold and Miss Susan Anna Jones, all of Laurens County, S. C.

On the 28th of December 1882, by Rev. A. C. Stepp, Mr. Wm. Austin Anderson and Miss Laura E. McPherson--all of Laurens County, S. C.

On the 28th of December, 1882, by Rev. F. C. Jeter, Mr. T. D. Lee and Miss Victoria Phillips, all of Union County, S. C.

Departed this life at the old Kincaid Mansion, on Cedar Creek, Fairfield County, S. C., on the 8th November, Mrs. Emma Eugenia Anderson, wife of Mr. Thomas Anderson, and sister of Mrs. Frank McBee, of Greenville... member of the little River Baptist Church.

Mrs. Sallie Etolia Duckett, wife of Thos. B. Duckett, and daughter of Dr. S. S. and Mrs. Permelia Knight, was born January 21st 1862, united with the New Harmony Baptist Church when about twelve years of age; was married to Thomas B. Duckett, December 27th 1881, and died at her home in Laurens County, S. C., August 21st 1882.

Issue of January 18, 1883

Tribute of Respect from Rosemary Baptist Church, November 4th, 1882, to W. T. Blanton.

Married on the 21st of December 1882, by Rev. J. W. Hutchins, at the residence of the bride's parents, in Pickens County, Mr. Forest Algood and Miss Annie Bowen.

On the 20th of January 1883, by Rev. T. W. Mellichamp, at the residence of the bride's father, Winnsboro, S. C., Mr. Wm. H. Willingham and Miss Lula Romedy, all of Fairfield County, S. C.

On the 21st of December 1882, by Rev. D. W. Cuttino, at the residence of the bride's mother, in Clarendon County, Mr. C. P. McKnight and Miss Loula Cuttino-- all of Clarendon County.

On the 14th of December 1882, by Rev. T. M. Galphin, at the residence of the bride's mother, Mr. Jehu W. Barnes and Miss M. Ella Jones--all of Orangeburg County.

Mrs. E. B. Whatley was born in Barnwell County, S. C., on the 11th day of March 1803, and died at her home in the city of Greenville, on the 12th day of December 1882, being in her 79th year. In the presence of her physician Dr. Earle, her daughters Miss Julia and Mrs. H. H. Hickman, and one of her grandchildren, she quietly fell asleep in Jesus. [eulogy] A. W. Lamar.

Issue of January 25, 1883

Tribute of Respect from Mt. Pleasant Baptist Church, January 13th 1883, to Brother E. W. Horne.

Mrs. Jemima Brooker died on the 21st of December 1882, at her grand-son's, Mr. Walter Brooker, near Blackville, aged ninety-four years. She was the wife of Rev. John Brooker, who died more than twenty years ago, fellow=laborer with Hansford Duncan and Darling Peeples, and mother of Rev. William Brooker, who died about four years ago. She was the mother of ten, five of whom, with grandchildren, great- and great-great-grandchildren survive her. Jno. G. Williams.

Issue of February 1, 1883

Married by Rev. Thomas Looper on the 18th January 1883, Mr. Marion Freeman and Miss Martha Williams, all of Pickens, S. C.

By Rev. W. D. Rice, at the residence of the bride's father, on the 14th January 1883, Mr. Benj. Chasereau and Miss M. Copeland, all of Barnwell County, S. C.

By Rev. J. B. Adger, D. D., at the residence of the bride's father, on Wednesday, January 10th 1883, Mr. W. W. Russell, of Anderson County, and Miss Minnie J. Edwards, of Orangeburg, S. C.

By Rev. J. W. Hutchins, at the residence of Mr. M. King, on the 16th January 1883, Mr. Robt. F. Ariail and Miss Susan E. Barrett, of Pickens County, S. C.

At the residence of the bride's father, on Wednesday, January 17th, 1883, by Rev. N. N. Burton, Mr. L. B. Jones of Columbia, S. c., and Miss Gelma F. Sawyer, of Aiken County.

December 21, 1882, by Rev. J. E. Rodgers, Mr. T. J. Debruhl and Miss S. A. Hough, all of Kershaw County.

December 24, 1882, by Rev. J. E. Rodgers, Mr. W. J. Newman and Miss E. G. Gardner, all of Kershaw County.

December 28, 1882, by Rev. J. E. Rodgers, Mr. F. J. Smith and Miss E. F. Barnes, all of Kershaw County.

January 3, 1883, by Rev. J. E. Rodgers, Mr. C. S. Boykin, of Sumter, and Miss M. E. Dorrity, of Kershaw.

January 3, 1883, by Rev. J. E. Rodgers, Mr. A. K. Lee and Miss M. F. Corbett, of Kershaw County.

Died on the 19th January, aged 32 years, Edmund W. Lawton, a beloved member of the Allendale Church and Sunday School. Last August his wife died, leaving three little orphans. Three other children preceded them to their home in heaven. J. A. L.

Issue of February 8, 1883

Married by Rev. R. Furman Whilden, Jan. 28th, 1883, at the residence of the bride's mother, Mr. Perry Odom, and Miss Martha, daughter of Mrs. Sarah Waldrop.

Issue of February 15, 1883

Died, December 11th, 1882, Rev. John Williams, in the seventy-first year of his age. He was baptized December 20th 1833, and lived a devoted, pious Christian's life. J. A. B. Williston, S. C., Feb. 8th 1883.

Issue of February 22, 1883

Married at the residence of the bride's father, Dec. 27, 1882, by Rev. C. T. Scaife, Mr. James Roy and Miss Janie Brandon, all of Union County, S. C.

At the residence of Mr. Adam Goudelock, on Jan. 16, 1883, by Rev. C. T. Scaife, Mr. John Foster and Miss Bettie Goudelock, all of Union County.

At the residence of the bride's mother, Feb. 6, 1883, by Rev. C. T. Scaife, Mr. W. J. D. Williams, of York County, and Miss Lizzie Duncan, of Union County, S. C.

In Darlington County, Jan. 31, 1883, by Rev. A. McA. Pittman, Mr. J. H. Bozeman and Miss A. H. Blackman.

Feb. 3, 1884, by Rev. J. W. Hutchins, Mr. E. D. Whitmire and Miss Sallie Moon, all of Easley, Pickens County, S. C.

In Darlington, S. C., Feb. 14th 1883, by Rev. A. McA. Pittman, Mr. H. L. Beck and Miss J. E. Byrd.

On the evening of the 15th inst., at the residence of the bride's mother, by the Rev. C. C. Brown, Mr. W. J. Young of Rafting Creek, and Miss Annie White, of Sumter.

On the 31st of January, little Annie Lou, youngest daughter of Mr. and Mrs. Thos Roberds. She was born May 28th 1881, at her father's residence, and died January, 1883, at her uncles in Lawtonville, S. C.

Issue of March 1, 1883

Married on the 15th February 1883, by Rev. J.D. Mahon, at the residence of the bride's mother, Mr. Thos. B. Chapman and Miss Carrie Bell Price-- all of Fairfield County.

On the 14th of February 1883, by Rev. J. D. Mahon, assisted by the Rev. W. W. Mills, at the residence of the bride's parents, Mr. Robt. Y. Clowney and Miss Sallie S. Crosby-- all of Fairfield County,

On the 22nd of February 1883, by Rev. J. H. Mahon at the residence of the bride's parents, Mr. M. C. Boulware and Miss Belle Stephenson-- all of Fairfield County.

Tribute of Respect from Big Stephens' Creek Baptist Church to A. J. Hammond.

Issue of March 8, 1883

Mrs. Fannie Garden Furman died last Sunday afternoon at the residence of her husband, Charles M. Furman, Esq. of this city. She was an only daughter of Alester Garden, of Sumter County, who died in her early childhood [eulogy].

Married at the home of the bride's father in Cleaveland County, N. C., by Rev. R. W. Sanders, Feb. 28, 1883, Mr. J. Harvey Smith, of Chester, S. C., and Miss Alice Graham.

At the residence of the bride's father, Mr. Allen Shuler, Feb. 28, 1883, by Rev. D. W. Key, Mr. Manly Hunkerpiller and Miss Ida Shuler, all of Orangeburg County.

Feb. 27, 1883, by Rev. S. A. Gary, Captain James A. Griffin and Miss Harriet C. Singleton, daughter of Rev. W. B. Singleton, all of Pickens County.

At the residence of the bride's father, Mr. W. J. Hix, Feb. 27, 1883, by Rev. G. H. Carter, Mr. Joe W. Shelor, of Walhalla, and Miss Lizzie Hix, of Fair Play.

Issue of March 15, 1883

Death of a Prominent Citizen. Dr. Samuel S. Marshall, of Greenville, was killed by an accidental discharge of a gun in the hands of his son, John B.

Marshall, whom he was visiting near Greenville, Fla. She sad accident took place on Monday, March 5th... [account] His remains were brought to Greenville, and the funeral took place at the Episcopal Church on Sunday last. Dr. Marshall was a native of Abbeville County, and many years of his life were spent in Florida. At the time of his death he was President of the Greenville Oil Mill.

Departed this life after a short but painful illness, Robert L. Williams, formerly of Colleton County, but for the past few years a resident of Barnwell County, in the 31st year of his age... 28th February 1883. W. D. R.

Died, in Pendleton, S. C., February 22nd, 1883, John Calhoun Cherry. Mr. Cherry was born in 1826 at Cherry Hill, near Old Pendleton C. H. he served as a soldier in the Confederate army. In August 1877, he became a useful member of the Pendleton Baptist Church....

Issue of March 22, 1883

Married on Thursday, March 15th, 1883, by H. M. Allen, at the residence of the bride's mother, Mr. B. F. Blackerby of Greenville, and Miss Lucy Brock, of Pickens County.

At the home of the bride's uncle, Mr. W. B. Gue, March 4th 1883, by Rev. S. B. Sawyer, Mr. Wade M. Gue, of Orangeburg County, S. C., and Miss Lucinda Lincoln, of Charleston County, S. C.

Died, at his residence, in Cleaveland Township, Greenville County, S. C., Mr. S. E. McJunkin, aged 69 years and seven months. He was buried in the family grave yard. His funeral was preached by Rev. E. J. Mullinax... He was a member of the South River Baptist Church. He leaves a wife and seven children.

Issue of March 29, 1883

Married by Rev. A. C. Stepp, on the 25th of March 1883, Mr. D. Fletcher Ballentine and Miss Mattie V. Murff, both of Laurens County.

At the residence of Mr. John Thompson, by Rev. J. L. Rollins, on 11th February, Mr. Wm. Coleman and Miss Ida Jones.

On 22d March, at the residence of the bride, by Rev. J. L. Rollins, Mr. J. F. Chandler and Miss Elizabeth Hanna. All of Williamsburg.

Died, in Liberty, Mo., March 4th, 1883, Mrs. R. A. Chambliss, wife of Rev. A. W. Chambliss, D. D., and daughter of Capt. Joseph Ellerby, in the 70th year of her age. Sister Chambliss was born in Chesterfield District, South Carolina, June 26th, 1813. She united with the Society Hill Baptist Church, South Carolina, in September 1829 and was baptized by Rev. Mr. Dossey. [eulogy] B. G. T.

Died at his residence in Laurens County, S. C., Deacon Abel Lyles, in the 70th year of his age. Deacon Lyles has been for more than fifty years a consistent member of Upper Duncan's Creek Church, and for thirty years a Deacon. He leaves a wife and several children. Pastor.

Issue of April 5, 1883

Married, Sunday afternoon, March 18, 1883, at New Hope Church, Lancaster County, by Rev. G. W. Gardner, Mr. Alick Cauthen and Miss Emily Caskey.

At the residence of the bride's father, by Rev. H. Lecroy, on Tuesday, March 29th, 1883, Mr. William Matthews, of Barnwell Co., S. C., and Miss Sarah E., youngest daughter of Rev. J. A. Seigler, of Aiken Co., S. C.

Issue of April 12, 1883

Rev. Silas Knight. The papers bring us the sad intelligence that Brother Knight is Dead. He had been in declining health for more than a year, and had lived beyond his three score years and ten, being about seventy-nine years old. The history of his ministerial life is interwoven with the history of the Reedy River Association. He entered the ministry as a Licentiate according to the Minutes in 1834.... spent his whole life in what is now Laurens County, S. C. He raised a large family of children, and two of his sons studied medicine and became practicing physicians, Dr. S. S. Knight, near Cannon's Store in this County, and Dr. James Knight, who commanded a cavalry company during the war, and who died shortly after the surrender. Silas Knight was twice married, but all of his children except one, were the fruits of his first marriage. He raised his family near Fowler's Cross Roads in the neighborhood of Warrior's Creek Church, where he lived until his second marriage, when he removed to near Durban's Creek Church. [long account and eulogy] A. C. Stepp.

Tribute of Respect from Saluda Hill Church, Pickens Co., S. C., March 24th 1883, to Bro. Daniel McJunkin, whose death took place 10th November 1882. His remains were interred in the burying ground at Saluda Hill Church....

Issue of April 19, 1883

Married by Rev. N. N. Burton, at the residence of the bride's mother, on Tuesday, April 10, 1883, Mr. W. J. Hardy and Miss Nannie Long-- all of Edgefield.

Tribute of Respect from First Creek Church, March 20th, 1883, on the death of Brother Zackariah Hall.

Mrs. H. E. Griffin, wife of Dr. W. K. Griffin, departed this life at her home in Greenville on the 31st ult. She was the mother of five children, two of which preceded her to the grave.... buried in Springwood Cemetery.

Died, March 29th, 1883, at the residence of her son, near Pendleton, S. C., Mrs. Amelia A. Norris. Mrs. Norris was born in St. Matthew's Parish,

Orangeburg District, S. C., January 24th 1812, and was baptized by Rev. H. W. Mahoney, joining Antioch Church of which she remained a member until the formation of Corinth Church.

Died, March 31st, 1883, at the same place, Nannie, daughter of D. K. and B. C. Norris, born May 30th, 1880.

Issue of April 26, 1883

Tribute of Respect to Elma Hill who died 26th March 1883, and Eliza Lawhon, who died 26th February 1883... Midway, S. C., April 13, 1883.

Married on the evening of the 18th inst., at the residence of the bride's mother, by Rev. Wm. Henry Strickland, Mr. Henry Briggs and Miss Lula McBee. All of City of Greenville.

On the 15th April 1883, by Rev. J. C. Furman, at the residence of the bride's father, Mr. Perry F. Cox and Miss Ella Lee Rice.

Mrs. R. T. Yarborough departed this life March 31st, 1883, in the 38th year of her age... left husband and devoted daughters R. W. M. The "Southern Christian Advocate" will please copy.

Issue of May 3, 1883

Married on the 22d of April 1883, at the residence of the bride's mother, by Rev. J. K. Fant, Mr. W. Edgar Harling and Miss Jane Minor. All of Edgefield County.

Mrs. E. A. Clinkscales, relict of Capt. A. Clinkscales, died on the 28th March 1883, leaving two sons, two daughters and many friends... member of Little River Church, Saluda Association. Due West, S. C.

Balus Hix died at his home in Fair Play, S. C., on the 27th day of March 1883, in the seventy-fifth year of his age. [eulogy]

Mrs. Rachel Woodruff died at Hartsville, S. C., 20th March 1883 [eulogy].

Issue of May 10, 1883

Married on the evening of the 25th April 1883, at the residence of the bride's father, by Rev. W. D. Rice, Miss Lizzie Connelly, of Barnwell County, and Mr. Gustavus Ott, of Orangeburg County.

On 1st May 1883, at the residence of the bride's father, by Rev. D. Weston Hiott, Mr. Wm. A. Cason and Miss Sallie, second daughter of Mr. B. Frank Mauldin. All of Anderson County.

Tribute of Respect to Rev. George Howe, D. D., LL. D., President of the Columbia Bible Society.

Mrs. N. W. Jones died at her home in Fairfield County, S. C., on the 7th March 1883, in the 63rd year of her age. She was the eldest daughter of John and Catharine Mobley. [eulogy] J. D. Mahon. Halselville, S. C.

Issue of May 17, 1883

Married on Sunday, May 6th, 1883, at the residence of the bride's father in Sumter County, Mr. Isadore M. Truluck to Miss N. C. Hinds.

Mrs. Rebekah Johnston, wife of Benjamin Harrison, and daughter of Rev. J. R. and Helen Johnston, deceased, died in Edgefield village on the 23rd April 1883, aged 58 years. She was a faithful member of the Ebenezer Baptist Church at Trenton... left husband, children, grandchildren, brothers, sisters and friends. Her Pastor, J. P. M.

Departed this life, Thursday, April 10th, at 11 o'clock P. M., Mrs. Sue Louise, wife of the late Hon. A. B. Wilson... Her remains were interred in Oak Grove Cemetery. Mrs. Wilson was a consistent member of the Baptist Church, and a daughter of Rev. A. M. Cartledge, of South Carolina, and was married in Chester County, in October 1875. The deceased was 32 years of age and leaves two children, a little boy of six and a little girl of three years... Greeneville (Tenn.) Herald.

Issue of May 24, 1883

Married at Monticello, Fairfield County, S. C., by Rev. C. G. Bradford, May 1, 1883, Mr. J. Ellison Jones to Miss Pauline Scott, daughter of B. R. Scott.

At Due West, S. C., at the residence of Mr. H. P. McGee, by Rev. Dr. Grier, May 7, 1883, Mr. J. B. Tappan, of Ringgold, Ga., to Miss Ida S. McKay, of Greenville, S. C.

Died, at Meador, Union County, S, C., May 11, 1883, Mr. Willie D. Steen, aged 25 years. On the 15th of March last, he was married to Miss Sallie Fant, a consistent member of Blackstock Baptist Church, Fairfield County... A. E. Fant.

Issue of May 31, 1883

Tribute of Respect from Mt. Ebal Sunday School to Miss Annie Howard.

Tribute of Respect from Edgefield Association on the death of brethren A. J. Hammond and J. P. Moss.

Tribute of Respect to our former pastor, Rev. Thos. W. Smith, from little River Baptist Church, Fairfield County, 6th May 1883.

Tribute of Respect from Glenn Springs, May 18, 1883, to Rev. Thomas Wilson Smith, Philadelphia Baptist Church.

Issue of June 7, 1883

Rev. H. Wade Eagerton, son of Rev. Council Eagerton, died April 21st, in the 34th year of his age. He joined the Willow Creek Church before he had completed his eleventh year. Three years ago he was licensed to preach by Calvary Church. He leaves a wife and four children. S. M. R. Mars Bluff, S. C.

Lewis Reynolds died at the home of his son-in-law, Dr. J. H. Strom, May 24, 1883, aged 69 years. He was born, he lived and he died in Edgefield County, S. C. J. K. F.

Issue of June 14, 1883

Died, at her home at Society Hill, S. C., May 21st 1883, Miss Louisa McIntosh.

On the 30th of April 1883, near Mt. Vernon, Edgefield County ,S. C., Mrs. Eugenia White Harrison, died, aged 29 years. In her 17th year, she was received into the Bethany Baptist Church. In her 18th year, she was united in marriage with J. C. Harrison. She leaves three little girls....

Issue of June 21, 1883

Tribute of Respect from Lyles Ford, Fairfield Co., S. C., to Rev. Thos. W. Smith.

Married June 14th, 1883, by Rev. R. N. Pratt, at the residence of the bride's father, Mr. E. R. Horton, of Liberty, S. C., and Miss Laura S. McDavid, eldest daughter of Dr. Quince McDavid, of Due West, S. C.

April 12th, 1883, by Rev. S. T. Russell, Mr. L. C. Kellahan and Miss S. E. Elliott.

Issue of June 28, 1883

Married by Rev. J. C. Furman, on Sunday, June 24th, Mr. Berry League to Miss Sallie, daughter of Mr. Rowland Cox.

Elizabeth Boyd, wife of John H. Boyd, Laurens County, S. C., died on 16th May 1883, being 63 years old. She was baptized by Rev. W. P. Martin into the fellowship of Poplar Springs Church forty-one years ago. A husband, five children, and many friends are left... A. C. S.

Died, at his residence in Natchitoches Parish, La., Benjamin Screven Sweat, aged 32 years and 3 months. He was a consistent member of the Saline Baptist Church, and was a devoted, son brother, husband, and father. And he was the only son of his mother and she was a widow.

Departed this life June 19th, 1883, at her residence in Abbeville County, S. C., Mrs. Agnes W. Reynolds, in the 81st year of her age. She was born 26th

March 1803, and in 1830 was baptized into the fellowship of the Baptist Church at Damascus, in Edgefield County, and in 1832 united with the Mt. Moriah Baptist Church, Abbeville county.... R. S. W., Jr.

Issue of July 12, 1883

In Memoriam. Death of Dr. J. M. Turner.

Died, May 3rd, 1883, Mrs. Rebecca Johns, wife of Isaac Johns, Colleton County, S. C. Sister Johns was about 71 years old... member of Little Salkehatchie Baptist Church.

Died, at Barnwell C. H., S. C., on the 5th of June 1883, at 12 m., Mrs. Angelia Suares, wife of Rev. M. R. Suares, in the 56th year of her age. She was a pupil of her husband in 1842 in her 17th year; in her 19th became his wife. [eulogy] M. R. S.

Issue of July 19, 1883

Died, at his home in Lancaster village, on July 4th, 1883, in the 56th year of is age, Richard Elliott. He united with Fork Hill Baptist Church two or three years ago, and later joined our church by letter. G. W. Gardner

Issue of July 26, 1883

Tribute of Respect from Methodist and Baptist Sunday Schools of Black's, S. C., to Miss Laura M. Sharpe, who died first instant at 8: 30 P. M.

Fell asleep in Jesus at Graniteville, S. C., on June 26th, 1883, Miss Martha S. Weathersbee, daughter of Mr. and Mrs. J. W. Weathersbee....

Issue of August 2, 1883

Died in Greenville County, July 16th, 1883, Mrs. Mary A. Smith, in the fifty-seventh year of her age. For more than thirty years she had been a consistent member of Rocky Creek Baptist Church.... C. M.

Died, at Bradley's, S. C., July 24, 1883, of typhoid fever, Miss Emma Holloway, aged 15 years and 6 months. She had gone to Bradley's on a visit, her home being at Ninety-Six. A step=daughter of our esteemed brother, E. S. Hale....

Issue of August 9, 1883

Married by A. C. Stepp, at the residence of Travis Medlock, the bride's father, on the 12th July 1883, Mr. John Henry Ballentine and Miss Clara A. Medlock, both of Laurens County, S. C.

On the 29th of July 1883, at the residence of bride's father, by Rev. J. L. Rollins, Mr. John Jones and Miss Elizabeth Coleman, all of Marion County, S. C.

On Sunday evening, July 29th, 1883, by Rev. J. A. Seglar, Mr. G. W. Garland of Darlington County, to Miss Amelia Reed, of Aiken County, S. C.

Died, May the 17th, 1883, Mrs. Matilda, wife of O. H. Jenkins, of Greenville County, in the 73rd year of her age....

Died, at her home in Hood County, Texas, on the 17th of July 1883, in the 52d year of her age, Mrs. Mary Elizabeth Rice Mobley, wife of Dr. Samuel F. Mobley. She was baptized and became a member of Springtown Baptist Church in Barnwell Co., S. C., Aug. 4, 1848. She afterwards lived in Fairfield County near Fellowship Church, until her removal to Texas, after the war. L. C. H. Texas Baptist Herald please copy.

Departed this life on the 25th July 1883, Mrs. Milly Blackwell, in the 87th year of her age. She was baptized into the fellowship of the Gum Branch Baptist Church, I suppose, of the Welsh Neck Association. At the time of her death she was a member of the Mt. Pisgah Church of the Moriah Association. She leaves several children and grandchildren. John S. Croxton.

Miss Virginia Lee Barton died on the 24th of July 1883, near Easley, S. C. [eulogy] J. C. Hudson.

Issue of August 16, 1883

On the 25th of July 1883, Deacon J. M. Carwile entered into the rest that remaineth for the people of God, aged 63 years. He had been a consistent and useful member of Little River Church for forty years, serving the church as deacon for twenty-five years. The funeral sermon was preached at Little River Church by Rev. J. S. Murray, his pastor.... left widow and children.

Died, August 6th, Miss Ella Hunter, after a long illness. She was a member of the church at Damascus, and was baptized by Rev. J. H. Dargan. She leaves a mother, sister and brothers.

Issue of August 23, 1883

Married at the residence of the bride's father, Mr. Milton Ulmer, August 12, 1883, by D. W. Key, Mr. John Fersener and Miss Livia Ulmer, both of Orangeburg County, S. C.

Tribute of Respect from Baptist Sabbath School at Conway, S. C., August 12, 1883, death of our teacher Mollie Jollie, 17th July 1883.

Little Carrie Lou Lawton was called by the Reaper at twenty minutes before eleven o'clock on the morning of the 7th of August 1883. Allendale, S. C.

Issue of August 30, 1883

Tribute of Respect to deacon Thos. P. Shaw, from Big Stephens Creek Baptist Church, 23 August 1883.

Died, July 14th, 1883, Mrs. Mary Ann McDowal, wife of A. A. McDowal, of Kershaw County, in the fiftieth year of her age. The deceased was born and raised on Lynches Creek, near Tiller's Ferry, in Kershaw county. She was married to A. A. McDowal in 1852. She and her husband joined the Bethany Baptist Church of Kershaw county in August 1856. She had lost two children by death. She leaves a husband and eight children.

Issue of September 6, 1883

Tribute of Respect from Pee Dee Baptist Church Sabbath School, August 27, 1883, to Mary Ida Davis.

Died at his home in Lancaster Co., on the 23rd of August, 1883, in the 76th year of his age, Rev. William F. Brasington. He was born in Sumter county, S. C., and in his fifteenth year, his widowed smother removing to the town of Camden, Kershaw County, was bound as an apprentice to learn the carpenter's trade... was received into the fellowship of Camden Baptist Church. In the year 1838 he was called to the pastorate of the Fork Hill Church, and served this church twenty-six years. John S. Croxton. "Lancaster Ledger" and "Camden Journal" please copy.

Issue of September 13, 1883

Died, in Charleston, S. C., July 26th, 1883, little Leotia Estella, youngest daughter of W. D. and T. E. Moore, aged one year and eleven months.

Died, on the 15th day of June 1883, Mrs. C. M. Taylor, wife of Mr. Lewis T. Taylor, aged sixteen years and eight months.

Died, August 24, 1884 [sic], at Ninety Six, S. C., of typhoid fever, Mr. Richard P. Quarles, aged 33 years. Mr. Quarles was a consistent member of the Ninety-Six Baptist Church. The Abbeville "Press and Banner" says: Mr. Quarles married Miss Lula Neville at Walhalla, in January 1881. He had built a handsome dwelling at Ninety-Six....

Issue of September 20, 1883

Married on Sept. 11, by Rev. J. D. Mahon, at the residence of the bride in Chester County, Mr. William J. Cornwell, of York Co., S. C., and Mrs. M. V. Colvin.

From Hebron Sunday School: Rosa Benton, a flower just blushing into womanhood, died August 4th.... Stephen Lexton Matthews was snatched away on August 30th. Had he been spared till November 7th, he would have been thirteen years old.

On the 2nd of September 1833, Daniel Nelson died in the 92nd year of his age. He had been an active and useful member of the Buffalo Baptist Church for more than sixty years... R. R. V. Blythewood, S. C., Sept. 6, 1883.

Died, near Due West, S. C., July 4th, 1883, Col. Wm. Clinkscales in the 71st year of his age. He was a consistent member of Little River Baptist Church.

Died at the residence of her mother in Williamston, August 1st, 183, Addie, youngest daughter of Mrs. Izabella P. Locket, in the 21st year of her age. Her funeral services were conducted at Standing Sprig Church, where her remains were interred, by her Teacher, Rev. Samuel Lander.

Issue of September 27, 1883

Died, of congestion, at the home of her parents in Clinton, S. C., September 14th, 1883, Emma Griffin, aged 12 years. M. E. B.

Married on the 20th of September, by Rev. A. J. McCoy, Mr. Geo. Kennington and Miss Michal Harris, all of Lancaster County, S. C.

Issue of October 4, 1883

Died of inflammation of the stomach, little Eva May, infant daughter of C. H. and Fannie A. Marshal, Sept. 24, 1883.. not quiet three years old. D. C. H.

Issue of October 18, 1883

Died, September 5th, 1838, Daisy, daughter of Mr. and Mrs. David T. Byrd, of Darlington County, S. C., aged 1 year and 11 months.

Died, near Ninety Six, S. C., September 29, 1883, Mr. Preston White... a loved member of Fellowship Church.

Rev. A. J. Joplin departed this life at his residence in Chesterfield Co., S. C., on 28th of July 1883, at the age of thirty-six. Bro. Joplin was born and read in the state of South Carolina. At the age of twenty he united with the Cross Roads Church, Chesterfield County. In the year 1870 he emigrated to Texas, where he remained a member of the Rock-west Baptist Church, Nevara County, until the year 1881, when he returned to his native state... He leaves a wife and many relatives and friends. He was a member of the Macedonia Baptist Church when he died. A. S. Willeford.

Married at the residence of the bride's father, in Walhalla, S. C., on Wednesday morning, 10th inst., by Rev. J. P. Smeltzer, D. D., Mr. J. C. Keys, Jr., of Charleston, and Miss Lizzie R., eldest daughter of Col. R. A. Thompson, of Oconee.

On October 14th, 1883, by Rev. R. W. Seymour, at the residence of Mr. J. C. Koon, Mr. E. G. Paul to Miss Sarah Ann King, all of Newberry County, S. C.

Issue of October 25, 1883

Married near Townville, Anderson County, S. C., October 16th 1883, by the Rev. Landy Wood, Mr. Wm. T. Hunt, to Miss Sallie, daughter of Wm. Woolbright, Esq.

Married near Townville, Anderson County, S. C., October 16th 1883, by the Rev. Landy Wood, Mr. Wm. T. Hunt, to Miss Sallie, daughter of Wm. Woolbright, Esq.

Died, on Friday evening, October 19th, 1883, at Anderson, S. C., Mrs. Sophie Divver, in the seventy-sixth year of her age.

On the 5th February 1883, his 19th birthday, W. H. Carson fell asleep in Jesus. W. B. Carson

Died, recently at her home in Barnwell Co., S. C., Mrs. Hanson Darlington, aged sixty-six years. Sister Darlington was the wife of the late Deacon James Darlington. In early life she united with the Cypress Chapel Baptist Church. J. J. M.

Died October 18, 1883, Florie Lee, daughter of Mr. and Mrs. O L. Sanders, of Chester Co., S. C., aged four years and six months. L. C. H.

Martha Louise Carter, oldest child of John L. and Mollie F. Carter, aged 4 years, 10 months and 18 days, died September 29th, 1883. G. W. Bussey.

At three o'clock A. M. of the 15th of September 1883, Mrs. Mary Hargrove, widow of the late Stephen Hargrove, of Marion County, S. C., died at her residence near Cat Fish Church, in the sixty-fifth year of her age.

Departed this life on Sunday morning September the 2nd, 1883, at the residence of his father in Graham's, Barnwell County, S. C., James Clark Cooper, youngest son of Capt. C. C. Cooper, in the twenty-first year of his age.... W. D. R.

Issue of November 1, 1883

Married at the residence of the bride's father, Mr. Charles Thompson, by Rev. I. W. Wingo, Mr. A. J. Dillard and Miss Nora Thompson, all of Spartanburg.

Died at her home in Abbeville County, Oct. 2nd, 1883, Mrs. Phena Latimer, wife of W. T. Latimer, in the 49th year of her age. She was a member of Turkey Creek Baptist Church for thirty-two years....

Died at the residence of her son, Washington H. Drummond, on the 12th of August, Mrs. Rebecca Meredith, in the 67th year of her age. She was first married to Harrison Drummond, of Spartanburg County, S. C. Her second marriage was to Samuel Meredith, of Laurens County, S. C. She was the daughter of Benjamin Martin. By Harrison Drummond, she had seven children, all of whom she saw married and settle din life except one which died in infancy. By her second marriage, she had one child only, the wife of Dr. J. A. Martin.

Died, at Ninety-Six, S. C., Oct. 28, 1883, of fever, Dr. Wm. M. Wakefield, aged 34 years. [eulogy]

Issue of November 8, 1883

Married on the 14th Oct., 1883, by Rev. W. D. Rice, at the residence of the bride's mother, Benj. S. Carter and Miss M. E. Fender, all of Barnwell County, S. C.

By Rev. W. D. Rice, on the 28th Oct., 1883, at Buford's Bridge, S. C., Josiah M. Dickinson and Miss M. Aurie Gaines.

Issue of November 15, 1883

Married at the residence of Col. Samuel W. Mobley, Chester, S. C., October 31st, 1883, at 8:30 p. m., by Rev. R. W. Sanders, Mr. Franklin L. Whitlock and Miss Mattie M. Walker, all of Chester.

Died, at the residence of her father, W. H. Long, Newberry County, S. C., on the 16th September 1883, Miss Nannie Long, in the 17th year of her age [eulogy] R. W. S., Jr.

Departed this life on Sunday, October 13th, 1883, at his residence in Greenville County, S. C., Mr. J. K. Bates. The large church at Ebenezer was filled with the large attendance of his friends and neighbors at his funeral.

Died, at the residence of her husband, Mr. Wm. T. Ray, August 23d, 1883, Mrs. Emma M. Ray, aged 19 years.

Issue of November 22, 1883

Tribute of Respect from Clinton Baptist Church Sunday School to Emma Griffin, who died September 14th, 1883.

Married, November 15th, 1883, at the residence of the bride's father, Mr. R. Turner, by Rev. I. W. Wingo, Mrs. Cora A. White, of Spartanburg County, and Mr. W. C. Thomson, of Camden.

On September 13th, 1883, at the residence of Mr. R. Hawkinson, by Rev. F. Jones, Mr. Lewis Page and Miss Lizzie Woodward, all of Aiken County, S. C.

On November 7th, 1883, at the Beech Island Baptist Church, by Rev. F. Jones, Mr. Span Page and Miss Mayo Page, both of Aiken County, S. C.

November 18th, 1883, at the residence of the bride's father, by Rev. M. E. Smith, Mr. W. P. Smith, of Henderson, N. C., to Miss Ester C. Baker, of Greenville County, S. C.

At Beech Island, S. C., on the 31st day of October 1883, died Miss Martha Robinson, formerly of Silverton in Aiken Co.

Departed this life October 19, 1883, B. A. Lowe, in the 39th year of his age... a member of Mount Zion Baptist Church.

Mrs. Mary Johnson as born May 5th, 1806, was baptized into the fellowship of the Rock Springs Baptist Church by the pastor, Rev. Zedekiah Watkinson, almost a century ago, and then came with her husband, Mr. isaac Johnson, from Orangeburg to Edgefield and united with the Rocky Creek Baptist Church. Here he died some years ago, and left her with a large family of sons and daughters to provide for.. She feel asleep in Jesus october 3, 1883.

Mrs. Elizabeth Mahaffey was born April 21st, 1810, and departed this life October 22d, 1883, in the 74th year of her age. She united with the church at Rabun Creek, Laurens County in 1832, and was baptized by Rev. Joseph Babb.... with her husband Allen Mahaffey moved to Anderson County and by letter united with Cedar Grove Church.

Issue of November 29, 1883

Mrs. Angie Callison Kemp, wife of Preston B. Kemp, and daughter of hon. Jas. Callison, has gone to the Christian laborer's rest... Bold Spring Church. J. S. Jordan.

Died, in the city of Augusta, Georgia, November 17th, 1883, Mrs. Lucy Dunbar, in the 77th yaer of her age.... Steel Creek Baptist Church in Barnwell County. Our sister was the relict of Maj. F. F. Dunbar. Sister Dunbar died at the residence of her daughter, Mrs. R. B. Wilson. L. H. Shuck. Charleston, S. C., Nov. 25th, 1883.

Married, November 13th, at the residence of Mr. T. C. Lipscomb, by Rev. T. M. Galphin, Mr. H. P. Galphin and Miss Mamie J. McSwain, all of Ninety-Six, S. C.

Issue of December 6, 1883

Death of Mrs. E. J. Forrester. The secular press has brought us the sad intelligence of the death of this most excellent lady. Her beloved parents and grandparents were among our most intimate and dearest friends. Mr. and Mrs. Hugh Lide (the latter the daughter of Evan Pugh of blessed memory), presented in old age one of the most attractive illustrations of happy wedded life. The mother of Mrs. Forrester was the youngest daughter, having married Rev. J. O. B. Dargan. Her oldest daughter Bessie became the wife of Rev. E. J. Forrester.

Married in Laurens County, S. C., on the 25th November, 1883, by Rev. J. K. Mendenhall, Mr. J. A. Traynham to Miss Pernicie Riddel.

At the residence of the bride's father, Mr. John N. Nicholson, in Lancaster village, Wednesday morning, October 31st, 1883, by Rev. G. W. Gardner, Mr. John Reid and Miss Belle Nicholson.

On the 20th November, 1883, by Rev. H. M. Barton, at the residence of the bride's father, Saml H. Maret, Esq., Mr. Robert C. Harris to Miss Emma P. Maret, all of Oconee.

Issue of December 13, 1883

Married, Nov. 6, at the residence of Mr. Andrew McClellan, by Rev. W. H. Hartin, Mr. Andrew McClellan and Mrs. Martha Wilson, all of Fairfield County, S. C.

Tribute of Respect from Woman's Mission Society of Lancaster Baptist Church, Dec. 3, 1883, to Mrs. Dora L. Gardner, consort of Rev. G. W. Gardner, who died on the 16th of November last.

Issue of December 20, 1883

Married, Dec. 12, by Rev. J. K. Fant, at the residence of Mrs. Frances Hammond, Aiken Co., S. C., Dr. C. M. Burckhalter and Miss Augusta G. Hammond.

Also, at the same time and place, with the same ceremony, Mr. Thomas P. Hammond and Miss S. Julia Hammond.

James L. Bobo, 4 years old, died of croup in Cross Keys Township, Oct. 15th 1883. L. C. Ezell.

Died in Richland County, on the night of December 1st, 1883, little Maggie, only daughter of J. J. and Othella L. Howell, aged two years and eleven months. J. D. H.

Willie E. Ford, son of Tracy R. and Mary C. Ford, of Marion County, was born June 28, 1875, and died June 19, 1883, aged seven years, eleven months and eleven days. A. W. P.

Issue of January 3, 1884

Married at Charleston, S. C., December 6, 1883, by Rev. A. J. S. Thomas, Mr. John Gelzer and Miss Nannie Axson, both of Charleston.

At the residence of the bride's mother, Mrs. Elizabeth Wolfe, in Orangeburg County, Wednesday morning, Dec. 19th, 1883, by Rev. G. W. Gardner, Mr. D. J. Gardner and Miss Maria Wolfe, all of Orangeburg County.

On Dec. 10th, 1883, at the residence of the bride's father, by Rev. D. Weston Hiott, Mr. Fred C. Clark and Miss Alice Duckworth, all of Anderson, S. C.

By Rev. F. O. S. Curtis, at the residence of the bride's father, on the morning of October 10th 1883, Mr. J. B. Burch and Miss Mary E. Napier, third daughter of Rev. Robert Napier, of Marion Co., S. C.

By Rev. F. O. S. Curtis, at the residence of the bride's father, on the evening of Dec. 20th 1883, Mr. J. B. McBride and Miss Angie Napier, youngest daughter of Rev. Robert Napier, of Marion Co., S. C.

By Rev. F. O. S. Curtis, at the residence of the bride's father, on the evening of Dec. 20th 1883, Mr. J. B. McBride and Miss Angie Napier, youngest daughter of Rev. Robert Napier, of Marion Co., S. C.

On the 13th of December 1883, at the residence of Mr. W. A. Merritt, Ridge Spring, by Rev. G. F. Williams, Dr. J. M. Quattlebaum and Miss L. Belle Merritt.

By Rev. L. C. Ezell, Dec. 20, 1883, at the residence of Dr. B. F. Kilgore, the bride's father, Mr. A. B. Stallworth, of Edgefield, and Miss Annie V. Kilgore, of Spartanburg.

At the residence of John Steele, near Rock Hill, on the 25th December, by Rev. L. C. Hinton, Mr. John R. Alexander and Miss Maggie W. Robbins.

At the residence of the bride's father, Dec. 13th, 1883, by Rev. G. W. Bussey, Mr. John Strom and Miss Lee Strom.

At the residence of the bride, Dec. 16th, 1883, by Rev. G. W. Bussey, Mr. Pomp. Cheatham and Miss Lula Williams.

At the residence of the bride's father, Dec. 20th ,1883, by Rev. G. W. Bussey, Captain Carroll and Miss Mattie Tucker.

At the residence of Mr. Wm. Quarles, Dec. 20th, 1883, by Rev. G. W. Bussey, Mr. Thomas Quarles and Miss America Holmes.

Died at Allendale, on the 9th of December, Mrs. Harriet Jaudon, aged 46 years.... J. A. Lawton.

In Memory of J. B. O'Bannon, Esq., the young lawyer who recently died at the home of his father, Dr. J. J. O'Bannon, Barnwell, S. C. [eulogy] C. N. Donaldson.

Issue of January 10, 1884

Married at Lawtonville, S. C., December 26th, 1883, by Rev. A. B. Estes, Mr. Alfred Johnston and Miss Susie Brunson, all of Hampton County, S. C.

In Atlanta, Ga., January 2d, 1884, by Rev. A. Buist, Mr. W. R. Kelly, of Blackville, S. C., and Miss Carrie A. Randal, of Atlanta, Ga.

December 23d, 1883, by Rev. J. K. Fant, Mr. P. Brooks Harling to Miss Hattie McDowell, both of Edgefield County, S. C.

By Rev. J. K. Fant, December 25th, '83, Mr. Chas. H. Edmonds to Miss Ella Harling, both of Edgefield County, S. C.

December 27th, '83, by Rev. J. K. Fant, Mr. N. A. Shirley to Miss Mary Fant, both of Anderson County.

At the residence of Mr. Marion Robinson, on the 2d of December 1883, by Rev. T. J. Taylor, Miss M. E. Murrell and Mr. A. P. Varner, both of Union Co., S. C.

On the 9th of December 1883, at Mount Joy Church, by Rev. T. J. Taylor, Miss Josie Turner and Mr. Ashby Kelly, both of Union County, S. C.

On the 16th of December 1883, at the residence of the bride's mother, near Goucher Creek Church, in Spartanburg County, by Rev. T. J. Taylor, Miss A. S. Littlejohn and Mr. H. H. Littlejohn.

On the 16th of December 1883, at the residence of the Rev. W. M. Foster, the bride's father, at West Springs, by Rev. T. J. Taylor, Miss Mollie E. Foster and Mr. S. Cabot Colton, both of Union Co., S. C..

On the 25th of December 1883, at the residence of Mrs. Mary Tolleson, the bride's grandmother, Miss M. A. Wilkins and Mr. W. S. Grant, both of Union County, S. C.

On the 25th of December 1883, at Mt. Joy Church, by Rev. T. J. Taylor, Miss Selma Kelly and Mr. Wm. Gault, all of Union County, S. C.

Died at Limestone of Pneumonia, Dec. 29th, 1883, 11 P. M., Maria Budd, aged 3 months and 13 days, daughter of Prof. R. O. and Emma A. Sams.

Issue of January 17, 1884

Married at the residence of the bride's mother, on the 25th of December, 1883, by Rev. A. C. Stepp, Mr. Robert Mills Preston Brooks Balentine and Miss Cleopatra Haseltine Victoria Emiline Lafayette Bolt, both of Laurens County, S. C.

Near Blackville, S. C., January 7th 1884, by Rev. A. Buist, Mr. G. Templeton, of Marion County, Fla., and Miss Ann Ray, of Barnwell County, S. C.

At Blackville, S. C., January 10th 1884, by Rev. A. Buist, Mr. Willie Odom and Miss Mary McClanan, both of Barnwell County, S. C.

On the 18th of December 1883, at the residence of the bride's father, by Rev. Wm. R. Puckett, Dr. W. B. Courtney to Miss Mary A. Walker, all of Aiken County.

January 9, 1884, by the Rev. Luther Broadus, Mr. James H. Hunt, of Cartersville, Ga., to Miss Emma McKellar, of Newberry, S. C.

On the 3d January 1884, at the residence of the bride's father, L. R. Marshall, by Rev. W. C. Lindsay, Dr. Rufus A. Cox, of Orangeburg, and Miss Lou O. Marshall, of Columbia, S. C.

At the residence of the bride's father, on the 26th of December, 1883, by Rev. E. A. Edwards, Mr. Willis Hodge to Miss Lou Wells, of Privateer, Sumter County, S. C.

Died, in Richland County, S. C., December 19th, 1883, little Harry the infant son of Oscar F. and Mattie M. Chapell, aged ten months and nine days. J. D. H.

Issue of January 24, 1884

Married on the 17th January 1884, at the residence of Mr. W. H. Perry, in Piedmont, by Rev. Mike McGee, Mr. J. S. Latimer of Piedmont, and Miss Fannie Hammond, daughter of H. S. Hammond, of Abbeville County, S. C.

On the 13th of December 1883, by the Rev. J. A. Martin, at the residence of the bride's father, Mr. John Grant, of Greenville, and Miss Margaret J. Cook of Laurens.

On the 15th of January 1884, at the parsonage of the Mineral Spring Baptist Church, in Marlboro County, S. C., by Rev. Rufus Ford, Mr. J. C. Dees to Miss Beulah Shooter.

Departed this life, of paralysis, on the -- day of December, 1884, at his residence in Fairfield County, S. C., A. J. Mobley, aged 53 years... J. D. M.

Issue of January 31, 1884

Married Jan. 20, 1884, at the residence of the bride's father, by Rev. G. W. Bussey, Mr. Jefferson Shelton and Mrs. Lizzie Jennings.

Jan. 24, 1884, at the residence of the bride's father, by Rev. G. W. Bussey, Mr. G. D. Mims and Miss Sallie Whatley, all of Edgefield County.

Mrs. Mary Walker died in Chester, S. C., Friday, January 18th, 1881, aged about ninety years. Her funeral took place at Liberty Church, four miles west of Chester at 2 p. M. Sunday, Jan. 20th, and her remains were laid to rest in the graveyard near the church. R. W. S.

Mrs. Laura C. Felton was born in Barnwell County, S. C., January 24, 1853, united with the Healing Springs Baptist Church; was married in 1875; leaves her companion and four motherless children, besides father, mother, brothers and sisters... departed this life 23rd November 1883. R. J. F. Texas Baptist Herald please copy.

Issue of February 7, 1884

Married at the residence of the bride's mother, by Rev. A. C. Stepp, on the 17th of January, 1884, Mr. W. C. Rasor and Miss Ella Clardy, both of Laurens County, S. C.

At the residence of the bride's mother by the Rev. A. C. Stepp, on January 17th 1881, Mr. W. C. Darby and Miss Margaret Bagwell, both of Greenville, S. C.

At the residence of the bride's father, by Rev. W. D. Rice, on Wednesday, January 23d, 1884, Mr. J. Frank Folk and Miss Frank E. Rents, all of Barnwell County, S. C.

On the morning of January 31st 1884, by the Rev. R. N. Pratt, brother-in-law to the bride, Mr. R. F. Stewart and Miss Emma L. McKay.

Bro. W. L. Parks, Sr., Deacon of the Baptist Church at this place, and he for whom Parksville was named, died very suddenly while sitting at the dinner table, January 14th 1884. Bro. Parks was about 64 years of age. United with the old Callaham's Baptist Church and was baptized by Bro. D. D. Brunson in 1845... leaves a wife, four sons and one daughter-- all of whom are members of the Baptist Church at this place. The oldest is also a Deacon. G. W. Bussey.

Issue of February 14, 1884

Married on Tuesday morning, 29th January 1884, at the bride's residence, by Rev. H. Lecroy, Rev. J. A. Seigler of Aiken Co., to Mrs. Mary E. Taylor, of Orangeburg Co., S. C.

February 5th 1884, at the residence of the bride's father, Mr. Jehu Spears, by Rev. I. W. Wingo, Mr. J. J. Gaffney, of Gaffney city, and Miss Hattie Spears, of Union Co., S. C.

In Chester, S. C., at the residence of the bride's uncle, Mr. J. J. Kain, Wednesday 8 p. m., February 6, 1884, by Rev. R. W. Sanders, Mr. B. Frank Massey and Mrs. Annie Brown.

On February 8th 1884, at the residence of the bride's father, by Rev. D. W. Hiott, John M. McConnell, Esq., of Anderson, S. C., and Miss Carrie, daughter of Wm. Duckworth of Hopewell Township, Anderson Co., S. C.

January 9th, 1884, by Rev. J. E. Rodgers, C. F. Adkisson and Adaline Adkisson, both of Sumter County, S. C.

On the 10th of January 1884, by Rev. J. E. Rodgers, J. A. Stafford and N. S. Boykin, both of Sumter County, S. C.

January 16th, 1884, by Rev. J. E. Rodgers, J. N. Christmas and M. A. S. price, all of Kershaw County, S. C.

Died, January 4th, 1884, of Consumption, Brother T. A. Davis, of Sumter County, S. C., in the 27th year of his age. He united with the Antioch Baptist Church, Kershaw county, in 1879, and was baptized by Rev. J. E. Rodgers. He joined with others in forming Cedar Creek Baptist Church. He was married January 22d, 1881, and leaves a wife and one child. J. E. Rodgers.

Issue of February 21, 1884

Married in Elko, S. C., in the Baptist Church, February 13, 1884, by Rev. A. Buist, Mr. L. A. Thomson, of Elko, and Miss Alice D. Wilson, of Campbell County, Virginia.

On January 2d, 1884, at the bride's residence, by Rev. L. D. Bass, Prof. C. A. Smith, of Reynolds, N. C., to Miss Fannie Lorena Byrd, of Timmonsville, S. C.

On January 23d, 1884, at the residence of the bride, by Rev. L. D. Bass, James O. Melton, of Society Hill, S. C., to Miss Mary E. Copeland, of Cartersville, S. C.

On January 24th, 1884, at the Baptist Church in Lake City, S. C., by Rev. L. D. Bass, Mr. B. O. Bristow to Miss Sallie McCutchen, all of Lake City.

February 13th, 1884, by Rev. L. D. Bass in the Timmonsville Baptist Church, Mr. R. Judson Bradham, of Manning, S. C., to Miss Florence Cook, of Timmonsville.

February 7th, 1884, at the residence of the bride's mother, by Rev. G. W. Bussey, Mr. Brooks Timmerman and Miss Leila Cartledge, all of Edgefield County, S. C.

At "Shady Grove" Presbyterian Church, Laurens County, on the 29th January 1884, by Rev. N. B. Williams, the Rev. H. Fowler of Laurens, and Miss Mary Scott, of Newberry Counties.

Died, of Bronchitis, January 28th 1884, B. W. Fanning, infant son of Brother B. Winton and Sister Laura C. Fanning, of Aiken County. Little Bennie, one year and a few days old....

Issue of March 6, 1884

Married February 19th, 1884, by Rev. G. W. Bussey, Mr. J. Agnew and Mrs. P. Ridge, both of Edgefield County, S. C.

February 21st, 1884, at the bride's grandmother's, by Rev. G. W. Bussey, Mr. James Reese and Miss Georgia Morgan, both of Edgefield County, S. C.

On Wednesday, February 13th, 1884, at the residence of the bride's father, Mr. William Miller and Miss Mamie Ash, both of Orangeburg County, S. C.

Feb. 27th, by Rev. G. W. Bussey, at the residence of the bride's father, Mr. John Bailey and Miss Irene McDaniel, all of Edgefield County, S. C.

On Sunday morning, Jan. 20th, 1884, at the residence of the bride's father, Mr. James A. Riddle, by Rev. J. A. Martin, Mr. William Alford Willis and Miss Emma M. Riddle, all of Laurens County, S. C.

On Feb. 20th 1884, at the residence of the bride's mother, by Rev. B. C. Lampley, Mr. Horace Curtis and Miss Maggie E. Brogdon, all of Sumter County.

On Feb. 20th 1884, at Camden, S. C., by Rev. M. E. Broaddus, Mr. A. Witherspoon Brown and Miss Kate Frietag, of Kershaw County.

On Feb. 13th, 1884, at Timmonsville, S. C., by Rev. L. D. Bass, Mr. R. J. Bradham, of Manning, and Miss Florence Cook, of Timmonsville.

Died, in Orangeburg, S. C., Feb. 16, 1884, Mrs. Irene C. Robinson, daughter of Dr. and Mrs. Wm. H. Hagood, Blackville, S. C.

Died, in Chester, S. C., Feb. 25th, 1884, Miss Kate Lattimer... member of the Baptist church at Chester. R. W. S.

Issue of March 13, 1884

Married in Johnston Baptist Church, March 4, 1884, at 8:30 p.m., by Rev. J. K. Pace, of Batesburg, Mr. W. Pierce Dean and Miss Sallie E. Wills, both of Johnston.

On the 17th February 1884, by Rev. L. D. Bass, Mr. J. E. Wingate and Miss Fannie Coker, at Timmonsville, S. C.

February 18th, 1884, by Rev. J. E. Rodgers, T. A. Myers and Mattie Bradley, all of Kershaw.

February 20th 1884, by Rev. J. E. Rodgers, H. R. Barnes and J. A. Davis, both of Sumter County.

March 3d, 1884, by Rev. J. E. Rodgers, Hardy Thorn and J. A. Dixon, all of Kershaw County.

At the residence of Mr. F. W. Boyd, February 14th, 1884, by Rev. S. T. Russell, Mr. H. Evans and Miss S. E. Boyd.

February 12th 1884, by Rev. W. P. Smith, Mr. J. B. Trail and Miss Hattie L. McCarley, all of Spartanburg County.

At the residence of Mr. S. Ott, at Kalmia, on Wednesday, Feb. 20, 1884, by Rev. S. T. Fuller, Mr. D. F. McEwen and Miss Allie P. Wise, both of Aiken.

In Johnston, Feb. 14th, 1884, at the residence of the bride's father, Mr. Aaron Dean, by Rev. H. A. Whitman, Mr. J. B. Watkins and Miss Lula Dean, all of Edgefield Co.

Died, near Ninety-Six, S. C., March 2, 1884, Mrs. Victoria Pinson, wife of Mr. B. P Pinson, Clerk of Siloam Baptist Church. Mrs. Pinson was a Methodist but was much beloved by her many Baptist friends and relatives.

Died, February 27th, 1884, Cecil, daughter of Mr. and Mrs. B. F. Peeples, aged 7 months.

Died, at Blackville, S. C., February 29, 1884, Olive Rebecca, daughter of Mr. and Mrs. Frank Richer, aged 3 months.

Issue of March 20, 1884

Married in Wassamasaw Church, March 2d, 1884, by Rev. E. H. Cuttino, Mr. P. L. Walling and miss Aura E. Winter, all of Berkeley County, S. C.

Died, at her home in Marion County, S. C., on the morning of the 20th February, Mrs. Rebecca B. McNeill, wife of William McNeill, of the same county. Besides her husband, she left four little children, the eldest of whom is twelve and the youngest four years old... F. J. B.

Died, Nov. 14, 1883, in the 80th year of her age, Mrs. Ann E. Fort, of Darlington County, S. C. For more than fifty years she had been a faithful member of the Black Creek Church.

Issue of March 27, 1884

Married, March 29th, 1884, 10 a. m., at the residence of the bride's uncle, Mr. John B. Cornwell, by Rev. R. W. Sanders, Mr. J. S. Turner and Miss Sallie D. Cornwell, all of Chester County, S. C.

In Baltimore, March 20, 1884, by Rev. Thos. D. Anderson, Mr. R. G. Johnson, of Ninety-Six, S. C., and Miss Emma Schooley, of Baltimore. Mr. Johnson, of the firm of Galphin & Johnson, is the genial and popular Clerk of the "96" Baptist Church, and is one of the rising business men of the place.

Died, at Ridge Spring, S. C., March 12th 1884, at 2 o'clock a. m., Mrs. E. M. Merritt, wife of Mr. Wm. A. Merritt...

Died, in Barnwell County, S. C., on the 26th February 1884, Mrs. Julia A. Free, wife of Bro. A. F. Free, of Springtown Church, in her fifty-third year. She was born on the 26th of December, married on the 26th of January ,and died on the 26th of February. She leaves a devoted husband and nine children. J. G. W.

Issue of April 10, 1884

Married on the 30th of March 1884, at the residence of the bride's father, by Rev. D. W. Hiott, Charles P. Barrett, Esq., of Spartanburg, S. C., and Miss Addie, second daughter of Major J. H. Ambler, of Pickens Co., S. C.

By Rev. J. A. Mundy, March 25th, 1884, Mr. W. R. Hale and Miss Annie Randolph, both of Greenville.

March 27th, 1884, at the house of the bride's father, by Rev. G. W. Bussey, Mr. Davis Thurmond and Miss Bettie Brooks, all of Edgefield County.

March 24th, 1884, by Rev. J. E. Rodgers, Levi Banks and Angelina Adkisson, all of Kershaw County.

March 30th, 1884, by Rev. J. E. Rodgers, J. H. Wooten and Margaret Curby, all of Kershaw County.

Mrs. Bettie Long was born February 11, 1852. She was the daughter of the late Moses Davenport; was married to Mr. Joseph Long, February 12, 1868, and died February 29, 1884, at Mt. Willing, Edgefield County, S. C. She united with the Methodist Church at about the age of ten years... J. Walter Dickson.

Died, in Pendleton, S. C., March 26, 1884, just as she had entered her seventy-ninth year, Mrs. Mary P. Maxwell, relict of Robert A. Maxwell. She was the only surviving child of Samuel Earle, who lived on Beaver Dam, now in Oconee County. She united in early life with the Washington Baptist Church in Greenville County, and resided in that vicinity for several years.

Issue of April 17, 1884

Married, April 13th, at the residence of Alfred Taylor, Esq., by Rev. Rich'd H. Griffith, Mr. Berry Southern and Miss Elsie Hawkins, all of Greenville County.

Resolutions on the Death of B. C. Bryan, and the Union Meeting of the Four Division of the Edgefield Association.

Deacon Samuel Riley died on 17th March 1884, aged 68 years, 6 months and 17 days, at his residence in Mount Pleasant, Berkeley Co., S. C. He was a native of Coosawhatchie, Beaufort co., but his boyhood was passed in Charleston, where he graduated at the Charles College in 1834... Marrying a daughter of R. M. Venning, Esq., deceased, of Christ Church Parish, who with two daughters survives him.... member of the first Baptist Church, Charleston.

The church at Rock Hill has sustained a heavy loss in the death of Bro. D. R. S. Blake, which occurred on the night of the 18th February 1884. He was born in York County, March 1832, being at the time of his death in the 52d year of his age. Serving faithfully during the late civil war, as a soldier in the Fifth Regiment, S. C. V.... In 1871, he was baptized into the fellowship of Harmony Church, Chester Co., where he served until 1878, a baptist church at Rock Hill was formed.

Dempsey Hartwell, infant son of D. R. S. and Jennie H. Blake, died in Rock Hill, S. C., on the 27th June 1883, aged one year, four months and seventeen days. A. P. P.

Rev. W. L. Hawes, a worthy and faithful Baptist minister, died at his home near Aiken, S. C., on the 4th of February, from diabetes, after a long and painful illness. He was born Oct. 14th, 1824, in Lincoln Co., Ga., was baptized into the fellowship of the Goshen Baptist Church by Rev. J. N. Bolton, and commenced to preach in his seventeenth year; was called to Plum Branch

Church and ordained to the gospel ministry at New Hope Church, Ga., in 1854. He leaves a wife, three sons and four daughters.... J. P. M.

Issue of April 24, 1884

Died, March 29th, 1884, near Blythewood, Fairfield County, S. C., Mrs. Charlotte W. Vann, beloved wife of Rev. R. R. Vann, sixty-seven years of age. [eulogy] C. G. B.

Departed this life on March 27th, 1884, Mrs. Emma Hester, of Pickens County, aged fifty-six years. She was the relict of Mr. Abraham Hester, who preceded her some eighteen or nineteen years. She had been a member of the Baptist Church for many years, a member of Secona Church for at least twenty-five years. She was buried near her own door.

Mrs. Susan Hawkins, of Pickens County, died March 3d, 1884, aged sixty-seven years. She was buried at Secona Church, and funeral services were conducted by Rev. W. B. Singleton.

Married at the residence of the bride's father, April 3rd, 1884, by Rev. S. t. Russell, Mr. F. G. Rhame and Miss Olivia Brockington.

At the residence of the bride's father, by Rev. W. D. Rice on the morning of the 13th April 1884, Mr. Samuel Zorn and Miss Emily Folk, all of Barnwell County, S. C.

Issue of May 1, 1884

Departed this life of paralysis, at his home in Chester County, S. C., Nicholas Colvin, Esq., aged eighty-one years, six months and seven days. [eulogy] J. D. M.

Died, at his home in Laurens County, S. C., on the 14th of January 1884, William Goggans, in the eighty-first year of his age. He was born in Newberry County, S. C., Feb. 29th, 1804. He lived a consistent member of the Baptist church for fifty-one years, and served as Deacon from July 1st, 1845. D. P. G.

Annie, only child of Mrs. Mary Richardson, of Hardeeville, S. C., died in the city of Charleston, April 2nd 1884. Annie was but a little over eight years of age.

Issue of May 8, 1884

Died at his home in Aiken County, S. C., on the night of the 10th inst., Mr. John V. Sawyer, one of Aiken's best citizens. Mr. Sawyer left a wife, three sons and three daughters....

Issue of May 15, 1884

Tribute of Respect from Ghent's Branch Sunday School, Barnwell County, to Mr. B. F. Rice.

R. D. Bruce was born in Greenville county, on May 23rd, 1850, and died at his home in Abbeville County, April 29th, 1884, after a long and weary illness. he was a member of the Baptist Church.

Issue of May 22, 1884

Married near Woodruff, S. C., May 8th, 1884, by the Rev. H. K. Ezell, Mr. Ben L. Parsons and Miss Sue H. Drummond, all of Spartanburg County.

In Orangeburg by Rev. T. M. Galphin, on May 15th, 1881, at the residence of the bride's mother, Miss A. E. Oakman, of Orangeburg, and Mr. L. R. Fell, of Blackville, S. C.

Departed this life, at the residence of his father, Mr. J. C. Hill, Laurens County, S. C., Mr. Charles Smith Hill, in the 30th year of his age... on 27th of April. R. S. W., Jr.

Issue of May 29, 1884

Died at Mannville, S. C., May 7th, 1881, of Catarrhal fever, little Bessie, daughter of John S. and Julia A. Cuttino.

Mr. J. W. Beard died in Barnwell County, May 19, 1884, in the 59th year of his age. He was a deacon of the Bethesda Baptist Church. J. F. Buist.

In Memoriam. Fell asleep in Jesus, at Lawtonville, S. C., on Monday morning, May 12th, 1884, Anna Belle Lawton, infant daughter of T. O. and M. P. Lawton, aged one year, two months and fourteen days.

Issue of June 5, 1884

In Memoriam. Mrs. Flora E., beloved wife of Mr. A. B. Cunningham and daughter of Mr. Alfred Taylor, quietly fell asleep in Jesus, Sunday evening, May 4th, 1884, in the 29th year of her age. Chick Springs, S. C.

In Memoriam. Deacon Tandy Lewis Martin was born 1807, born again 1838, married 1829, widowed 1863, and died 1884, May 21st. J. K. Fant.

Married at the residence of the bride's father, May 13th, 1884, by Rev. J. A. Martin, Mr. A. Judson White of Winnsboro, S. C., to Miss Corrie J. Jones, of Laurens County, S. C.

May 25th, 1884, by Rev. W. P. Smith, Mr. John W. Wilson and Miss E. Rowena Carroll, all of Spartanburg County, S. C.

On the 20th of May 1884, by Rev. D. W. Hiott, Mr. H. C. Shirley and Miss Mary Brock, both of Central.

On Tuesday, May 20th, 1884, by Rev. T. T. Eaton, D. D., Rev. W. J. Williams, of Nicholasville, Ky., and Miss Lillie M. McMullen, of Louisville, Ky.

On the morning of the 14th of May 1884, Mrs. Elizabeth McKnight passed quietly away at her residence in York County, S. C., in her 73rd year.. J. E. Covington.

Died, May 20, 1884, Mrs. Josephine Burns, wife of Mr. J. W. Burns, and the mother of three children. Her maiden name was McDowell. She was a consistent member of the Baptist Church, and leaves her husband, parents, relatives...

Issue of June 12, 1884

Reuben Sharp departed this life May 29th, 1884, in the 82nd year of his age. He was in the constitution of Harmony Church, Orangeburg County.... E. H. G.

Died, at her home in Darlington County, S. C., May 19th 1884, Mrs. Joanna Burch, age 80 years and 4 days. She was for thirty-five or forty years a member of the Ebenezer Baptist Church. J. Q. A.

Issue of June 19, 1884

Missouri, wife of William W. Leathers, was born May 30th, 1863; joined the Beaverdam Baptist Church in August, 1880; was married December 4th, 1883, and died June 10th 1884.

Died at the residence of her son, Mr. P. B. Sligh, Newberry County, S. C., May 20th, 1884, Mrs. Elizabeth Sligh, in the 67th year of her age... united with Enoree Baptist Church.

Died, at Reevesville, Colleton Co., S. C., on the morning of Tuesday, June 3d, 1884, little Annie E., daughter of Robert S. and Eugenia C. Weeks, aged one year, nine months and six days.

Died, of measles, at Clifton, S. C., May 3d, 1884, Miss Alice Pettit, daughter of Nathan and Agnes Pettit, and on June 6th, near the same place, of the same disease, her cousin M. C. Thompson, daughter of Wm. R. and C. E. Thompson. These two cousins, Alice and Millie, of only seventeen summers, had been members of Cowpens Baptist Church.... G. P. Hamrick.

Issue of June 26, 1884

In Memoriam. Passing this week by the Milford Church, I went and stood uncovered by the grave of my late friend and brother Washington Taylor... T. J. Earle

Married at Modoc, June 17th, 1884, by Rev. G. W. Bussey, Mr. James Moultry and Miss Carrie Lanham.

Elizabeth J. McDowell, daughter of Johnson and Jane Coggins, was born August 22nd 1834, and died March 6, 1884. G. S. A.

Joseph Sandifer died at his residence in Barnwell Co., S. C., on the 11th inst., in the 57th year of his age. J. F. Buist.

Issue of July 3, 1884

Died, near Dunbarton, S. C., 7th of June 1884, after an illness of only four days, little Anderson, eldest son of I. A. and Virginia C. Killingsworth, in the eighth year of his age. C. K.

Rev. J. S. C. Hoffman died at his home near Orangeburg, Wednesday morning, June 18th, 1884. He was born in Orangeburg County, April 12th, 1812... joined Mt. Carmel Baptist Church. His funeral services were conducted at his home, where he was buried.... D. W. Key.

Issue of July 10, 1884

Married at the residence of the bride's mother, Newberry, S. C., July 3d, 1884, by Rev. William Hanckel, of Pendleton, Hon. James N. Lipscomb, Secretary of State, and Miss Ella Motte, of Newberry.

Mrs. Nellie Sharpton, wife of David Sharpton, of Edgefield Co., S. C., was born September 7th, 1852, married December 16th, 1873, and entered into rest April 25th 1884. Samuel J. Bethea. Parksville, Edgefield Co., S. C., June 20, 1884.

Issue of July 17, 1884

Mr. and Mrs. J. R. Littlejohn of Union, S. C., lost their son Kenneth, aged two years, five months and seventeen days. W. D.

Died, at Ninety-Six, S. C., July 5, 1884, Mr. J. Davis Johnson, aged 23.

Died, at Athens, Ga., June 10th, 1884, Cornelius DuPre Barrett, in the 32d year of his age. His mother is the sister of the lamented Mrs. E. Gerard, and his father W. G. Barrett, had no superior as a man and Christian. J. E. DuPre. Smithville, S. C.

Mrs. Eliza Hunnicut, wife of M. R. Hunnicut, departed this life on the 23d of June, 1884. She was the daughter of Rev. Thomas Dawson, and was born Sept. 11, 1823, at Indian Station, North Carolina, when her father was at that place teaching school for the Indians. She was married to M. R. Hunnicut, December 12th 1838, and joined the Baptist church in the fall of 1847. She was the mother of fourteen children, and eleven of them are still alive. H. N. Hayes.

Tribute of Respect from Bamberg, S. C., July 6th, 1884, to Robert Green.

Issue of July 24, 1884

Mrs. Nicy D. K. Gregory was born August 10th, 1822, joined the Fairview Baptist Church by baptism, Nov. 1, 1874, died on the night of July 5th ,1881, having nearly completed her 62nd year. She was a kind hearted woman, a tender mother....

Died, at Lowndesville, Abbeville County, S. C., July 16th, 1884, of cholera infantum, little Ellen Harley, infant daughter of Dr. O. R. and Mrs. L H. Horton, aged ten months and six days.

Issue of July 31, 1884

Little Edwin Andrew, infant son of Mr. and Mrs. W. A. Sanders, of Chester, S. C., died Wednesday, July 16, 1884, at the residence of the grandfather, Mr. Jesse H. Hardin. This child was only about five months old. R. W. S.

Issue of August 7, 1884

Tribute of Respect from Mineral Spring Baptist Church, July 26th, 1884, to sister Mattie Ford.

Married on Wednesday evening, July 23rd, 1884, in the Greenville Baptist Church, by Rev. J. A. Mundy, D. D., Mr. Charles H. Lanneau and Miss Antoinette Williams, both of Greenville.

Died, at her residence in Chester, S. C., July 29th, 1884, after long illness, Mrs. Eliza Melton, aged about 80 years. She had been for many years a member of the Baptist Church at Chester. R. S. W.

Mrs. Elizabeth Sparks Pettigrew died at the residence of her son-in-law, Dr. J. H. Blackwell, in the town of Florence, on the 4th of July 1884, at the age of 72 years and 21 days.

Bro. Henry Dunlap, aged 36, years, died near his home in Spring Hill, Sumter Co., S. C., July 15th, 1884. J. J. Myers.

Issue of August 14, 1884

Married on the 31st July 1884, at Ninety-Six, at the residence of the bride's father, by Rev. Samuel Lander, D. D., Mr. John C. Bailey, editor of the "Enterprise and Mountaineer," and Miss Laura J. Gaulden, of the Williamston Female College.

Mrs. Mary L. Huggins died in Greenwood, S. C., on the morning of July 29th, 1884, in the 59th year of her age. Deprived of a mother in infancy, soon after her playmate brothers, and then of a father....

Issue of August 21, 1884

Tribute of Respect from Bethlehem Church, Clark's Hill, S. C., to Margaret Meriwether.

Died, at his residence near Skull Shoals, Union County, S. C., on the 31st of July 1884, Deacon Ervin Wood in the thirty-ninth year of his age. T. J. Taylor.

Died, August 3rd, 1884, after an illness of about twenty hours, James Barnie, infant son of J. S. and M. J. Floyd, aged four months. M. J. F.

Issue of August 28, 1884

In Memoriam. Mrs. Mary L. Haynsworth, on the twentieth of June, Mary L., wife of Brother W. F. B. Haynsworth passed hence... [eulogy] C. C. Brown. Sumter, S. C.

Died, on the 20th of August, 1884, little Thomas, the infant son of Maj. J. W. and Marian Wilkes. J. D. H.

Died, recently at Silverton, S. C., Mr. Jacob Foreman, Jr., eldest son of Dr. and Mrs. Isaac Foreman, and grandson of Mrs. Jane Rountree and the late Capt. Wm. Rountree. J. J. M.

Mrs. Jane E. Wood died in Abbeville, Ga., July 27th, 1884, in the 24th year of her age. She was a member of the Blackville Baptist Church. J. J. H. Stoudemire.

Issue of September 4, 1884

Tribute of Respect to Deacon William L. Rowell from the Britton's Neck Baptist Church.

Died suddenly at her residence in Barnwell County, S. C., July 27th, 1884, Mrs. Z. E. Turner, widow of the late Dr. John M. Turner, in the sixty-ninth year of her age. James F. Buist.

At Easley, S. C., on Sunday night, July 20th, 1884, Mrs. Maggie howard quietly passed away. J. C. Hudson.

Died, on the 20th of June 1884, Lewis M. Orr, aged about 56 years and 7 months. The deceased was baptized by Rev. R. J. Edwards in 1859... fellowship of the St. George's Baptist Church of the Charleston Association. He afterwards transferred his membership to the Branchville Baptist church.... R. J. E.

Issue of September 11, 1884

Tribute of Respect from Beaverdam Woman's Mission Society, September 1, 1884, to Mrs. Missouri Leathers, who died June 10, 1884.

Tribute of Respect to Rev. J. E. Rodgers from Antioch Church.

July 31, 1884, sister Annie Brown, wife of pastor Rev. W. L. Brown, died. L. J. Paris, Texas.

Death of Herbert Lee, son of Deacon John C. Willingham, on 16th July 1884, aged one year... five brothers and a sister preceded him. J. A. L.

Due West, S. C., has lost one of her most estimable citizens and the Little River Church, Saluda Association one of its most worthy members in the person of Deacon Edwin Cox who died of Bright's disease, 18 April 1884. Bro. Cox was a native of Greene county, Ala., but for the last twenty years had resided in South Carolina.

Harmony Church has been called upon to mourn the loss of sister Martha N. Ferguson, wife of W. P. Ferguson, of Chester County, S. C., She died on the 20th of August 1881, in the 56th year of her age. A. P. P.

Issue of September 18, 1884

Married, July 27th, 1884, by Rev. J. A. Martin, in the Cedar Shoal Baptist Church, Spartanburg Co., S. C. Mr. William McGill and Miss Sallie Morgan.

On Sunday morning, August 3, 1884, at the bride's father's, by Rev. J. A. Martin, Mr. Willie J. Anderson and Miss Lula Todd, both of Woodruff, Spartanburg Co., S. C.

On Sunday evening, August 31st, 1881, at the bride's father's, by Rev. J. A. Martin, Mr. Willie L. Stone and Miss Laura J. Johnson, both of Cross Anchor, Spartanburg Co., S. C.

Tuesday, Sept. 3, 1884, at St. Matthews, S. C., John Ernest, infant son of John R. and M. E. Mack, died at the age of eight months and twenty-three days. D. W. Key.

Mrs. Frances R. Wolfe, wife of John Wolfe, died at her home near St. Matthews, Sept.9, 1884, at the age of fifty-two years and eight months. D. W. Key.

Died, in Darlington County, on the 6th of August 1884, little Nellie Bass, daughter of Mr. and Mrs. C. B. Bass, both members of Swift Creek Baptist Church. A. McA. Pittman

Died, in the town of Abbeville, Wilcox, Co., Ga., on the 26th of July 1884, Mrs. Janie E. Wood, wife of Mr. W. L. Wood in the 22nd year of her age. The deceased was converted and baptized into the fellowship of the Blackville Church, Barnwell County, at a very early age... Jno. G. Williams.

Issue of September 25, 1884

Married on Tuesday evening, September 16th 1884, at the Baptist Church, by Rev. A. C. Wilkins, Mr. Matthew O. White and Miss Julia F. Danner, both of Beaufort, S. C.

On Sunday morning, the 7th of September, 1884, by Rev. J. D. Mahon, in the presence of a large audience in the Beaver Creek Church, Prof. D. B. Busby of the Crosby Institute, and Miss M. E. Faucett, the Assistant in the same.

On Thursday, September 4th, 1884, by Rev. W. D. Rice, at the residence of the bride's mother, Mr. John A. richardson and Miss Julia Brabham, all of Barnwell County.

Died, at Silverton, S. C., Anselm Ernest, infant son of Mr. and Mrs. J. A. Bates.

Died, at Silver hill, near Silverton, S. C., Paul Jackson, son of Mr. and Mrs. C. C. Meyer.

Died, at Peter's Pond, near Silverton, Jacky, infant son of Mr. and Mrs. Jesse Foreman.

Died, on Tim's Branch, near Silverton, Mattie, infant daughter of Mr. and Mrs. Wm. Key. J. J. M.

Departed this life on the 4th of September, 1884, Mrs. Martha Shedd, in the 52nd year of her age. J. D. H.

Died, in Barnwell County, S. C., on the 4th of August, 1884, Willie H. Hyrne, son of Mr. Henry and Mrs. Elizabeth Hyrne, aged about 13 years. B. W. Whilden.

Died, at her husband's residence, near Barnwell C. H., on the 11th September 1884, Mrs. Frances Cave, at the age of sixty-three years.

Died, August 8th, 1884, Mattie beloved and only daughter of Mr. Jesse P. McGee, of Anderson County, S. C. She was born January 3rd, 1850....

Tribute of Respect from Lower Duncan's Creek Church, September 14th, 1884, to Baruch Duncan.

Issue of October 2, 1884

Married, at Hodge's, S. C., Sept. 25th 1884, by Prof. Geo. D. Purinton, at the residence of the bride's brother, Mr. Henry Arnold, Mr. Chas. N. Cason and Miss Janie Arnold, both of Hodge's, S. C.

At Clifton, S. C., Aug. 28th, 1881, by Rev. G. P. Hamrick, Mr. C. B. Scollefield and Miss J. A. Culberson.

Sept. 23rd 1884, by Rev. G. P. Hamrick, Mr. J. S. Thomas and Miss Lizzie Barnes, all of Spartanburg Co., S. C.

In Laurens Co., Sept. 21, 1884, by Rev. H. K. Ezell, Mr. John L. Burdett and Miss N. E. Mitchell.

Died, near Ninety-Six, S. C., Sept. 17, 1884, Mr. Thomas E. Lake, aged 30 years... member of Fellowship church. Washington, D. C., Sept. 23, 1884.

Issue of October 9, 1884

Tribute of Respect to Franklin Easterling, from Beaverdam Church and Sabbath School.

Tribute of Respect to Payne Kenyon, a bright and pious boy, from Georges Baptist Sabbath School. St. George's S. C., Oct. 1, 1884.

Tribute of Respect from Bethel Church, September 28, 1884, to Thomas M. Dickey, A. M., and graduate of Wofford College.

Married on Tuesday evening, Sept. 23, 1884, in the Baptist Church at White Pond, S. C., by Rev. Arthur Buist, Dr. J. Rierson Smith, of Barnwell County, to Miss Carrie E. McCreary, of Aiken County.

At the residence of her daughter, Mrs. D. K. Rone, about 9:30 o'clock a. m., on Thursday, 14th September 1884, Mrs. M. B. Yarbrough quietly sank to rest. Seventy-four years measured the time of her sojourn....

David M. Smoak died at Branchville on Monday, September 1st, 1884. He was just entering his seventeenth year....

Issue of October 16, 1884

Married on the evening of the 9th of October 1884, at the residence of the bride's father, by Rev. B. F. Miller, Mr. James W. Sproles, of Greenwood, S. C., to Miss M. Lizzie McGee, second daughter of Mr. M. B. McGee, all of Abbeville County, S. C.

On August 30th, 1884, little William Rowe, eldest and only son of Rev. J. J. H. and Mrs. Mamie Stoutenmire, died at his father's home, Holly Hill, Charleston Co., S. C....

Departed this life August 27, 1884, Albert Ferguson White. Deceased was born near Chesterfield C. H., S. C., February 3rd, 1859. F. N.

Mrs. Camilla Whitfield Dinkins, widow of L. J. Dinkins, was born in Charleston, Nov. 21, 1821, and fell on sleep, August 19th, 1884, at her home in Mayesville, S. C. J. Howard Carpenter. Sumter "Watchman and Southron" please copy.

Issue of October 23, 1884

Ellie H., infant son of Mr. and Mrs. A. J. Quattlebaum of Ninety-Six, S. C., died of congestion, September 18th 1884. Little Ellie was a year old.

Departed this life October 5th, 1884, at the residence of her son-in-law, Edwin Harper, Harper's, S. C., Mrs. Sarah A. Davidson, consort of the late Robt. J. Davidson, Sr. The Georgetown "Times" will please copy.

Married by Rev. N. N. Burton, Oct. 7th, 1884, at the residence of the bride's mother, Mr. Arthur E. Eidson, of Clintonward, to Miss Alice Turner, of Graniteville.

In Darlington County, S. C., on Sunday evening, Sept. 21, 1884, by Rev. A. McA. Pittman, Mr. J. F. Hill and M. E. Carter.

In Darlington Co., S. C., on Sunday evening, Oct. 5th, 1884, by Rev. A. McA. Pittman, Mr. Zelates Bryant and Miss Fannie Rhodes.

Issue of October 30, 1884

Married, October 16th, 1884, at the residence of the bride's father, by Rev. M. L. Jones, Mr. Holbert Lynch to Miss Sunie Eadens, all of Pickens County, S. C.

At the residence of C. P. Shuler, Chester County, S. C., October 23rd, 1884, 12:15 p. m., by Rev. R. W. Sanders, Mr. C. L. Refo and Miss M. E. McBride, all of Fairfield County.

On October 21st 1884, by Rev. J. C. Furman, D. D., in the Baptist Church at Greenville, S. C., Mr. Henry W. Allen and Miss Mary I. Mendenhall, daughter of Rev. J. K. Mendenhall, of Greenville.

September 16th, 1884, at Fork Shoals Church, by Rev. J. K. Mendenhall, Mr. Wm. Cason and Miss Bettie Pepper, daughter of W. A. Pepper of Greenville County.

Dr. E. T. Rembert died at his home in Berkeley County, S. C., October 14th, 1884, at 5 o'clock p.m. He was about 65 years old and had been an officer in the M. E. Church for a number of years. he leaves a wife, who is a member of the Baptist Church. M. L. Ball

Died, near Hattieville, on the Port Royal and Augusta R. R., October 2nd 1884, of typhoid fever, Miss Hattie Rountree. She was a member of Steel Creek Church... J. F. M.

Died, near Barnwell C. H.., S. C., October 11, 1884, Mrs. Mary A. Sanders, wife of Jesse M. Sanders, in the 29th year of her age.... a native of Augusta, Ga., but married and became the adopted daughter of South Carolina. In early life Mrs. Mary A. Sanders was trained by Roman Catholic influence, but at mature age... united with the Mt. Olivet Baptist Church. She leaves a husband, five children, and a brother out West.

Issue of November 6, 1884

Married at the residence of Maj. S. P. Brooks, October 22nd 1884, by Rev. J. S. Jordan, Mr. Joseph Lake, of Phoenix, and Miss Lillie Nicholson, of Greenville, S. C.

October 28th, 1884, by Rev. W. P. Smith, Mr. Stonewall J. Knight, grandson of Rev. Silas Knight, and Miss Elvina Paulk, both of Union County, S. C.

Issue of November 13, 1884

Married at the residence of Dr. S. S. Knight, on Sunday morning, November 2d, 1884, by Rev. Graves L. Knight, Mr. D. L. Jones and Miss Corrie White, all of Greenville co., S. C.

October 28th, 1884, by Rev. W. F. Chaplin, in the Baptist Church at Orangeburg, S. C., Mr. Chas. B. Glover, Jr, to Miss Ida C. Zeigler.

At Woodruff, S. C., November 1st, 1884, by Rev. H. K. Ezell, Mr. J. A. Godfrey and Miss L. C. Hudson, all of Spartanburg County.

Tribute of Respect to Franklin Easterling... Marlboro County.

Rev. Joel Allen gently passed away at mid-day October 18th, 1884. He was born on the eastern border of Marion County, near the North Carolina State line, March 2nd, 1815. When about eighteen he came to Marlboro with his widowed mother and her family, and united with the Brownsville Church by letter. [long account]

Died, at her residence in Barnwell County, S. C., Oct. 29th, 1884, Mrs. Rebecca J. Beard, in the thirty-third year of her age. J. F. Buist.

Died, on the 8th of November 1884, Lila, only daughter of Mr. and Mrs. F. L. Milam, wanting one month and three days of being nineteen years old. She joined the Huntsville Baptist church in Laurens county.... J. D. P.

Issue of November 20, 1884

In Memoriam. Died on the 16th of November 1883, Mrs. Dora L. Gardner, wife of Rev. George W. Gardner, in the 25th year of her age. E. L. P.

Married on Thursday night, November 6th, 1884, in the Greenwood Presbyterian Church, by Rev. J. P. Martin, Mr. John R. Leavell, Jr., and Miss Hessie Blake. Also, at the same time and place, Mr. R. R. Calhoun and Miss Mary P. Blake, all of Greenwood.

At the residence of the bride's father, near Blackville, S. C., by Rev. W. D. McMillan, November 12th, 1884, Mr. Isaac W. Eubanks of Aiken County, to Miss Mattie C. Blume, daughter of John L. and Lydia Blume, of Barnwell County.

On Thursday, October 23d, 1884, by Rev. C. A. Stiles, Mr. James Kelly and Miss Ellen Kennedy, formerly of Fairfield, now of Richland County, S. C.

On Sunday evening, October 26th, 1884, by Rev. C. A. Stiles, Mr. W. J. Stack and Miss Alice C. James, all of Richland County, S. C.

On Sunday, November 2nd, 1884, at Macedonia Church, by Rev. A. S. Willeford, Mr. --- Sowell and Miss Fannie Segars, all of Kershaw County, S. C.

Died, after a long illness, at his residence in Chester, S. C., November 9th, 1884, Mr. James McNinch... left wife and five children. R. W. S.

Died, November 10th, 1884, Mrs. Roxie Culpeper, wife of Dr. J. F. Culpeper, of Timmonsville, S. C. She leaves a devoted husband and two little boys. S. P. M.

Issue of November 27, 1884

Married, November 15th, 1884, by Rev. G. W. Bussey, at Mr. E. Hite's, Mr. Henry Amos and Mrs. S. Shaffer, both of Edgefield.

On the 15th of November 1884, by Rev. J. K. Mendenhall, Mr. A. M. Warren, of Augusta, Ga., to Miss Lilis Epting, of Greenville, S. C.

Issue of December 4, 1884

Married, by Rev. L. C. Ezell, on the morning of Nov. 25th, 1884, at the residence of Mrs. Nancy Ray, the bride's mother, Mr. R. W. Harris and Miss Lula A. Ray, all of Union Co.

On the 27th of November, at the residence of the bride's father, by Rev. J. D. Huggins, Mr. Willie R. Lee and Miss M. J. Brakefield, all of Chester Co.

Died, at 8 p.m., on Tuesday, Nov. 25, 1884, Thomas Peter, infant son of D. T. and M. T. Smith, of Greenville, S. C.

Died, in Barnwell County, S. C., Oct. 23rd, 1884, Mr. John Johns, in the 45th year of his age... J. F. Buist.

Died, Oct. 6th, 1884, William B. Lewis, aged about 85 years. Bro. Lewis was born a number of years a worthy member of the Blackstock (S. C.) Church. J. A. B.

Died, Oct. 31, 1884, Mr. Lewis Odom, aged 71 years... a deacon of the Healing Springs Baptist Church.

Sister Martha J. Griffin died of typhoid fever at her home in Spartanburg County, on the 13th of November, in the 38th year of her age. T. J. Taylor.

Departed this life, Oct. 30, 1884, little Carrie Lula Porter, youngest daughter of brother Roger and sister Anna Porter, aged one year, eight months and twenty-nine days. W. H. Hartin. Ridgeway, S. C.

Mrs. Mary H. Whilden, wife of Rev. Bayfield W. Whilden, ex-missionary to China, died at her home at Allendale, S. C., on the 23rd of October 1884, in the 64th year of her age... J. A. L.

Died at home, July 15, 1884, Mrs. Jane B. Miller, wife of Dr. Stephen H. Miller, of the Lynchburg section of Sumter County, S. C. The deceased was the eldest child of Robert and Mary B. Fraser; was born October 25, 1821, near Bishopville, in the same county, and was married in the same place December 24, 1839. Twins sons were born to her November 10, 1841, but they both died in infancy on the same day, June 43, 1843. Against she became a mother August 15, 1853, but the little "Benny" was called up higher November 25, 1855, leaving her childless. [eulogy] C. E. S. Yorkville, S. C.

Tribute of Respect to Mary Lee Hartzog from Bamberg Baptist Sunday School.

Tribute of Respect to Willie O'Brien.

Issue of December 11, 1884

Married, December 2nd, 1884, at the residence of the bride's grandmother, Mrs. N. A. Fant, in the town of Union, by Rev. G. W. Gardner, Mr. Joseph H. McKissick and Miss Lilian Gilliam, both of Union, S. C.

On Tuesday, November 25th, 1884, at the residence of the bride's father, by the Rev. John F. Morrall, Mr. James Irby Fair, of Newberry, and Miss Lizzie Rountree, daughter of Judson Rountree, of Hattieville, Barnwell County, S. C.

By the Rev. A. C. Stepp, November 6th, 1884, Mr. John F. Fowler to Miss M. Alice McPherson, both of Mt. Pleasant, Laurens Co., S. C.

On November 13th, 1884, by Rev. A. C. Stepp, Mr. James W. Simpson to Miss Ella E. Beeks, both of Poplar Springs, Laurens County, S. C.

On 23rd November 1884, by Rev. A. C. Stepp, Mr. Charles W. Benson, formerly of New York, to Miss Sophie Fowler, of Warrior Creek, Laurens County, S. C.

On the 27th November 1884, by Rev. A. C. Stepp, Mr. William Davis to Miss Cora Bagwell, both of Line Creek, Greenville County, S. C.

Tribute of Respect from Healing Springs Church, November 22d 1884, to Deacon Lewis Odom.

Issue of December 18, 1884

Deacon Thomas S. Budd has recently passed away from this world. His death occurred at Limestone Springs, S. C., on Sunday, November 30th, 1884. For many years I was his pastor in Charleston, and as deacon of the First Baptist Church, I was thrown intimately and constantly with him... L. H. Shuck. Paducah, Ky., December, 1884.

Married, October 26th, 1884, at the residence of the bride's father, M. R. Sturgess, Esq., by Rev. F. O. S. Curtis, Mr. T. P. David, of Marlboro County, and miss Lille R. Sturgess of Marion County.

At Rehoboth Church, on the 4th December 1884, by the Rev. J. K. Fant, Mr. N. L. Broadwater, of Edgefield County, and Miss Zabrina Moor, of Hampton County.

Death of Morgan S. Hill, 3rd of September 1884, a young man only twenty-eight years old. R. B. M.

Died, at Grenada, Miss., on the 10th of September, 1884, Mrs. Nancy Miller, wife of Mr. Archie Miller, and daughter of Mr. John D. and Mrs. Elizabeth Smith, in the fifty-seventh year of her age. She was born in Greenville county, S. C., and joined the Rocky Creek Baptist Church in 1847.

Tribute of Respect from Upper Marion Union to Rev. Joel Allen.

Tribute of Respect from Yorkville Baptist Church to Deacon Zadok Darby Smith.

Issue of December 25, 1884

Married at the residence of the bride's father, on the 17th of December 1884, by Rev. J. D. Huggins, Mr. Willie T. Moore, of York County, and Miss Laura A. Ferguson, of Chester County, S. C.

At the residence of the bride's father, on the 18th of December 1884, by Rev. J. D. Huggins, Mr. Sidney Z. McMachin, of Chester County, and miss Kate Cranford, of York County.

At the residence of the bride's mother, in Abbeville County, at 10 a. m., on the 16th of December 1884, by Rev. S. M. Richardson, Mr. James Clinkscales and Miss Ella Kay, both of Abbeville County, S. C. The happy pair started on the same day for New Orleans.

On Thursday evening, December 11th, 1884, at the residence of the bride's father, John C. Douglass, Esq., by Rev. B. F. Miller, Mr. R. J. Warren to Miss Willie Bell Douglass, all of Abbeville County.

December 13th, 1884, at the residence of the bride's father, by Rev. W. A. Gaines, Mr. John P. Barrott, of Abbeville County, to Miss Mattie E., eldest daughter of Rev. J. S. Jordan, of Edgefield County.

December 18th, 1884, at the residence of Maj. S. P. Brooks, by Rev. J. S. Jordan, Dr. P. H. Adams and Mrs. Lizzie A. Dargan, nee Townes, all of Abbeville County.

At the residence of the bride's father, on the 3rd December 1884, by Rev. A. C. Wilkins, Mr. Fred. Smith of Charleston, and Miss Dora Finckney, of Beaufort, S. C.

At the residence of the bride's father at McNeill's Station, A. & P. R. R. on the 17th December 1884, by Rev. A. C. Wilkins, Mr. George R. Doane of Beaufort, S. C., and Miss J. E. Cummings, of McNeill's, S. C.

By Rev. J. K. Fant, at the residence of the bride's father, Mr. George Outzs, December 9, 1884, Mr. Brantly Outzs and Miss Fannie Outes.

By Rev. J. K. Fant, December 11th, 1884, at the residence of the bride's father, Capt. Robert Cheatham, Mr. Thos. P. Morgan to Miss Bettie H. Cheatham.

At Phoenix, S. C., by Rev. J. S. Jordan, December 4th, 1884, Mr. R. R. Tolbert of Greenwood and Miss Annie Henderson, of Phoenix.

At Phoenix, S. C., December 10th, 1884, by Rev. J. S. Jordan, Mr. J. B. Baker, of Bradley's and Miss Mattie Bentley, of Whitehall.

At Phoenix, S. C., December 14th, 1884, by Rev. J. S. Jordan, Mr. M. P. Burnett and Miss Eula, eldest daughter of Mr. A. C. Stallworth.

December 16th, 1884, by Rev. G. W. Bussey, Mr. Asa Barden and Miss Mamie Walls.

December 18th, 1884, by Rev. G. W. Bussey, at the home of the bride, Mr. Wm. McDaniel, Jr., and Miss Sallie Wood.

December 18th, 1884, by Rev. G. W. Bussey, at the house of Dr. Mason, Mr. J. J. Griffis and Miss Iola Mason.

By Rev. G. W. Bussey, December 26th, 1884, at the house of the bride's mother, Mr. Willie Cothran and Miss Jennie Strom.

Issue of January 15, 1885

Married in Greenville, Wednesday, Dec. 17, 1884, by the bride's father, assisted by Rev. Dr. Mundy, Miss Annie M. Furman, of Greenville, to Harry J. Haynesworth, Esq. of Williamsburg, S. C.

At the residence of S. P. Brooks, Phoenix, S. C., Dec. 23, 1884, by Rev. J. S. Jordan, Miss Kate F., daughter of Col. G. F. Townes, of Greenville, S. C., to Dr. L. Geo. Corbett, of Mayesville, S. C.

At Black Creek church, on the evening of Dec. 24, 1884, by Rev. R. W. Lide, Rev. L. T. Carroll and Miss Annie L. DeLorme, both of Dovesville, S. C.

Dec. 24th, 1 o'clock p. m., at the residence of the bride's father, Capt. Thomas, by Rev. R. W. Sanders, Mr. Fred A. Nunnery and Miss nannie Jane Thomas, all of Chester County, S. C.

At the residence of the bride's father, Dec. 24, 1884, by Rev. C. A. Stiles, Mr. E. S. Owens to Miss Lizzie, eldest daughter of E. F. Smith, Esq., all of Richland Co., S. C.,

At Darlington, S. C., Dec. 18, 1884, by Rev. W. J. Alexander, Mr. James B. Law and Miss Carrie Player.

Near Whitaker's, S. C., Dec. 23, 1884, by Rev. G. P. Hamrick, Mr. D. F. C. Harry to Miss Fannie Gold.

At the residence of the bride's father, in Cleveland Co., N. C., Dec. 25, 1884, by G. P. Hamrick, Mr. E. R. Broom to Miss m. T. Moore.

At Whitaker's, S. C., Dec. 25, 1884, by Rev. G. P. Hamrick, Mr. D. J. Allen and Mrs. M. J. Bell.

At the residence of the bride's father, Dec. 18, 1884, by Rev. A. Buist, Mr. I. L. Buckhalter and Miss Lilla Wise, both of Aiken County.

By Rev. J. D. Mahon, in Beaver Creek church, Dec. 10, 1884, Mr. Robert Cameron and Miss Ella Price, all of Chester.

By Rev. J. D. Mahon, in Beaver Creek church, Dec. 16, 1884, Mr. Johnston Cameron and Miss Nannie Belle Price, all of Chester.

By Rev. J. D. Mahon, at the residence of the bride's mother in Chester co., Dec. 30, 1884, Mr. S. M. Hafner and Mrs. F. P. McAlilly.

By Rev. L. C. Ezell, Dec. 11, 1884, at the residence of Mrs. Elizabeth Thomas, the bride's mother, Mr. S. P. Parker and Miss J. A. Thomas, all of Spartan-burg Co.

By Rev. L. C. Ezell, Dec. 18, 1884, at his residence, Mr. D. P. Lanford and Miss B. E. Weathers, both of Spartanburg Co.

By Rev. L. C. Ezell, Dec. 21, 1884, at Padgett's Creek church, Mr. James Eubanks and Miss C. H. Holcomb, both of Union Co.

By Rev. L. C. Ezell, Jan. 6, 1885, at the residence of Mr. J. B. Button, the bride's father, Mr. Wm. P. Burlington and Miss Olivia J. Button, both of Woodruff, S. C.

Dec. 14, 1884, at Mayesville, S. C., by Rev. J. Howard Carpenter, Mr .W. H. Rembert and Miss Hettie V. Smith.

Dec. 23, 1884, at Augusta, Ga., by Rev. J. Howard Carpenter, Mr. C. T. Smith and Miss V. E. Carpenter.

At the residence of Mr. W. W. Kleugh, Coronaca, Dec. 30th, 1884, by Rev. S. M. Richardson, Mr. W. Warren Fouche and Miss Melissa Franklin, all of Abbeville County.

At the residence of the bride's brother, Dec. 10, 1885, by Rev. Lucius Cuthbert, Mr. Geo. W. Curtis and Miss Carrie C. Wise, both of Aiken, S. C.

Jan. 1, 1885, 1 p. m., by Rev. R. W. Sanders, at the residence of Mr. John Knox, Chester County, S. C., Major C. W. McFadden and Miss Lizzie J. Pankey.

Dec. 23, 1884, by Rev. J. S. Jordan, Mr. William Miller and Miss Ledie Reynolds, both of Edgefield Co.

Dec. 23, 1884, by Rev. J. S. Jordan, Mr. Lucian Casey and Miss Mattie Bell, both of Abbeville Co.

Dec. 25, 1884, by Rev. J. S. Jordan, Mr. David Rash, Jr., and Miss Minerva Shaw, both of Edgefield Co.

Dec. 21, 1884, by Rev. J. S. Jordan, Mr. F. P. Hollingsworth and Miss Ellen Stevens, both of Edgefield Co.

At the residence of the bride's mother, Mrs. J. B. Rosemond, Jan. 4, 1885, by Rev. T. W. Reid, Mr. W. I. Kendrick and Miss Mary E. Rosemond, all of Greenville County.

Dec. 23, 1884, by Rev. G. W. Bussey, Mr. Pickens Bailey and Miss Sallie Parkman.

Dec. 23, 1884, by Rev. B. F. Miller, at the residence of the bride's uncle, Deacon R. E. Henderson and Miss Beulah A. McKellar, all of Abbeville Co., S. C.

Dec. 23, 1884, by Rev. B. F. Miller, at the residence of the bride, Mr. W. Y. Quarles and Mrs. Mary Johnson, both of Edgefield Co., S. C.

At the residence of the bride's father, Dec. 24, 1884, by Rev. N. N. Burton, Mr. Benj. Brooks and Miss Emmie Nicholson, all of Edgefield.

Nov. 12, 1884, by Rev. S. T. Russell, at the residence of Mr. T. R. Smith ,Mr. Julius E. Ammons and Miss Martha A. B. Smith.

Dec. 18, 1884, by Rev. W. P. Smith, Mr. R. C. Cathcart and Miss N. Carrie Fleming, all of Spartanburg Co.

Dec. 18, 1884, by Rev. W. P. Smith, Mr. R. F. Thomas, of Tennessee, and Miss C. Cornelia Morrow, of Spartanburg Co.

On January 6th, 1885, at Hartsville, S. C., by Rev. R. W. Lide, assisted by Rev. John Stout, Rev. E. J. Forrester and Miss Maggie L. Dargan.

Died, in Blackville, S. C., Dec. 21, 1884, Fannie, infant daughter of Mr. and Mrs. James Thomson, aged seven weeks.

Died, near Mt. Ebal, in Aiken County, on the 24th of December 1884, Cornelia Kneece, in her 20th year. She was baptized into the fellowship of Mt. Ebal Baptist Church about four years ago, by Rev. A. J. S.Thomas. C. L. J.

Died, on the morning of Dec. 15th, at her home in Sumter, Mrs. Juanita Hoyt, eldest child of Rev. W. D. Rice, and wife of Mr. J. A. Hoyt, aged 23 years. She had been married about two years... C. C. B.

Died, in Chester, S. C., Jan. 4th, 1885, at 10 a. m., in the 77th year of her age, Mrs. Adelaide Erwin. Sister Erwin was converted in early life and connected herself with the Presbyterian Church, but subsequently she became a Baptist... R. W. Sanders.

J. W. Hawkins entered into rest on Monday morning, Dec. 22, 1884... member and deacon of Lynchburg Baptist Church. J. Howard Carpenter.

Issue of January 22, 1885

Married at Pendleton, S. C., January 6th 1885, by Rev. C. P. Ervin, Mr. E. Y. Hunnicutt and Miss Carrie M. Moore.

On the 14th of January 1885, at the residence of Mr. J. A. Meyer, near Hattieville, S. C., by the Rev. F. J. Sanders, Mr. Robert W. Knight, of McBean, Ga., and Miss Laura A., daughter of Col. J. J. Meyer, formerly of Silverton, now of Hattieville.

January 8th, 1885, by Rev. N. N. Burton, at the residence of the bride's mother, Mr. Jesse L. Hart and Miss Hattie E. Horne, both of Edgefield, S. C.

January 6th, 1885, by Rev. G. W. Bussy, Mr. Foster Christian and Miss Carrie Reynolds, both of Edgefield County, S. C.

By Rev. G. W. Bussey, January 13th 1885, Mr. John Turner and Miss sallie Sharpton, both of Edgefield County.

By Rev. G. W. Bussey, January 15th, 1885, Mr. Thomas Howle, Jr., and Miss Maggie Brooks, all of Edgefield County.

In Memoriam. Mrs. Juanita Rice Hoyt, daughter of Rev. W. D. Rice of Barnwell County, was born March 4th, 1861, was received into the Baptist Church, Newberry County, S. C., in 1876, was married to H. A. Hoyt in 1883, removed to Sumter, S. C., 1883, and died at her home December 16th, 1885, aged twenty-three years, nine months and seven days. J. F. Buist. Bamberg, S. C.

Issue of January 29, 1885

Married in Charlotte, N. C., at the residence of the bride's father, by Rev. O. F. Gregory, Mr. Jno. T. Burris, of Anderson, S. C., and Miss Jannie E. Fromm, youngest daughter of C. H. Fromm, of Charlotte, N. C.

On Thursday afternoon, January 22, 1885, at the residence of the bride, by Rev. B. F. Miller, R. J. Felton, Esq., of Georgia, to Mrs. M. J. Dorn, of Edgefield County, S. C.

At the residence of the bride's father, Dec. 25th, 1884, by Rev. R. W. Burts, Miss Katie Rasor to Mr. J. E. Moore, all of Abbeville County. S. C.

By Rev. R. W. Burts, January 11th, 1885, Miss Clara Kay, of Abbeville County, to Mr. Wylie Murff, of Laurens, S. C.

By Rev. R. W. Burts, Jan'y 20th 1885, Mr. John Cox, of Anderson County, and Miss Sue Foster, of Abbeville County.

By Rev. J. A. Hoffman, December 18th, 1884, Mr. Willie Dukes to Miss Martha Sturkey, daughter of David Sturkey.

By Rev. J. A. Hoffman, January 8th 1885, Mr. Willie C. Smoke to Miss Rena Bonnett.

By Rev. J. A. Hoffman, January 15th, 1885, Mr. Washington Ash to Miss Anna Metts, all of Orangeburg County, S. C.

Mrs. Caroline F. Crocker, a devoted member for almost forty years of the Beaufort Baptist Church, died on Thursday, the 15th instant. Left a son Dan... A. C. Wilkins. Jan. 20, 1885.

Mrs. Thos. J. Pyles was born May 30th, 1830, jointed the Beaverdam Baptist Church by baptism in the summer of 1864, and died on the night of December 23rd, 1884....

Died, near Aiken, S. C., Jan. 16, 19885 ,Ernest Eugene, infant son of Mr. and Mrs. Felder Rankin, aged 10 months 11 days.

James Harrison, son of J. L. and Annie H. Wideman, on the 17th inst., of membraneous croup, aged 10 months.

Issue of February 5, 1885

Married at the residence of the bride's father, in Florence, S. C., January 20, 1885, by Rev. B. G. Covington, Miss Alice Temple to Mr. Geo. T. Twitty, of Barnwell Co.

January 21, 1885, in the Baptist Church in Florence, by Rev. B. G. Covington, Miss Mollie Reynolds, to Mr. A. T. Vernon, all of Florence.

January 6, 1885, in the Baptist church at Mayesville, by Rev. B. G. Covington, assisted by Rev. J. H. Carpenter, Miss Adelaide F. Foxworth to Mr. A. A. Stubbs, of Bennettsville.

January 29, 1885, at the residence of the bride's father, Joseph Nevil, Esq., by Rev. G. T. Gresham, Mr. Joe B. McJunkin and Miss Lucy Nevil, both of Oconee Co., S. C.

January 22, 1885, in West Marion, by Rev. S. M. Richardson, Rev. Duncan McDuffie and Mrs. M. P. Matthews, all of Marion Co.

December 24, 1884, by Rev. J. Q. Adams, Mr. Robert Cannon and Miss Lou Burch, all of Darlington Co., S. C.

January 22, 1885, by Rev. J. Q. Adams, Mr. Thos. Green and Miss Lorena Wilson, all of Darlington.

January 13, 1885, by Rev. H. L. Henderson, the bride's father, at his residence, Mr. Thos. R. Bell and Miss Julia Henderson, all of Greenville County.

At the residence of Capt. Walmsey, Graniteville, S. C., January 28, 1885, by Rev. J. F. Buist, Mr. J. W. Goodson of Barnwell Co., and Miss Jennie Padgett, of Aiken Co.

At the residence of the bride's uncle, January 11, 1885, by Rev. E. M. Hicks, Mr. Anson Caulder and Miss Hattie Dubose, all of Williamsburg Co.

Mrs. Susan L. Burn, relict of Rev. James W. Burn, died at her residence in Society Hill, on Wednesday, Sept. 18th, in the seventy-fourth year of her age. Mrs. Burn was the daughter of Rev. John R. Roberts, D. D., who was one of the honored teachers of the Furman Institute when it was located at the High Hills of Santee. here father died when she was young, her mother had preceded him to the grave, and she was left at a tender age to the care of relatives. She was married at the age of nineteen to the good man with whom for fifty years she lived a helpmeet indeed....

Issue of February 12, 1885

Married, Thursday morning, February 5th, 1885, at the residence of the bride's grandmother, Mrs. T. C. Reed, by Rev. J. S. Murray, Mr. J. B. Haltiwanger of Edgefield County, and Miss Carrie H. Brown, of Anderson.

December 23d, 1884, by Rev. S. T. Russell, at the residence of the bride's father, Mr. Samuel Tisdale and Miss Martha B. McCullough.

On the 4th of February 1885, at the residence of Rev. L. C. Hinton, in Chester County, by the bride's father, assisted by Rev. R. W. Sanders, Mr. Joseph D. Means and Miss Kate E. Hinton.

Little Mary Dean, daughter of Rev. I. W. and Lula Dean Wingo, died at Gaffney's, on Tuesday, 20th of January 1885. T. J. E.

Silas Lanier was born in Edgefield County, S. C., August 22d 1797, and died December 2d, 1884. He was baptized in 1827 and became a member of Big Stevens Creek Baptist Church, commonly known as Hardy's Church. On the

17th anniversary of the death of his wife, he lay down to endure his mortal illness... Hugh F. Oliver.

Issue of February 19, 1885

Married at Pendleton, S. C., February 4, 1885, by Rev. C. P. Ervin, Mr. J. C. Moore and Miss Corrie Mounce.

At the residence of the bride's father, Reuben O'Shields, in Union Co., S. C., Feb. 8, 1885, by Rev. J. S. Ezell, Mr. Davis H. Williams and Miss Madeline O'Shields.

February 15th, 1885, at the residence of the bride's father, Mr. R. Y. H. Lowery in Seneca City, S. C., by Rev. Geo. D. Purinton, Miss Virginia B. Lowery and Mr. W. O. Hamilton, both of Seneca City, S. C.

By Dr. G. W. Rogers, January 15th 1885, Dr. J. N. Mendenhall, of Guide, Texas, and Miss Effie Routh, of Sherman, Tex., daughter of the late Rev. Jacob Routh.

Died on pneumonia, February 3rd, 1885, Joe Amos, the oldest son of Bro. C. M. Amos. W. T. D.

Died, on the 6th of February 1885, little Maggie Bomar, the youngest child of Maj. John Earle Bomar, of Spartanburg, S. C.

Fell asleep in Jesus on the morning of the 29th January, Mr. Abner Atkinson, aged about sixty-two. Bro. Atkinson had been for nearly thirty years a consistent member of the Beech Island Baptist Church.

Mrs. Annie M. Durant. Twice within a month has the Lynchburg Church been visited... on the 22nd of December, Bro. J. W. Hawkins "finished the course," and at the close of the 25th day of January, the 4th Sabbath, sister Durant, consort of J. J. Durant.... J. Howard Carpenter. Mayesville, S. C. Feb. 10, 1885. Southern Christian Advocate and Watchman and Southron copy.

Issue of February 26, 1885

Married by the Rev. J. L. Rollins, at the residence of Mrs. Roe, on the 13th of February, Mr. Thomas Fobs to Miss Minnie Roe, all of Georgetown County, S. C.

February 19th, 1885, by Rev. A. Buist, Mr. John Creech and Miss Lizzie Miles, both of Barnwell County, S. C.

February 18th, 1885, by the Rev. W. M. Rankin, Mr. Albert Latta, of Monroe, N. C., to Miss Jessie Garland, of White Plains, S. c.

Thursday, January 22d, 1885, by Rev. L. C. Ezell, at the residence of the bride's father, Mr. A. S. McAbee to Miss P. A. Turner, all of Spartanburg County.

January 28th 1885, at the residence of the bride's father, by Rev. W. J. Snider, Mr. Marcy Hill and Miss C. Alice Cuttino.

Departed this life Feb'y 6th, 1885, in Georgetown County, S. C., Mrs. Sarah E. Williams. The subject of this sketch was born May 1st, 1824. She was brought up under Methodist influence. About fifteen years ago, she was baptized into the fellowship of the Baptist church by Rev. Alford Nobles.... J. L. R.

Issue of March 5, 1885

Married by Rev. A. C. Stepp, on the 22d January, 1885, Mr. Thadeus P. Davis and Miss Nancy Tallulah Thompson, both of Greenville County, S. C.

By Rev. A. C. Stepp, on the 26th February, 1885, at the residence of Henry Reddin, the bride's father, Mr. Henry M. Wright, formerly of Newberry, now of Laurens, and Mrs. Mollie T. Washington, of Laurens County, S. C.

On the 25th of February 1885, at the residence of the bride's father, by the Rev. Dan'l Durant, Mr. T. W. L. Cox to Miss Susan G. Myers, all of Williamsburg County, S. C.

By the Rev. A. Buist, at the residence of Mr. H. W. Scott, White Pond, S. C., on the 26th of February 1885, Mr. Arthur Williams and Miss Belle McCreary, both of Aiken County.

Departed this life on Sabbath morning, Feb. 15th, 1885, Mrs. Martha Walker, wife of Mr. James B. Walker, near Ridgeway, S. C. For thirty or forty years sister Walker has been a member of Concord Baptist Church.... She leaves a husband, five children and a number of grandchildren. W. H. Hartin.

Issue of March 12, 1885

Married at the residence of the bride's father, in Berkeley County, S. C., February 19, 1885, by Rev. J. J. H. Stoudenmire, Miss Victoria Rast to Mr. J. M. Parlor, all of Berkeley County, S. C.
By Rev. E. H. Graves, at his residence, Feb. 19, 1885, Mr. Jno. S. Oliver to Miss Fletcher L. Herlong, all of Orangeburg Co., S. C.

By Rev. E. H. Graves, at his residence, Jan. 20, 1885, Mr. Govan Seawright to Miss Sarah Crider, all of Orangeburg Co., S. C.

Near Blackville, S. C., March 4, 1885, by Rev. A. Buist, Mr. Joseph Odom and Mrs. Mary Baxley, both of Barnwell Co.

February 23d 1885, at the residence of the bride's mother, Mrs. S. W. McIver, by Rev. G. B. moore, Capt. W. C. Coker to Miss Lavinia McIver.

February 25th, 1885, at the residence of the bride's sister, Mrs. Edwin Dargan, by Rev. G. B. Moore, assisted by the Rev. J. G. Law, Mr. Theodore DuBose to Miss Anna Hart.

At Swift Creek Parsonage, Darlington Co., S. C., on the 22d of February 1885, by Rev. A. McA. Pittman, Mr. William Bryant and Miss Bettie Lunn, daughter of Capt. T. J. Lunn.

Died on the 5th of February 1885, Mrs. Sallie C. Smith, wife of Deacon E. E. Smith, aged 40 years, 3 months and 18 days. [eulogy] W. P. S.

Mrs. Curtis Rhodes departed this life on the 21st of February 1885, in the 71st year of her age. For many years she had been a thoughtful member of Swift Creek Baptist Church. A. McA. Pittman.

Issue of March 19, 1885

Married at the residence of the bride's mother in Union County, S. C., on the morning of the 8th of March 1885, by Rev. J. S. Ezell, Miss Mary A. Alexander to Mr. Javan B. Kirby, of Pacolet, Spartanburg County, S. C.

At the residence of the bride's parents, Feb. 3rd, 1885, by Rev. R. J. Edwards, Mr. Robert Riley and Miss Henrietta Shuler, all of Orangeburg County, S. C.

Mr. Matthew H. Watson died at his residence in Marion County, February 26th, 1885. Brother Watson was born April 12, 1813, and died in the seventy-second year of his age. He was married March 12, 1839, and baptised into the fellowship of the Antioch Church in August, 1841. A. W. P.   Mullins, S. C., March 10, 1885.

Issue of March 26, 1885

Married by Rev. S. T. Russell, at the residence of Mr. Cooper Altman, March 8th, 1885, Mr. James Altman and Miss Sarah C. Burrows.

Died at his residence in Allendale, Barnwell County, S. C., on the 4th of March 1885, Rev. Andrew Broadus Estes, aged fifty-three years. He was the only son of Rev. Elliot Estes. Early in life A. B. Estes married Miss Anna Cornelia Willingham, and soon after united with the Baptist church at Lawtonville. He leaves a wife, five sons and four daughters, all of them members of the Baptist church. One son of great promise died a few years ago in Rome, Ga. Jos. A. Lawton.

Issue of April 2, 1885

Married February 26th, 1885, at the residence of the bride's uncle, J. Mat. Finley, by the Rev. J. D. Pitts, Mr. John W. Payne, of Newberry, and Miss Eugenia Sidney Finley, of Laurens County, S. C.

Thursday evening, March 28th, 1885, by Rev. N. N. Burton, at the residence of Mrs. C. A. Meyer, the bride's mother, Mr. Wood H. Loman and Miss Sallie A. Meyer, both of Batesburg, S. C.

In Union County, S. C., Sunday afternoon, March 22d, 1885, at the residence of Mr. E. W. Hames, by Rev. G. W. Gardner, Mr. James H. Parr and Miss Mamie Smith, both of Union County.

By the Rev. J. D. Pitts, on the 19th March 1885, at Mr. B. A. Cunningham's, Mr. John Q. Brown and Miss Lena E. Cunningham.

After a short illness, Mrs. Eliza Ulmer, wife of Ephraim Ulmer, died at her residence in Barnwell County, S. C., March 14th, 1885, in the 73rd year of her age. J. F. Buist.

Issue of April 9, 1885

Married at the residence of the bride's father, near Merrittsville, Greenville County, on Tuesday morning, March 31st, 1885, by Rev. J. A. Mundy, D. D., Mr. Patrick Henry Rielly, of this city, and Miss Leila Goodwin, daughter of Col. John H. Goodwin.

On the 25th of March 1885, at the residence of the bride's father, Mr. S. L. Getzen, by the Rev. J. P. Mealing, assisted by the Rev. S. P. Getzen, Mr. T. W. Fortson, of Fortsons's, Muscogee County, Ga., and Miss M. F. Getzen, of Curryton, S. C.

Died, on the 18th inst., Mrs. Delilah Turkett, aged 88 years. She was a member of the Buffalo Baptist Church for more than sixty years. J. N. Entzminger.

Died, on March 30th, 1885, little Clarence Latimer, youngest child of Mr. and Mrs. S. N. Latimer of Anderson County, S. C.

Tribute of Respect to Silas Lanier from Hardy's Church.

In Memoriam. Mrs. Martha Sarah Willingham, wife of John C. Willingham, died at Allendale on 26th March 1885. She was in her thirty-eighth year. She was born and reared in the neighborhood where she lived and died. The eldest daughter of Dr. B. W. Lawton... studied at Limestone Female College [eulogy].

Issue of April 16, 1885

Tribute of Respect. Lynchburg, S. C., April 11, 1885, to Annie M. Durant.

Died at the residence of her husband, Graham's, S. C., April 1st 1885, Mr. B. T. Hane, in the forty-first year of her age. Sister Hane united with the Ghent's Branch Baptist Church in September 1870. W. D. R.

Died, at her home in Orangeburg, on the morning of the 3rd of April 1885, Mrs. Lenore Bailey Chaplin, wife of Rev. W. F. Chaplin.

Mrs. Mary Steedly Hughes, wife of Brother A. Jackson Hughes, of Barnwell County, S. C., died on the 8th day of February 1885, in the fifty-sixth year of her age. She was baptized some thirty-four years ago by Rev. J. M. hoover, at the old Bethesda Church.   W. D. R.   Graham's, S. C.

Issue of April 23, 1885

Married, at Clifton, S. C., March 8th, 1885, by Rev. G. P. Hamrick, Mr. E. R. Cash to Miss M. L. Byrd, both of Spartanburg Co., S. C.

At Clifton, S. C., March 17th, 1885, by Rev. G. P. Hamrick, Mr. J. E. Dodson to Miss Idella Whitaker, both of Spartanburg County, S. C.

By Rev. G. P. Hamrick, at the bride's mother's, in Spartanburg, S. C., April 5, 1885, Mr. E. S. Kirby to Miss L. M. Cooper, both of Spartanburg County, S. C.

Tribute of Respect from New Hope Baptist Church, Lancaster County, S. C., April 12, 1885, to Mrs. Mattie Thomas Barton.

Issue of April 30, 1885

Tribute of Respect from Mr. Carmel Baptist Church, Jamison's, S. C., April 26, 1885, from the Woman's Mission Society to Mrs. Martha Hoffman, consort of the late Rev. J. S. C. Hoffman.

Tribute of Respect from Charlottesville, Va., April, 4 1885, from Albemarle Female Institute to Lilian McGee.

Died, at the residence of her grandmother, Mrs. H. T. Sweat, Natchitoches Parish, La., on the 18th of April 1885, Alice Edgerton Pinchard, only daughter of Thomas and Bettie Pinchard.

Died, at her home near Orangeburg, April 21, 1885, Mrs. Martha Hoffman, wife of Rev. J. S. C. Hoffman, at the age of sixty-six. Her husband preceded her ten months ago.   D. W. K.

Issue of May 7, 1885

In Memoriam. Elizabeth Caroline Mahoney, wife of that aged servant of God, Rev. H. W. Mahoney, passed to her rest, January 23d, 1885. Our sister was born November 11, 1812, in the fork of Black River, Clarendon County. In February 1828, She was baptized into the Moriah church by Rev. Jesse Hartwell, by whom also, on Nov. 3, 1831, she was joined in marriage to Rev. H. W. Mahoney... C. C. B.   Sumter, S. C.

Issue of May 21, 1885

The Late Prof. George W. Riggan, D. D., died 18th April 1885. Tribute from Faculty of Southern Baptist Theological Seminary. Louisville, April 23, 1885.

Married by Rev. J. Howard Carpenter, April 30, 1885, Mr. J. E. W. Chandler to Miss Sallie Truluck.

May 3d, 1885, by Rev. H. K. Ezell, Mr. W. M. Pinson and Miss C. L. Pool, all of Woodruff, Spartanburg County, S. C.

At the residence of the bride's father, on 30th April 1885, by Elder D. Weston hiott, Mr. Martin J. Welborn, of Oconee County, and Miss Annie, youngest daughter of Thos. R. Price, Esq., of Pickens County, S. C.

In Williamston, S. C., April 26th 1885, by Elder D. W. Hiott, Mr. Matthew S. Moore and Miss Lille Beeks, all of Pelzer, S. C.

Mrs. Caroline Sanders Dorrill, wife of the late Augustus Dorrill, of Charleston, died on the morning of May 34d, 18854, in Barnwell County, S. C. She died in her 62nd year, was baptized into the fellowship of the First Baptist Church of Charleston, S. C., by Dr. Brantley, Sr. J. F. Buist.

Nathan D. Williams was born in Richland County, S. C., near Gadsden, April 12th, 1823, and died at his residence near Bishopville, S. C., of typhoid pneumonia, January 1st, 1885. He joined the Piedmont Baptist Church in August 1872. W. J. L. "Christian Neighbor" please copy.

Died, at the residence of her husband, E. H. Poore, Esq., in Anderson County, on the morning of the 5th of May, Mrs. Flora Poore... C. M.

Issue of May 28, 1885

Married on the 12th of May 1885, at the residence of the officiating minister, Rev. C. B. Stewart, Mr. James P. Johnson, of Laurens County ,and Miss Laura A. Williams, of Greenville County, S. C.

At the residence of the bride's parents, in Berkeley County, S. C., on the 20th of May, 1885, by Rev. S. T. Russell, Mr. W. P. Russell to Miss L. F. Eagerton.

Died at the residence of its grandmother, in Camden, S. C., April 28thk 1885, Fred Evans, Mathis, aged one year and eleven months,son of brother and sister F. E. Mahtis of our church.

Died, at Ridge Spring, S. C., April 13th, 1885, Joseph R. Crouch, in the 18th year of his age.

Issue of June 4, 1885

Died, at Belton, S. C., May 27th, 1885, Mrs. G. W. Taylor, daughter of the late Rev. Robert King. C. M.

Herbert Key, infant son of S. H. and Catharine Mack, of St. Matthew's, S. C., died on May 13th, 1885, at the age of ten months and sixteen days.

Died, in Fairfield County, S. C., May 20th, 1885, in the sixty-eighth year of his age, Mr. Reuben Motley, leaving a family of three daughters.... T. W. M.

Died, suddenly, of heart's disease, May 25, 1885, at Ninety-Six, S. C., Dr. John W. Calhoun, aged 63. Dr. Calhoun was a Methodist....

Issue of June 11, 1885

Died, in Bamberg, Barnwell County, S. C., May 8th, 1885, Mrs. Narcissa Ray, wife of Capt. H. M. Ray, in the 52nd year of her age. The deceased had been a member of Springtown Baptist Church for many years... J. G. W.

Died, in Bamberg, Barnwell County, S. C., May 20th 1885, Capt. Hugh M. Ray, in the 55th year of his age. Twelve days after the death of his wife, Bro. Ray died of the same disease... both are sleeping in the Springtown cemetery. At the organization of Capt. T. W. Sanders' company, he was elected a lieutenant, and when the war ended he was captain of the same company, Co. H. 17th Regiment.... J. G. W.

Issue of June 18, 1885

Died, at the hold home in Edgefield County, S. C., on the 4th of June '85, Mrs. Elizabeth Ann Coleman, relict of the late Rev. J. w. Coleman, aged 78 years. She was a Miss Harris, a native of Abbeville County. She survived her husband not quite three years. W. A. G. Gaines', S. C., June, 1885.

Issue of June 25, 1885

Bro. Curran H. Sloan is no more [eulogy]. Wm. Henry Strickland. Nashville, Tenn., June 14, 1885.

Mr. Simeon Patterson was born in Edgefield County, S. c., Feb. 28th, 1832, and in early manhood removed to Colleton County, S. C., where he died Dec. 1st, 1881, leaving a wife, five children, and many grandchildren. R. S. W.

Died, at St. George's, S. C., May 5th,1885, Mrs. Marsenah Elinor Kenyon, wife of Joseph A. Kenyon, in the 44th year of her age....

Issue of July 2, 1885

In Memoriam. Leta and Florence Pringle, from the home of Dr. W. J. Pringle. Sumter, S. C., June 28th, 1885.

Tribute of Respect to Robt. C. Harris, from South Union Sunday School, June 21, 1885.

Married at Beech Island, S. C., June 4th, 1885, at the residence of Mr .John Wright, by Rev. F. Jones, Mr. W. F. Martin, of Madison, Ga., to Miss Mary Lamar Wright, of Beech Island.

On the 15th of June 1885, by the Rev. W. H. King, Mr. Z. H. Carwile, of Oconee County, and Miss Essie J. Latham, of Anderson Co., S. C.

On Tuesday evening, June 9, 1885, at Greenwood, S. C., by Rev. Chas. Manly, D. D., Mr. L. L. McGee, of Belton, and Miss Carrie Cobb, of Greenwood, S. C.

Issue of July 16, 1885

Married at the residence of the bride's father, at Allendale, S. C., on Sunday afternoon, July 5th, 1885, by the Rev. John T. Morrison, Oliver P. Arnold, of Wartrace, Tenn., to Miss Annie Willingham, daughter of E. G. Willingham.

Died, at Summerville, S. C., on the 4th of July 1885, little Robby Taylor, son of Mr. and Mrs. L. P. Taylor. Maggie Hunter. Abbeville, S. C., July 6, 1885.

Mrs. E. Janie Berry, wife of Mr. Thomas N. Berry, departed this life at Chester, S. C., June 28th, 1885. Mrs. Berry, formerly Miss E. Janie Kennedy, granddaughter of Maj. John Kennedy, who was so long and favorably known in Chester... R. W. S.

Died, at Belton, June 26th, Francis Stakely Poore, the youngest child of Jas. W. and Corrie Poore, aged 18 months and 21 days.

In Memoriam. Little Jerry Eugene, youngest child and only son of Mr. and Mrs. B. M. McGee, who died July 4th, 1885, aged twenty-one months. R. C. H.

Issue of July 23, 1885

Tribute of Respect to Deacon John Williamson from Flint hill Church, June 28th, 1885.

Mrs. Washington Poole died near Spartanburg, S. C., July 9th, 1885. For nearly twenty years, Mrs. poole was a consistent member of the Baptist Church... W. T. Tate.

Issue of July 30, 1885

Tribute of Respect from Springtown Church to Hugh M. Ray

Married at the residence of the bride's step-father, John P. McKissick, Wednesday, 12 m., July 15, 1885, by Rev. G. W. Gardner, Mr. Eugene G. Evans, of Pendleton, and Miss Nannie E. Glenn, of Union, S. C., only daughter of Mrs. Mary McKissick.

On the evening of July 21st, 1885, by Rev. S. H. Miller, M. D., Mr. Solus Truluck to Miss Vermelle Player, youngest daughter of Christopher Player, Esq., all of Sumter co., S. C.

Mrs. Emeline S. Grimes died in Charleston, July 23d, 1885, aged fifty-eight years. In her death, Branchville Church loses a useful member. D. W. K.

Mrs. E. C. Ferguson of Darlington County, S. C., died on the 6th of May 1864, in the seventy-ninth year of her age. Mrs. Ferguson was an earnest member of Black Creek Church. W. H. H.   Ridgeway, S. C.

Departed this life July 13th, 1885, at Providence, S. C., S. C. Martin, son of Mr. and Mrs. S. W. Mobley. J. J. Myers.

Issue of August 6, 1885

In Memoriam. From my Welford congregation, Mr. Randolph Turner died at his home on the evening of the 21st inst., aged fifty-nine years. I. W. Wingo. Gaffney City, July 28, 1885.

Mr. S. W. Nicholson, the postmaster at Elmwood, Edgefield County, one of the wealthiest citizens in the county, died on the 19th of July.

In Memoriam. Departed this life at her childhood's home in Williamston, Tuesday July 17, 1885, Mrs. Maimee Mauldin Tribble, in the 26th year of her age. In 1882 she united her life to that of Mr. R. M. Tribble, and they resided in Seneca City until about a year ago....

Issue of August 13, 1885

Married, July 20th, 1885, by Rev. W. A. Gaines, Mr. Willie Hollingsworth to Miss Anna Maria Whatley, both of Edgefield.

Died, on the 27th of June 1885, Horace Ford Youngblood, eldest child of Mr. and Mrs. Frank Youngblood of Beech Island.

Departed this life on the morning of the 27th of July 1885, Mrs. Rachel Amelia Beverly, wife of W. D. Beverly, pastor of the Baptist Church at this place. She was a native of South Carolina, born at Society Hill, in Darlington County, May 13th, 1828... fellowship of the Black Creek Church. She was united in marriage to Rev. W. D. Beverly December 27th, 1851.

Issue of August 20, 1885

Tribute of Respect from the Long Branch Baptist Church to Brother I. P. Harley.

Married at the residence of the bride's father, F. J. Buyck, Aug. 13, 1885, by Rev. D. W. Key, Mr. John McLaughlin, of Richland County, and Miss Mamie Buyck, of St. Matthews.

Died on Sabbath morning, June 28th, 1885, at the home of brother James Morgan, Barnwell County, Capt. John B. Coward, aged 82 years... member of Cypress Chapel Church. J. J. M.

Died near Honea Path, Anderson County, on the 3rd of August, 1885, May, eldest living child of Joel and Mary Jane Harper, aged 7 years and 2 months. W. A. G. Gaines', S. C., Aug. 1885.

Died, of pneumonia, 7th Feb. 1885, Alice, second daughter of J. and Cornelia Corley, of Edgefield County. W. A. G.   Gaines', S. C., 1885.

Issue of September 3, 1885

Tribute of Respect to Manchester Padgett from Bethel Church.

Married at the residence of the bride's father, Lanes, S. C., on the evening of August 5th, 1885, Miss ____ Davis, to Mr. Wm. Peagler, by Rev. J. D. Andrews.

At the residence of the bride's father, in Kingstree, on the morning of July 30th, 1885, by Rev. J. D. Andrews, Miss Ammie Keels to Mr. F. E. Thomas, of Wedgefield, S. C.

On the 21st of August 1885, Miss Millie Fowler, a lady of eminent piety, and a member of Abner's Creek Church, passed away after two days' illness. S. M. H.

Departed this life at the residence of Mr. J. M. Kirby, in Abbeville, July 16th, 1885, Mrs. America M. Farr, in the thirtieth year of her age. The subject of this notice was born at Williamston, and was married to Mr. J. W. Farr in 1874... member of Big Creek Baptist Church. She left a husband and three small children.

Issue of September 10, 1885

Tribute of Respect to brother F. G. Stansell from Washington Church.

Tribute of Respect to brother M. S. Messer from South Union Sunday School.

Issue of September 17, 1885

Married, September 3rd, at 1.45 p. m., by Rev. R. W. Sanders, at the residence of the bride's mother in Chester, S. C., Mr. J. W. Dyches, of Lady Lake, Florida, and Miss M. E. Cornwell, of Chester.

Walter Lee, infant son of Colonel and Mrs. E. T. Atkinson, died in Chester, S. C., September 5th, 1885, at 9.15 p. m., of typhoid fever and bronchitis... two years and six months old. R. W. S.

Died, in Hardeeville, S. C., on Thursday, September 3d, after a painful illness, Miss Louisa A. Raymond. A. S. W. Greenville, S. C., Sept. 9th, 1885.

Issue of September 24, 1885

Married at the residence of the bride's father, Mr. I. P. Garrison, York County, S. C., September 10th, 1885, by Rev. J. K. Fant, Mr. B. S. Ferrell to Miss N. Theodocia Garrison.

Died in Pendleton, S. C., September 17, 1885, Robert Maxwell, in his 63rd year.

Died, at his residence in Barnwell, S. C., on the 2nd Sept. 1885, Bro. J. Aaron Green, in his seventy-sixth year. F. J. S. Williston, S. C.

Mrs. Annie E. Perry, wife of Mr. E. A. Perry, born November 30th, 1843, did at their home in Ridge Spring, September 10th, 1885... left husband and children... member of Ridge Spring Baptist Church.

Issue of October 1, 1885

Died, September 4th, 1885, Mrs. Maggie A. Garick, wife of Mr. John P. Garick, eldest daughter of Daniel D. and Mary E. Bonnett, aged 41 years. J. D. Bonnett.

On the evening of the 16th of September, 1885, at his residence, near Cross Hill, Laurens County, S. C., Deacon David Reed fell asleep in Jesus. He was born May 9th, 1813, and lived almost in sight of the place where he first saw the light. He connected himself with the Liberty Spring Presbyterian Church at Cross Hill... later was baptized into the fellowship of the church at Bethabara. R. W. Seymour, Jr. Laurensville "Herald" please copy.

Issue of October 8, 1885

Married, September 20th, 1885, by Rev. G. W. Bussey, at the bride's home, Mr. Bonham Hamilton and Miss Hellen Green, both of Edgefield County, S. C.

September 29th, 1885, by Rev. D. W. Key, Miss Bessie Hammond and Mr. Albert E. Willis, both of Barnwell County, S. C.

On Wednesday evening, September 30, 1885, by Rev. W. D. Rice, at the residence of the bride's mother, Mr. John Crews, of Orangeburg, and Miss Jennie Turner, of Barnwell, S. C.

Died, at Buford's Bridge, Barnwell County, S. C., September 3rd, 1885, Gussie, daughter of Thomas and Rosa Clayton, aged one year and three months.

John David Stuart, of Coronaca, S. C., was born Dec. 29, 1863 and died September 21, 1885. He joined the Siloam Baptist Church in the summer of 1881. Greenwood, S. C. H. C. S.

Issue of October 15, 1885

Married at Swift Creek Parsonage, on the third Sunday morning in September 1885, by Rev. A. McA. Pittman, Mr. Judson Blackman and Miss Maggie Lunn, daughter of Capt. T. J. Lunn.

After a short illness, passed away quietly on the 6th of October 1885 at Blackville, S. C., Hampton Buist, son of Rev. and Mrs. Arthur Buist, in the twenty-first year of his age. J. F. Buist.

On September 14, 1885, Mrs. Annie Thackston, wife of E. R. Thackston, passed away in her forty-second year. She leaves a bereaved husband and eight children. S. M. Hughes.

Capt. Augustus F. Edwards of Palmetto, S. C. is no more. on Tuesday morning, the 29th ult., he visited the Florence Baptist Parsonage and in company with his pastor visited the Mt. Hope cemetery... Capt. Edwards was born in Spartanburg County, S. C., on the 17th day of May 1826. In 1838 the family removed to a place that is now in the corporate limits of Cartersville, Ga., where their father died and was buried. On the 15th of October 1841, he with B. W. and their elder brother, was baptized into the fellowship of the Petit's Creek Church by Dr. John W. Lewis, who was afterwards a member of the Confederate Congress. The three brothers returned to South Carolina to get their education and remained in the State... B. G. C.

Issue of October 22, 1885

Married at the residence of the bride's father, Mr. Walter Eubanks of Aiken County k,by Rev. W. D. McMillan, on October 7th, 1885, Mr. Milledge G. Hair of Barnwell County, to Miss Laura E. Eubanks.

At the residence of S. P. Brooks, the brother-in-law of the bride, of Abbeville County, on Thursday, Oct. 15th, 1885, by Rev. J. S. Jordan, Mr. J. M. Harris of Mano--, Texas, and Miss Annie L. Townes, of Greenville, S. C.

On September 17th, 1885, at the bride's father's, Mr. Thos. Humphries, near Gaffney, S. C., Mr. M. A. Sarratt to Miss L. M. Humphries, Rev. G. P. Hamrick officiating.

Oct. 8th, 1885, at the residence of the bride's father, Mr. P. D. Cureton, by the Rev. W. H. Araial, Mr. Charles W. Stokes to Miss Minnie A. Cureton, all of Greenville Co., S. C.

Louise Ruth Long was born in Fairfield County, June 21st, 1821, died August 12th 1885. She had been a member of Little River Church about twelve years. T. W. M.

Issue of October 29, 1885

Married at her father's home in Edgefield County, S. C., Oct. 18th, 1885, by Rev. J. S. Jordan, Miss Annie M., daughter of Mr. Tillman Harling, to Mr. H. Alex Rush.

Oct. 8th, 1885, by Rev. R. W. Burts, Mr. J. C. Milford to Miss Sallie A. Latimer, all of Abbeville County, S. C.

By Rev. R. W. Burts, October 16th, 1885, Mr. Marion F. Gambrell, of Williamston, to Miss M. J. Robinson, of Pelzer.

At the Baptist parsonage in Chester at 7 P. M., Oct. 12th, 1885, by Rev. R. W. Sanders, Dr. Sidney E. Hancock and Miss M. Eugenia Coleman, all of Chester.

October 15th, 1885, at the home of the bride's father, by Rev. I. W. Wingo, Mr. C. Virgil Bostic, of Shelby, N. C., and Miss Mamie Smith, of Pendleton, S. C.

At the residence of the bride's father in Florence, S. C., by the Rev. B. G. Covington, on the 21st of October 1885, Mr. Horatio L. Dare, Jr., of Sumter, to Miss Julia Brown.

At the residence of the bride's father, Deacon S. P. Blankenship, on the 20th of October 1885, by Rev. J. K. Fant, Mr. Zeb. V. Kendrick to Miss Edra E. Blankenship, both of Flint Hill church.

Mrs. Annie Henderson Talbert, daughter of the late Nathaniel Henderson, and wife of Robert R. Talbert, died at the home of her mother, at Phoenix, on the 6th day of October 1885. Less than one year ago occured the pleasant pastoral duty of celebrating her marriage... J. S. Jordan.

Departed this life on the 11th day of October 1885, sister Annis T. Hare, the beloved wife of brother A. D. Hare. She leaves a loving husband, eight children and many relatives... baptized in the fellowship of St. John's Baptist Church by Rev. R. J. Edwards.   Sand Ridge, S. C.   E. H. C.

Issue of November 5, 1885

News of the daeth of Rev. Luther Broaddus, son of the Rev. Andrew Broaddus, D. D., of Virginia, who is held in high esteem in his native State.

[another column] Rev. Luther Broaddus was born at White Plain, Sparta, Caroline County, Va., i 1846. A son of Rev. Andrew Broaddus, D. D., and M. Jane Broaddus, educated at the University of Va., and at the Southern Baptist Theological Seminary. In 1863 he left the University of Va. to join Allen's Company of the 24th Regiment, which was a protion of Gen. M. W. Gary's Brigade of Cavalry.... died on the 26th of October [long account] *Newberry Observer.*

Married, Tuesday, Oct. 27th, 1885, 8 p. m., in Chester, S. C., at the residence of the bride's mother, Mrs. P. Nail, by Rev. R. W. Sanders, Mr. Jno. A. Blake and Miss Rowena B. Nail, all of Chester.

On the evening of October 1st, 1885, in the Baptist Church at Cheraw, S. C., by Rev. R. W. Lide, Miss Kate A. Wilson and Mr. Wm. H. Malloy.

On Wednesday, October 21st, 1885, at the residence of the bride's father, by the Rev. A. Buist, Mr. W. Elmore Ashley to Miss Carrie I. Foreman, daughter of Dr. Isaac Foreman.

Died, 24th August 1885, at the home of Bro. Calvin Metts, Martha Metts, aged 16 years... Canaan Baptist Sunday School. J. D. Bonnett.

Died, at the residence of her father, J. H. Matthews, of this city, Thursday, Oct. 22nd, 1885, 8½ p. m., Mrs. Sophia Anderson, of heart disease and dropsy of the chest, aged forty-one years.

Issue of November 12, 1885

Married at the residence of the bride's father, Mr. Benj. Simons, Charleston, S. C., by Rev. T. M. Galphin, on the afternoon of Nov. 5th, 1885, Dr. L. S. Wolfe and Miss Lottie A. Simons.

At Swift Creek parsonage, on Sunday morning, Nov. 1st, 1885, by Rev. A. McA. Pittman, Mr. Everett Rhodes and Miss Rosa Lewis.

Darling Lee died at his home near Williston, S. C., October 28th, 1885, at the age of seventy-four years, two months and twenty-seven days... D. W. K.

Issue of November 19, 1885

Married October 12th, 1885, at the home of Dr. Robt. Pratt, Due West, S. C., by Rev. J. S. Jordan, his youngest daughter, Miss Laura E., to Mr. T. P. Henderson, of Phoenix, S. C.

At the home of the bride's mother in Union County, S. C., Nov. 10th, 1885, by Rev. I. W. Wingo, Mr. W. W. Gaffney, of Gaffney City, and Miss R. M. Macomson.

Meta Lou, only daughter of John Allen Weathersbee, died October 30th, 1885, aged seven years and ten months. Williston, S. C.

Eveline Elizabeth Sprawls, died Nov. 11, 1885, aged forty-nine years. She had been a member of Rosemary Baptist Church for thirty years. Williston, S. C.

Married on the morning of the 17th of november, 1885, at the residence of the bride's father, in Kershaw County, by Rev. A. S. Williford, Mr. J. A. P. Blackman, of Lancaster County, and Miss Mollie Mickle, of Kershaw County.

On the 15th of November, 1885, at the home of the bride's mother, by Rev. G. W. Bussey, Mr. Willie Carter, of Laurens County, and Miss Addie Lanham, of Edgefield County.

At Swift Creek parsonage, on Thursday morning, November 19, 1885, by Rev. A. McA. Pittman, Mr. Jesse Bryant, Sr., and Miss Emma Blackwell.

At Manning, S. C., Nov. 17th, 1885, by Rev. R. B. Mahony, assisted by Rev. L. D. Pass, Mr. Washington Broadway and Miss Lizzie Mahony.

In Clarendon County, by Rev. L. D. Bass, on the 11th November 1885, Mr. Logan and Miss Ard.

On the evening of the 12th November 1885, by Rev. B. F. Miller, of Abbeville county, at the residence of the bride's mother, Mrs. S. D. Cheatham, Mr. Luke D. White to Miss Lou Cheatham, all of Edgefield County, S. C.

At the residence of the bride's father, on the evening of the 19th of november 1885, by the Rev. C. A. Stiles, Miss Ada V. Rhame and Mr. J. R. Cloud, all of Richland County, S. C.

November 17th, 1885, at the home of W. H. Richardson, by Rev. I. W. Wingo, Mr. S. R. Thackston, of Union County, and Miss S. M. Littlejohn, of Spartanburg County.

At the residence of the bride's father, Thos. E. Rickenbaker, by Rev. D. W. Key, November 25th, 1885, Rev. T. M. Galphin and Miss Lizzie Rickenbaker.

By the Rev. A. G. Collier, at the residence of the bride's father, the Hon. J. P. Blackwell, on November 22d, at 4 o'clock p. m., Mr. J. H. Tompkins and Miss Carrie S. Blackwell.

November 25th, 1885, by Rev. J. Howard Carpenter, Miss Fannie C. Hicks, of Sumter County, to Mr. J. Calhoun Baker, of Clarendon County, S. C.

November 24th, 1885, at the residence of the bride's father, in Anderson County, S. C., by Rev. H. M. Allen, Miss Lucia Walters, daughter of Col. W. E. Walters, to Mr. R. P. Wheeler, of Putnam County, Ga.

Died, November 13th, 1885, James W. Latimer, fourth son of Mr. and Mrs. S. N. Latimer, aged twenty years and eleven months.

Mrs. Ann Jane Scott departed this life on Sunday, October 11th, 1885, at her residence near Gadsden, S. C., in the 78th year of her age. She was the relict of deacon John Scott, who was for many years well known to the members of the Charleston Baptist Association. She was a member first of the Congaree and afterwards of the Good Hope churches.

Fell asleep in Jesus, on the 16th of November 1885, in Long Town, Fairfield County, S. C., Mrs. Pauline Scott Jones, wife of Mr. Ellison Jones, aged twenty-six years. She was the only surviving child of Mr. B. R. and Mrs. E. P. Scott. She has left husband, two babes, parents.... J. K. M.

On Sunday, the 25th of October 1885, was buried at Graham's, S. C., the remains of Perry H. Cooper. For two years past he had made his home in Florida.... J. C. B.

Issue of December 10, 1885

In Memoriam. From Baptist Sunday School at Clinton to Mrs. F. L. Williams, the mother of Rev. N. B. Williams.

Oscar L. Stringer departed this life November 9, 1885, at the residence of his father, A. J. Stringer, Esq., in Belton, S. C. He was born May 3d, 1867. C. M.

Married at the home of the bride's father, Dec. 3rd, 1885, by Rev. G. W. Bussey, Mr. M. L. Red, of Aiken, and Miss Ella Jennings.

Died, October 2nd 1885, at her home in Clinton, S. c., Mrs. Sarah Crowder, aged forty-four years, ten months and nine days. She leaves a husband, three children and an aunt (who was the only mother she ever knew).

In Memoriam. Just before leaving my charge in South Carolina, I buried Byron, the youngest son of Mr. and Mrs. Ellis Hill, Cartersville, S. C. R. B. Mahony. Stanford, Ky., Nov. 27, 1885.

Issue of December 17, 1885

Married on the 26th of Nov., 1885, at the residence of the bride's mother, Mrs. Mary A. Bolt, by Rev. A. C. Stepp, Mr. O. H. Perry Woolbright, of Oconee County, and Miss Ida Bolt, of Laurens County.

At the residence of the bride's mother, Nov. 15, 1885, by Rev. W. A. Gaines, Mr. Madison Medlock, to Miss Mary Emma Reynolds, both of Edgefield County, S. C.

At the residence of the bride's father, Hon. James Strom, on 10th December 1885, by Rev. W. A. Gaines, Mr. C. H. B. Williams to Miss Annie Lela Strom, both of Edgefield County.

December 3, 1885, at Storeville, S. C., by Rev. H. M. Allen, Miss Ida Simpson to Mr. Marion Barnes.

On the evening of the 9th inst., at the residence of the bride's mother, B. T. Rice, Probate Judge for Barnwell County, and Miss Lizzie Walker, a daughter of the late N. G. W. Walker, for so many years Sheriff of Barnwell County. Paul Willis. Barnwell, Dec. 11, 1885.

Issue of December 24, 1885

Married at the residence of the bride's father, Dr. J. W. Lowman, by Rev. T. M. Galphin, Mr. M. B. Randle, of Arkansas, and Miss Estelle Lowman, of Orangeburg, S. C.

Dec. 29, 1885, at the residence of the bride's mother, by Rev. Joab Edwards, Mr. Valentine Poole and Miss Rosa Able, both of Aiken County, S. C.

December 6th, 1885, at the residence of the bride's father, by Rev. G. N. Askew, Mr. J. B. Armstrong, of Appleton, and Miss Bessie Miller, daughter of Dr. J. C. Miller, both of Barnwell County, S. C.

At the residence of S. N. Merritt, the bride's father, December 15, 1885, by Rev. J. K. Fant, Mr. John Bellen and Miss Ida Merritt.

December 17, 1885, at Fort Mill, S. C., by Rev. J. K. Fant, Miss Estelle McDowell and Mr. A. A. Munn.

By Rev. J. D. Mahon, at the residence of Mr. J. W. Weir, on the 18th November 1885, Mr. Martin F. Pope and Miss Minnie Cassels, all of Fairfield.

By Rev. J. D. Mahon, at the residence of the bride's father, on the 26th of November 1885, Mr. C. E. Waters and Miss Fanny D. Kerr, all of Fairfield.

By the Rev. T. W. Reid, on the 20th December 1885, at the residence of the bride's father, J. J. Watson, Esq., Mr. Thomas Benson and Miss Annie Watson, all of Greenville County.

By the Rev. T. W. Reid, on the 20th December 1885, at the residence of the bride's father, Mr. J. D. Cooper, Mr. Jasper Watson and Miss Mollie Cooper, all of Greenville County.

Tribute of Respect from Clinton Baptist Church to Francis L. Williams and Sarah J. Crowder.

Tribute of respect to Mrs. Pauline S. Jones from Longtown Baptist Church.

Issue of January 7, 1886

Married at the residence of the bride's parents, by Rev. R. J. Edwards, December 17th, 1885, Mr. Luther Smith and Miss Ellen Shuler, all of Orangeburg County, S. C.

November 5th, 1885, by Rev. M. W. Rankin, Mr. William Hancock to Miss Ellen Thorne.

December 17th, 1885, by Rev. M. W. Rankin, Mr. Gilliam Horton to Miss Alice Hough.

By Rev. A. C. Stepp, on the 23d December 1885, at the residence of B. F. Moseley, Esq., the bride's father, Mr. James B. Johnson to Miss Ida McSwain Moseley, all of Greenville County, S. C.

On Thursday, December 24th 1885, by Rev. J. S. West, at the residence of Mr. J. M. Edwards, the bride's father, Mr. J. V. Young and Mrs. M. J. Martin, all of Greenville.

December 29th, 1885, at the residence of the bride's father, Mr. W. J. Wingo, in the city of Spartanburg, by Rev. T. H. Law, Miss Ida L. Wingo to Mr. H. E. Leach, of Greenville.

At the residence of the bride's father, on December 15th, 1885, by Elder D. W. Hiott, Mr. J. R. Bailey and Miss Lena, youngest daughter of William Duckworth, Esq., all of Anderson County, S. C.

By Elder D. W. Hiott, at Williamston, S. C., on December 17th ,1885, Mr. W. H. Hicks and Miss N. A. Cartee, all of Anderson County, S. C.

On the 17th December 1885, by Rev. Jno. F. McMillan, Mr. S. W. Still and Miss Eliza Whatley, all of Edgefield County.

On the 23d of December 1885, by Rev. Jno. F. McMillan, Mr. Wm. L. Johnson to Miss Prannie Ouzts, of Mountain Creek, Edgefield County, S. C.

Died, at his residence in Colleton County, S. C., the Rev. S. Wilson, in the eightieth year of his age... He joined the church when about twenty years of age, and at about fifty years of age was called to the ministry of the Baptist church. Sallie.

Issue of January 14, 1886

Married at the bride's home, December 24th, 1885, by Rev. G. W. Bussey, Mr. Jonathan Christian and Miss Maggie White.

By Rev. G. W. Bussey, December 31st, 1885, Mr. J. L. Stone and Miss Virginia Stone.

At the residence of the bride's mother, in Edgefield County, S. C., December 22nd 1885, by Rev. J. A. Bell, Mr. D. J. Seigler to Miss P. E. Seigler, all of Edgefield County.

December 31st, 1885, by Rev. D. W. Key, at the residence of Mr. S. S. Walter, Branchville, Mr. M. A. Michaels and Miss Emma M. Patrick, all of Orangeburg County.

December 24th, 1885, at the residence of the bride's grandparents, by Rev. G. T. Gresham, Miss Hattie E. Mills, of Oconee County, and Mr. John Shearer, of Anderson County.

December 29th, 1885, by Rev. G. T. Gresham, at the residence of the bride's parents, Miss Eliza Crawford, of Oconee County, and Mr. W. W. Thomas, of Georgia.

By Rev. Jno. F. McMillan, on January 6th, 1886, Mr. Henry J. Kemp, of Lady Lake, Sumpter County, Fla., to Miss Alice Whatley, of Mountain Creek, Edgefield County, S. C.

Mrs. Elizabeth L. Ulmer of Barnwell County, S. C., died December 31st, 1885, aged forty-five years. The deceased was a faithful wife, devoted mother.... J. F. Biased.

Issue of January 21, 1886

Married by Rev. L. C. Ezell, at the residence of Mrs. Martha Kelly, December 27th, 1885, Mr. A. C. Hughes and Miss Sallie A. Kelly.

By Rev. L. C. Ezell, at the residence of Capt. H. E. Drummond, December 29th, 1885, Mr. J. D. Calmes and Miss Mamie L. Drummond.

By Rev. L. C. Ezell, January 5th, 1886, at the residence of the late James Leatherwood, Mr. W. W. Miller and Miss S. Jane Leatherwood.

At the bride's residence on December 31st, 1885, by Rev. W. O. Petty, Mr. C. B. Rhodes and Miss Jeanette Parrott, all of Darlington County, S. C.

At the residence of Mrs. Patrick, Augusta, Ga., December 23d, 1885, by Rev. F. Jones, Mr. Walker Meyer of Beech Island, S. C., to Miss Fanny Hicks, of Georgia.

At the residence of the bride's parents, by Rev. E. H. Graves, January 5th, 1886, Mr. W. K. Johnson, of Aiken county, and Miss L. A. Bates, of Orangeburg County.

At the residence of James Duckworth, Esq., the bride's father, on the 13th January 1886, by Rev. A. C. Stepp, Mr. Joel A. Ellison of Greenville County and Miss Emma Duckworth, of Williamston, S. C.

By Rev. T. J. Earle, at Capt. G. W. Holtzclaw's, on the 6th of January 1886, Mr. Lawrence Blakeley and Miss Lula Holtzclaw, all of Greenville.

On Thursday, January 14th, 1886, at the residence of Mr. T. L. Clinkscales, near Storeville, S. C., by Rev. S. Lander, D. D., Rev. John M. Lander, of the Williamston Female College, and Miss Sallie Thompson Hall, of Anderson County, S. C., recently a teacher in the Norfolk (Va.) College.

At the bride's home, near Timmonsville, S. C., on Sunday evening, December 27, 1885, by Rev. A. McA. Pittman, Mr. J. S. Lewis and Miss Ella Stokes.

In the Mt. Elon Baptist Church, on December 31st, 1885, by Rev. A. McA. Pittman, Mr. Lee Bass, son of Capt. J. E. Bass, and Miss Lizzie Josey.

At Swift Creek parsonage, on Wednesday evening, January 13th, 1886, by Rev. A. McA. Pittman, Mr. Luther Bateman and Miss Lela Blackman.

At the home of the bride in Darlington County, S. C., on Thursday morning, January 13th, 1886, by Rev. A. McA. Pittman, Mr. J. D. Rhodes and Miss A. J. Bozeman.

In Memoriam. Died at his home in Allendale, Barnwell County, S. C., November 7, 1885, Dr. George P. Harley, in the fifty-second year of his age. The deceased was the son of Mr. Jacob Harley, one of Barnwell's best known citizens about twenty-five years ago.... sending him first to South Carolina College, and afterwards to Harvard University, Mass., where he finished his course.... J. G. W.

Tribute of Respect to Joseph A. Clark from Johnston Baptist Church.

Died, on the 7th of January 1886, in the 33rd year of her age, at Lowrysville, in Chester County, S. C., at the home of Dr. A. T. Anderson, Mrs. Mary L. Anderson, consort of D. G. Anderson, and daughter of E. H. and C. C. Abell.

Issue of January 28, 1886

Married at the residence of the bride's mother, by Rev. J. H. Stoudenmire, December 24, 1885, Mr. J. H. Singletary and Miss O. M. Hart, all of Berkeley County, S. C.

Departed this life at the residence of her brother-in-law, Mr. J. C. C. Feaster, December 3rd, 1885, Mrs. Elizabeth Porter, wife of the Rev. C. M. porter, who died about three years ago. After remaining at her home a few months, she was moved to her sister, Mrs. Feaster's, near Columbia... Sister Porter had long been a member of Poplar Spring Baptist Church, Fairfield County. W. H. Hartin. Ridgeway, S. C.

Mrs. Jane Rountree, born 1798, died 1885, departed this life in September last at the home of her son-in-law, Dr. Isaac Foreman, near Silverton, S. C. Mrs. Rountree was the wife of that noble Christian gentleman, the late Capt. William Rountree, who preceded her to the grave 25 years. Mrs. Rountree leaves two sons and three daughters.... Hattiesville, S. C. Jan. 1st, 1886.

Rev. Moses B. Boynton expired at his home in Barnwell County, S. C., January 6th, 1886, in the forty-sixth year of his age. [long account] J. F. Buist.

Issue of February 4, 1886

Married on Tuesday, January 26th, 1886, by Rev. C. P. Scott, at the residence of the bride's aunt, Mr. Wm. F. Ewart and Miss Cora L. Cannon, all of Newberry Co., S. C.

On Wednesday, January 17th 1886, by Rev. C. P. Scott, at the residence of the bride, Mr. Burr F. Goggans and Mrs. Amanda J. Cash, both of Newberry, S. C.

On the 14th, by Rev. B. F. Miller, at the residence of the bride's father, Maj. B. E. Gibert, Mr. Andrew LeRoy and Miss Addie Gibert, all of Abbeville Co., S. C. Three persons, great-grandmother of the bride, grandfather of the groom, sister of the grandfather were present, whose aggregate ages were 154 years, 93, 85, 76, respectively.

Issue of February 11, 1886

Married by Rev. J. Howard Carpenter, December 17, 1885, Mr. W. D. Truluck of Sumter County, S. C., and Miss Bonnie Perkins, of Lake City, S. C.

By Rev. J. Howard Carpenter, December 24, 1885, Mr. Jno. A. Burgess to Miss Edith A. Carraway, all of Sumter County, S. C.

December 25th, 1885, by Rev. J. Howard Carpenter, Jno. R. Keels, Esq., of Sumter C. H., S. C., to Miss Eunice Keels of Sumter Co., S. C.

January 14th 1886, by Rev. J. Howard Carpenter, Mr. S. D. M. Chandler of Clarendon County, S. C., to Miss Belle McCutchen, of Williamsburg County, S. C.

January 21st 1886, by Rev. J. Howard Carpenter, Mr. John M. Welsh to Miss Vermelle Hicks, all of Clarendon County, S. C.

By Rev. A. C. Stepp, on the 29th of January, 1886, Mr. Geo. W. Davis, of Dunklin Township, Greenville County, and Miss Isabella Simpson, of Williamston, S. C.

Issue of February 18, 1886

Married, Tuesday, January 19th, 1886, at the residence of the bride's father, by Rev. J. J. Getsinger, Mr. J. D. Fickling, of Barnwell, and Miss Elizabeth Jefcoat, of Orangeburg.

February 9th 1886, by Rev. G. W. Bussey, Mr. Joseph Sharpton and Miss Savannah Crawford.

At the residence of the groom's uncle, Dr. James Cartledge, on the 11th February 1886, by Rev. J. A. Bell, Mr. D. P. Self to Miss Mamie F. Price, all of Edgefield County, S. C.

By the Rev. H. K. Ezell, February 9th 1886, at Lower Fairforest Church, Union County, S. C., Mr. J. G. Greer, of Spartanburg, and Miss Lou Barnett, of Union.

January 16th 1886, by D. N. Bethea, Esq., at the residence of D. N. Bethea, Mr. S. A. Cook to Miss Harriet Herring, all of Marion County, S. C.

December 31st 1886, by Deacon A. R. Surles, at the residence of A. R. Surles, Mr. C. J. Cook to Miss Mary D. Surles, all of Marion Co., S. C.

Mrs. Mattie L. McCarley died at Winnsboro, S. C., January 18th 1886, in the thirty-fifth year of her age. Mrs. Oxner, her mother, is a devoted member of the Baptist Church.... At a very early age the deceased was baptized by Rev. William Elkin, at the Hormah Baptist Church. C. G. B. Winnsboro, S. C., Jan. 26, 1886.

Mrs. Eliza Jane Hinton, formerly Miss Eliza Jane Kennedy, was born in Chester, March 9th, 1832, and departed this life at her home in the same town, January 28th 1886. She was the daughter of Major John Kennedy [eulogy]. R. W. S.

Died, on the 9th of February 1886, at his late residence, near Leavensworth, Darlington Co., S. C., James A. Williams, in the sixty-first year of his age... for thirty-three years he served the Black Creek Church as Deacon... R. W. Lide.

Departed this life January 14th 1886, Mrs. Robert Harley, aged thirty years.... a member of Mt. Arnon Baptist Church. Left husband and step-children....

Tribute of Respect from Salem Sunday School to Mrs. Sarah R. Burriss.

Issue of March 4, 1886

Married on the 21st February 1886, at Fingerville, S. C., by Rev. T. V. Gowan, Mr. Jas. F. Clark and Miss Mollie E. Morrow, all of Spartanburg County, S. C.

By Rev. R. W. Barber, February 21, 1886, in Wolfe Creek Church, Mr. J. L. Greene to Miss Anna M., only daughter of Mr. L. F. Prince, both of Landrum's, S. C.

At Bristol, Ashe County, N. C., January 19, 1886, by H. J. Church, Esquire, Mr. McIver Stuckey, of Darlington County, S. C., to Miss Clara Baldwin of Ashe County, N. C.

On Thursday evening, February 18th 1886, at the residence of the bride's father, by Rev. J. R. Earle, assisted by Rev. Walter Daniel, Mr. Willis Hudgens to Miss Nettie Daniel, all of Oconee County, S. C.

By Rev. W. T. Derieux, on the 17th of February 1886, at the bride's home in Spartanburg County, Miss Kate Bomar to Mr. W. D. Hollis.

At Blackville, S. C., February 18th 1886, by Rev. A. Buist, Mr. Jack Alrige and Mrs. Ellen E. Birt.

February 18, 1886, at the home of the bride's father, Dr. T. E. Jennings, by Rev. G. W. Bussey, Mr. A. V. Bussey and Miss Maria Jennings.

On February 25th 1886, at 3 o'clock p. m., by Rev. H. C. Smart, at Sylvania, the residence of the bride's father, J. H. Wideman, Maj. J. T. Youngblood of Troy, formerly of Williston, to Miss Mamie W. Wideman, of Abbeville.

At the residence of Mr. J. T. Chandler, by Rev. S. T. Russell, Mr. B. F. Brockington of Williamsburg to Miss Emma Chandler, of Clarendon County, S. C.

February 25th, 1886, by Rev. G. H. Carter, at the residence of the bride's father, T. W. Roe, Mr. B. M. moore to Miss Minnie Roe, of Greenville County, S. C.

Little Effie, daughter of J. R. and Sallie Wolfe, of Pineville, N. C., died December 6th, 1885, aged four years. Just eight weeks afterwards, Carl, their baby son, aged twenty-two months... J. K. F.

Departed this life, at his home near Blackville, Barnwell County, S. C., February 2nd, 1886, Mr. John A. Burckmyer, in the sixty-first year of his age. The deceased was a native of Charleston, removed to Blackville during the war. Our friend leaves a devoted wife and thirteen children, four of them by a former marriage, and three sisters, Mrs. Judge B. C. Pressley, Mrs. Judge John C. Pressley, of California, and Mrs. Winkler, widow of the late Dr. Winkler. J. G. W.

Mrs. Sarah Baker, wife of Elisha Baker, died at her home near White Plains, S. C., 16th January 1886, in the sixty-ninth year of her age. [eulogy]

Issue of March 11, 1886

Charles Franklin Spearman, son of Robert F. Spearman, was born in Laurens County, S. C., in 1859, and united with the church of his fathers at Bathabara. On 27th December 1884, he was united in marriage to Miss Jane S. Bozeman, daughter of D. L. and J. F. Bozeman.....

In Memoriam. Died, at the residence of Mrs. Rebecca McKay, in Greenville, on Thursday, February 18th 1886, John McKay, son of William and Rebecca McKay in the 22nd year of his age.

Married February 24th, 1886, by Rev. M. W. Rankin, Mr. James Cato, of Kershaw County, to Miss Margaret Knight, of Chesterfield Co., S. C.

On the afternoon of the 25th February 1886, at the residence of the bride's parents, by Rev. J. L. Rollins, the bride's father, Mr. F. E. Rogers to Miss Mary J. Rollins, all of Williamsburg County, S. C.

On the 21st of February 1886, by Rev. J. C. Furman, at the home of the bride's mother, Mr. R. H. Alverson, of Simpsonville, to Miss J. C. Locke.

Issue of March 18, 1886

Married at the residence of Capt. J. E. Bass, the step-father of the bride, in Darlington County, S. C., on Wednesday evening, February 24, 1886, by Rev. A. McA. Pittman, Mr. B. A. Johnson, of Manning, S. C., and Miss Kimmie Lucas.

By Rev. B. G. Covington, on the 2nd Feb. 1886, at the home of the bride, Mr. G. C. L. Cox, of Scranton, S. C., to Miss Minnie E. Weatherford, of Florence, S. C.

By Rev. N. B. Clarkson, on the 17th of Feb., 1886, Mr. Alonzo Stowe, to Miss Vermell Frierson, all of Williamsburg County, S. C.

By the Rev. C. T. Anderson, on the 3rd March, '86, at the home of the bride, Mr. L. N. James, of Williamsburg County, to Miss Rebecca Hudson, of Marion County, S. C.

On Thursday, March 11th, 1886, at the residence of the bride's father, Dr. B. P. West, by Rev. J. K. Mendenhall, Rev. J. E. Covington, of Yorkville, S. C., and Miss Sallie West, of Greenville County, S. C.

Died, at her home near Barnwell, S. C., on 27th February 1886, Mrs. Mary Horn Sanders, at the age of sixty-five. Mrs. Sanders was a native of Augusta, Ga., but in youth as a bride came with her husband, the last Moses Sanders to this State....

Issue of March 25, 1886

Died, February 23rd, 1886, Eva, eldest daughter of Mr. and Mrs. Claudius Ashley, aged ten years.

Herbert James, the eldest child of Thos. E. and Cornelia E. Rickenbacker, departed this life on March 16th, 1886. He was born 24th July 1867... received into the fellowship of Four Holes Baptist Church. Orangeburg, S. C., March 21, 1886.

Mrs. Kate Hinton Means, wife of Mr. Joseph D. Means, and daughter of Rev. L. C. Hinton and Mrs. Kate Hinton, departed this life at her home in Chester, March 13th, 1886, 2:38 a. m. She was born in Chester, March 28th, 1860, and was married but little more than a year ago. R. W. S.

Married at the residence of the bride's father, Hon. A. A. Myers, by Rev. Thos. H. Burruss, on the evening of March 20th 1886, Mr. Manly T. Barrett, of Anson County, N. C., to Miss Sallie H. Myers, of Marion County, S. C.

Issue of April 1, 1886

Married by Rev. W. H. Hartin, March 24, 1886, at the residence of the bride's mother, Mrs. Jane Wiggins, Mr. Benjamin Cloud of Fairfield Co., and Miss Olivia Higgins, of Richland Co., S. C.

By Rev. W. H. Hartin, Feb. 11, 1886, at the home of Mr. Wm. Cloud, Mr. Henry Rains and Mrs. Z. Boney, all of Fairfield Co., S. C.

By Rev. W. H. Hartin, Feb. 4, 1886, at his residence, Mr. James Marthers and Miss Little Sweatman, all of Fairfield Co., S. C.

On the 18th March 1886, at H. A. James', the residence of the bride's brother, near Bishopville, S. C., by Rev. W. O. Petty, Mr. Henry Woodward and Miss Mary James, all of Sumter County, S. C.

At Elko Church, March 21, 1886, by Rev. D. W. Key, Mr. F. A. Fairy, of Orangeburg Co., S. C., and Miss Julia Wade, of Barnwell Co., S. C.

At the residence of the bride's father, March 25th, 1886, by Rev. D. W. Key, Mr. Brooks A. Parler and Miss S. Parniece Cuttino, all of Orangeburg County, S. C.

On the 3rd of March 1886, by Rev. C. T. Anderson, at the residence of the bride's mother, Mr. Louis N. Jones, of Williamsburg Co., to Miss s. R. Hudson of Marion Co., S. C.

Little Susie, aged two years, infant daughter of Mr. and Mrs. L. C. Paysuer, died on 15th March 1886... S. T. F.

Issue of April 8, 1886

Tribute of Respect from Lower Three Runs Church to S. G. Ellis, senior deacon.

Married on Sunday, March 21, 1886, at Black Mingo missionary station, by Rev. J. L. Rollins, Mr. J. B. Sanders to Miss G. A. Moore, all of Georgetown County, S. C.

After long sickness, Aggie Belle Withers, second daughter of J. S. and M. M. Withers, died in Chester, S. C., March 31st, 1886, in the 17th year of her age. R. S. W.

Issue of April 15, 1886

Death of Mrs. Dr. Bailey. On Thursday evening, April 8th, a large number of friends were gathered in Springwood Cemetery in this city, at the burial of the remains of Mrs. Alice Kierulff Bailey, wife of Dr. T. M. Bailey, Corresponding Secretary of the Baptist State Mission Board. She was a native of the Danish West Indies, was educating in Hamburg, was married in 1856....

Issue of April 22, 1886

Deacon John G. Milnor. Citadel Square Baptist Church... John Glenn Milnor was born in the city of Savannah, 21st February 1818, but removed to Charleston at the eight of eight years. His early religious training was among the Presbyterians. Tribute of Respect.

Married on the 18th of April 1886, by Rev. T. V. Gowan, Mr. William H. Cantrell, of Spartanburg, and Miss Mittie S. Johnson, of Columbia, S. C.

At the residence of the bride's mother, by Rev. R. W. Seymour, April 8th 1886, Mr. Frank Cobb, of Laurens County, and Miss Mattie Calhoun, of Abbeville.

Died, in Williamsburg County, S. C., January 15th, 1886, Mrs. Eutula E. Matthews, aged thirty-two years... united with Scranton Baptist Church.

Lizzie Hutto, wife of Henry Hutto, Jr., daughter of C. R. and J. Sturkie, died in her 20th year, and had three children, one five weeks old. E. H. G. Lexington *Dispatch* will please copy.

Rev. Jas. A. Woodward died March 28th, 1886. Mr. Woodward was born in April 1881. He was baptized into the fellowship of Rosemary church, June 1824, with his brother, Rev. S. E. Woodward, now the only surviving member of the family. he spent several years of his early manhood in Georgia.... H. W. M.

Issue of April 29, 1886

Mr. Willis Hair died April 12th 1886, at the age of three score and ten.... member of Rosemary Church.

Mrs. Ellen M., wife of Mr. Wm. Matthews, died at her home near Elko, April 12th, 1886, at the age of forty-one... member of Rosemary Church. D. W. K.

Married on the 22nd of April 1886, by Rev. C. C. Brown, Mr. W. F. Cook to Miss Lula Brogdon, all of Sumter, S. C.

Issue of May 6, 1886

Married at the home of the bride's father, in Augusta, April 27th 1886, by Rev. G. W. Bussey, Mr. J. M. McCain, of Edgefield County, S. C., and Miss Mamie Henderson, of Augusta, Ga.

Julia Gladys, infant daughter of Wm. E. and Mrs. Emma McMichael, died April 26th, 1886, at the age of one year and three months. Williston, S. C. D. W. K.

Issue of May 13, 1886

Mrs. Mary Mims, wife of Mr. Robert Mims, died at Elko, April 23, 1886, at the age of forty-seven. She was a member of Elko Church.... D. W. K.

Mrs. Mary E. (familiarly known as Aunt Polly) Mitchell, died at her home on Saluda, in Edgefield County, Nov. 23, 1885, in the 73rd year of her age... joined Sardis Baptist Church, and was baptized by Rev. Zedekiah Watkins. She was married in early life to Frank Mitchell to whom were born four children. Two of these died in childhood....

Married on the 22nd of January 1886, by Rev. F. Jones, at the residence of Mr. J. C. Hawkinson, Beech Island, Mr. Frank Hawkinson and Miss Ida Stallings, both of Aiken Co.

On the 28th of April, 1886, by Rev. F. Jones, at the residence of Dr. James Galphin, Beech Island, Mr. Albert Barnes and Miss Anne Galphin, both of Aiken County.

Issue of May 20, 1886

Death of Rev. James F. Buist, May 13th, a native of Charleston, born 29th September 1839. His parents died when he was quite young, and he was taken in charge by his uncle E. T. Buist, D. D., who was pastor of the Presbyterian Church, and one of his brothers was a pastor in the same denomination, the late Rev. E. H. Buist of Cheraw. Another brother is the Rev. Arthur Buist of Blackville.

Married in the First Baptist Church, on the 28th of April 1886, by Rev. A. J. S. Thomas, Mr. Tristram Tupper Hyde and Miss Minnie Ball Black, all of Charleston.

Departed this life on the morning of March 12th, 1886, Mrs. Sarah Rallings, wife of Lewis Rallings, at her residence near White Plains, S. C., in the sixty-fifth year of her age... baptized into the fellowship of the Baptist Church at White Plains by Elder Joseph T. Copeland... G. W. B.

Died, suddenly, in Orangeburg County, S. C., May 8th 1886, Mr. Jeremiah Riley, in the seventy-eighth year of his age. In early life joined Antioch Baptist Church. Shortly afterwards he joined the Four Holes Baptist Church... He united with others in constituting Walnut Grove Baptist Church. He left a wife and children. D. W. C.

Issue of May 27, 1886

Tribute of Respect to Rev. James F. Buist who died May 13, 1886.

Tribute of Respect from Mt. Tabor Church to Solomon R. Hennecy.

Married April 29th, 1886, at the home of J. D. Collins, by Rev. J. Q. Adams, Mr. R. P. Ferguson and Miss Barbara Fudge, all of Chester County, S. C.

Died, on the 14th of May 1886, at his home in Abbeville County, S. C., Augustus H. Morton, in his sixty-ninth year. He was an honored deacon in the Beulah Baptist Church, Abbeville Association. He leaves a wife, four daughters and one son.

Paul C., son of John and Florence Lee, died at home near Williston, S. C., May 12, 1886, aged twelve years and seven months. D. W. K.

Mrs. Sallie J. Perry died in Birmingham, Ala., on Monday, May 17th,1886, at the residence of her brother, Capt. F. N. Walker, who went from Spartanburg, S. C., to Birmingham about two years ago. She was the only sister of Mrs. J. C. Hudson. J. C. H.

Mrs. Eliza Starr died at the home of Col. J. H. Burckhalter, Williston, S. c., May 12, 1886, at the advanced age of ninety-five. She lived a widow for sixty-two years, and was the mother of seven children... D. W. K.

Benjamin Daniel Gardner departed this life at his home in Kershaw County, S. C., on the 28th of March 1886, aged thirty-eight years, four months and three days. Bro. Gardner was the fourth son of his parents, and was born near Flat Rock, Kershaw County, November 25th, 1847. He was joined in married with Miss Sarah E. Jones, January 10th 1872... received into the fellowship of Sand Hill Baptist Church, Kershaw County. A. S. Willeford.

Issue of June 3, 1886

Tribute of Respect to Rev. J. F. Buist from Allen's Chapel Church.

Married at the residence of Mr. J. J. Dale, on the 25th of May, by Rev. S. G. Wilkins, Mr. Duncan G. Wilson, Sr., to Mrs. Annie Butler, all of Beaufort, S. C.

Died at Pelzer, S. C., on the 15th of April last, of consumption, Alice Lindsay, aged fifteen years... W. E. O.

Mrs. Emma F., wife of W. E. McMichaels, Williston, S. C., Died May 25, 1886, aged thirty-nine years and three months. She was born at Aiken.... D. W. Key.

Died, in Williston, May 11, 1886, Terrill Smith, infant son of Dr. and Mrs. W. C. Smith, aged one year and two months.

Issue of June 10, 1886

Married at the residence of Mr. Wm. Crouch, on Wednesday, June 2nd, 1886, at 11 o'clock a. m., by Rev. N. N. Burton, Mr. Charles M. Ranton and Miss Carrie E. Crouch, all of Edgefield County, S. C.

Augustus H. Morton. Early in the present century, a young man by the name of Thomas W. Morton, married and settled in the upper western section of Edgefield County, near liberty Hill. His wife was Miss Talbert. The oldest son John B. graduated with honor in the South Carolina College... The second son, too, passed with either in childhood or youth. The only surviving one was August H. Morton, who was born Dec. 24th, 1817. At the age of twenty-two became a member of Bethany Church, of Liberty Hill. In 1833, he married Miss E. A. Payne, the younger half-sister of Deacon Thomas Payne, of Fellowship. Tribute of Respect.

Tribute of Respect to John Asbury Zeigler, who was born in Orangeburg County 14 Nov 1833, and died at his home in our town 3rd May 1886....

Issue of June 17, 1886

Married at the residence of the bride's father, Rev. W. M. Foster, on Tuesday morning, June 8th, 1886, by Rev. G. W. Gardner, Mr. F. G. Treszer and Miss Florence F. Foster, both of Union village, S. C.

On Thursday, May 13, 1886, at the residence of the bride's father, by Rev. W. D. Rice, Mr. Wade H. Zimmons and Miss Willie Way, all of Barnwell County, S. C.

On June 2nd, 1886, at the residence of Dr. Isaac Foreman, Silverton, S. C., by Rev. F. Jones, Mr. William I. Bush to Miss Florence Foreman, all of Aiken County.

Died, at Blackville, S. C., May 12th, 1886, Roger A. Risher, infant son of Mr. and Mrs. Frank Risher. Aged eight months and seventeen days.

John W. Reese died at his home in Newberry County, on the night of the 23rd of April 1886. He died young, leaving a young wife and three small children. J. D. Huggins.

Departed this life on May 28th, 1886, Mrs. Mildred Fant, in her 99th year, at the residence of her son, Dr. F. M. E. Fant, Fairfield County, S. C. She was the daughter of Francis Edrington, who emigrated from Virginia to South Carolina in 1774, and the consort of Wm. Fant, Esq., who died in union County, S. C., 1854. They were both consistent members of Black Rock Baptist Church, Union County. W. Edrington.

Mrs. Jennie Turner Crews, daughter of the late G. W. Turner, of Graham's, S. C., was born August 13, 1863, married 30th September 1885, and died March 17th 1886. W. D. R.

Tribute of Respect upon the death of Rev. Jas. F. Buist.

Issue of June 24, 1886

Mrs. Fannie, wife of Dr. Boyce Brooker, died at the residence of Dr. L. Brooker, Williston, S. C., June 15, 1886, at the age of twenty-seven. She was born in Chambersburg, Pa.... D. W. K.

Died, on June 6th, 1886, Mellichamp, infant son of Mr. and Mrs. E. J. Burch, in Darlington County, S. C., aged nineteen months.

Mrs. Antho T., wife of Bro. J. W. Jones, of Laurens, died 1st of June 1886, at forty-six years of age.... left husband and six children. J. D. P.

Mrs. Mary Young, wife of Mr. Alfred Young, and daughter of Mr. Sam Joe Burch, of Darlington Co., S. C., departed this life at her home, near Ebenezer, on the morning of May 12, 1886, in the twenty-sixth year of her age...

Mrs. Mary Sauls, wife of Isaac Sauls, of Smoak's X Roads, Colleton County, S. C., died June 10th 1886, aged forty-three years, five months and nine days. S. W. A.   Round, S. C., June 16, 1886.

On the night of the 14th of June 1885 [sic], died Ferdinand Munson Gregory. For sixty-seven years he had served his generation... He leaves widow, two daughters and a son, who are members of the Citadel Square Church; a son in Florida a member of the M. E. Church, and the writer of this notice, who is the eldest son. O. F. Gregory. Baltimore, Md., June 15, 1886.

Issue of July 1, 1886

In Memoriam. Sister J. W. Peak, who died on the 15th inst.... tribute of respect from McCormick Baptist Church.

In Memoriam. Dr. David William Cuttino, with his wife Susan Parneice Pack, lived and practiced medicine at Georgetown, S. C., where on the 17th day of November 1819, their son David William Cuttino was born. in his early childhood his father died... his widowed mother with little David made Columbia her home. Tribute of Respect from Santee Church.

Departed this life in Chester, June 22nd, 1886, at 2:40 a. m., Mrs. Margaret Woods, in the seventy-seventh year of her age. Sister Woods was the oldest daughter of Major John Kennedy, and was one of the first members of the Chester Baptist Church. R. W. S.

Mrs. J. W. Peake was born October 10, 1853. She was the third daughter of Dr. Joseph and Mrs. C. Jennings, the latter dying when this daughter was quite young. She was baptized into Plum Branch Baptist Church. She was married to Mr. W. H. peak in December 1872. In 1878 she was let a lone widow. After spending several years teaching, she was married at her residence in Abbeville County in January 1884 to a younger brother of her former husband, Mr. James Peak... J. A. B.

Issue of July 8, 1886

Departed this life on the 28th of June 1886, Mrs. E. M. Williams, wife of Rev. H. A. Williams, of Cross Plains, Ala., in the 73d year of her age. *Christian Index* please copy.

Died of dysentenr, June11th, 1886, James Watson ,youngest son of W. H. and Lizzie Daniel, aged 10 months and twelve days.

Died in Williamston, S. C., June 11, 1886, little Victor, son of G. heyward and Mary Brown Mahon... D. W. Hiott.

Hilton Jones, for forty-odd years a member of the Sand Hill Baptist Church, Kershaw County, fell on sleep on the 20th inst., in the 80th year of his age, at his home. He leaves an aged widow and a number of children. A. S. Willeford.

This tribute is to the memory of Mr. Claudius A. Scott, of Richland County, S. C., who departed this life on 29th of April last, in the 74th year of his age.

Died, in Chester, S. C., June 24th, 1886, Mrs. Jane Y. Dickson, wife of Mr. John Dickson, in the 30th year of his age. She leaves a husband and one child. R. S. W.

Departed this life in Chester, S. C., June 26, 1886, in the 11th month of his age, little John Wesley, infant son of Mr. J. W. and Mrs. Ellen Rothrock. R. W. S.

Died on June 24, 1886, at the residence of her brother-in-law, J. C. Heaner, Mrs. Sallie A. Ayres, aged about 42 years. The deceased was the wife of Mr. John M. Ayres, of Orangeburg County, S. C., and daughter of Rev. Richard and Elizabeth Foster Woodruff, of Woodruff, S. C... united with Four holes Baptist Church of Orangeburg County, R. J. E.

Robbie J. Winter, son of Mr. Robert and Mrs. L E. Winter, of Clarendon co., S. C., departed this life at his home near Ladson Road, june 27, 1886, in the 26th year of his age. Mr. Winter early united with the Clarendon Church near his home. To his sister and brother, whom he stayed with until his marriage on the 17th of January 1886, he was loving and affectionate... Maggie Hunter. Anneville, S. C., June 28, 1886.

On Friday, 25th June, at the home of his father, near Anderson, died James R. Tribble, eldest son of Rev. L. W. Tribble, aged 19 years. He was buried at the Barker's Creek Church. R. P. B.

Wm. J. Daniel died 25th February 1883, in the 64th year of his age. He was born in Williamsburg County, April 1822. Baptized by Rev. J. A. W. Thomas in 1856, and remained a member of the Bennettsville Baptist Church until he moved to Clarendon in 1879... L. D. B.

Tribute of Respect to Rev. D. W. Cuttino from Charity Lodge, No. 62, A. F. M.

Tribute of Respect to Rev. James F. Buist.

Tribute of Respect to Miss Annettie A. Henderson from Standing Spring Sunday School.

Issue of July 15, 1886

Married at the residence of the bride's father, Alexander McDougall, Glasgow, Scotland, Miss Mary McDougall, formerly a student of the Greenville Female College, and afterwards of Tallahassee, Fla., and Mr. Robert Twiggins, of Glasgow, Scotland.

Issue of July 22, 1886

Olive Hewitt, infant daughter of Mr. and Mrs. N. W. Macaulay, fell asleep July 7th, aged six months.

Miss Josephine Hazel, the eldest of three granddaughters of Deacon Joseph Hazel, died 4th of July 1886, at her home in Beaufort, S. C. A. C. W.

Robert Cliett, son of Jno. G. and Sarah G. Thompson, died June 27, 1886, aged one year and twelve days. Williston, S. C. D. W. K.

Died, at Pelzer, S. C., June 26th, 1886, Witsell James, son of Mrs. S. A. James, formerly of Spartanburg county, S. C., in the twentieth year of his age.

On the 7th of July 1886, died Pinkey, aged four years, daughter of brother and sister W. D. Russell, of Pineville, N. C.   J. K. F.

Johnny, son of Brother and sister J. W. Capps, of Flint Hill, died on the 9th inst., aged seven months. J. K. F.

Issue of July 29, 1886

Tribute of Respect to sister E. L. Harbuck.

Married on the 14th of July 1886, at Ocala, Fla., by Rev. R. H. Weller, D. D., Mr. George G. Griffith, formerly of Charlotte, N. C., but now of Jacksonville, Fla., and Miss Maggie Finley, daughter of Gen. J. J. Finley, of Ocala, Fla.

At the residence of the bride's father, Alexander McDougall, Glasgow, Scotland, Miss Mary McDougall, formerly a student of the Greenville Female College, and afterwards of Tallahassee, Fla., and Mr. Robert Twiggins, of Glasgow, Scotland.

Miss Nettie Connelley, daughter of B. D. and S. L. Connelley, of Ninety-Six, S. C., died 8th July 1886, in her seventeenth year.

Died, July 2nd, 1886, Annie Eliza, infant daughter of James M. and Mattie A. McGee, of Greenville, S. C.

Issue of August 5, 1886

On the morning of the 21st inst., died Weston Martin Hiott... J. K. M.

Departed this life on Wednesday morning, July 28th, 1886, Mrs. Sallie Rhodes, a member of Swift Creek Church, and wife of Bro. G. Q. S. Rhodes. A. McA. Pittman.

Died at his home in upper Edgefield, Saturday July 3d, 1886, Deacon John T. Coleman, in the 54th year of his age. He was the oldest son of Rev. J. W. Coleman, and nephew and namesake of Col. John T. Coleman, late of Greenville. W. A. G.

Bro. James Thomas Garrison, son of Re.v J. M. Garrison was born August 12, 1837, married in 1857 to Miss Emily Smith (who for 29 years made him one of the best of wives), died July 19, 1886. J. K. Fant.

Issue of August 12, 1886

Married on Thursday, August 5th, 1886, at the residence of the bride's mother, by the Rev. J. M. Rose, Rev. J. F. Sheppard, of South Easton, Penn., and Miss Mary A. McKay, of Greenville, S. C.

In Greenville, S. C., on August 4th, 1886, by the Rev. Charles Manly, D. D., William G. Whilden and Mrs. E. Julia Mauldin, daughter of Thos. P. Smith, Esq. of Charleston, S. C.

At the residence of Washington Garrett, the bride's father, on the 27th of July 1886, by Rev. A. C. Stepp, Mr. Willie H. Barksdale and Miss Mollie C. Garrett, both of Laurens County, S. C.

By the Rev. A. C. Stepp, on the 5th of August 1886, at the residence of Joseph Bagwell, the bride's father, Mr. G. W. Darby and Miss Ida Lee Bagwell, all of Dunklin, Greenville Co., S. C.

Miss Atlie Loadholt, daughter of J. J. and M. P. Loadholt, of Campbellton, S. C., passed from earth on the 30th day of July 1886, aged sixteen... member of the Harmony Baptist Church.

Mrs. Ella Pounds died at Bradley, S. C., August 1st, 1886, in her 29th year... H. C. S.

Death of little Robert Key Riley, aged two years and nine months...

Died, near Dunbarton, S. C., June 18th, 1886, little Bertha, only child of Mrs. Rosa Killingsworth, aged one year and six months.

Issue of August 19, 1886

Tribute of Respect to Samuel E. Woodward who died 25 July 1886 from Rosemary Baptist Church.

Died on Monday morning, 19th July 1886, at his home in Barnwell County, S. C., Mr. William P. Bates, in the 61st year of his age... member of Pleasant Mountain Baptist Church. J. J. M.

Issue of August 26, 1886

Died in Chester, S. C., August 14th, 1886, little Earle McNinch, infant son of Mr. Amzai and Mrs. Ella McNinch. R. W. S.

Mrs. Sarah Catharine Cline departed this life in the town of Chester, S. c., at 4 p. m., August 17th, 1886. She was born in Salisbury, N. C., January 24th, 1822... for a long time member of the M. E. Church, South... later joined the Baptist Church at Chester. She raised six children, one of them, Rev. A. J. McCoy. R. W. S.

Issue of September 2, 1886

Married at Piedmont, S. C., on Tuesday, August 17th, 1886, by Rev. J. S. Murray, Mr. R. Duff Sloan and Miss M. Lillian Trowbridge, daughter of Mr. S. F. Trowbridge.

At the residence of the bride's father, E. M. Hill, by Rev. M. r. hill, Mr. J. E. Hill and Miss Ellen Hill, all of Darlington County, S. C.

On the morning of the 11th of July 1886, Miss Elizabeth Walker, the aged sister of Capt. J. N. Walker, died at Appleton, S. C. The deceased was aged eighty years and ten months. She leaves one brother, the only surviving member of a family of thirteen....

Issue of September 16, 1886

Married September 1st, 1886, in the Rock Hill Baptist Church, by Rev. J. Q. Adams, Mr. William Freel and Miss Sallie Sturgis.

By Rev. J. Q. Adams, Sept. 2nd, 1886, at the home of the bride's father, Mr. F. C. White and Miss Sallie E. Ferguson.

On Thursday, August 26th, 1886, at the residence of the bride's father, by Rev. H. M. Allen, Mr. E. M. Duckworth to Miss M. L. Martin, daughter of Mr. Welborn Martin, all of Anderson County, S. C.

By Rev. T. M. Galphin, on the evening of Sept. 8th, 1886, at the home of Mrs. D. W. Cuttino, the bride's mother, Miss Annie E. Cuttino, and Mr. James A. Parler, all of Elloree, S. C.

Rebecca Warren, only daughter of Mr. Jas. R. and Mrs. Isabel M. Hill, died in Elko, S. C., August 16th, 1886, at the age of one year, seven months and twelve days.

Mrs. Rosa A. Parker, wife of Samuel Parker, of Society Hill, died on the 2nd of Sept. 1886. The deceased was a daughter of the venerable J.W. Burn...

John Morgan Kneece, son of Dr. J. K. and Louisa Kneece, was born June 26th 1862, and died August 17, 1886... member of Batesburg Baptist Church. J. K. Pace.

Issue of September 23, 1886

In Memoriam. Wilhelmina, daughter of W. R. B. and Louisa Virginia Farr, was born at Chick's Springs, near Greenville, 13 July 1859. At the Greenville Female College she received her education.. became a member of Chick Springs Baptist Church... On 28 June 1882, she married Rev. William J. Snider... died Saturday, 28th August.

Issue of September 30, 1886

Married at Modoc, S. C., Sept. 16th, 1886, by Rev. G. W. Bussey, Mr. Thomas Quarles and Miss Mattie Boddick.

Mrs. D. A. Whitmire died at her home in Newberry County, on 5th September 1886, in the sixty-ninth year of her age. J. D. Huggins.

Testa Kyle Berry, of Cranesville, Marion County, was born March 24, 1868, and died April 4, 1886. G. P. B.

Died, in Chester County, S. C., Sept. 16th, 1886, Mrs. Holley Ferguson, at the advanced age of eighty-four years. Mrs. Ferguson was born January 2nd, 1802... joined Harmony Church. Mrs. Ferguson leaves three daughters, one son and many grand-children.

Mrs. M. Jennie Himan, of Abbeville, was born 8th June 1860, and died 13th August 1886... death of her daughter Fannie, 7th September 1885, in the sixth year of her age.

Issue of October 7, 1886

Tribute of Respect to J. Clifton Holley and A. J. Wise, died 3rd of july and 11th of September 1886, from Milbrook Baptist Church.

Married on the 15th September 1886, by Rev. J. K. Mendenhall, Mr. William H. Hammett to Miss Janie B. Scott, daughter of Mr. Robert Scott.

Died, at Pelzer, S. C., on the 27th July 1886, Milly Florentine Rhoads, aged thirty years.

Mary Louise, infant daughter of Rev. Wm. J. Snider, died 25th September 1886.

Issue of October 14, 1886

Married at the residence of Mr. J. T. Richardson, the bride's father, on Sunday,Sept. 12th, 1886, by Rev. B. P. Estes, Mr. L. E. Cooner, of Branchville, and Miss Mamie J. Richardson, of Midway, S. C.

At the bride's residence, Sept. 30th, by Rev. John D. Mahon, Mr. Walter J. Kellar and Mrs. Sarah F. Hill, of Fairfield County.

At the residence of the bride's father, Oct. 7th, by Rev. T. P. Bell, Mr. Albert G. Means and Miss Annie M., daughter of Sylvester Bleckley, Esq., of Anderson.

Departed this life, at Reevesville, S. C., on Sept. 27th, 1886, John C. Brothers, aged twenty-five years and three months. W. D. M.

David Henry Smith, son of Savage and Elizabeth Cuttino Smith, was born February 26th, 1817 at Georgetown, S. C., where he died of apoplexy, at 3 p. m., Monday, September 27th, 1886. His brother Thomas P. Smith, of Charleston, a lineal descendant of Landgrave Thomas Smith, the first rice planter in America... H. F. O.

Issue of October 21, 1886

Married at the residence of the bride's father, Oct. 10th, 1886, by Rev. J. R. Pentuff, Mr. Preston Wood and Miss Patie Harris, all of Spartanburg County, S. C.

Roxsy May, daughter of Mr. Solomon and Mrs. Martha Keel, died October 4th, 1886, at the age of three years, one month and sixteen days.

Died, at his residence in Clarendon County, S. C., Bro. N. H. Welch, born June 27th, 1820, and died 9th April 1886... Bethel Church, Welsh Neck, Association. S. H. Miller. Clarendon *Enterprise* please copy.

Demise of Mrs. Fannie Durham Tindal, wife of Mr. E. A. Tindal, took place at Summerton, Clarendon County, S. C., October 7th, 1886. She was a daughter of Dr. A. K. Durham of Greenville, S. C. She was twenty-seven years, and eleven months old. At the age of sixteen years, she joined the Baptist Church at Camden. She married Mr. E. A. Tindal and moved to Clarendon County. I. L. E. Clarendon, S. C. Oct. 16.

Tribute of Respect from Pineville Lodge, No. 2,622, Knights of Honor, to Thomas J. Garrison.

Issue of October 28, 1886

Married on Sabbath morning, October 17th, 1886, by Rev. B. F. Miller, at the residence of the bride's father, Mr. B. L. Clinkscales, to Miss E. M. Wilson, second daughter of Mr. J. R. F. Wilson, all of Abbeville County, S. C.

Issue of November 4, 1886

Died, on the 27th July 1886, little Brennie Manly, the only child of Mr. and Mrs. J. J. Cherry, aged one year and four days. A. S. W.

Died, October 14th, 1886, Mary Francis, wife of J. R. Cheatham and daughter of B. B. Harvey... member of Bethany church, Edgefield Co. J. S. Jordan.

Died on the 15th inst., in Orangeburg County, S. C., at the residence of her parents, Bro. Stephen E. and sister Mary Early, Fannie Early, aged about six years. R. J. E.

Died, at the residence of her husband, in Fairfield County, Mrs. E. S. Corley, wife of Rev. B. F. Corley, on 17th October in the sixty-fifth year of her age. She was buried on the 19th of October at her church, Crooked Run.

Died, August 7th, 1886, Martin R. Kee. He was born October 31st, 1844... Leaves wife and eight children.

Entered into rest, October 31st, 1885, Mrs. Emily C. Carter, wife of J. B. Carter, of Columbia, S. C., in the 49th year of her age.

Donie Moye Chandler, wife of Grigsby E. Chandler, Esq., of Columbus, Ga., and eldest daughter of Col. Thomas J. Counts, fell asleep at her father's house, Bamberg, S. C., October 26th, 1886. Born September 17, 1863. On November 5, 1885, she was married to Mr. Chandler, and removed to Columbus, Ga.... left infant child.

Married October 12th, 1886, at Earlesville, S. C., by Rev. T. J. Earle, Mr. George A. Harrison of Anderson County, and Miss Hannah, daughter of Mr. O. P. Earle, of Spartanburg County, S. C.

By the Rev. C. L. Stewart, at the residence of the bride's father, on the 27th of October 1886, Mr. Eugene Owens and Miss Minnie Harde.

At the residence of the bride in Chester County, October 26th, by Rev. J. D. Mahon, Gen. Edward Taylor, of Fairfield County, and Miss Mary Williams.

At the residence of the bride's parents, Oct. 27, by Rev. J. D. Mahon, Mr. J. K. Cornwell and Miss Corrie V. Colvin, all of Chester County.

Issue of November 11, 1886

Married by Rev. G. W. Gardner, at residence of Mr. Thomas Eison, October 29, 1886, Mr. Oliver F. Roux, of Gainesville, Fla., and Miss Corrie Eison, of Union, S. C.

By Rev. S. E. Morris, at the residence of the bride's mother, on the evening of October 27, 1886, Mr. J. B. Rice of Graham's, to Miss Sallie A. Roach, of Bamberg, S. C.

On Sunday morning, Nov. 7th, at the residence of Mrs. John B. Williams, by Rev. W. H. Arial, Mr. B. F. McDavid, of Greenville County, and Miss Emma J. Osborne, of Anderson.

At the residence of Mr. J. W. M. Simmons, Wednesday, Nov. 3rd, 1886, by Rev. C. P. Scott, assisted by Rev. J. S. Cozby of the Presbyterian Church, Mr. Samuel A. Boozier and Miss Berdie Rook, both of the city of Newberry, S. C.

Our lamented sister, Susan Toole, was born February 9th 1825, married at Beech Island, Aiken county, S. C., Feb. 1st, 1844, to Mr. G. L. Toole, and died at her home in Montmorenci, S. C., 21st September 1866. H. L. B.

Dr. John Richard Mobley was born in Edgefield County, S. C., on the 28th of February As. D. 1824. While yet under twenty-one years of age, he graduated at the medical college in Charleston, S. C. In 1847 he married Miss Mary E., daughter of Col. B. S. Griffin, of Newberry County, who after bearing him seven children, preceding him to the grave. He afterwards married Emma C. Griffin, a sister of his deceased wife, who also bore him seven children.... joined Bush River Baptist Church with his wife Mary.   B. G. Covington, Florence, S. C.

Married at the residence of the bride's mother, Nov. 7th, by Rev. E. H. Graves, Mr. J. F. Graves and Miss Mamie Joiner, all of Orangeburg County, S. C.

On Thursday, November 4th, at home, by Rev. A. J. S. Thomas, J. T. E. Thornhill, of Augusta, Ga., to Lula M., daughter of Theodore A. Wilbur, of Charleston, S. C.

By Rev. F. M. Satterwhite, at the Marion Baptist Church, Nov. 19th, 1886, Rev. John F. McMillan, of Edgefield Co., S. C., and Miss Annie Loula Holliday, of Horry Co., S. C.

At the residence of bride's parents, Tuesday, 9th inst., Mr. J. Richard Earle, of Anderson, to Miss Lula P. Hix, of Oconee, Rev. J. R. Earle officiating.

Died on the 31st of October 1886, Mr. Henry Blackman, Sr., aged 97 years, 10 months and 17 days. He was thirty five years old when he married and was married but once. his wife was in her sixteenth year when he married her. She died sixteen years ago. They were blessed with nineteen children, nine girls and ten boys. Ten are still living, four girls and six boys. The youngest child is now in his 36th year. The grand-children and great-grand-children number at least 200. Mr. Blackman was in the war of 1812... A. McA. Pittman.

Issue of November 25, 1886

Married, November 11th, 1886, at the residence of the bride's mother, by Rev. H. K. Ezell, Mr. Wm. Fowler Bobo of Union, S. C., and Miss Bettie Thomas, of Union County, S. C.

November 29th, 1886, by Rev. G. W. Bussey, at the home of the bride's mother, Mr. S. P. Wright and Miss Fannie Hamilton, all of Edgefield County, S. C.

By Rev. G. W. Bussey, November 16th, 1886, G. W. Broadwater and Annie Reynolds.

November 3rd, 1886, by Rev. W. A. Gaines, Mr. T. J. Burnett to Mrs. Martha Parkman, both of Edgefield.

November 18th, 1886, in the Rock Hill Baptist Church, by Rev. J. Q. Adams, Mr. E. E. Lunn, of Atlanta, Ga., and Miss Anna L. Davis, of Rock Hill, S. C.

Harry Key Willis, son of M. T. and Mrs. Mattie E. Willis, died at Williston, S. C., Nov. 25, 1886, at the age of nine months. D. W. K.

Died at the residence of her son, Mr. C. E. Tyler, Graham's T. O., S. C., July 5, 1886, Mrs. Mary A. Nealy, in the 61st year of her age. Mrs. Nealy was the eldest daughter of our beloved brother, Rev. Thomas Mason, deceased. S. B. S.

Issue of December 2, 1886

Married on the morning of November 28th, 1886, at the residence of the bride's father, by Rev. S. A. Gary, Mr. E. H. Poor, of Belton, S. C., and Miss Eva Wyatt, of Pickens Co., S. C.

At the residence of Mrs. Keturah Bolt, the bride's mother, on Thursday evening, Nov. 18th, 1886, by Rev. A. C. Stepp, Mr. William Luther Ballentine and Miss Corrie E. Bolt, both of Laurens County, S. C.

At the residence of William Ellison, the bride's father, by Rev. A. C. Stepp, on Tuesday evening, November 23rd, 1886, Mr. Gideon Kemper Willis and Miss Minnie Lee Ellison, both of Greenville County, S. C.

November 24th 1886, by Rev. G. W. Bussey, at the home of the bride's mother, Mr. John Crafton and Miss Fannie Thurmond.

By Rev. G. W. Bussey, on November 24th, at the home of the bride's mother, Mr. Louis Thurmond and Miss Jennie Culbreth, all of Edgefield County.

Harry, infant son of W. W. and Mrs. A. E. Harley, died at Elko, S. C., October 23d, 1886, aged on month and nine days.

Died, October 28th, 1886, A. S. Goudelock, in his ninety-first year. The subject of this notice was born September 12th, 1796, within one-half mile of where he lived and died. He joined the Baptist Church at ElBethel, October 1833, and served the church as Clerk thirty-three years. He was married January 3, 1842, to Miss Polly Littlejohn, and they lived together for sixty-five years. He was the father of twelve children--six of whom preceded him to the grove. He furnished four sons for the Confederacy, one of whom died from disease contracted by wading Bull Run at the first battle of Manassas. Another died from gunshot wounds received in the battle of Missionary Ridge. Another, narrowly escape having been severely wounded in the famous battles around Richmond. "Uncle Adam" was a kind and loving husband.... J. R. J.

Died, suddenly at her home in Jonesville, Oct. 29, 1868, Mrs. Mary Ann Perrin Foster, in the seventy-sixth year of her age. For fifty years she was the wife of Gen. B. B. Foster... member of Jonesville Baptist Church. Two of her sons died in the war. She leaves her husband and three daughters. G. W. Gardner, Union, S. C., Nov. 16, 1886.

Departed this life November 3rd, 1886, Flurnoy Weathersbee, infant daughter of Mr. and Mrs. W. F. Weathersbee, aged fourteen months.

Issue of December 9, 1886

Married December 1st, 1886, by Rev. G. W. Bussey, at the home of the bride, Mr. Charlie Quarles and Miss Monteith Wood, all of Edgefield County, S. C.

At the residence of the bride's father, Mr. Allen Riley, by Rev. D. w. Key, Mr. R. L. Antley and Miss Annie E. Riley, Nov. 23d, 1886, all of Orangeburg County.

At Elko, S. C., Dec. 1st, by Rev. D. W. key, Mr. Wm. C. Matthews and Miss Mamie E. Johnson, all of Barnwell County.

Maj. J. J. Brown, died November 26th 1886. He was only fifty-two years old. [long account] I. W. W.

Issue of December 16, 1886

Married on Sabbath afternoon, Dec. 5, 1886, by Rev. B. F. Miller, at the home of Mr. Thomas W. Nichols, Mr. Vincent Griffin to Miss M. Amelia Bond, all of Abbeville Co., S. C.

Dec. 5th, 1838, by Rev. S. T. Russell, Mr. D. N. Kellehan and Miss Sarah Brown, all of Williamsburg County.

On Thursday evening, 2nd Dec. 1886, at the residence of Willis Cheek, the bride's father, by Rev. A. C. Stepp, Mr. Marion Bolt and Miss Ida Cheek, both of Laurens Co., S. C.

On Sunday evening, 5th Dec., 1886, at the residence of the late David Ellison, father of the bride, by Rev. A. C. Stepp, Mr. J. C. Ragsdale, of Anderson County, and Miss Mamie Ellison, of Greenville Co., S. C.

At Evergreen, S. C., on the 1st Dec. 1886, by Rev. M. McGee, Mr. Baylis Earle Cooley and Miss Ola Earle, daughter of Maj. E. J. Earle, all of Anderson County.

By Rev. J. K. McCain, Dec. 2nd, 1886, at the residence of Mr. Robert T. Yarborough, the bride's father, Mr. Willie D. Davis, of Monticello, to Miss Jessie H. Yarborough, all of Fairfield Co., S. C.

At the residence of Mr. William Brown, on Dec. 1st, 1886, by Rev. W. H. Hartin, Mr. J. F. Brown and Miss Mary Langford, all of Fairfield Co., S. C.

On Dec. 2nd 1886, at the residence of the bride's parents, Mr. Wm. C. Wooten and Miss Mary E. Dunn, all of Fairfield Co., S. C.

Died, at Silverton, S. C., Oct. 31st, 1886, Mrs. Sallie Bates, in her 58th year. In early life joined the Church at Cypress, afterwards joined at Matlock.

Died in November, at her home in Barnwell County, Mrs. Sallie Dunbar, in her 84th year... J. J. M.

Died, at his new home in the county of Newberry, in October last, Mr. Judson Rountree, aged 52 years. Bro. Rountree was a native of Barnwell County, and was a member of Steel Creek Baptist Church. He leaves a wife and one daughter.

Died, near Robbin's, Barnwell County, in October, Mr. Alex. Benson, in his 22nd year. Bro. Benson was a member of Steel Creek Baptist Church. J. J. M.

Mrs. Fannie Bates, wife of Mr. Milledge Bates, died at her home near Elko, S. C., Dec. 2nd, 1886, at the age of twenty-six. She was a member of Healing Springs Baptist Church. D. W. K.

Carrie, daughter of Mr. Edward and Mrs. Mary A. Baker, died in Williston, S. C., Dec. 6th, 1886, aged nine years and six months. D. W. K.

Mrs. Pauline E. Clarke, daughter of the late Dr. B. W. Lawton, died at Allendale, in Barnwell County, on the 27th of November last, in the twenty-first year of her age. She joined the Allendale Baptist Church. J. A. L.

Died, near Anderson, S. C., nov. 11, 1886, in the eleventh year of her age, little Nannie, eldest daughter of Dr. and Mrs. D. S. Watson. C. O. B.

Died, November 17th, 1886, R. Earnest Culp, in the eighteenth year of his age.... Harmony Baptist Church, Chester County, S. C.

Departed this life, December 4th, 1886, Mrs. Ann Graham, relict of Rev. Noah Graham, who died in 1877. Mrs. Graham had reached her seventy-ninth year... Her little grandson John, son of Col. and Mrs. J. D. Graham was buried at the same hour. C. C. Brown, Sumter. S. C.

Issue of December 23, 1886

Married at the bride's home, near Timmonsville, S. C., on December 16th, 1886, by Rev. A. McA. Pittman, Mr. C. H. Ham and Miss Addie Hill.

In the city of Orangeburg, at the residence of Maj. T. B. Whatley, on the afternoon of the 14th December 1886, by Rev. T. M. Galphin, Miss Viola Hydrick and Mr. Jno. C. Ulmer, all of Orangeburg.

November 5th 1886, at the home of the bride, by Rev. T. H. Burruss, Mr. T. Cannon of Darlington County, to Miss F. M. Lee, of Williamsburg County.

Nov. 24th, 1886, at the home of the bride, by Rev. T. H. Burruss, Mr. A. B. Newton to Miss Vindoll Matthews, all of Williamsburg County.

Dec. 12th, 1886, at the home of the bride, by Rev. Nathan Hall, Mr. James Miller to Miss Hellen Cockfield, all of Williamsburg County, S. C.

On the 25th November 1886, at the residence of the bride's mother, near Buffalo Baptist Church, Abbeville Co., by Rev. J. A. Bell, Mr. J. P. Lovelace, of Edgefield Co., to Miss M. E. Palmer.

On the 2nd of December 1886, at the residence of Mr. Holder, near McCormick, by Rev. J. A. Bell, Mr. John Seigler to Miss J. Coleman, all of Edgefield County.

On the 7th December 1886, at the residence of the bride's mother, near Buffalo church, Abbeville Co., by Rev. J. A. Bell, Dr. T. E. Jennings of Modoc, Edgefield Co., to Miss M. E. Truitt.

On the evening of the 8th December 1886, in the McCormick Baptist church, by Rev. J. A. Bell, Mr. John R. Kay to Miss Talula B. Howard, daughter of Mr. and Mrs. W. S. Howard, all of McCormick.

Died, at her home in Williamsburg county, S. C., December 8th, 1886, Mrs. Martha H. James, consort of the late Rev. S. C. James. Mrs. James had very nearly reached four score years.

Died at the home of his son, Col. C. C. Rush, in Blackville, November 2nd, Mr. John W. Rush in the 94th year of his age. The deceased was born in St. Matthews Parish, Orangeburg county, which was then a part of Barnwell District, so that it may be said that he was born, lived and died in Barnwell County. The deceased laves a brother in Alabama, Mr. Daniel Rush, only a few years his junior... J. G. W.

In Memoriam. Died on the morning of the 7th of December 1886, at her home in Columbia, S. C., Mrs. L. A. Ransom, daughter of Mr. Chastain Cock, of Powhatan County, Virginia. W. C. Lindsay.

In Memoriam. William L. Hart, died March 22nd, 1886, in the 33d year of his age and James A. Hart, died 26th September following, in his 27th year, at their home in Springville, Darlington county, S. C.

In Memoriam. On Thursday evening, November 18th, 1886, deacon Nimrod Donaldson, died in Greenville County, S. C., in the 84th year of his life [eulogy] C. N. D. Portsmouth, Va.

Issue of January 6, 1887

Married at Elko Church, December 22, 1886, by D. W. Key, Mr. W. D. Wade and Miss S. L. Bates, daughter of Mr. P. Bates, all of Barnwell County.

At the residence of the bride's father, Mr. Allen Woolly, By D. W. Key, Dec. 28, 1886, Mr. G. W. Parker and Miss Lulu Woolly.

At the residence of the bride's father, Mr. John Bracknell, near Dornville, Edgefield County, by Rev. J. A. Bell, Dec. 26, 1886, Mr. Thomas Faulkner and Miss Carrie Bracknell.

At the residence of the bride's father, Mr. C. P. Holly, near Dornville, by Rev. J. A. Bell, Dec. 30, 1886, Mr. J. W. Bracknell and Miss M. J. Holly, all of Edgefield County.

By Rev. G. W. Bussey, at the home of the bride, Dec. 22, 1886, Mr. W. R. Cooper and Miss Dora Walker.

By G. W. Bussey, at the bride's home, Dec. 12, 1886, Mr. J. Pickle and Mrs. Mamie Outzs, all of Edgefield County.

By G. W. Bussey, Dec. 16, 1886, at the residence of the bride's father, Mr. Albert Talbert and Miss Lizzie Prescott, all of Edgefield County.

By the same under the same ceremony, Mr. Charlie Key and Miss Alice Pater, all of Edgefield County.

At the residence of Mr. James Tisdale, by Rev. S. T. Russell, at 3 o'clock, Dec. 22, 1886, Mr. Willie McCrea to Miss Estelle Tisdale.

By Rev. S. T. Russell, Dec. 22, 1886, at the residence of Mr. William Brockinton, Mr. P. A. Alsbrook and Miss M. L. Brockinton.

At Plum Branch, S. C., Dec. 27, 1886, at 3½ o'clock p. m., by Rev. A. G. Collier, Hon. J.P. Blackwell and Mrs. M. A. Lanham

At the residence of the bride's step-father near Cartersville, S. C., Dec. 19, 1886, by Rev. S. M. Richardson, Theo. T. Fountain and Fannie Olivia Carter.

In Timmonsville, S. C., Dec. 23, 1886, by Rev. S. M. Richardson, Lee J. Rollins and Leila Ragsdale.

On Thursday evening, Dec. 23, 1886, by Rev. B. F. Miller, at the Elmore Place, near Mount Moriah Baptist Church, Mr. Tilman Fuller of Laurens County, and Miss Mamie, eldest daughter of Mr. and Mrs. Pinckney Teague of Abbeville County.

By Rev. J. K. Pace, Dec. 23, 1886, at the residence of Dr. J. K. Kneece, Mr. L. Hartley, Jr., and Miss Nannie Kneece, all of Lexington Co.

Dec. 21, 1886, by Rev. I. W. Wingo, in the Baptist Church at Black's, Mr. Augustus B. Stephens and Miss Alice R. Gale, both of Black's.

Dec. 23, 1886, at the residence of the bride's mother, by Rev. R. J. Williams, Mr. Timmerman Roper and Miss Mamie Clark, all of Greenville.

On Thursday, Dec. 16, 1886, by C. B. Bobo, Esq., Mr. John Davis to Miss Ada Spillers, all of Cross Keys, Union County, S. C.

At the residence of the bride's mother, Dec. 16, 1886, by Rev. J. A. Brown, Mr. Ed. Woodward and Miss Tillie Mobley, both of Fairfield Co., S. C.

Dec. 26, 1886, by Rev. R. J. Williams, Mr. Henry Granger and Miss Nannie Carmell, all of Greenville.

Dec. 22, 1886, by Rev. J. Q. Adams, Mr. P. M. Berry, of Greenville, S. C., and Miss Nannie Hoke, of York Co., S. C.

Dec. 22, 1886, by Rev. J. Q. Adams, Mr. J. F. Wingate, of North Carolina, and Miss Lucy Allen, of York Co., S. C.

Died, at her home in Barnwell County, S. c., Dec. 26, 1886, Mrs. Sibby Loadholt, the wife of the late John Loadholt. She was in her 78th year.

Mrs. Hattie A. Bass, wife of B. L. Bass and daughter of Rev. John and Mary Huggins, was born in Marion County, S. C., Jan. 2, 1861, and died Dec. 6, 1886. An aged mother, brothers and sisters, a devoted husband, and a one-year old daughter remain....

Departed this life, on Dec. 1, 1886, at the residence of his son, J. J. Antley, in Orangeburg county, Abram Antley, aged between 102 and 104 years.... a soldier in the War of 1812, and served for a time at Fort Moultrie, in Charleston harbor. His pension was fully paid after the late war between the states, and up to the time of his death. He married, at about the age of 37. In 1836 he with others united in constituting the Canaan Church, having obtained a letter from Ebenezer church. W. D. M.

In Memoriam. Nov. 25th, 1886, Mrs. Alice Jarnigan died. Mrs. S. Alice Bailey Jarnigan, daughter of Charles and A. C. Bailey, was born May 15th, 1852 in Kershaw County, was married to Dr. J. E. Jarnigan of Marion County, s. C., May 4th, 1875, and died of neuralgia at the home of her husband. She was raised by a pious mother, having lost her father when quite young, and in early girlhood joined the Methodist church at Smyrna, in her native county... in her sixteenth year she lost her mother. She enjoyed the facilities of a good education at Mecklenburg and Spartanburg Female Colleges. J. F. McM.

Issue of January 13, 1887

Married by Rev. R. J. Edwards, at the residence of the bride's parents, Dec. 30, 1886, Mr. Harrison Shuler and Miss Carrie Bozard, eldest daughter of Mr. Canady and Mrs. Rebecca Bozard, all of Orangeburg County.

At the residence of Major Isaac Boles, Jan. 4, 1887, by Rev. John F. McMillan, Mr. B. B. Freeman, of Lincoln County, Ga., and Miss Maggie E. Shadrach, of Edgefield County.

Jan. 5, 1887, by Rev. J. Q. Adams, Colonel J. J. Waters, of Rock Hill, and Miss Ida Brice, of Blackstock.

At Mount Joy Church, after the morning service, Jan. 9, 1887, by Rev. H. K. Ezell, Mr. B. F. Gault and Miss C. L. Inman. By the same, at the same time and place, Mr. G. W. Going and Miss Janie Vaughn, all of Union County.

On the Knob, at the residence of Willis Burns, the bride's father, Dec. 26, 1886, by Rev. A. C. Stepp, Mr. W. Z. Baldwin and Miss Essie Lee Burns, both of Laurens County.

Deacon James A. McCrorey fell asleep Dec. 28th 1886, aged 64 years. Bro. McCrorey was a deacon of the Blackstock Baptist Church... left wife and children....

Early on the morning of Dec. 24th, Janie E. Metts died, having scarcely seen her seventeenth summer. Her many young friends around Martin's Depot and Kinard's Turnout, in Laurens County will read this announcement with pain. About four years ago she joined the Sandy Springs Church and was baptized by Elder A. C. Stepp. Greenville, Jan. 4, 1887.

Departed this life, Dec. 9th, 1886, at her home in Edgefield County, S. C., Mrs. Mary Ann Johnson, consort of Mr. J. P. Johnson, in the 53rd year of her age. The deceased had been twice married, and left by her first marriage two sons and one daughter, by the second four sons, who with her grief-stricken husband, her aged parents, and five brothers survive to mourn... united with the Good hope Baptist Church, later of Phillipi Baptist Church. W. H. Timmerman.

Tribute of Respect to Angelia P. Hair, who died Dec. 22, 1886, from Ashleigh Church.

Tribute of Respect to James A. McCrorey.

Issue of January 20, 1887

Married by Rev. J. L. Ouzts, at the residence of the bride's mother in Edgefield County, Jan. 12, 1887, Mr. S. H. D. Adams and Miss Lucy A. Quarles.

On the afternoon of Jan. 6, 1887, at the residence of Mr. William Kinard, near Rocky Creek Church, by Rev. John F. McMillan, Mr. W. W. Johnson and Miss Florence Allen, all of Edgefield County.

At Mr. A. J. Frier's, Marion County, Dec. 27, 1886, by Rev. S. M. Richardson, Richard B. McRoy and A. Regina Keeffe.

Near Cartersville, S. C., Jan. 5th, 1887, by Rev. S. M. Richardson, Charles B. Nichols and Annie Carter.

Near Cartersville, S. C., Jan. 6, 1887, by Rev. S. M. Richardson, J. P. Lane and Minnie Carter.

By Rev. J. M. Hood, at his residence, on the night of Dec. 23, 1886, Mr. Ed. Dunn and Miss Bannie Braswell.

By Rev. J. M. Hood, at the residence of the bride's father, Jan. 11, 1887, Mr. Marion A. Hogan and Miss Louisa A. Joiner, all of Fairfield.

Dec. 7, 1886, at the residence of the bride's father, by the Rev. Dr. Adams, of Augusta, Ga., Mr. W. S. Radford, of Augusta, and Miss Lizzie L., daughter of Mr. Wiley Bailey, of Barnwell County.

At the bride's residence, in Elko, Jan. 9, 1887, by Rev. D. W. Key, Mr. Willie Johnston and Mrs. Hettie Shaw.

At the residence of Mr. G. L. Cauthen, of Lancaster County, the bride's father, Dec. 23, 1886, by Rev. A. S. Willeford, Mr. F. E. C. Gainer and Miss A. R. Cauthen, all of Lancaster County.

On the 29th of December, 1886, at the residence of Mr. William Jordan, of Chester Co., the bride's uncle, by Rev. A. S. Willeford, Mr. David Stover, of Lancaster County, and Miss Minnie Cherry, of Chester County.

Died on the 18th of December 1886, in the fifth year of her age, Tallulah, daughter of D. Townsend and M. Tallulah Smith, of Greenville, S. C.

Died, in Chesterfield County, on the 9th of January 1887, George Harman, infant son of brother and sister J. F. Myers, aged four months and nine days.

Died, at his home near Jackson Station, Aiken County, on Sunday, Dec. 5, 1886, Mr. W. Harrison Brown, in his 45th year. Mr. Brown had long been a consistent member of Matlock Baptist Church. He leaves a wife and several little children. J. J. M.

Departed this life in the 47th year of her age, on Dec. 5th, 1886, Mrs. Mattie Perry, wife of Mr. E. A. Perry, of Ridge Spring, S. C. G. F. W.

Died, at Bamberg, S., C., Dec. 30, 1886, Fannie Lou, youngest daughter of Dr. Wm. B. Rice. She was born July 2, 1872.

Died, in Blackville, Barnwell County, S. C., Dec. 7th, 1886, Capt. E. W. Perry, in the 78th year of his age. The deceased was born in Edgefield County, where the great part of his life was spent. In his early years his father moved to Barnwell County, and it was here that he was converted and baptized by Rev. Darling Peeples, by whom he was also married. Returning to Edgefield, he became a member of the Bethel church, and afterwards of the Ridge Spring church. About seven years ago, he made his home with Dr. J. H. E. Milhouse, who married his only daughter and youngest child. J. G. W.

In Memoriam. Mrs. Ann Elizabeth Coker, wife of Mr. Josiah M. Coker, a deacon in Lake Swamp Baptist Church, was born near Cheraw, S. C., April 25th, 1824, and died near Timmonsville, S. C., December 23d, 1886. She joined Antioch Baptist Church in Darlington County in 1841, and was baptized by Rev. Gregory Rollins. On moving from upper Darlington to lower Darlington, she became a member of the Lake Swamp Baptist Church.She was the mother of eight sons and five daughters, of whom two sons and two daughters passed away before her. A. McA. Pittman.

Issue of January 27, 1887

Married at the residence of the bride's father, Dr. Alexander Storne, near Blackville, S. C., on the evening of Jan. 20, 1887, by Rev. W. D. McMillan, Dr. J. H. Price and Miss Ida Storne, both of Barnwell County.

On the morning of Dec. 19, 1886, at the residence of the bride's father, Dr. B. P. West, by Rev. J. E. Covington, Mr. James H. Woodside and Miss Anna H. West, both Of Greenville County.

Jan. 19, 1887, at the residence of the bride's mother, in Marion County, by Rev. S. M. Richardson, John B. Timmons and H. Lou Hudson.

Jan. 29, 1887, at the residence of M. R. Sanders, Esq., in Marion County by Rev. S. M. Richardson, Ben Whitehead and Ida M. Sanders.

Died, in Spartanburg County, on the 15th of December 1886, Hattie Lee, daughter of brother J.P. and sister Mary Lee, aged five yours, nine months, and four days.

Died, at her residence in the city of Columbia, Nov. 28, 1886, Mrs. A. b. Burkett. She was for many years a member of the Baptist Church in Columbia, but at the time of her death her membership was with the Baptist church in Greenville, S. C. W. C. Lindsay.

On Monday night, Jan. 17, 1887, Mrs. M. Nimmons died. She was a member of the George's Creek Baptist Church, Barnwell County, S. c. W. D. R.

Mrs. Rebecca Lancaster Dyches died Dec. 12, 1886, at her home at Lee's, Barnwell County, S. C., in her 35th year.. Leaves a large family circle, among them an infant only three months old. W. D. R.

Departed this life on Thursday morning, Jan. 6, 1887, at the residence of M. L. Thompson, son-in-law of the deceased, Deacon Elijah Farmer, aged 84 years. Bro. Farmer was born in Lunenburg County, Va., and when fourteen years of age removed with his parents to Greenville County, S. C. Arriving at manhood, he married Elizabeth Berry, daughter of Rev. Nathan Berry, a Baptist minister of Greenville county. For a number of years he resided on Grove Creek, and had membership in the Washington Baptist Church. In 1880 he left Greenville and since that time lived with his children in Anderson and Oconee Counties, holding members in Townville Church. He leaves a wife and seven children.

Departed this life at Blackville, S. C., on Jan. 15, 1887, Mrs. Christian Odom, aged sixty two years and nine months. She was baptized into the fellowship of the Healing Springs Church and after the constitution of Blackville Church, in 1839, removed her membership there. W. D. M.

In Memoriam. Stephen D. Woodward was born near bishopville in Sumter county, S. C., 21 July 1848, of one of the best families of the country. Died in Bishopville, 1st October 1886. B. G. Covington. Florence, S. C. Dec. 27.

Issue of February 3, 1887

Married at the residence of the bride's father, in Orangeburg, S. C., by Rev. A. Pope Norris, Jan. 25th, 1887, Mr. Foster Fant, of Anderson, and Miss Minnie B. Norris, daughter of the officiating clergyman.

At the residence of Mr. E. A. Searles, near Plum Branch, S. C., Jan. 23d, 1887, by the Rev. A. G. Collier, Mr. W. A. Roberts and Miss Bessie Hill, of Burke County, Ga.

Caleb Peay departed this life January 17, 1887, aged eighteen years.... member of Blackstock Baptist Church.

Issue of February 10, 1887

Married at the residence of the bride's father, Dr. O. J. Bond, in Chester, S. C., Feb. 3d, 1887, at 1 p. m., by Rev. R. W. Sanders, Mr. Lucius S. Matthews of Graham's to Miss Mary E. Bond.

At the residence of Mrs. Boyd, near Silverton, Wednesday, Jan. 26, 187, by Rev. Fred'k Jones, Mr. Ben Foreman and Miss Mamie Butler, all of Silverton.

At the residence of Mrs. Henry Nail, Beech Island, S. C., on Monday, Jan. 31, 1887, by Rev. Fred'k Jones, Mr. George T. Barnes and Miss Mary F. Foreman, both of Silverton, S. C.

At the parsonage of the Beech Island Baptist Church, on Wednesday, Jan. 19, 1887, by Rev. Fred'k Jones; Mr. Willie Meyer and Miss Amelia Foreman, both of Silverton, S. C.

Near Kirksey's, S. C., Jan. 19, 1887, by Rev. John F. McMillan, Mr. Lee Faulkner and Miss Jennie Timmerman.

Jan. 25, 1887, by Rev. W. P. Smith, Mr. F. L. Floyd and Miss N. Widdie Strange, both of Spartanburg County.

Matilda Wallace, born in Marlboro Co., S. C., March 17th 1826, consort of Rev. B. F. Parrott, died at her home in Darlington, Jan. 12, 1887.

Janie Estel Kidd died Jan. 3rd, 1887, after a few day's illness, in the fourth year of her age. She was the daughter of Simpson and Ella Kidd....

Died, Jan. 15, 1887, Calvin Brice Ferguson, infant son of Calvin and Sallie Ferguson, aged one year and three months.

Lottie Culp, daughter of W. S. and Mary Culp, died Jan. 18, 1887, in the 91th year of her age. She was a member of Harmony Baptist Church....

Died, Jan. 28, 1887, at the residence of her son-in-law, Rev. D. H. Crosland, near Aiken, Mrs. S. A. Wise, nearly 75 years of age.... member of Treadway Baptist Church.

Died, in Barnwell County, Dec. 21, 1886, Mrs. Ann J. Kennedy, in the 65th year of her age. The deceased was the wife of Bro. H. w. Kennedy, who died about ten years ago and who for many years one of the pillars of Springtown Church. J. G. W.

Death of Jodie J. Stone, a young man of the Halsellville neighborhood, Chester Co., 27th December 1886.

Died, on the 1st of January 1887, in Hartsville, S. C., Mrs. Rennie Lawton, wife of Mr. T. P. Lawton, and only daughter of Dr. J. D. Erwin, Jr., and of Laura Ann Erwin, deceased, both of Barnwell County, S. C. Mrs. Lawton departed this life at the age of twenty years. On the 8th of April 1883, she was joined in marriage to Mr. T. P. Lawton, a son of the late Hon. B. W. Lawton, M. D., of Barnwell County, S. C. In September last they removed to Hartsville, carrying with than an infant daughter only a few months old.... Her remains were placed in the family lot at Erwinton, S. C.

Issue of February 17, 1887

Married on Sabbath morning, Feb. 6th, 1887, at the home of the bride's father, by Rev. B. F. Miller, Mr. H. Mack Wilkinson to Miss Maggie A. Kohn, all of Abbeville Co., S. C.

Zadock Paschal Hudson died of Catarrhal fever near Greenville, S. C., January 27th, 1887. He was within a few months of the "three score years and ten." He was a member of the Berea Baptist Church. He married Susan G. Rector, daughter of Rev. Louis Rector, of precious member, and they continued in mutual affection forty-six years. They have five sons-- Irby P., Elliott A., Jason C., William R., and J. Belton Hudson, and the aged mother is still living. He was buried in the old Hudson-Rector family grave-yard, eight miles east of this city.

Rev. John M. Hoover died at his home in Barnwell County, December 4th, 1886, in his 73d year. When an infant he was left without father or mother, but was adopted by a godly old man by the name of Harrison, who did a father's part by him, and left him all his property. He grew up a sober, industrious and moral youth... baptized into the fellowship of the Great Salkehatchie church. He was married twice, and leaves a wife, and two sons and two daughters by his former marriage. His last wife was the widow of the Rev. Thos. W. Sanders, once so well known in Barnwell County. One of his sons, Col. Geo. H. Hoover, is a leading citizen of Hampton County, and another son gave up his life for his country at Manassas... Jno. G. Williams.

Issue of February 24, 1887

Married by Rev. J. A. Hoffman, on the 9th of Jan., 1887, at the residence of the bride's father, Mr. J. J. Antley, Mr. Malachi Smoak and Miss Sue Antley, all of Orangeburg Co., S. C.

By Rev. J. A. Hoffman, on the 23rd of Jan. ,1887, at the residence of Mr. Jno. Hartzog, the bride's father, Mr. John Ayers and Miss Fannie Hartzog, all of Orangeburg County, S. C.

At the bride's home, February 17th, 1887, by Rev. G. W. Bussey, Mr. Cromwell Jackson and Miss Emma Reel, both of Edgefield Co.

On Sabbath morning, Feb. 20, 187, at the residence of the bride's father, by Rev. B. f. Miller, Mr. James A. Sharp to Miss Carrie E., eldest daughter of Mr. W. F. Broderick, of Coronaca, Abbeville Co., S. C.

Died, in the city of Augusta, Ga., Feb. 24th, 1885, one year ago, Mrs. Kate Bignion, in the thirty-ninth year of her age. It was a severe bereavement to her husband and two children, to her widowed mother and her sister and brothers. Lucius Cuthbert.

Hattie Smith Crook was born June 10th, 1862 and died February 1st 1887... She was the mother of four bright children. She married Henry Crook just six years and three days before her death. J. K. Fant. *Southern Christian Advocate* and Yorkville *Enquirer* please copy.

Died, in Bamberg, S.C., February 10th 1887, in her thirty-second year, Sallie Elizabeth Moye, devoted and beloved wife of M. A. Moye. Mrs. Moye was born December 10, 1855, was married in her seventeenth year, and in 1872 was baptized by Rev. J. F. Buist into the fellowship of Philadelphia Church....

Issue of March 10, 1887

William Wilks, Sr., aged 72, years 10 months, and 10 days, departed this life on Sunday evening, at 4 o'clock, Jan. 16, 1887. He was born in Chesterfield County, S. C., on 6th March 1811. He was married to Miss L. Rowell by Rev. Gregory Rollins, Feb. 9th, 1839. He joined the Antioch Baptist Church in upper Darlington, S. C., later in life and was baptized by Rev. J. W. Burn. In 1831 became a member of Lake Swamp Baptist Church. He was the oldest male member in the Lake Swamp Church. A. McA. Pittman.

Married Feb. 1, 1887, by Rev. W. P. Smith, Mr. C. S. Moore and Miss Sue J. Thomas, all of Spartanburg County.

Feb. 17, 1887, by Rev. W. P. Smith, Mr. J. D. Brown and Miss E. Odelia Thomas, all of Spartanburg County.

At the home of the bride, Feb. 16, 1887, by Rev. A. C. Wilkins, Mr. Sam'l W. Byrd and Miss Mary L. Moore, both of Darlington Co.

In the Baptist church at Jamison's, on Feb. 22, 1887, by Rev. T. M. Galphin, Mr. Newton Bell and Miss Maud Paulling, all of Orangeburg.

Feb. 24, 1887, at Modoc, by Rev. G. W. Bussey, Mr. James Callaham, Jr., and Miss Lee Jackson, all of Edgefield County.

By Rev. R. J. Edwards, on the afternoon of Thursday, Jan. 27, 1887, at the residence of the bride's parents, Mr. John O'Cain and Miss Lela Moorer, all of Orangeburg County, S. C.

In the afternoon of March 3d, 1887, by Re.v B. F. Miller, at the residence of Mr. John McNeil, of Verdery, S. C., Mr. J. W. Felts to Miss Beulah McNeil, all of Abbeville County, S. C.

January 9th 1887, at the home of the bride's parents, by Rev. W. H. Hartin, Mr. Robert Hollis to Miss Belle hood, all of Fairfield County, S. C.

At the residence of the bride's father, February 9th 1887, by Rev. W. H. Hartin, Mr. Henry Rains to Miss Hattie Wooten, all of Fairfield County, S. C.

By the Rev. W. H. Hartin, at his residence, February 24th 1887, Mr. James Rains to Miss Mary Motley, all of Fairfield County, S. C.

Issue of March 17, 1887

Married at the residence of the bride's father, Z. T. Bailes, by Rev. J. K. Fant, March 10th 1887, Mr. Henderson Coltharp to Miss Mollie C. Bailes, both of York County, S. C.

At the residence of the bride's uncle, near Lee's, S. C., on the 23d January 1887, by Rev. W. D. Rice, Mr. J. B. Gillam and Miss Lizzie Conneif, all of Barnwell County, S. C.

At the residence of Dr. S. S. Knight, on the 3rd March 1887, by the Rev. J. D. Pitts, Dr. T. B. Duckett, of Mississippi, and Miss Olivia A. Knight, of Fountain Inn, S. C.

On the 3rd of March 1887, Mr. Samuel Reed, who was in the 77th year of his age, departed this life. Bro. Reed united himself to the fellowship of the Healing Springs Baptist Church about fifty years ago. G. N. A.

Mrs. Matilda Brown Edwards was born February 7, 18078, and died Feb. 26, 1887. She was twice married, first to Wm. Manson, and he dying about one year after marriage, she became the wife of Matthew Edwards, Sr. J. K. Fant.

Carlos Hill, youngest son of the late Henry H. Hill, departed this life on Friday, 21st January 1887, at the home of his mother, in Barnwell County, S. C., in the 21st year of his age. W. D. R. Graham's, Feb. 21, 1887.

Robert H. Kennedy of Barnwell County, S. C., died on the 5th of February 1887, at the residence of his son, in the sixty-ninth year of his age. He united with Springtown Baptist Church of the same county, some fifty years ago. Some time after he moved his membership to the Friendship Church. When the George's Creek Church was organized, some thirteen years ago, he became one of the constituent members. W. D. R. Graham's, S. C., Feb. 25, 1887.

Mrs. Vashti Burgess departed this life Monday afternoon, February 21st 1887, at her home in the city of Anderson. She was a daughter of Robt. C. Sharpe, and was born January 12th 1828, near Due West, Abbeville County. In 1850 she was married to Dr. E. G. Gaines of Pickens County who died in 1865, when she returned to make her home with her father. In 1859, she was married to the late Milford Burress, of Anderson County, who died December 25th, 1869. She was the mother of two children, one son and one daughter.

The son was by her first marriage and died in infancy; the daughter was by her last marriage and survives her. Mrs. Burress was raised by pious parents, members of the Associate Reformed Presbyterian Church. W. W. K., Greenville, S. C., March 1887.

Issue of March 24, 1887

Married by Rev. C. A. Stiles, on 9th March 1887, at the residence of the bride's mother, Rev. C. D. Rowell, of the South Carolina Conference, and Miss Sallie E. Taylor, of Richland County, S. C.

On March 17, 1887, at the home of the bride's father, Mr. Burr John Harrison, of Columbia, S. C., to Miss Isoletter Dubose Garrison, of York County, S. C., Rev. J. K. Fant officiating. Columbia *Register* please copy.

In the Foreston Baptist Church, on Thursday March 17th, 1887, by Rev. B. C. Lamplet, Mr. H. L. Orvin, of Williamsburg, and Miss Hattie L. China, of Clarendon.

December 20th, 1886, Mrs. Sallie E. East, wife of late W. W. East, and daughter of Nathan and Mrs. Edna Whitmire, deceased, passed away. [eulogy]

Issue of March 31, 1887

Married at the residence of Wm. Ellison, on the 6th March 1887, by Rev. A. C. Stepp, Mr. Edmond S. Smith, of Piedmont, and Miss Emma Maddox, of Triangle, Laurens County, S. C.

March 24th, 1887, at the home of the bride's father, by Rev. G. W. Bussey, Mr. Charlie Stalmaker and Miss Annie Prescott, all of Edgefield County, S. C.

At the residence of T. A. Pack, Esq., of this city, on Thursday, the 24th inst., by the Rev. B. M. Pack, of Georgia, W. H. Hill, Esq., and Miss Mary E. Pack, both of Greenville.

Fell asleep in Jesus on the 13th of March 1887, little George Landrum, son of J. V. and E. J. Mayfield, in the sixth year of his age. his body was interred in the graveyard at Beaverdam church, after funeral services by Rev. D. I. Spearman.

Little Luther Cook, child of Mr. and Mrs. Frank Cook, of our church at Troy, died on the morning of the 12th of this month at their residence. Little Luther was about four years of age.. H. C. S. Troy, S. C., March 23, 1887.

J. Turner Owens died at his home in Laurens County, S. C., on the 15th February 1887, from effect of measles. He was born on Warrior's Creek on the 15th November 1851, near where he settled, lived and died. In 1872, he was married to Sarah E. Fowler, whom he leaves with six children. In 1881, he joined the Church at Warrior's Creek [long account]. A. C. S.

In Memoriam. Mrs. Louisa C. Fouche, wife of W. C. Fouche, was born 22nd January 1830 and passed away 25th of February 1887. She was a member of the Baptist church,-- first at Siloam and then of Coronaca church, near her late home in the county of Abbeville. B. F. M.

Mrs. Mamie Wideman Youngblood died on the afternoon of Thursday, the 17th of this month, at her home in Troy. She was the daughter of Col. James A. Wideman of Abbeville County, S. C., was born 14th July 1862. In February of last year she was married to Capt. J. T. Youngblood, formerly of Williston, but now of Troy. H. C. S., Tryon, S. C., March 23, 1887.

Issue of April 7, 1887

Married on 24th March 1887, at the residence of the bride's mother, York Co., S. C., Mr. Leander G. Wilson to Miss Maggie A. Blackwelder, Rev. J. K. Fant, officiating.

At the residence of the bride's father, Mr. J. W. Mitchell, March 6th, 1887, by Rev. D. W. Key, Miss Lula Mitchell and Mr. Wm. H. Woolly, all of Barnwell County.

At Blanton, Hill County, Texas, March 20th, 1887, Prof. M. L. Davis, formerly of Oconee County, S. C., to Miss Nannie Edney, of Washington county, Texas.

Died of measles, in Spartanburg County, S. C., March 5th 1887, Miss Nancy Coggin, aged forty-eight years and sixteen days. She joined the Cedar Springs Baptist Church at the age of eighteen.

Mrs. J. A. Turner died at her home near Providence, Fla., December 23, 1886. She was born in Edgefield County,, South Carolina, January 22, 1830; married J. A. Turner, July 1, 1847. She joined the Mountain Creek Baptist Church (South Carolina) in the fall of 1848 and removed with her husband and family to Florida, December 6, 1848. She was for about twenty-five years a member of Providence Church.

Issue of April 14, 1887

Tribute of Respect from Beulah Baptist Church to Deacon S. A. Y. McQuarters.

Married, March 27, 1887, by Rev. W. P. Smith, Mr. W. G. Shands and Miss Emma Nicholls, both of Spartanburg County, S. C.

April 7th, 1887, by Rev. W. P. Smith, Mr. A. M. Smith and Miss Barbara A. Bearden, both of Spartanburg County, S. C.

April 8th, 1887, at the home of Mr. Henry Cogburn, by Rev. G. W. Bussey, Mr. R. H. Leckie, of Edgefield, and Miss Bettie Murphrey, of Augusta, Ga.

Mrs. S. A. Whitlock, nee Kitchings, died in Chester County, December 12th 1886. She was born October 18th, 1821, and was baptized into the fellowship of Calvary Church, Chester Association when a young lady. Removed to Union C. H., after marriage to Mr. Harvey Whitlock, about 1850. She, with my father's family and Col. McKissick, composed the church at Union C. H. at its constitution. She leaves several children... C. T. S.

Issue of April 21, 1887

Married by Rev. I. W. Wingo, at the Baptist Church of Gaffney, April 6th, 1887, Mr. W. C. Carpenter to Miss Carrie Brown, all of Gaffney, S. C.

On the evening of April 14th, by Rev. G. F. Williams, assisted by Rev. A. J. S. Thomas, in the Baptist church at Ridge Spring, S. C., Rev. J. Hartwell Edwards, of Oxford, Miss., and Miss Kate McIver, daughter of R. B. Watson, of Ridge Spring.

Death on April 11 of little Georgie Smith, youngest child and only daughter of Bro. and sister W. P. Smith. She was only twenty-one months and four days old. W. T. Derieux.

Issue of April 28, 1887

Married at the residence of Rev. A. C. Stepp, the officiating minister, on the 20th of April 1887, Mr. Milton H. Traynham and Miss Lee Annie Davis, all of Dunklin, Greenville County, S. C.

Died, April 17th, 1887, at the residence of her husband in Alachua County, Florida, Elvira Miller, wife of Wade H. Harrison, and daughter of the late Gen. Miller of Spartanburg.

Mr. W. C. Patterson of McCormick, departed this life on 11th April 1887... He was thirty years of age. H. C. S.   Troy, S. C., April 25, 1887.

Died, on Tuesday morning, 19th of April 1887, Mr. John B. Hudgens. Bro. Hudgens was born in Laurens County in the year 1823. He united with Chestnut Ridge Baptist church in Laurens some twenty or more years ago. Soon after the war he removed to the Fork Township in Anderson County and joined the church at Townville... His remains were interred in the cemetery of Townville Baptist Church, on the 20th inst.

Death of Samuel McGrath, of Lewis T. O., Chester County, died on the 7th inst., in the 78th year of his age. L. C. H.

Departed this life at his home, Dunbarton, Barnwell County, on the night of the 29th of March 1887, Caleb Killingsworth, aged 58 years and 5 months. He was born October 20th, 1828. He the year 1853 he was baptized by Rev. H. D. Duncan into the fellowship of the Joyce's Branch church. In 1877 he moved his membership to the Cypress Chapel church [long eulogy]. W. D. M.

Issue of May 5, 1887

Married at the residence of G. W. Bussy, the officiating minister, April 29th, Mr. W. M. Bird and Miss Annie L. Thomas.

On the evening of the 27th April, by the Rev. H. C. Smart, Mr. Thomas Clinkscales to Miss Mollie Britt, all of Abbeville County.

On the evening of the 28th April, at the residence of the bride, by Rev. H. C. Smart, Mr. Toole, of Montmorenci, to Mrs. Fannie Perrin, of Abbeville County.

At the residence of the bride's father, by Rev. W. A. Betts, Tuesday afternoon, April 16th, Mr. Hammond Webb, of Anderson, and Miss Gertrude Brownlee, daughter of Mr. Geo. P. Brownlee, of Anderson County.

Died, in Graham's, April 16, 1887, Joseph Guess, Jr., infant son of Mr. and Mrs. Joseph Guess. T. E. J.

Issue of May 12, 1887

Married at Mt. Joy Church, April 28th, 1887, 7 p. m., by the Rev. H. K. Ezell, Mr. Jack W. Smith of Kelton, S. C., and Miss Ada Gorder, of Mississippi.

By the Rev. A. G. Collier, at the residence of Mr. T. C. Wise, near Blythe Station, Lincoln County, Ga., Mr. S. H. Roberts, of Richmond County, and Miss Mary A. Lucky, of Richmond County, Ga., at 11 o'clock a. m., on May 1st.

Issue of May 19, 1887

Married at the residence of Mr. M. C. Hitt at Plum Branch, S. C., by Rev. A. G. Collier, on May 12th, 1887, at 9½ a. m., Mr. W. A. Crawford and Miss Maggie Freeland.

At the Baptist Church, Blackville, S. C., on the evening of May 4th, 1887, by Rev. W. D. McMillan, Dr. D. K. Briggs to Miss Ida, eldest daughter of Capt. Henry Dodenhoff, all of Blackville.

On the evening of the 3rd May 1887, at the residence of the bride's father, by Rev. W. D. Rice, Mr. W. B. Chitty and Miss Ida Browning, all of Barnwell County, S. C.

At the residence of the bride's father, May 4th, 1887, by Rev. E. H. Cuttino, Mr. M. C. Muldrow and Miss Janie King, all of Darlington, S. C.

Departed this life, after a short illness from measles, Mrs. Isa Darlington, daughter of Mr. Caleb Killingsworth, and wife of Mr. Benj. Darlington, aged twenty-six years and eleven months. Scarcely had three weeks elapsed since her lamented father was laid to rest.... She was baptized into the fellowship of Cypress Chapel Church by Rev. A. Buist in 1875. W. D. M.

In Memory of Mrs. B. M. McGee [poem and long eulogy]. A. M. G.

Issue of May 26, 1887

Married at the residence of the bride's father, near Blackville, S. C., on the afternoon of May 18, 1887, by Rev. C. P. Ervin, Mr. Thomas J. Martin of Williamston, S. C., and Miss Blanche, eldest daughter of Mr. Judson E. Hair.

On Sunday, May 14th, 1887, in Lane's Baptist Church, by Rev. J. L. Rollins, Mr. J. M. Lockhart, of Darlington County, to Miss Willie McClary, of Williamsburg County.

Died, April 21st, 1887, aged one year and sixteen days, Gazelle Francis Moore, infant daughter of B. P. and W. P. Moore. The little one was laid away to rest in the cemetery at Townville.

Issue of June 9, 1887

Married on the 28th April 1887, at the residence of the bride's father, in the County of Marion, Mr. Edward B. Watson to Miss Addie W. Bethea, the Rev. H. C. Bethea officiating.

Mrs. Martha Bass, a member of Swift Creek Church, and wife of the late Josiah Bass, was born November 20th 1815 and died May 3rd, 1887. Two of her sons are honored officers in our church. A. McA. Pittman.

Died at his home in Cross Keys Township, April 8th, 1887, Adolpus D. Estes, from the effects of measles. The deceased was the youngest of four brothers and two sisters, natives of Union County. He was in the prime of life... a member of the Padgett's Creek Baptist Church, under the pastorate of Rev. L. C. Ezell. Our brother leaves a wife and four small children. Shelton, S. C., May 31, 1887.

Issue of June 16, 1887

In Memoriam. Minnie Cuttino Hoyt. To-day (June 11th) we laid aside from mortal view the remains of this dear girl, just a year and five days from the day when we preformed the same said duty for her honored father, Bro. W. H. Cuttino. On December 17, 1882, I united her in marriage to Mr. C. I. Hoyt. C. C. Brown. Sumter, S. C.

Tribute of Respect to Mrs. Floride Coleman.

Helen, the two year old baby of Capt. Hugh and Mrs. Mary Jane Robinson, of the Little River Church, Saluda Association, died on 11th day of February 1887.

Died, in Clarendon County, May 9th, 1887, William Weaver, who was born January 20th, 1897, and was married to Miss Eliza Phillips, of Darlington County, October 29th, 1831. The subject of this notice is the father of Rev. John M. Weaver. He leaves an aged widow and several children. J. L. R.

Died, at Yorkville, S. C., June 19th, 1887, little Frederick Chiles, son of F. c. and J. S. Hickson, aged six months, lacking one day.

Hayne F. Rowell died after an illness of only three days, at his father's home near Graham's, S. C., on the 17th day of May 1887, aged one year, ten months and seven days. In less than a week after, on the 91th May, in the same room, his brother Leland Rhett Rowell, in the ten year of his age. W. D. R.

Late in the afternoon on the 1st day of June, 187 ,little Ernest, aged six years and four months, son of Dr. George T.l and Hattie Walker, of Glendale, S. c., died.

Edwin Joseph Bostick died in Charleston, S. C., April 1st 1887. This dear young brother was born in Marion County, S. C., November 1st 1869, and was baptized by Rev. C. T. Anderson in 1882, and was a member of Mt. Zion Baptist Church. f. O. S. C.

Mrs. Enoree Thompson Suber died at her residence in Newberry County, s. C., June 3rd, 1887, in the forty-fifth year of her age. She was added to the church while at school in the Johnson Female University at Anderson, S. C. J. D. Huggins.

Mrs. Loula B. Gignilliant was born April 24th, 1856, in Newton County, Ga. She was the daughter of Mr. John M. and Mrs. Amanda Bostwick. Mr. Bostwick was an honored deacon of the Baptist church in Conyers, Ga. In 1874, she was baptized by her pastor, Rev. J. M. Britton. The same year she moved to Atlanta and was married to Mr. H. J. Gignilliat, December 7th 1875. For one year she resided at Norcross, Ga., thence moved to Easley, S. C., October 1st 1876, where she lived until her death, May 12th 1887. J. K. M.

Married at Black's, S. C., June 15th, 1887, by Rev. J. A. White, Mr. Joseph Blalock to Miss Eva Bridges.

At Black's, S. C., June 16th, 1887, by Rev. J. A. White, Mr. S. J. Bell to Mrs. L. E. Hall, all of Black's.

On the 26th instant, at the residence of the bride's father, Mr. J. J. Traynham, Greenville County, S. C., by Rev. J. K. Mendenhall, Mr. J. F. Riddle to Miss Addie E. Traynham.

Died at the home of the parents in Chester, S. C., June 26th, 1887, aged two years and six months, Katie Ferguson, youngest daughter of Mr. and Mrs. A. Ferguson. R. W. S.

Died, on the 13th of April, 1887, Mrs. Mary Hanna, who was born April 19th, 1818. She had been a consistent member of Black Mingo Church for many years... J. L. R.

Mrs. Amanda Williams was baptized at Flat Creek Church, Lancaster County, of which she remained a member during her married life. She afterwards became a member of Beaver Creek Church and remained there up to 1881, when she, with her children, three sons and a daughter, aided in the constitution of Laurel Hill Church, Lancaster County. Two of her sons are now honored deacons of Laurel Hill Church... A. S. W. Taxahaw, S. C.

C. C. Brunson died May 31st, 1887, in the 78th year of his age. He was born in Barnwell County and there spent the greater part of his life. He moved to the upper part of the state during the war and in 1866 was baptized by the Rev. Mr. Picket. J. Q. A.

It was on the third Sunday in February last, when the writer was summoned to the dying bedside of a Christian woman some nine miles away. Such was the scene in the home of Mr. Lawrence Fowler, when a mother was taken from her children. Mrs. Fowler (Rosa J.) was a member of the Rocky Creek Church. Born 23d May 1861, dying 20th February 18878. J. C. F.

Mrs. Marion Glover Mobley Wilkes died at her home, Wilkesburg, S. C., on the evening of June 17, 1887. She was married to Major John W. Wilkes February 9th 1876, and was baptized and united with Brush Fork Baptist Church in 1876. At the time of her death she was a member of Calvary Baptist Church. F. O. S. Curtis.

On Sunday afternoon, May 1, 1887, Mrs. Sarah Smith Howe died, aged nearly ninety-one years. She was the only child of Capt. Oliver Fuller. She was born in Selkirk, Miss., May 17, 1796; married July 4, 1816, by Dr. Richard Furman, to Silas Howe, formerly of Northboro, Miss., but then a wealthy merchant of Charleston, S. C. Her husband died April 19, 1856. She was baptized by the same pastor into the fellowship of the First Baptist Church, Feb. 1823. She never had any children of her own, but adopted as her child, the present Mrs. E. R. Doucin. [long account] O. F. Gregory.   Baltimore, June 21, 1887.

Issue of July 14, 1887

Death of little Bruce McLean, son of Mr. and Mrs. J. S. McLean, of McCormick, 10th June. H. C. S.

Deacon John C. Hayes of Buffalo Church, Abbeville County ,was born in the month of September 1802; died June 9th 1887, and was buried at the old homestead at Long Cane. h. C. S.

In Memoriam. Lucinda Arnett, Cedar Spring Church.   She was born December 31st, 1801, and died May 30th, 1887. Her birth place on Fair Forest is just two miles from Cedar Spring, and there she rests in the family cemetery beside her father and grandfather, who were honored revolutionary soldiers.

Married at the residence of the bride's mother, Dunbarton, S. C., on the evening of June 30th, by Rev. W. D. McMillan, Mr. Henry B. Matthews to Miss Mary J., daughter of the late Caleb Killingsworth, all of Barnwell County.

Tribute of Respect from Woman's Missionary Society of Liberty Baptist Church, Chester County, June 26, 1887, to sister Marion Mobley Wilkes.

Issue of July 21, 1887

Married, July 13, 1887, at the home of the officiating minister, Rev. G. W. Bussey, Mr. J. C. Bussey and Miss E. L. Heath, all of Edgefield County.

Departed this life on the 26th of April, 1887, at the home of her son, J. E. DuPre, Smithville, S. C., Mrs. Priscilla A. DuPre, aged about seventy years. The subject of this brief notice was born near Bishopville, S. C. She joined the Baptist church early in life. She married the Rev. James DuPre....

Died, at his home in Greenwood, S. C., July 17, 1887, Maj. Peter McKellar, of an apoplectic stroke. The deceased was born in Greenock, Scotland, March 20th, 1810, and at the age of five came with his father to the United States. his father settled at Scotch Cross, Abbeville District, S. C. Peter McKellar went to school in Spartanburg County. Maj. McKellar was twice married. His first wife was Miss Agnes Lipscomb, and after her death he married Miss Almina Sale. He survived her many years. He joined the Mt. Moriah Baptist Church of Abbeville County, under Rev. Nicholas W. Hodges. Left children and grandchildren.... A. S. T.

Issue of July 28, 1887

Mrs. Frances M. Revell, wife of Mr. James C. Revell, died in Florence, on the evening of the 11th of July 1887, in the 48th year of her age. She joined the church at Antioch, near Camden, in early life, and was baptized by Rev. J. E. Rodgers. She has left a husband, three sons and one daughter. B. G. Covington.

Bro. William Jordan, a native of Crawfordsville, Ga., united with the Baptist Church at Langley, S. C., previous to 1877. On January 1st 1882, he and Bro. J. F. Lamb were elected deacons. On May 9th 1887 he died, aged about sixty-one years. W. A. McCrackan.

Departed this life at Beech Island, on Sunday, March 13th, 1887, Mrs. Mary Gardner, wife of Mr. Garrett Gardner, of the above place. [eulogy]

Departed this life at Blackville, S. C., on June 30th, Miss Eliza J. Hagood, aged forty-six years, six months and twenty days. She was a member of Blackville Baptist Church. W. D. M.

Issue of August 11, 1887

Tribute of Respect from Baptist Sunday School at Greer's to Richard Lee Greene.

Married, July 19th, 1887, at the residence of Mr. C. C. Ellzey, Mr. Walter Ellzey, of Orangeburg County, S. C., to Miss Camilla Bozeman, of Scriven County, Ga., Rev. J. A. Hoffman officiating.

In the Baptist Church at Bennettsville, S. C., July 28th 1887, by Rev. R. N. Pratt, Mr. Marion G. Wilson and Miss Annie E. Ellerbe, of Bennettsville.

Died, at Williston, S. C., on the 1st of August, Edna Virginia Sanders, daughter of Rev. and Mrs. F. J. Sanders. This little girl was just two years, four months, and four days old.

Departed this life on the 26th of July 1887, in Orangeburg County, S. C., Dr. J. A. J. Hildebrand, in the 60th year of his age. He was a member of Providence Baptist Church. He leaves a wife and six children. E. H. G.

Fell asleep in Jesus, at her home in Greenville County, S. c., May 13th, 1887, Mrs. Frances Moon, aged thirty-three years. The deceased was the daughter of Joel B. and Mary J. Garrison, and the wife of J. P. Moon, clerk of Bethuel Baptist Church. She left eight small children, one of whom has since died. R. J. W.

Issue of August 25, 1887

Tribute of Respect from Lower Fair Forest Baptist Church, Union Co., S. C., Aug. 6, 1887, to Mrs. E. H. Lawson. W. S. Harrison

Tribute of Respect from Lower Fair Forest Baptist Church, Union Co., S. C., to sister Jane Grier, who died February 24th, 1887. G. C. Grier, C. C.

Rev. Randal McDaniel departed this life August 16th, 1887, at his home in Mullins, S. C. He was born May 22, 1816, and united by baptism with Cedar Creek Church of Cumberland Co., N. C., when fourteen years of age. His life was mostly spent in Fayetteville, N. C., where his occupation was farming and merchandising. he was ordained to the full work of the gospel minister 7 January 1872 at the Gapway Church of Marion County, S. C. T. P. L.

Died in Lexington, Mo., August 9th 1887, Charles Gildersleeve Lanneau, son of Prof. John F. and Louise S. Lanneau-- and grandson of Mrs. Thos. M. Cox, of Greenville, S. C. He lacked a month and a day of living five years. J. F. L.

William H. Hill was born August 3rd, 1861, and died of typhoid fever August 6th, 1887, at the home of his father, the late lamented C. J. Hill, six miles above Greenville City. A few months before his death he was married to Miss Mary E. Pack, of Greenville City. R. W. Barber.

On Tuesday morning, August 16th, our village folk were moved by the sudden death of Mrs. Rachel Coker. Her only child, Bro. Thomas H. Coker. She was the relict of Mr. Thomas Coker, whom death claimed years ago. She was a member of Welsh Neck Church. Society Hill, S. C.

Issue of September 1, 1887

Tribute of Respect. On 16 July 1887, the church at Bruton's Fork was called the mourn the death of Mrs. Elizabeth R. Liles, who was born in this community and spent her life here with the exception of a few years of her early married life at the home of her noble husband, H. W. Liles, who preceded her by nearly thirty years. J. A. W. Thomas. Pearson P. O., S. C., Aug. 25, 1887.

Married on the 21st instant, by Rev. J. L. Sifly, Mr. Patrick V. Matthis and Miss Mary Barr, all of Barnwell Co., S. C.

Died at Woodruff, S. C., on the 23th of August 1887, John Trap Henderson. He is deeply mourned by his young wife and child. C. M.

Died at Blackstock, Aug. 5th, 1887, Mrs. Lucretia M. McCrorey, aged 54 years... member of Blackstock Baptist Church. J. A. B.

Entered into heaven's rest, July 17th, 1887, Mrs. Annie G., daughter of Dr. John Galphin, of Beech Island, S. C., and wife of Mr. Albert Barns, of Silverton, of the same state.... Beech Island Baptist Church.

Miss Ellen J. Gifford, youngest daughter of Mr. Ebenezer Gifford, deceased, died at her residence, Aug. 25, 1887. She was born Nov. 3d 1826, joined Beech Branch Church under Rev. Gilbert Williams, Sept. 1st 1855. J. T. M.

Issue of September 8, 1887

Married, on Sunday 28th August 1887, by Rev. W. A. Gaines, Mr. W. J. Gaines, of the Augusta *Chronicle*, to Miss Anna M. Gaines, eldest daughter of the officiating minister.

Died, near Aiken, S. C., August 20th 1887, Teresa, daughter of Mr. and Mrs. W. J. Price, aged nine years.

Sallie, daughter of William and Margaret Anderson, died August 25, 1887, aged six years and two months. D. W. K., Williston, S. C.

Infant son of J. C. and Emma Stansel died Aug. 19, 1887, aged one year and eight months. D. W. K., Williston, S. C.

Bertha Ruth, only child of Hampton and Jane M. Hair, died August 30, 1887, aged seven months and twenty days. D. W. K., Williston, S. C.

Rev. A. M. Noble departed this life August 8th, 1887. The subject of this notice was born in Robeson County, N. C., in 1805. He united with the Methodist church. He afterwards joined the Baptist church and was licensed to preach A. D. 1846. Friendfield, S. C.   C. T. A.

Died at her home near Darlington C. H., S. C., June 4th, 1887, after an illness of ten days, Mrs. Margaret Ann Smith, in the thirty-ninth year of her age. Mrs. Smith was the second daughter of Mr. Max Gandy. She was baptized by Dr. J. O. B. Dargan into the fellowship of Black Creek Church, August 18th 1870. On the 12th of February 1880, Miss Margaret Ann Gandy was married to Mr. Henry M. Smith. R. W. Lide.

Miss Hattie S. Moye departed this life on Monday the 8th of August 1887, at the home of her sister, Mrs. Donie O'Neal, in the town of Bamberg, S. C., in the sixtieth year of her age. Thirty-nine years ago she was baptized at Philadephia Church, near Buford's Bridge, Barnwell County, S. C. One mile distant is the burying ground where he loved ones rest. W. D. R. Grahams, S. C., Aug. 29, 1887.

Issue of September 15, 1887

Mrs. Sarah Ann Gregory passed away July 19, 1887, at her home in Charleston, S. C. She was born in Providence, R. I., April 6, 1820. She was baptized at the age of fourteen by Rev. Basil Manly. She was married by the elder Dr. W. T. Brantly to Ferdinand M. Gregory, June 23, 1842. They lived long enough to see their children godly and active Christian men and women, and one of them O. F. Gregory, D. D., of Baltimore, a useful minister.

Tribute of Respect from Woman's Mission Society of Blackstock Baptist Church to Mrs. L. M. McCrorey.

Issue of September 22, 1887

Married at the residence of the bride's parents, Ronald, Va., Sept. 14th, 1887, by Rev. J. A. Brown, assisted by Rev. N. C. Burnett, Mr. Elisha Bomar, of Clifton, S. C., and Miss Bessie Brown.

By Rev. T. J. Earle, at the lady's home, on the 13th Sept. 1887, Col. F. H. Fuller and Mrs. Sarah Donnald, all of Greenville Co.,

Tribute of Respect from Middle Tyger Church, July 10, 1887, to Mrs. Elizabeth Ann Greer, daughter of James A. and Ellen Hadden, one of the founders of this church, formerly from Mount Zion.

Died, at the home of her parents, Mr. and Mrs. C. A. Rodgers, in Greenville, S. C., little Edith Leach Rodgers, aged nine months.

Died, at her home, July 29, 1887, Mrs. Georgia Ann Griffin... a member of Corinth Church since Sept. 9, 1868. She leaves a husband and several children. R. P. G.

Died, at Chesterfield C. H., S. C., Sept. 11th, 1887, Deacon William Malloy, aged sixty-eight years....

Departed this life while on a visit to Summerton, S. C., Sept. 6, 1887, Mr. John Phillips of Providence, Sumter County, S. C., in the 71st year of his age. He was a consistent member of the High Hills Baptist Church. He leaves two daughters, three sons... J. J. M.

Edgar F., son of Bro. John Hart, entered into heavenly rest Sunday evening, June 19, 1887. Bro. E. F. Hart was born March 10th 1870... baptized by Bro. D. W. Cuttino into the fellowship of Corinth Church of the Charleston Association, Oct. 19th, 1884. R. P. G.

Died, at his residence near Crosbyville, in Fairfield Co., S. C., Dr. C. C. Estes, aged thirty-eight years, nine months and six days. Dr. Estes had been a member of the Beaver Creek Baptist Church about twenty-two years... J. D. Mahon. Halsellville, S. C.

On Wednesday, September 7th, at a little before six o'clock in the afternoon, our young brother, Mr. Edward Kirkley, died at the home of his father, Bro.D. C. Kirkley... C. A. Fulton, Camden, S. C., Sept. 17, 1887.

Issue of September 29, 1887

Married by Rev. J. L. Ouzts, September 22d, 1887, at the residence of Mr. J. K. Harvley, Edgefield County, S. C., Mr. B. R. Quarles and Miss Flonnie Adkins.

John W., only son of W. T. and S. K. McGregor, died of cholera infantum, Sept. 20th, 1887, aged four months and twelve days.

Died, very suddenly, of heart disease, on Saturday night, July 23d, 1887, Mrs. Martha M. Oxner, aged 70 years, 1 month and 8 days. Sister Oxner was the oldest member of the Winnsboro Baptist Church. her husband who preceded her only seven years ago, was for many years the deacon, clerk and earthly pillar of the church. J. Howard Carpenter.

Died, July 17th, 1887, of typhoid fever, Mr. Ray F. McNeil Turner, only son of Mr. G. R. and Mrs. M. J. Turner, the latter of this place. The subject of this sketch was in his seventeenth year at the time of his death. At the time of his death he was in the employ of Captain B. F. Pennington, supervisor of railroads, and a resident of this place. Chas. R. Willeford.

Issue of October 6, 1887

Married, September 27, 1887, at the bride's residence at Williston, S. C., by Rev. J. W. Elkins, Miss Janie E. Holland to W. J. Snider, of Elloree, S. C.

On the night of the 21st of September 1887, at the residence of the bride's mother, by Rev. J. E. Covington, assisted by Rev. C. T. Scaife, Mr. Henry T. Price, of Rockwood, Tennessee, to Miss Eva Knight, of Union Co., S. C.

Died, at the residence of their father, Mr. George Rabin, in Fairfield Co., S. C., little Hattie and Dorcas Rabin, in about three hours of each other, with diphtheria, and both were buried in the same coffin and same grave... W. H. H.

On the 16th of the same month, and in the same neighborhood and with the same dreadful disease, Miss Rebecca Gregg, about eighteen years old. Only a few weeks before she united with Pine Grove Church, Kershaw County.

Died, September 19, 1887, in the 72nd year of her age, Mrs. Elizabeth Rhodes, wife of C. B. Rhodes, Sr., of Darlington County, S. C. Elizabeth Hicks was born in Darlington County, Feb. 25th, 1816. In 1837 she was married to C. B. Rhodes, and in 1856 was baptized into the fellowship of Swift Creek Church.... left husband and children.

Mrs. E. C. Watson died on September 6th, at her home in Ridge Spring, S. C. G. F. Williams. Milwood, Va.. Sept. 19, 1887.

Issue of October 13, 1887

Married, October 5th, 1887, at the home of Mr. and Mrs. John C. Walker, near Ninety-Six, their eldest daughter, Miss Bettie, to Mr. Wm. P. Lipford, Rev. J. S. Jordan, officiating.

Tribute of Respect to O. T. Whatley.

Tribute of Respect to pastor John A. Dill, who departed this life September 19, 1887, from Lima Baptist Church.

Tribute of Respect from Sandy Springs Baptist Church, Greenville Co., S. C., to William J. West, who joined the Standing Spring Church on July 23d, 1857, was elected church clerk in 1867, and served until he united with Sandy Spring Church on October 20, 1877, at this time he wa also received as deacon of this church.

Issue of October 20, 1887

Departed this life October 4th, 1886,Mrs. R. A. Owens. One year ago to-day.... Her Children.

Sister Sarah Morgan, daughter of John and Rebecca McManus, was born in Lancaster County, S. C., March 8th, 1815, and died in Cheraw, September 26,k1887.

Little James Joppa McHugh, the eldest son of Brother Andrew McHugh, of Abner's Creek Church, died Aug. 21, 1887....aged two years.

Mr. Wm. Lemuel Lee died near Williston, October 9th 1887, at the age of thirty-nine years and six months. He was twice married and leaves a wife and five children... member of Rosemary Church. D. W. K.

Died in Seneca, S. C., Oct. 10th, 1887, Mrs. Clara Hewitt Macaulay, wife of Prof. N. W. Macaulay, and youngest daughter of Maj. and Mrs. A. R. Broyles, in the thirty-third year age. C. M.

Died in Abbeville, on Sunday night, October 9th, 1887, James LeRoy, son of J. L. and Anna M. Wideman, aged one year, nine months and nineteen days.

Death in the family of Mr. J. L. E. Jones, residing in the forks of Buncombe and Rutherford streets, infant boy of nine months of age... borne to the cemetery of Abner's Creek Church, Spartanburg County.

Married at his residence on the 2d inst., by Rev. D. I. Spearman, Mr. S. M. Richey to Miss Jane McAlister, all of Anderson County, S. C.

At the residence of the bride's father, Oct. 6th, 1887, by Rev. D. I. Spearman, Mr. John Hammond to Miss Emma Martin, all of Anderson County.

At Barnwell, S. C., Oct. 5th, at 3 o'clock p. m., by Rev. C. G. Bradford, Mr. C. W. Rentz, of Bamberg, S. C., to Miss Lizzie Shuck.

At Red Oak, Barnwell County, Oct. 5th, at 8½ p. m., by Rev. C. G. bradford, Mr. C. C. Caliph to Miss Sarah Cave.

On the evening of the 11th Oct., at the residence of Mr. C. B. Fowler, Jonesville, Union County, S. C., by Rev. Chas. R. Willeford, Mr. W. A. Cranford and Miss Mattie E. Rowell, daughter of the late Rev. C. D. Rowell, of the South Carolina Conference.

Issue of October 27, 1887

Tribute of Respect from Adelphian Literary Society of Furman University to Mr. Henry T. Wilson.

Married on the 12th day of October 1887, at the residence of the bride's father, Mr. John Reese, in Richland County, Miss Kate Reese to Mr. J. e. McKinnon, Rev. B. C. Lamplet officiating.

At the residence of the bride's mother, near Plum Branch, at 5 p. m., the 18th instant, by Rev. J. A. Bell, Mr. Bartow Thomas to Miss Gussie Blackwell, all of Edgefield County.

At the residence of Mr. B. Howell, near Lydia, S. C., on the 13th instant, by Rev. W. O. Petty, Mr. Henry Harrell and Miss E. J. Harrell.

By Rev. W. O. Petty, near Timmonsville, at the bride's home, Mr. J. C. Revill, of Florence, and Miss Alberta Jordan.

Died, at Cheraw, S. C., October 18th 1887, Vereen McNair, son of W. Hyman and Pauline E. Gurganus, aged nine months and nineteen days.

Died, September 28th, 1887, at his home near Bishopville, in the 45th year of his age, H. A. James.   Bishopville, Oct. 10, 1887.

It was my sad duty on yesterday, at the Jonesville church, to funeralize Mr. Joseph R. Fowler, who departed this life a few weeks since. Chas. R. Willeford, Jonesville, Oct. 17.

Died, August 29th 1887, Miss Gussie Rice, third daughter of Dr. W. B. and Mrs. F. U. Rice, aged seventeen years, two months and thirteen days. J. G. Williams.

THE BAPTIST COURIER

Married, Oct. 18, 1887, at the residence of the bride's father, by Rev. I. W. Wingo, Mr. Charles Christman and Miss Pearl A. Lipscomb, all of Gaffney, S. C.

October 25th, at the residence of the bride's father,by Rev. I. W. Wingo, Rev. F. Bee Gaffney and Miss Laura M. Tanner, both of Saluda, N. C.

Oct. 27th, at the Baptist church in Gaffney, by Rev. I. W. Wingo, Mr. H. L. Spears and Miss Gracie Gaffney, all of Gaffney, S. C.

At Abbeville C. H., Oct. 13th, by Rev. R. N. Pratt, Mr. Willie E. Miller of Charleston, and Miss Georgia Gordon, of Abbeville.

Died at Barnwell, S. C., September 17, 1887, Robert Frederick, infant son of Mr. and Mrs. W. L. Kirby, aged nine months and two days. This sweet child, named for his uncle, Rev. Frederick Hickson.... C. G. Bradford.

On the night of the 19th of October, John T. Rice died....

Died, at her home near Baldock, Barnwell County, S. C., 11th October 1887, Mrs. Ella C. Wilson, wife of Mr. O. D. A. Wilson, and daughter of the late W. R. Ulmer... united with the Great Salkehatchie Baptist Church. J. G. Williams.

On Sept. 6, 1887, Nannie Green, the beloved wife of C. C. Grubbs, passed away. Sister Grubbs was born Oct. 17th, 1844, and united with the church at Barker's Creek in August 1865. D. W. Hiott. Williamston, S. C.

Mrs. S. C. Perryclear departed this life June 1st 1887. She was baptized into the church of her parents in Savannah, Ga., at the age of 14 years. In 1851 she married Rev. James S. Perryclear of Beaufort, S. C.

Married by Rev. W. T. Derieux, in Spartanburg, Oct. 26, 1887, Mr. W. B. W. Veazy and Miss Hattie Mitchell.
Oct. 30, 1887, at the residence of the bride's father, by Rev. D. Weston Hiott, M.r J. Frank Talbert and Miss Dora, youngest daughter of Capt. Robert A. Gray, all of Williston.

By Rev. F. C. Hickson, at the residence of the bride's father, Oct .13, 1887, Mr. Calhoun Clarke and Miss Mary Ellen Ferguson, both of York.

Nov. 1st, 1887, in Chester County, at the residence of the bride's father, Mr. William Hollis, by Rev. R. W. Sanders, Mr. J. Yongue Murphy and Miss Anna A. Hollis.

Oct. 30, 1887, by Rev. W. D. Rice, Miss Florie Rice and Mr. E. J. Bryan, all of Barnwell County.

At the residence of the bride's mother in Edgefield Co., by Rev. J. L. Ouzts, Oct. 22, 1887, Mr. J. D. Quarles and Miss M. R. Holmes.

At the Baptist parsonage near Lydia, S. C., by Rev. W. O. Petty, Oct. 30th 1887, Mr. Robert Galloway, of Charleston, and Miss P. L. Howell, of Darlington County.

At the home of the bride's mother, by Rev. H. L. Baggott, Oct. 15, 1887, Mr. J. L. Brooker and Miss M. B. Whetstone, both of Lexington County, S. C.

At the home of the bride, by the Rev. H. L. Baggott, Oct. 3, 1887, Mr. Edward Curtis and Miss Nellie Patterson, both of Montmorenci, S. C.

Died in Fairfield Co., S. C., Oct. 27th 1887, Mrs. Emma Nicholson, aged about 55 years. This sister was the widow of the late Rev. Peter Nicholson... She was for years a member of the Blackstock Baptist Church.

Mr. John Dickey, was born Feb. 14, 1808, and died at his home near Fishing Creek Factory, in Chester County, S. c., May 26th, 1887. His remains were laid away in Union Church Cemetery. M. A. Connolly.

Died, at Belton, S. C., October 28th, 1887, Mrs. Sarah Agnew. Had she lived another month she would have completed her ninety-eighth year. C. M.

Issue of November 17, 1887

Married at the residence of the bride's father, Mr. James Wideman, near Plum Branch, by Rev. James A. Bell, on the 8th inst., at 4 p. m., Mr. G. H. W. Smith, of Germany, to Miss M. M. Wideman.

At the residence of the bride's mother, on the 3rd inst., by Rev. T. J. Earle, assisted by Rev. M. M. Landrum, Capt. Peyton Ballenger and Miss Emily Wall, of Spartanburg County.

By the pastor, in the Baptist Church at Greenwood, November 9, 1887, Mr. Warren Strawhorn and Miss Mary McKellar.

November 3rd, 1887, at the bride's home by Rev. G. W. Bussey, Mr. O. M. Burnett and Miss Carrie DeLaughter, all of Edgefield.

At the residence of the Hon. J. W. Lyles, on the morning of the 9th instant, by Rev. J. D. Mahon, Rev. B. F. Corley and Miss Mary L. Morris, all of Fairfield.

By Rev. J. D. Mahon, at the residence of the bride's mother, Mrs. Mary Ann Pope, Nov. 2, 1887, Mr. J. C. Stone and Miss Minnie E. Pope, all of Fairfield County.

Mrs. L. A. Wilkes, late relict of Mr. W. M. Wilkes, was born in Darlington County, Oct. 19, 1816. She joined New Providence Church (then called Boggy Swamp) in early life. After her marriage she and her husband became members of the Antioch Church. In 1861 the moved near Lake Swamp Church and transferred their membership to the same. Sister Walker died August 26, 1887. A. McA. P.

Frank Curtiss, son of G. Johnnie and Hattie Varn, departed this life October 15th, 1887, aged four years and eight months. J. F. P.

Issue of December 1, 1887

Married at the residence of the bride's father, Oct. 30th, 1887, by Rev. F. O. S. Curtis, Mr. E. Alston Wilks and Miss Mattie Byars, daughter of T. T. Byars, Esq., all of Chester County.

At the residence of the bride's father, Nov. 20th, 1887, by Rev. F. O. S. Curtis, Mr. G. W. Cornwell and Miss Lela Belle Gregory, eldest daughter of Pickens Gregory, all of Chester County.

November 15th, 1887, at the bride's home, by Rev. J. A. White Mr. John B. Meritz, Sr., of York Co., S. c., and Mrs. Fannie Beehtler, of Cleveland Co., N. C.

At the residence of the bride's father, by Rev. J. A. White, on the 19th inst., Mr. J. D. Paine, of Greenville County, to Miss Hattie C. Owen, of Black's.

At Mrs. Sarah Seigler's, the bride's mother, by Rev. A. G. Collier, on the 24th inst., Mr. E. M. Watley and Miss Francis E. Seigler, all of Edgefield County.

On Thursday night, October 27, 1887, at the residence of the bride's step-father, by Rev. B. P. Estes, Mr. M. Perry Autley and Miss Annie D. Inabinit, all of Jamison, S. C.

At the Blackville Baptist Church, on the evening of Tuesday, Nov. 8th, 1887, by Rev. W. D. McMillan, Mr. N. P. Padgett to Miss Jennie Turner, all of Barnwell County.

At the residence of Judge Tompkins, Edgefield County, on November 8, 1887, Mr. J. Mc. Kinard and Miss Betty Gallman, Rev. J. S. Jordan officiating.

November 16, 1887, at the home of the bride's mother, by Rev. G. W. Bussey, Mr. James Thurmond and Miss Emma Williams, all of Edgefield County.

On the 16th of November 1887, in the city of Greenville, S. C., by Rev. J. H. Stoudenmire, Mr. C. Robertson to Miss Mary Bishop, all of Greenville.

At the home of the bride's father, by Rev. J. A. Hoffman, Sept. 22nd, 1887, Mr. Charlie Ethridge and Miss Mary Ann Myers, both of Orangeburg Co., S. C.

At the home of the bride's mother, by Rev. J. A. Hoffman, Oct. 20, 1887, Mr. A. D. Dempsey and Miss Annie Beickle, both of Orangeburg Co., S. C.

By Rev. J. A. Hoffman, Nov. 11th, Mr. Edward Judge, of Colleton County, and Miss Margaret Myers, of Orangeburg County.

Rufus Alonzo Reese, born February 25th, 1883, died November 8th, 1887. Little Rufus' father crossed the river a little more than a year ago. J. D. Huggins.

Gentle Fay, daughter of J. R. and Sallie J. Wolfe, of Pineville, N. C., died Nov. 2nd, 1887, aged one year, lacking nineteen days. J. K. Fant.

Reuben Cooper Hilton died 20th October, aged thirty years. Thirteen years ago he entered the Christian service, affiliating with a Methodist Church in Alabama..... J. S. Jordan.

Departed this life June 17, 1887, at the home of her son-in-law, Mr. John Fenley, of Fairfield Co., S. C., Mrs. Sallie Entzminger, aged seventy-nine years and six months. Sister Entzminger had been a member of Buffalo Baptist Church for at least fifty years. She leaves six children, quite a number of grandchildren.... W. H. H.

Mrs. Melissa Sample, wife of J. W. Fouche, departed this life at their home at Ninety-Six, on the 8th of November 1887. She was fifty-eight years old, and became a member of Siloam Baptist Church in 1852.

Issue of December 15, 1887

Married at the residence of the bride's father, Mr. Delaware Powell, on the afternoon of Dec. 1, 1887, by Rev. D. H. Crosland, J. D. Rankin to Miss Lula M. Powell, all of Aiken County.

December 1st, 1887, at the residence of the bride's father, by Rev. M. W. Rankin, Mr. W. K. Williams, of Lancaster, to Miss Nannie Beatty, of Kershaw.

Departed this life on the 8th inst., Rev. H. M. Barton, at Fair Play, S. C. He was born about the year 1810 on Tugaloo River, in Oconee County. Bro. Barton was twice married. His first wife was a Miss King, of Anderson County. She died about the close of the war. His second wife was a Mrs. Glenn, daughter of Bro. Levi Burris, late an honored and faithful deacon of Mountain Creek Church, Anderson County. He leaves a wife and five children... W. W. Leathers.

Issue of December 22, 1887

Married on Wednesday, Dec. 7, 1887, by Rev. W. D. Rice, at the residence of the bride's mother, Mr. J. K. Fender and Miss Mattie Carter, all of Barnwell County.

At the residence of James B. Higgins, the bride's father, Nov. 9, 1887, by Rev. A. C. Stepp, Mr. John A. Madden and Miss Cora Higgins, all of Laurens Co.

Dec. 6, 1887, at the residence of James Owens, the bride's father, by Rev. A. C. Stepp, Mr. S. Stewart Boyd and Miss J. Lenora Owens, both of Laurens Co.

Dec. 8, 1887, at the residence of N. L. Barksdale, the bride's father, by Rev. A. C. Steep, Mr. Charles B. Bobo, of the firm of Orr, Owens & Bobo, Laurens, S. C., and Miss Mattie Barksdale, of Highland Home, S. C.

At the residence of the bride's father, near Williston, by Rev. D. W. Key, Dec. 8, 187, Mr. M. D. Bell and Miss V. G. Woods.

At the residence of the bride's brother, Mr. Melvin Hair, by Rev. D. W. Key, Dec. 14, 1887, Mr. Fletcher Anderson of Augusta, Ga., and Miss Ellen J. Hair, of Barnwell County.

On the evening of Dec. 15, 1887, at the residence of the bride's father, by Rev. J. J. Myers, Mr. E. S. Gardner and Miss Maggie J. Gauf, both of Kershaw Co.

On the evening of Dec. 8, 1887, at the residence of the bride's father, Hon. J. W. Beasley, Mr. Henry Lee, son of Dr. Henry Lee, of Lydia, and Miss Annie Beasley-- Rev. W. O. Myers, officiating.

At the residence of the bride's mother, Dec. 4, 1887, by Rev. J. A. Hoffman, Mr. Hampton Ott and Miss Fannie Hughes, both of Orangeburg Co.

At the residence of the bride's father, Dec. 7, 1887, by Rev. J. A. Hoffman, Mr. Lawrence Metts and Miss Henrietta Wallin, all of Orangeburg Co.

By Rev. J. A. Hoffman, Dec. 11, 1887, Mr. H. C. Murphey and Miss Cora Smoak, all of Orangeburg Co.

In Foreston Baptist Church, Dec. 11, 1887, Mr. C. M. Mason and Miss Dora A., eldest daughter of Maj. C. W. Land-- Rev. B. C. Lampley, assisted by Rev. T. J. Rooke, officiating.

December 8th, 1887, in the Baptist Church at Ninety-Six, S. C., by Rev. Geo. H. Carter, Mr. J. N. Griffin, and Miss Annie Galphin.

On the morning of November 27th, 1887, by Rev. J. K. Mendenhall, Mr. William Mac Ridgeway to Miss Mary Jane Traynham, daughter of Mr. Nimrod Traynham.

Died, at Mannville, S. C., November 21, 1887, little Bessie, daughter of Mr. and Mrs. W. S. Scarborough, aged three years.

John R. Abel died at his home, near Blythewood, Fairfield County, on the 16th of November 1887, in the 70th year of his age,leaving his wife and three sons....

Died, Sept. 27, 1887, little Frank Montgomery, infant son of Mr. and Mrs. R. R. Willkins, of Gaffney, S. c., aged four months and ten days.

Died in Bamberg, S. C., Dec. 11, 1887, Miss Elizabeth S. Hewitt, in her 56th year. In early life she connected herself with the church under the preaching of Rev. Richard Fuller, in Charleston, S. C., and her membership continued with the Citadel Square Baptist Church until she removed to Bamberg.

302

BEE, Eliza G. (Fogartie) 35
  John S. 35
  Robert (--) 26
BEEHTLER, Fannie (--)-
(Meritz) 297
BEEKS, Ella E. (Simpson)
222
  Lille (Moore) 235
BEICKLE, Annie (Demp-
sey) 297
BELL, 156
  A. M. (Towill) 35
  Ada C. (Clabaugh) 147
  Angie (Towill) 81
  G. 126
  George 81,171
  Henrietta (Timmerman)
126
  J. A. 247, 250, 270, 271,
294
  James A. 296
  Julia (Henderson) 229
  L. E. (Hall) 286
  M. D. 299
  M. J. (--)(Allen) 225
  Mattie (Casey) 226
  Maud (Paulling) 279
  Newton 279
  S. J. 286
  Susan M. (--) 156
  T. A. 36
  T. P. 147,264
  Thos. R. 229
  V. G. (Woods) 299
BELLE, Hayne 81
  P. G. (Workman) 81
BELLEN, Ida (Merritt) 246
  John 246
BELLOT, Janie B. (Porter)
117
BELLOTTE, A. D. 171
  Kate (Rowland) 171
BENNETT, E. H. 136
  Indiana (Rountree) 136
  Josephine (Clary) 149
BENNITTE, Julia (Spillers)
123
  W. C. 123
BENSON, Alex. 270
  Annie (Watson) 246
  Charles W. 222
  Elvira (Goodlet) 144
  Nannie T. (White) 6
  Sophie (Fowler) 222
  Thomas 246
BENTLEY, Mattie (Baker)
224
BENTON, Rosa 196
BERRY, E. J. (Kennedy)
170
  E. Janie (Kennedy) 237
  Elizabeth (Farmer) 276
  J. Pauline (Mendenhall)
118,138
  Juliet (Bull) 131
  M. J. (Foster) 183
  Nannie (Hoke) 272

Nathan 276
P. M. 272
Testa Kyle 264
Thomas N. 118,170,237
W. R. 183
BEST, Julia (Lafitte) 149
BETHEA, Addie W. (Wat-
son) 285
  D. N. 250
  H. C. 285
  Samuel J. 213
BETTS, W. A. 284
BEVERLEY, Meta Adaline
27
  R. A. (--) 27
  W. D. 27
BEVERLY, Beulah Marie
77
  Emma E. (Clark) 12
  R. A. (--) 77
  Rachel Amelia (--) 238
  W. D. 7, 8, 12, 18, 36, 58,
77, 238
BEWLEY, Anna (Cathcart)
129
  W. C. (--) 129
BIASED, J. F. 248
BIGBY, James A. 36
  Mollie (Wilson) 36
BIGGS, Cornelia E. (Spen-
cer) 169
  Jas. R. 169
BIGNION, Kate (--) 279
BILTON, Mary (Mims) 171
BIRD, Annie L. (Thomas)
284
  W. M. 284
BIRT, Ellen E. (Alrige) 251
  J. E. 158
  John E. 157
  Mattie A. (Keele) 146
BIRTS, Judson M. 134
  Maggie (Templeton) 134
BISHOP, Laura I. (Davis)
172
  Lewis 68
  Mary (Robertson) 297
  R. J. 109
  Sarah A. (Garick) 109
  Sinie (Bishop) 68
BISSEL, 88
BLACK, Charlie 167
  Georgia 167
  Hattie (--) 92
  J. B. 92
  J. R. 47
  Mary (--) 52
  Minnie Ball (Hyde) 256
BLACKERBY, B. F. 189
  Lucy (Brock) 189
BLACKMAN, 155
  A. H. (Bozeman) 187
  Henry 267
  J. A. P. 243
  Judson 240
  Lela (Bateman) 248
  Maggie (Lunn) 240

Mollie (Mickle) 243
BLACKMON, A. E.
  (Metts) 162
BLACKWELDER, Maggie
A. (Wilson) 282
BLACKWELL, Annie L.
(Fletcher) 106
  Carrie S. (Tompkins) 244
  Emma (Bryant) 243
  Gussie (Thomas) 294
  J. H. 214
  J. P. 37,244,272
  Jas. W. 167
  Lottie S. (McIntosh) 167
  M. A. (--)(Lanham) 272
  Millie J. (Simpson) 171
  Milly (--) 195
BLAKE, D. R. S. 209
  Dempsey Hartwell 209
  Hessie (Leavell) 220
  Jennie H. (--) 209
  Jno. A. 242
  Mary P. (Calhoun) 220
  Rowena B. (Nail) 242
BLAKELEY, Lawrence 248
  Lula (Holtzclaw) 248
BLAKENSHIP, Emma T.
(Grier) 131
BLALOCK, Eva (Bridges)
286
  Joseph 286
BLANCH, Eva 38
BLANKENSHIP, A. F.
(Hill) 44
  Edra E. (Kendrick) 242
  H. V. 131
  M. J. (Epps) 30
  S. P. 242
BLANKINSHIP, 115
BLANTON, W. T. 185
BLEASE, H. H. 73
  Lizzie (Satterwhite) 73
BLECKLEY, Annie M.
(Means) 264
  Sylvester 264
BLOOM, Rebecca (McMil-
lan) 104
BLOUNT, M. E. (Thomas)
101
  S. F. 101
BLUME, John L. 220
  Lydia (--) 220
  M. A. 76
  Mattie C. (Eubanks) 220
BLUNT, Mariah (Hill) 115
  W. A. 115
BOAZMAN, Dempsy 53
  Elizabeth (--) 53
  John B. 50
  M. Corrie (Holloway) 50
  T. N. (Spearman) 56
BOBO, 299
  Bettie (Thomas) 267
  C. B. 272
  Charles B. 299
  James L. 201
  Mattie (Barksdale) 299

(BOBO), Wm. Fowler 267
BOCHETTE, G. F.
(Bochette) 100
J. F. 100
BODDICK, Mattie
(Quarles) 263
BODIE, Carrie E. (White-
mon) 83
BOGGS, Alice (Cochran)
128
Annie (Hamilton) 152
C. C. 94
Martha E. (Ellis) 94
W. E. 9
BOLES, Isaac 273
BOLLES, Edwin A. 112
Felicia Perry Bergman
(Holcombe) 112
Harriot A. (--) 112
BOLLING, L. C. (--) 182
Rosa (Irvine) 182
Rosa 22
BOLT, Cleopatra Haseltine
Victoria Emiline Lafayette
(Balentine) 203
Corrie E. (Ballentine) 268
Edwin B. 149
Ida (Cheek) 269
Ida (Woolbright) 245
J. Stobo 113
Keturah (--) 268
Leah E. (Reddin) 157
Marion 269
Mary A. (--) 245
Mary E. (Baldwin) 113
Mary Jane (Bagwell) 37
Mattie I. (Daniel) 149
BOLTON, J. N. 209
Joseph 184
Sarah (--) 184
BOMAR, Bessie (Brown)
291
Elisha 291
John Earle 230
Kate (Hollis) 251
Maggie 230
BOND, M. Amelia (Griffin)
269
Mary E. (Matthews) 277
O. J. 277
BONEY, Z. (--)(Rains) 253
BONNER, A. L. (Ellis) 139
B. 139
Elder B. 126
J. I. 12
BONNETT, Daniel D. 240
J. D. 240,243
Maggie A. (Garick) 240
Mary E. (--) 240
Rena (Smoke) 228
BONNETTE, David 14
Rufus W. 14
BONY, M. M. (Collins) 44
BOOKER, Wm. 98
BOOKHART, Cynthia (--)
57
E. A. (Shuler) 108

E. M. (Gaines) 138
James 138
Kate 57
Lotta F. (Derieux) 148
S. W. 57,148
BOON, Daniel 78
Fannie (Copeland) 78
Z. 78
BOONE, J. B. 109
BOOZER, C. P. 55
BOOZIER, Berdie (Rook)
266
Samuel A. 266
BORSTEL, Cassandra H.
(--) 90
F. C. V. 90
BOSTIC, C. Virgil 242
Mamie (Smith) 242
BOSTICK, Alice P. (Petti-
grew) 140
Edwin Joseph 286
Paul I. 111
Saline J. (Myers) 111
BOSTWICK, Amanda (--)
286
John M. 286
Loula B. (Gignilliant) 286
BOSWELL, A. 63
J. P. 63
Laura (Shelnits) 63
BOTSFORD, A. P. 145
BOUCHELL, J. 83
BOUKNIGHT, Mary (-
Quattlebaum) 83
BOULWARE, Belle (-
Stephenson) 188
M. C. 188
Minnie M. (Woodward)
164
Thomas M. 164
BOWDEN, Patsy (Cross)
31
BOWEN, Annie (Algood)
185
BOWERS, Lucy (Foreman)
93
Samuel 93
BOX, C. M. 92
Mary J. (Davis) 92
BOYCE, James P. 31
BOYD, 277
C. B. 90
Eliza (Hellams) 134
Elizabeth (--) 193
Etta (Wearn) 94
F. E. (Lowry) 90
F. W. 207
Fannie E. (Smith) 31
J. B. 5,170
J. C. 94
J. Lenora (Owens) 299
John 100
John H. 193
Lucy (Donald) 5
Mattie J. (Payseur) 170
Pheraby 88
R. J. 31

R. W. 165
S. E. (Evans) 207
S. Stewart 299
Wm. M. 134
BOYKIN, A. J. 135
Adaran E. (Corbitt) 135
C. S. 187
C. S. M. (McCaskill) 110
Dorcas (--) 44
H. L. 135
M. E. (Dorrity) 187
Mary (Yates) 67
N. S. 205
S. M. 67,110
Sallie E. (Bridges) 135
BOYLES, Mary Ann (Mey-
er) 103
BOYLSTON, A. 99
BOYNTON, Catherine 168
Moses 111
Moses B. 249
Samuel 35
BOZARD, Canady 273
Carrie (Schuler) 273
Rebecca (--) 273
BOZEMAN, A. H. (Black-
man) 187
A. J. (Rhodes) 248
Camilla (Ellzey) 288
D. L. 252
David L. 14
J. F. 252
J. H. 187
Jane S. (Spearman) 252
BRABHAM, Julia (Rich-
ardson) 217
Ogreta (Dunbar) 88
Sallie (Moye) 43
BRACKNELL, Carrie
(Faulkner) 271
J. W. 271
John 271
M. J. (Holly) 271
BRADDY, Elizabeth S.
(--)(McLaughlin) 77
BRADFORD, 81
C. F. (Nettles) 82
C. G. 101,103,121,192,-
294,295
Charles 140
F. B. 82
J. D. 82
Jessie H. (Nettles) 66,67
Maggy (Nettles) 82
R. 11
Samuel J. 66,67
BRADHAM, Florence
(Cook) 206,207
R. J. 207
R. Judson 206
Rosa (Ridgill) 173
BRADLEY, Anna (Wood-
ward) 170
E. E. (Reynolds) 80
F. (--)(Campbell) 122
J. 122
J. J. 78

(BRADLEY), M. E. (Johnson) 169
M. H. (Reynolds) 78
Mattie (Myers) 207
Pinckney 32
Rebecca (Butler) 32
S. B. 31
Sarah (Cato) 31
Sarah A. (Barnes) 55
Z. H. 80
BRADWELL, Ellen (Hurford) 54
William 54
BRADY, Sallie E. (Davis) 109
BRAKEFIELD, M. J. (Lee) 221
BRAMLETT, Elias 163
M. Lavinia (Gould) 163
Mattie A. (Jameson) 165
Z. D. 165
BRAND, F. K. 177
Rebecca E. (Johnson) 177
BRANDON, Janie (Roy) 187
BRANLLEY, M. L. (Estes) 183
BRANT, Bettie (Wilson) 169
D. W. 153
Simpson (Croft) 21
BRANTLEY, 235
BRANTLY, Mattie (Marston) (Walker) 25
W. T. 24,291
BRASINGTON, William F. 196
BRASWELL, Bannie (-Dunn) 274
BRAZEALE, Augustus B. (Malone) 6
David K. 6
Elizabeth (--) 6
BREAKER, D. M. 91
Mary Jane (Ross) 91
BREZEALE, B. B. 1
Rachel L. (Anderson) 1
BRICE, Ida (Waters) 273
R. W. 179
Walter S. 179
BRIDGES, Eva (Blalock) 286
Sallie E. (Boykin) 135
BRIGGS, D. K. 284
E. C. 133
Gist 69
Henry 191
Ida (Dodenhoff) 284
Jennie (Spears) 69
Laura S. (Calmes) 133
Lula (McBee) 191
BRIGHAM, James Cochran 115
Lizzie (Cochran) 101
W. H. 101
Wm. H. 115
BRISTOW, B. O. 206

Ella C. (Herring) 158
Sallie (McCutchen) 206
BRITT, B. M. 149
E. A. (Howard) 149
Mollie (Clinkscales) 284
Sarah 94
BRITTON, J. M. 286
BROADDUS, Andrew 242
L. 29
Luther 18,20,242
M. E. 109,130,168,207
M. Jane 242
Sallie F. (Bryan) 29
BROADUS, J. A. 14
Luther 203
BROADWATER, Annie (Reynolds) 267
G. W. 267
Mattie (Getsinger) 88
N. L. 223
Robert 88
Zabrina (Moor) 223
BROADWAY, M. S. (Rich) 28
N. G. 28
Washington 244
BROCK, Anderson 4
Lucy (Blackerby) 189
Mary (Shirley) 211
BROCKINGTON, B. F. 251
B. O. 148
Emma (Chandler) 251
Jane (Lockhart) 148
L. D. (Brown) 184
Mary J. (Wilder) 33
Olivia (Rhame) 210
W. J. 184
BROCKINTON, M. L. (Alsbrook) 272
William 272
BROCKMAN, Elizabeth (--) 158
BRODERICK, Carrie E. (Sharp) 279
W. F. 279
BRODIE, Elizabeth C. (Segler) 98
John W. 98
Judson 80
Maggie (Porter) 76
Mary E. (Prothro) 80
Mary P. (Hogg) 104
Mattie (Cook) 39
Robert 174
Sarah (--) 98
Susan North (Thayer) 174
Thomas Furman 37
BRODWAY, Lizzie (Mahony) 244
BROGDON, Anna Eliza (Tindal) 72
John 72
Lula (Cook) 255
Maggie E. (Curtis) 207
BRONSON, Louisa S. (Pegues) 116

BROOKBANKS, Charles N. 49
Emma C. (Layne) 49
BROOKER, Boyce 258
Fannie (--) 258
J. L. 296
Jemima (--) 186
John 30,186
L. 258
M. B. (Whetstone) 296
W. 85
Walter 186
William 22,186
BROOKS, Benj. 226
Bettie (Thurmond) 208
Ella (Coleman) 133
Emmie (Nicholson) 226
Hattie A. (Lawton) 146
John F. 44
Josephine (Lynch) 65
L. B. (Townes) 71
M. A. E. (Deas) 96
Maggie (Howle) 227
Margaret S. (Anderson) 156
Mary E. (Adams) 44
R. R. 108,111,156
S. B. 71
S. E. 96
S. P. 20,219,223,224,241
Stanmore 141
Stanmore Butler 182
Tahpenes (Lipscomb) 141
Tahpenes L. (--) 142
W. I. 146
BROOKSHIRE, Drucilla (Hawkins) 143
BROOM, E. R. 225
G. L. 102
J. Wiley 102
M. T. (Moore) 225
BROTHERS, John C. 264
BROWN, A. Witherspoon 207
Allen 127
Amanda (Davis) 78
Ann Talula (Wilson) 121
Annie (--) 215
Annie (Massey) 205
B. H. 72
Benj. F. 201
Bessie (Bomar) 291
C. C. 84, 103, 117, 122, 133, 188, 215, 255, 270, 285
C. E. (Mahaffey) 129
C. W. 81
Carrie (Carpenter) 283
Carrie H. (Haltiwanger) 229
Catherine (West) 81
Clementine H. (--) 72
Cornelia Elizabeth (--) 122
D. B. 129
Daniel 78
E. Odelia (Thomas) 279
Essie A. (Thompson) 182

(BROWN), Gasper 127
H. P. 121
Henry 166
J. A. 272,291
J. D. 279
J. D. A. 93
J. F. 269
J. H. 177
J. J. 269
John Q. 233
Julia (Dare) 242
Kate (Frietag) 207
L. D. (Brockington) 184
L. H. (Fry) 169
Lena E. (Cunningham) 233
Lula E. (Hodges) 150
Mamie (McCord) 177
Mary (Langford) 269
Mary (Mahon) 259
Mary F. (Traynham) 78
Mary J. (--)(Mattison) 1
Matilda (Edwards)(Manson) 280
Peter R. 182
Rebecca (Marsh) 69
Sallie (Gossett) 201
Sallie (Wright) 133
Sarah (Kellehan) 269
Sarah A. (Hancock) 47
Susan (Hudson) 166
Susan M.' (--) 78
W. H. 88
W. Harrison 275
W. J. 51
W. L. 18,28,36,55,67,69,-71,135,140,215
William 47,269
William H. 78
BROWNE, Birdie 150
J. C. 150,164,178
Leila 150
M. A. (--)(Ray) 178
BROWNING, Ida (Chitty) 284
BROWNLEE, Geo. P. 284
Gertrude (Webb) 284
BROYLES, A. R. 8,293
Clara Hewitt (Macaulay) 293
Lula L. (Baker) 8
BRUCE, J. P. 93
Joseph G. 81
Mary Ann (Hough) 81
Meta 93
O. M. 93
R. D. 211
BRUNSON, C. C. 287
D. D. 205
Fannie M. (Penn) 18
James B. 137
James P. 48
Joseph 131,136
Josephine (Alexander) 142
M. R. (Wilder) 90
Mary (Forester) 131
Mary (Forrester) 136

Mary F. (Crosby) 48
R. Durant 90
Susie (Johnston) 202
W. H. 18
BRYAN, Annie Laurie (Norris) 146,161,162
B. C. 29,146,162,171,209
E. J. 295
Florie (Rice) 295
Lulie J. (Cullum) 171
Sallie F. (Broaddus) 29
BRYANT, Bettie (Lunn) 232
Emma (Blackwell) 243
Fannie (Rhodes) 219
Jesse 243
Mary Julia (Reeves) 185
U. G. 185
William 232
Zelates 219
BUCHANAN, Harriet (Young) 78
John 78
Wm. 3
BUCKHALTER, I. L. 225
Lilla (Wise) 225
BUCKNER, Adie E. (Ruth) 105
B. F. 89,162
Carrie (DuBois) 103
J. L. 103
P. F. 33,105
BUDD, Caroline 36
T. S. 36
Thomas S. 222
BUFORD, C. 133
Ella (Davis) 133
BUIST, A. 58, 62, 63, 76, 78, 80, 81, 85, 97, 100, 103, 110, 111, 113, 117-119, 123, 124, 133, 134, 137, 139, 140, 144-146, 151, 152, 154, 157, 161, 181, 182, 202, 203, 206, 225, 230, 231, 243, 251, 284
A. A. (--) 144
Arthur 218,241,256
E. H. 256
E. T. 256
Hampton 241
J. F. 32, 38, 43, 65, 66, 70, 74, 79, 80, 84, 88, 93, 95, 99, 102, 112, 115, 116, 119, 120, 123-125, 130, 132, 134, 137, 143, 150, 155, 182, 211, 213, 220, 221, 227, 229, 233, 235, 241, 249, 257, 279
J. L. 111, 144
J. T. 125
James F. 62, 158, 215, 256, 258, 260
L. C. (Cave) 111
Linna C. (--) 144
Lula 144
Samuel Arthur 144
BULL, Amanda (Felder) 58
Amanuel 58
Harriet C. (--) 17

John B. 131
Juliet (Berry) 131
W. H. 17
BULLOCK, Maria (Polattie) 134
William S. 114
Willie A. (Reddick) 114
BUNCH, Moses 109
BURCH, E. J. 258
Henry 123
J. B. 104,201
Joanna (--) 212
Leana (Lee) 123
Lou (Cannon) 229
Mamie W. (Fort) 122
Mary (Young) 258
Mary A. (Timmons) 104
Mary E. (Napier) 201
Mellichamp 258
Sam Joe 258
BURCKHALTER, Augusta G. (Hammond) 201
C. M. 201
J. H. 256
BURCKMYER, (Winkler) 252
John A. 252
BURDETT, John L. 217
N. E. (Mitchell) 217
BURGE, J. C. 142
BURGESS, Edith A. (Carraway) 250
Jno. A. 250
Lizzie (Kennedy) 151
Vashti (Sharpe)(Gaines) 280
BURISS, S. Elizabeth (Cater) 8
BURKE, A. J. 37
G. A. 89
M. E. (Richbourg) 89
Mary Agnes 37
BURKETT, A. B. (--) 276
H. (--) 50
Robert 50
BURKHALTER, Charles M. 152
Frances A. (--) 152
BURLEY, Adam 48
Adam J. 29
Elizabeth (Yarborough) 48
BURLINGTON, Olivia J. (Button) 225
Wm. P. 225
BURN, J. W. 27, 133, 135, 263, 279
James W. 143, 229
Rosa A. (Parker) 263
Susan L. (Roberts) 229
BURNETT, A. E. (Hudson) 152
Carrie (DeLaughter) 296
D. G. 24
Eula (Stallworth) 224
Fannie (Ward) 134
Fannie K. (Taylor) 68

310

312

ELLERBE, Annie E. (Wilson) 289
ELLERBY, Joseph 189
R. A. (Chambliss) 189
ELLIOTT, Louise Hay (Mellichamp) 43
Richard 194
S. E. (Kellahan) 193
ELLIS, A. L. (Bonner) 139
Clara H. (Barmore) 131
J. Milton 131
J. R. 139
Jas. 154
Laura L. (McGee) 131
Martha E. (Boggs) 94
S. G. 94,254
Walter K. 131
ELLISON, Abbie (Gaines) 126
David 269
Emma (Duckworth) 248
J. T. 126
Joel A. 248
Mamie (Ragsdale) 269
Minnie Lee (Willis) 268
William 268,281
ELLZEY, C. C. 288
Camilla (Bozeman) 288
Walter 288
ELMORE, 272
EMERSON, John Allen 4
Sallie S. (Kay) 4
ENGLISH, Elsey (Rogers) 46
Emma S. (Robinson) 65
Harriet (--) 112
Mattie (Cook) 97
R. R. 83
Sallie E. (Baldwin) 65
Sallie E. E. (Stokes) 83
ENTREKIN, Clanchis 137
Eugenia (Burns) 137
ENTZMINGER, J. N. 233
Sallie (--) 298
EPPS, Emma O. (Davenport) 152
G. (Harris) 31
James Hardy 152
Joe 31
M. J. (Blankenship) 30
S. H. 30
EPTING, H. T. 12
Lilis (Warren) 221
Mary Jane (Hill)(Knox) 12
ERVIN, C. P. 227,230,285
ERWIN, Adelaide (--) 227
Annie (Martin) 56
J. D. Jr. 278
Laura Ann (--) 278
Rennie (Lawton) 278
ESKEW, Amanda E. (Burriss) 4
Emma (Beam) 149
J. B. 162
John 4,162
Mary (Crump) 14
Simeon 149

W. E. 14
ESTES, A. B. 51, 79, 129, 133, 166, 167, 174, 177, 183, 202
Adolpus D. 285
Andrew B. Jr. 183
Andrew Broadus 232
Anna Cornelia (Willingham) 232
B. P. 264,297
Benjamin Lawton 167
C. C. 292
Cornelia (Willingham) 167
E. Annie (Chewning) 177
Elliot 79,232
Julia (Ross) 79
M. J. (Anderson) 21
M. L. (Branlley) 183
Phoebe S. (Hickman) 129
T. B. 21
ETHEREDGE, Edwin 142
Elizabeth (--) 142
G. M. 142
ETHRIDGE, Charlie 297
Mary Ann (Myers) 297
EUBANKS, Brantley 65
C. H. (Holcomb) 225
Emily (Green) 65
Isaac W. 220
James 225
Laura E. (Hair) 241
Mattie C. (Blume) 220
Walter 241
EVANS, C. L. 158
Elizabeth Jane (Miller) 158
Eugene G. 237
H. 207
Hattie L. (White) 184
J. C. 28
J. D. 79
J. L. 46
Marie (Leavell) 28
Mary J. (McLeod) 79
Nannie E. (Glenn) 237
S. E. (Boyd) 207
S. E. (Simpson) 46
Susan E. (--)(Cox) 85
EVEANS, Mary E. (Shiver) 97
EWART, Cora L. (Cannon) 249
EWART, Wm. F. 249
EZELL, H. K. 211, 217, 220, 235, 250, 267, 273, 284
J. J. 143
J. S. 230,232
L. C. 108, 128, 168, 201, 202, 221, 225, 230, 248, 285
M. S. (--) 108
Maggie 128
FAGG, Ellen (Cheatham) 156
John F. 156
FAIR, James Irby 222
Lizzie (Rountree) 222
FAIRY, (Grimes) 110

F. A. 254
John D. D. 110
Julia (Wade) 254
FALLOW, Abner P. 82
Antonette L. (Woodard) 82
FANNING, B. Winton 206
Bennie W. 206
Laura C. (--) 206
FANT, A. E. 192
Catharine (--) 121
F. M. E. 258
Foster 276
J. K. 98, 114, 191, 201, 202, 211, 223, 224, 239, 242, 246, 261, 279-282, 298
James K. 91,112
Jane E. (Clinkscales) 7
Kittie (Jackson) 2
Mary (Shirley) 202
Mildred (Edrington) 258
Minnie B. (Norris) 276
N. A. (--) 222
Sallie (Steen) 192
W. A. 2
Wm. 258
FARIS, S. C. (Culp) 30
FARMER, Elijah 276
Elizabeth (Berry) 276
G. A. (Earle) 18
N. O. 18,143
FARR, America M. (--) 239
Henry W. 181
J. W. 239
Louisa Virginia (Snider) 263
Mattie E. (Merchant) 181
W. R. B. 263
Wilhelmina 263
FARRER, Mary A. (Speaks) 52
FAUCETT, M. E. (Busby) 216
FAULKINBURY, Amos 82
FAULKNER, Carrie (Bracknell) 271
Jennie (Timmerman) 277
Lee 277
Robert 95
Thomas 271
FAULT, Ellen (Duncan) 119
J. E. 119
FAWCETTE, Hattie R. (Slater) 57
FEASTER, Annie I. (Coleman) 67
D. R. 30
David R. 67
J. C. C. 249
V. E. (--) 67
FEE, L. A. (Withers) 110
L. M. 110
FELDER, Amanda (Bull) 58
Bessie C. (Johnson) 125
Fannie C. (Hat) 38

(FELDER), J. M. 44
N. Y. 125
Sallie J. (Hooten) 44
V. D. (Dantzler) 120
W. L. 120
FELL, A. E. (Oakman) 211
L. R. 211
FELTON, Laura C. (--) 204
M. J. (--)(Dorn) 228
R. J. 228
FELTS, Beulah (McNeil) 279
J. W. 279
FENDER, J. K. 298
M. E. (Carter) 199
Mattie (Carter) 298
FENLEY, John 298
FENTERS, E. (Williams) 184
Elizabeth (Williams) 184
Francis H. 184
John T. 184
FERGUSON, A. 286
Barbara (Fudge) 256
Calvin 277
Calvin Brice 277
E. C. (--) 238
Holley (--) 264
Isabella (Culp) 70
Katie 286
Laura A. (Moore) 223
Martha N. (--) 216
Mary (--) 29
Mary Ellen (Clarke) 295
R. P. 256
Sallie (--) 277
Sallie E. (White) 263
W. P. 216
William 29
FERRELL, B. S. 239
N. Theodocia (Garrison) 239
FERRISON, Addie O. (Cook) 63
FERSENER, John 195
Livia (Ulmer) 195
FEWELL, J. W. 146
Lula (Sturgis) 163
Maggie J. (Sturgis) 146
FICKLING, Carrie L. (-Gardner) 113
Charles R. 113
Elizabeth (Jefcoat) 250
J. D. 250
Joseph L. 156,157
Wm. J. 156
FINCHER, S. J. 158
FINCKNEY, Dora (Smith) 223
FINLEY, Allie E. (Fuller) 67
Della (Watts) 63
Eugenia Sidney (Payne) 232
Harrison 63
J. J. 261
J. Mat. 232

Maggie (Griffith) 261
William Watts 67
FISHBURNE, C. C. 174
FISHER, Carrie (Henderson) 6,181
Jennie (Williamson) 19
FITZGERALD, Sallie E. (Gregory) 32
FLEMING, Mary F. (Mattison) 29
N. Carrie (Cathcart) 226
Warren S. 29
FLETCHER, Annie L. (Blackwell) 106
Wm. R. 106
FLOYD, Amelia (Burton) 25
Barnabas 25
F. L. 277
J. B. 87
J. S. 215
James Barnie 215
John S. 61
Josephine S. (Peterson) 61
Lura C. (Lark) 48
M. J. 215
Mary Ann M. (Williams) 87
N. Widdie (Strange) 277
Washington 48
FOBS, Minnie (Roe) 230
Thomas 230
FOGARTIE, B. M. 35
Eliza G. (Bee) 35
FOGLER, F. H. 136
Florence C. (Strange) 136
Sallie (Rourk) 121
FOLK, Emily (Zorn) 210
Frank E. (Rents) 205
George 68
H. W. C. 33
J. Frank 205
Mary C. (Woodward) 94
Rosa E. (Ruth) 68
FOLSOM, E. (Kelly) 55
FORD, Mary C. (--) 201
Mattie 214
Rufus 204
Tracy R. 201
Willie E. 201
FOREMAN, Amelia (Meyer) 277
Ben 277
Carrie I. (Ashley) 243
Florence (Bush) 258
Isaac 174,215,243,249,258
Isaac W. 93
Jacky 217
Jacob Jr. 215
Jesse 121,217
Lucy (Bowers) 93
Mamie (Butler) 277
Mary F. (Barnes) 277
Mittie H. (Howell) 174
FORESTER, Mary (Brunson) 131

FORRESTER, Bessie (-Pugh) 200
E. J. 107,200,226
Maggie L. (Dargan) 226
Mary (Brunson) 136
FORT, Alice (Gorden) 49
Ann E. (--) 208
J. G. 49
Josiah (--) 70
Josiah A. 10
Mamie W. (Burch) 122
Warren 122
Willie W. 102
FORTSON, M. F. (Getzen) 233
T. W. 233
FOSTER, B. B. 18,268
Bettie (Goudelock) 187
Elizabeth (Woodruff) 260
Eunice E. (Kennedy) 18
Fannie (Merrick) 75
Florence F. (Treszer) 257
John 187
L. S. 75,87,88
M. J. (Berry) 183
Mary Ann (Perrin) 268
Mollie E. (Colton) 203
Sue (Cox) 228
W. M. 203,257
Z. Frank 183
FOUCHE, J. W. 298
Louisa C. (--) 282
Melissa (Franklin) 225
Melissa (Sample) 298
W. C. 282
W. Warren 225
FOUNTAIN, Adela A. (Jones) 41
Fannie Olivia (Carter) 272
Theo. T. 272
Wm. H. 41
FOUSHEE, Rosa 22
FOWLER, C. B. 294
H. 206
John F. 222
Joseph R. 294
Lawrence 287
M. Alice (McPherson) 222
Mary (Scott) 206
Millie 239
Rosa J. (--) 287
Sarah E. (Owens) 281
Sophie (Benson) 222
FOX, Ella V. (Myers) 47
J. J. 47
FOXWORTH, Adelaide F. (Stubbs) 228
FRACHUER, Lucinda (--)(Walden) 5
T. Dickens 5
FRANKLIN, Melissa (Fouche) 225
Vicky (Pinson) 109
FRANKS, Nancy Alice (Page) 136
FRASER, Benny 222
Jane B. (Miller) 222

(FRASER), Mary B. 222
Robert 222
FRAZIER, Ella (Sanders)
20
John M. 28
M. 20
Mary (Cartmell) 28
FREDERICKS, Balus 5
Harriet (McKay) 5
FREE, A. F. 208
Allen W. 62
J. W. 62
Janie E. (Ulmer) 65
Julia A. (--) 208
M. E. 62
FREEL, Sallie (Sturgis) 263
William 263
FREELAND, Ida C. 177
Maggie (Crawford) 284
Mary P. (--) 177
S. E. 177
FREEMAN, B. B. 273
Gilbert 142
Lizzie (Gibson) 166
Maggie E. (Shadrach) 273
Marcus 166
Marion 186
Martha (Williams) 186
Mary Jane (Taylor) 142
FRENCH, Alene (Clem-
ents) 178
J. Adolphus 115
Jesse T. 178
FREY, J. R. 118
Sarah (--) 118
FRIDAY, S. T. (Walker) 67
FRIER, A. J. 274
FRIERSON, Vermell (-
Stowe) 253
FRIETAG, Kate (Brown)
207
FROMM, C. H. 227
Jannie E. (Burris) 227
FRY, C. F. 169
G. 46
L. H. (Brown) 169
M. J. (--)(Rawley) 46
FUDGE, Barbara (Fergu-
son) 256
FULLER, Alla (Barksdale)
171
Allie E. (Finley) 67
F. H. 291
H. Eugene 98
H. Omer 91
Harrison 178
Hattie E. (Barksdale) 91
John R. 67
Lida A. (Coleman) 98
Lizzie (--) 178
Mamie (Teague) 272
Oliver 287
P. H. E. 171
S. T. 207
Sarah (Donnald) 291
Sarah Smith (Howe) 287
Tilman 272

W. A. 178
FULTON, C. A. 292
FULTZ, Julia (Winter) 172
FUNCHES, Ida S. (Kenne-
dy) 161
FURMAN, Annie M.
(Haynesworth) 224
Charles M. 188
Fannie (Garden) 188
J. C. 25, 55, 64, 118, 140,
153, 164, 191, 193, 219,
252
Jas. C. 103
Martha (Riley) 94
R. W. 94
Richard 103,287
Samuel 103
FURSE, Helen (--) 111
James Edgar Cochran 111
Richard 94,111
GADSDEN, C. P. 37
GAFFNEY, Emma C.
(Kerr) 30
F. Bee 295
Gracie (Spears) 295
Hattie (Spears) 205
J. J. 205
J. L. 30
Laura M. (Tanner) 295
R. M. (Macomson) 243
W. W. 243
GAINER, A. R. (Cauthen)
275
F. E. C. 275
GAINES, Abbie (Ellison)
126
Anna M. (Gaines) 290
B. S. 172
Bessie Pendleton 38
Bettie (--) 35
E. G. 280
E. M. (Bookhart) 138
Elizabeth (Austin) 146
James H. 17
John Milton 64
Kiziah J. (Arnold) 17
Loutetia Emeline
(Mattison) 50
M. Aurie (Dickinson) 199
M. E. (Hester) 169
Manie (Williams) 64
Marshal B. 50
Mary E. (--) 10,38
Nannie E. (Henderson) 21
Pascal 38
Strother D. 21
T. R. (--) 38
T. R. 20
Thomas Pascal 10
Tilman R. 16,22,30
Vashti (Burgess) (Sharpe)
280
W. A. 10, 16, 18, 21, 38,
46-48, 59, 64, 133, 136,
138, 141, 223, 238, 245,
267, 290
W. J. 290

Wm. P. 169
GALE, Alice R. (Stephens)
272
GALLMAN, Betty (Kinard)
297
GALLOWAY, P. L. (How-
ell) 296
Robert 296
GALPHIN, 208
Anne (Barnes) 255
Annie (Griffin) 299
Annie G. (Barnes) 290
George 173
H. P. 200
James 255
John 290
Lizzie (Rickenbaker) 244
Mamie J. (McSwain) 200
T. M. 186, 200, 211, 243-
245, 263, 270, 279
GAMBRELL, Adaline
(Whit) 10
Anna Law (Davenport) 19
Emeline (--)(Smith) 4
James 1
John F. 3
M. J. (Robinson) 242
Marion F. 242
P. Emeline (McCaster) 3
William 10,19
GANDY, Margaret Ann
(Smith) 290
Max 290
N. Lena (Odum) 165
Samuel B. 165
GANO, Stephen 164
GARDEN, Alester 188
Fannie (Furman) 188
GARDNER, Anna E.
(Livingston) 95
Benjamin Daniel 257
Carrie L. (Fickling) 113
D. J. 201
Dora L. 201, 220
Dora L. (West) 139
E. G. (Newman) 187
E. S. 299
G. W. 142, 150, 170, 175,
176, 185, 190, 194, 200,
201, 222, 233, 237, 257,
266, 268
Garrett 288
George W. 139,220
H. H. 86
Ida 86
Lula (Crouch) 91
Maggie J. (Gauf) 299
Maria (Wolfe) 201
Mary (--) 288
Minerva (Hydrick) 86
Nannie (Munn) 114
Percy A. (Cooper) 65
Sarah E. (Jones) 257
W. B. 65
GARICK, John P. 240
Maggie A. (Bonnett) 240
Sarah A. (Bishop) 109

GARLAND, Amelia (Reed) 195
G. W. 195
Jessie (Latta) 230
GARNER, Bettie (Nichols) 168
GARRETT, Mollie C. (Barksdale) 262
Washington 262
GARRISON, Ann Starr 105
Emily (Smith) 261
Fanny R. E. (--) 23
Frances (Moon) 289
Hannah (Davis) 26
I. P. 239
Isoletter Dubose (Harrison) 281
J. M. 261
J. Milton 105
J. R. 23,26
James Thomas 261
Joel B. 289
Mary J. (--) 289
Mattie (Wherry) 163
N. Theodocia (Ferrell) 239
Thomas J. 265
William 163
GARVIN, Sue (Harley) 133
Wm. H. 133
GARY, Eliza (--)(Griffin) 32
M. W. 242
Mary Simpson (--) 160
S. A. 188,268
T. R. 11
GATES, Christian 98
Mary (--) 98
GAUF, Maggie J. (Gardner) 299
GAULDEN, Laura J. (Bailey) 214
GAULT, B. F. 273
C. L. (Inman) 273
Wm. 203
GAULY, Selma (Kelly) 203
GAYDON, Mattie (Love) 133
GEDDES, Hattie (Monk) 138
James 138
GEDDINGS, Francis (-Hodge) 148
Henry 148
GEIGER, Emma A. (--)-(Goodlett) 157
GELZER, Cornelia (Singletary) 182
John 201
Nannie (Axson) 201
William 182
GENNINGS, George 95
Julia (Slater) 95
GEORGE, J. Z. 65
Lienizzar (Harvesson) 68
Mary (Leavell) 65
GERARD, E. (Barrett) 213

GETSINGER, J. J. 27, 44, 98, 132, 140, 155, 250
Maggie (Smoak) 140
Mattie (Broadwater) 88
R. (--) 27
Rebecca (--) 132
William 155
William J. 27
GETZEN, M. F. (Fortson) 233
S. L. 233
S. P. 233
GIBBES, Fannie (Cogburn) 121
GIBBS, John 123
GIBERT, Addie (LeRoy) 249
B. E. 249
GIBSON, John Q. 184
Laura A. (Clark) 184
Lizzie (Freeman) 166
R. B. 166
GIFFORD, Ebenezer 290
Ellen J. 290
GIGNILLIANT, Loula B. (Bostwick) 286
GIGNILLIAT, H. J. 286
GILBERT, Milton L. 129
Sallie E. (Morrell) 129
GILL, A. J. 61
Addie 61
Lucien 163
Marie C. (Moise) 33
Minnie (Shurley) 163
Washington 33
GILLAM, J. B. 280
Lizzie (Conneif) 280
GILLIAM, Lilian (McKissick) 222
GILLISON, Hetty (--)(Lincoln) 5
Thos. 5
GILMORE, Fannie (Dixon) 113
GILREATH, Herman G. 125
Mattie L. (Cauble) 125
GIST, Ella (Allsbrooks) 97
George 97
GIVENS, A. (Pendar) 151
GLASSCOCK, Hattie (-Robertson) 148
GLEAVE, Margaret E. (Reasoner) 68
GLENN, (Burris) (Barton) 298
J. M. 3
Martha E. (McGee) 3
Mary (--)(McKissick) 237
Nannie E. (Evans) 237
W. J. T. 43
GLOVER, Chas. B. Jr. 220
Ida C. (Zeigler) 220
Imogen (Hord) 156
J. Clarence 156
John M. 43
Lizzie C. (Davis) 43

GOBER, Ella Y. (Willard) 179
Zack 179
GODFREY, J. A. 220
L. C. (Hudson) 220
GOFF, L. (Smith) 55
GOGGANS, Burr F. 249
William 210
GOIN, Emma C. (Royall) 114
GOING, Eliza (Owens) 32
G. W. 273
Janie (Vaughn) 273
GOLD, Fannie (Harry) 225
GOLDING, David 56
Fannie (Hitt) 56
GOLDSMITH, Lillie G. (Reilly) 178
Sadie N. (Rowland) 147
Thomas 12,138
Wm. 147,178
GOLIGHTLY, David 23
GOLNICH, Jacob 124
Sarah (Singelton) 124
GOODLET, Elvira (Benson) 144
Moses 144
GOODLETT, Emma A. (--)(Geiger) 157
J. F. 161
R. P. 150
Robert C. 157
GOODMAN, Bluford 21
GOODSON, A. J. (--) 154
J. W. 229
Jennie (Padgett) 229
GOODWIN, J. B. 103
John H. 233
Leila (Rielly) 233
GOOGE, Jerry 34
GORDEN, Alice (Fort) 49
Benjamin R. 49
GORDER, Ada (Smith) 284
GORDON, E. C. 22
Georgia (Miller) 295
J. J. (--) 90
GORE, D. N. 139,169
D. W. 157
S. F. (Hughes) 169
GOSSETT, J. P. 201
Sallie (Brown) 201
GOUDELOCK, Adam 187
Adam S. 268
Bettie (Foster) 187
Polly (Littlejohn) 268
GOULD, M. Lavinia (Bramlett) 163
S. W. 163
GOURE, Charles 63
Mary (Pipkin) 63
GOWAN, T. V. 183,251,254
GRADEN, L. F. (Rhame) 159
GRAHAM, Alice (Smith) 188
Ann (--) 270

319

HAIR, Angelia P. 274
Bertha Ruth 290
Blanche (Martin) 285
C. A. J. (Nix) 60
Charity (--) 71
David S. 60
Ella H. (Templeton) 137
Ellen J. (Anderson) 299
Hampton 290
J. Walton 86
Jane (Johnson) 86
Jane M. (--) 290
John Pinckney 49
Judson E. 285
Laura E. (Eubanks) 241
M. J. (Keele) 97
Maggie (Kennedy) 149
Melvin 299
Milledge G. 241
S. A. 97
Wiley I. 76
Willis 255
HALBERT, Elizabeth (--) 15
Susannah (Acker) 14,15
William 15
HALE, Annie (Randolph) 208
E. S. 194
W. R. 208
HALFORD, Isabella (--) 121
John Alexander 87
HALL, Addison 34
Catharine (Hallman) 152
Elizabeth Alice (Murff) 136
J. B. 135
Joseph K. 183
L. E. (--)(Bell) 286
Lem. 152
Mary E. (Ramseur) 183
Nathan 270
Sallie Thompson (Lander) 248
Thomas 57
V. L. (Reynolds) 135
W. M. P. 136
Z. 6
Zackariah 190
HALLMAN, Catharine (Hall) 152
Elliott 152
Martha (--) 74
HALTIWANGER, Carrie H. (Brown) 229
Ellen M. (Morgan) 28
George 28
J. B. 229
HAM, Addie (Hill) 270
C. H. 270
HAMES, E. W. 233
HAMILTON, Annie (-Boggs) 152
Bonham 240
C. Earle 152
E. F. 144

Fannie (Wright) 267
Hellen (Green) 240
J. R. 93
J. R. H. 93
Janie (Jeter) 110
Nina (Jordan) 144
P. P. 110
Rachel (--) 93
Virginia B. (Lowery) 230
W. O. 230
HAMMETT, Bettie (Orr) 53
H. J. 53
Janie B. (Scott) 264
William H. 264
HAMMOND, A. J. 188,192
Albert 93
Augusta G. (Burckhalter) 201
Bessie (Willis) 240
Emma (Martin) 294
Fannie (Lane) 93
Fannie (Latimer) 204
Frances (--) 201
H. S. 204
John 294
S. Julia (Hammond) 201
Thomas P. 201
HAMPTON, 105
Joannah S. (--)(Campbell) 13
Phillip L. 13
HAMRICK, G. P. 212, 217, 225, 234, 241
HANCKEL, William 213
HANCOCK, Berry 97
Ellen (Thorne) 246
G. 79
Jane (Taylor) 82
M. Eugenia (Coleman) 242
Matilda (Yates) 79
N. J. V. (Reynolds) 97
Sarah A. (Brown) 47
Sidney E. 242
Thomas 82
William 246
HANE, B. T. 233
HANEY, J. S. 67
Kate (Spears) 67
HANKINSON, J. P. 55
K. M. (Williams) 54
Laura (Phillips) 115
R. J. Jr. 54
Virginia (Rountree) 81
Wade 81
HANNA, Elizabeth (Chandler) 189
Mary (--) 286
HANNER, E. R. (Cooper) 136
HANSBERY, Ellenor (--) 48
HARBIN, B. W. 2
J. A. (McLees) 2
HARBUCK, E. L. 261

HARDE, Minnie (Owens) 266
HARDEE, F. P. (--) 113
HARDEN, Alexander 112
Ellen (Cave) 112
Mattie 117
Ora Allein 176
W. A. 176
HARDIN, A. 22
D. C. 133, 148, 151, 152, 161, 164, 173
Eliza Jane (Whisonant) 21
Ira Jr. 21
Jane (Morris) 120
Jesse H. 214
HARDY, Anna E. (Willis) 80
Nannie (Long) 190
W. J. 190
HARE, A. D. 55, 185, 242
Annice T. (Carson) 55
Annis T. (--) 242
HARGROVE, Emma (A-brams) 34
Joseph C. 34
Mary (--) 198
Stephen 198
HARLAN, Nannie (Douglas) 136
HARLEY, A. E. (--) 268
A. M. 76, 98, 115, 176
Annie H. (McMillan) 83
Arthur Buist 174
E. H. (--) 145
George P. 51,249
Harry 268
Harry Eugene 144
I. P. 238
Isabel (Snider) 145
J. Edward 66
Jacob 249
Jefferson Preston 115
John H. 145
John P. 63
Kittie C. (Willis) 63
Lizzie (--) 144
Lucy (--) 176
Mary Eliza 76
Mary G. (--) 168
Preston 174
Robert (--) 251
Sue (Garvin) 133
W. B. 144
W. W. 268
HARLING, Annie M. (Jordan) 241
Ella (Edmonds) 202
Hattie (McDowell) 202
Jane (Minor) 191
P. Brooks 202
Tillman 241
W. Edgar 191
HARPER, Edwin 218
Joel 238
Joel M. 50
John R. 2
Laura A. (Chapman) 2

(HUDSON), J. Belton 278
J. C. (Walker) 256
J. C. 63, 85, 129, 152, 169, 195, 215
J. H. 168
Jason C. 278
L. C. (Godfrey) 220
P. J. 152
Rebecca (James) 253
S. R. (Jones) 254
Selma 172
Susan (Brown) 166
Susan G. (Rector) 278
William R. 278
Willie C. (Williams) 168
Zadock Paschal 278
HUGGINS, Hattie A. (Bass) 273
J. D. 221, 223, 258, 263, 298
J. DuBose 137
Jessie L. (Howell) 137
John 273
Julia C. (Moore) 133
Mary (--) 273
Mary L. (--) 214
HUGHES, A. C. 248
A. Jackson 233
Fannie (Ott) 299
Mary Steedly (--) 233
N. N. 184
S. F. (Gore) 169
S. M. 241
Sallie A. (Kelly) 248
W. J. 169
HUGHSON, J. S. 126
John S. 84
Lessie E. (Quattlebaum) 126
W. E. 61,106
HUMPHRIES, Barnet 71
L. M. (Sarratt) 241
Thos. 241
HUNGERPILLER, James 84
Laura E. (Parler) 84
HUNKERPILLER, Ida (Shuler) 188
Manly 188
HUNNICUT, Eliza (Dawson) 213
M. R. 213
HUNNICUTT, Carrie M. (Moore) 227
E. Y. 227
HUNT, Emma (McKellar) 203
James H. 203
Sallie (Woolbright) 198
Wm. T. 198
HUNTER, Ella 195
F. E. (--) 105
Florence E. (Reeves) 99
G. M. 99
J. W. 99
John P. 150
Laura (--)(Hickson) 150

Maggie 237,260
HURFORD, Ellen (Bradwell) 54
HURST, Nancy (McLeod) 101
S. D. 101
HUSBANDS, Josephine E. (Self) 147
HUSSEY, Elizabeth (Rigby)(Grimes) 110
John 110
HUTCHINS, J. W. 180, 181, 185-187
HUTCHISON, Mary (Johnson) 14
HUTSON, George (--) 54
HUTTO, D. H. 152
David 69
E. C. 57
Florence (Wright) 57
Francis (Patrick) 100
Gatsey (Still) 84
Henry Jr. 255
James 84
Lizzie (Sturkie) 255
Mary V. (Ray) 152
Z. L. (Weeks) 69
HYDE, Kate T. (Sloan) 59
Minnie Ball (Black) 256
S. 59
Tristram Tupper 256
HYDRICK, A. J. 86
Minerva (Gardner) 86
V. U. (Riley) 86
Viola (Ulmer) 270
HYRNE, Edward D. 153
Elizabeth (--) 217
Emma Frances (Grant) 153
Henry 217
Mary (Jones) 185
Willie H. 217
IKE, Joseph 183
Rosa (O'Bryan) 183
INABENETT, John 86
INABINET, Frances (New) 108
Annie D. (Autley) 297
INABNET, Lizzie E. 106
INGHAM, H. P. 184
Meta (Sompayrac) 184
INGLESBY, Joseph Scriven 52
Mary C. (Grant) 52
Wm. 52
INGRAM, Estelle (Hagood) 57
INMAN, C. L. (Gault) 273
IRVINE, D. H. 182
Rosa (Bolling) 182
IRWIN, C. M. 24
Cattie (Culp) 123
T. J. 123
ISBELL, S. 39
JACKSON, Cromwell 278
Daniel 25
Ellen (Rosier) 25

Emma (Reel) 278
John 43
Kittie (Fant) 2
Lee (Callahan) 279
Lizzie (Smith) 43
P. Victoria (McGee) 59
Sallie 22
William C. 59
JAMES, A. D. 158
Alice C. (Stack) 220
B. A. 89
Bettie (Crews) 58
Cornelia C. 160
E. J. (Barret) 119
Florence (Hudson) 161
Frederick 161
G. A. (Scarborough) 89
H. A. 253,294
John Hill 58
L. N. 253
Lizzie M. (DeLorme) 32
Martha H. (--) 271
Mary (Woodward) 253
Mary J. (Williams) 80
Mattie E. (--) 158
Mattie J. (Woodward) 135
Phebia (Shockley) 143
Rebecca (Hudson) 253
Robert 32
S. A. (--) 261
S. C. 271
S. E. (Mitchel) 85
Sarah Alberta 89
Spartan 143
W. A. 89,119
W. S. 85
William Thomas 158
Witsell 261
JAMESON, Bettie E. (Wingo) 151
J. 151,165
Mattie A. (Bramlett) 165
JANNEY, Catherine M. (--) 53
Jas. C. 53
JARNIGAN, J. E. 273
S. Alice (Bailey) 273
JARRETT, D. P. 144
Susie (Albright) 144
JARROLD, 101
JAUDON, Harriet (--) 202
JEFCOAT, Elizabeth (Fickling) 250
JEFFCOAT, Barney 120
Rosa (Swann) 120
JEFFERS, Rachel (Grooms) 113
William 178
JEMISON, Mary A. (Moore) 152
JENKINS, J. Mercer 45
Mamie E. (Cuttino) 124
Matilda (--) 195
O. H. 195
JENNINGS, C. (--) 259
Ella (Red) 245
Hannah 155

(LAWTON), Lucinda W. 91
  M. P. 211
  Martha Sarah (--) 138
  Martha Sarah (Willing-
ham) 233
  Pauline E. (Clarke) 270
  Rennie (Erwin) 278
  S. G. 146
  T. O. 211
  T. P. 278
  W. A. 91,101,112
LAYNE, Emma C. (Brook-
banks) 49
  John Y. 49
LEACH, H. E. (Wingo) 247
  P. Warren 95
  Victoria (Campbell) 95
LEAGUE, Berry 193
  S. R. 70
  Sallie (Cox) 193
LEATHERS, Missouri (--)
212,215
  W. W. 298
  William W. 212
LEATHERWOOD, James
248
  S. Jane (Miller) 248
LEAVELL, Hessie (Blake)
220
  John R. Jr. 220
  Marie (Evans) 28
  Mary (George) 65
  Rob't Y. 28
  W. H. 28
  William Hayne 65
LECKIE, Bettie (Mur-
phrey) 282
  R. H. 282
LECROY, H. 63,76,98,-
190,205
  LEE, A. K. 187
  A. M. (--)(Anderson) 157
  Annie (Beasley) 299
  Darling 243
  E. M. 69
  F. M. (Cannon) 270
  Florence (--) 256
  Florence I. (McCullough)
184
  Hattie 276
  Henry 299
  J. P. 276
  James 172
  John 256
  Julia V. (Robinson) 6
  Leana (Burch) 123
  M. F. (Corbett) 187
  M. J. (Brakefield) 221
  Mary (--) 276
  Mary (Williams) 172
  Mary E. (--) 127
  Paul C. 256
  R. H. (--) 184
  Rachel (Turner) 123
  S. H. (Moseley) 69
  Sophronia A. (Armstrong)
78

T. D. 185
  Tyre 177
  Victoria (Phillips) 185
  William 6
  William Lemuel 293
  William S. 123
  Willie R. 221
LEITNER, Celia Davis 45
  George 45
  Maria Eunice 45
LeROY, Addie (Gibert)
249
  Andrew 249
LESESNE, Anna M. (Mc-
Nulty) 143
  Bettie M. (Daniels) 173
  E. R. 143,173
  Marvin 143
LEWIS, A. G. (McCants)
69
  Anna H. (Rawls) 30
  Ella (Stokes) 248
  F. M. (Rowland) 20
  Geo. 183
  J. H. 30
  J. S. 248
  J. W. 5
  James 60
  John W. 241
  Joseph 69
  M. J. (McKeown) 60
  Martha (Reddick) 183
  Rosa (Rhodes) 243
  S. A. (Millwee) 5
  W. W. 60
  William B. 221
LIDDELL, Charles Gaillard
13
  James Simpson 12,13
  Samuel Baylis Alfred 13
  Wm. Anderson 13
LIDE, Annie E. (Reaves)
183
  Annie E. (Wilson) 148
  Carrie M. (Hawkins) 28
  Elizabeth D. (Sparks) 116
  Evan P. 183
  Hugh (Pugh) 200
  R. W. 121, 148, 224, 226,
242, 251, 290
  T. P. 48, 116, 183
  T. P. Jr. 148
  Theodora Lydia (--) 121
  Thomas P. Jr. 28
LILES, Elizabeth R. (--)
289
  H. W. 290
LIMERICK, Mamie E.
(Matthis) 181
  W. W. 181
LINCOLN, Heman 5
  Hetty (--)(Gillison) 5
  Lucinda (Gue) 189
LINDSAY, Alice 257
  Maggie 114
  W. C. 57, 110, 117, 122,
124, 203, 271, 276

LINDSEY, Dillan 56
  John 122
  Martha (Miller) 56
  Melvina (Mobley) 122
LINGLEY, Jas. 162
  Lena (Carr) 162
LIPFORD, B. L. 146
  Bettie (Walker) 293
  M. E. (Simmons) 146
  Wm. P. 293
LIPSCOMB, Agnes (Mc-
Keller) 288
  Elenora (Parker) 36
  Elizabeth (--) 141
  Ella (Motte) 213
  James N. 213
  Nathan 170
  Neddie 170
  Pearl A. (Christman) 295
  T. C. 200
  Tahpenes (Brooks) 141
  Thomas 141
LITTLE, John H. 4
  Martha L. (Robinson) 4
LITTLEJOHN, A. S. (Lit-
tlejohn) 203
  H. H. 203
  J. R. 213
  Kenneth 213
  Polly (Goudelock) 268
  S. M. (Thackston) 244
LIVINGSTON, Anna E.
(Gardner) 95
  Geo. 95
LOADHOLT, Atlie 262
  J. J. 262
  John 273
  M. P. 262
  Nancy (Lynes) 21
  Sibby (--) 273
LOCK, J. A. 19
  Levi 19
  Malinda (--) 19
LOCKE, Absalom 165
  J. C. (Alverson) 252
  Lizzie (Campbell) 165
  Mary Ann 152
LOCKET, Addie 197
  Izabella P. (--) 197
LOCKHART, J. M. 285
  Jane (Brockington) 148
  Willie (McClary) 285
LOGAN, (Ard) 244
  Emma (Herndon) 19
  J. R. 17,19
  Sarah (Patterson) 17
LOMAN, Sallie A. (Meyer)
232
  Wood H. 232
LONDOND, Josephine
(Newman) 55
LONG, A. J. 73
  Bettie (Davenport) 209
  Elizabeth (--) 106
  Henry 149
  Joseph 209
  Josephine (Seele) 111

329

(MERRITT), S. N. 246
  W. A. 202
  Wm. A. 208
MERRIWEATHER, Ware
130
MERRIWETHER, W. 128
MESSER, M. S. 239
METTS, A. E. (Blackmon)
162
  Adella A. 132
  Anna (Ash) 228
  Calvin 243
  Eleanor (--)(Judy) 59
  Fannie (Marshall) 134
  Henrietta (Wallin) 299
  Janie E. 274
  Laura (Riser) 21
  Lawrence 299
  Martha 243
  O. V. 86
  T. C. 162
  V. H. (Player) 86
  W. F. 21
  William B. 132
MEYER, A. D. 120
  Amelia (Foreman) 277
  C. A. (--) 232
  C. C. 140,217
  Cecil 140
  Charlie C. 121
  Fanny (Hicks) 248
  Ida (Stallings) 121
  J. A. 60
  J. J. 227
  Laura A. (Knight) 227
  M. Estelle (Norris) 152
  Mary Ann (Boyles) 103
  Paul Jackson 217
  Ruth (--) 53
  Sallie A. (Loman) 232
  Sallie H. (Miller) 99
  W. M. 103
  Walker 248
  Willie 277
MEYNARDIE, E. J. 53
MICHAELS, Emma M.
(Patrick) 247
  M. A. 247
MICKLE, Mollie (Black-
man) 243
MILAM, F. L. 220
  Lila 220
  Mattie (Duckett) 33
  Rhett 33
  Willie 180
MILER, B. F. 54
  Jonathan M. 145
MILES, Lizzie (Creech) 230
  London 173
  Rosannah F. (Walker) 173
MILFORD, J. C. 241
  Sallie A. (Latimer) 241
  W. J. 125
MILHOUSE, J. H. E. 275
MILLAN, J. F. 165
MILLARD, T. J. 94
MILLER, 283

A. E. (Doughety) 155
A. F. 155
Alice (Smith) 96
Anselm Irvin 145
Archie 223
B. F. 22, 44, 58, 112, 117,
159, 165, 181, 218, 223, 226,
228, 244, 249, 265, 269, 272,
278, 279
B. H. 156
Belle (Wright) 140
Benjamin F. 79
Bessie (Armstrong) 246
Bettie M. (Davis) 156
Carrie (King) 5
E. B. 164
Elizabeth (--) 158
Elizabeth Jane (Evans)
158
Elvira (Harrison) 283
Emmala T. (Reed) 9
Fannie (Taylor) 147
George W. 9
Georgia (Gordon) 295
Hellen (Cockfield) 270
Henry C. 160
J. C. 246
J. D. 13
Jacob 175
James 270
Jane B. (Fraser) 222
John S. 158
Jonathan M. 156
Ledie (Reynolds) 226
Lizzie H. (Morton) 44
Lou (Shuttle) 140
Mamie (Ash) 206
Margaret S. (--) 156
Martha (Lindsey) 56
Mattie (Wells) 58
Nancy (Smith) 223
Nettie (McQuatters) 160
Noah J. 140
S. C. (Cromer) 13
S. H. 237,265
S. Jane (Leatherwood)
248
Sallie H. (Meyer) 99
Stephen 99
Stephen H. 222
W. B. 58
W. W. 248
William 206,226
Willie (Moore) 164
Willie E. 295
MILLFORD, Anna M.
(Walters) 6
  W. J. 6
MILLS, 82
  Hattie E. (Shearer) 247
  Lucinda (King) 73
  W. W. 188
MILLWEE, S. A. (Lewis) 5
MILNOR, John G. 164
  John Glenn 254
MIMMS, Aiken A. 25

MIMS, Cornelia A. (Walk-
er) 118
  Edith C. (Spear) 135
  Fannie (Powers) 67
  Fannie B. (Hartley) 154
  G. D. 204
  James S. 135
  Julia (Jones) 152
  Lessie N. (Walker) 119
  M. 171
  Mary (--) 255
  Mary (Bilton) 171
  Robert 255
  Sallie (Whatley) 204
  Willie S. 118
MINN, Lewis 150
MINOR, Jane (Harling)
191
MINUS, Luella (Walker)
152
MITCHEL, A. H. 81
  Emma S. (Wooley) 81
  Martha (Sanders) 4
  Newton 4
  S. E. (James) 85
MITCHELL, Frank 255
  Hattie (Veazy) 295
  J. W. 282
  Lula (Woolly) 282
  Mary E. "Aunt Polly" (--)
255
  N. E. (Burdett) 217
MITCHUM, Amarintha
(Hood) 153
  Benjamin 153
MITHELL[sic], B. 149
  Lizzie (Armstrong) 149
MIXON, Ellen (Tuten) 103
  Frank 103
  Michael 90
  Ovile (--)(Grooms) 68
  Sarah Eugenia (--) 90
MOAK, Grace (Campbell)
156
  Moses 156
MOBBY, Amelia C. (Gwin)
4
MOBLEY, A. J. 204
  Bettie Madge (Scaife) 118
  Catharine (--) 101,192
  Emma C. (Griffin) 266
  Florence (Wilbourn) 57
  H. P. 118
  John 126,192
  John Richard 266
  L. Y. D. (Dye) 177
  Lizzie (Croxton) 118
  Marion (Wilkes) 288
  Marion Glover (Wilkes)
287
  Mary E. (Griffin) 266
  Mary Elizabeth (Rice) 195
  Melvina (Lindsey) 122
  N. W. (Jones) 192
  Ora (Willard) 135,136
  Richard 135
  S. W. 238

335

O'NEAL, Augusta E. (Sullivan) 85
  Donie (Moye) 291
  Mike 145
  Othello (Burriss) 145
O'QUINN, Elijah 110
  Rebecca (Beard) 110
O'SHEALS, 123
  Mariah (Lawson) 123
O'SHEILDS, Savilia 93
  Madeline (Williams) 230
  Reuben 230
OAKMAN, A. E. (Fell) 211
OATES, Fannie (Outes) 224
ODELL, Mattie (Robinson) 146
  Perrin 146
ODOM, Christian (--) 276
  Eugenia (Eaves) 85
  J. H. 86
  Joseph 231
  Lewis 221,222
  Lizzie A. (Grimball) 22
  Martha (Waldrop) 187
  Mary (--)(Baxley) 231
  Mary (McClanan) 203
  Nellie (Ray) 86
  Perry 187
  Willie 203
ODUM, N. Lena (Gandy) 165
OESTERREICHER, Joseph Pelot 41
  America (Anderson) 58
  D. S. 58
OLIVER, Ella (Stuart) 144
  Fletcher L. (Herlong) 231
  Hugh F. 152,155,230
  Jno. S. 231
ONEAL, F. R. (Moye) 74
  James 74
ORR, 299
  Abi S. (Roberts) 141
  Benjamin Franklin Lawrence 130
  Bettie (Hammett) 53
  C. (--) 177
  James L. Jr. 53
  John B. 182
  John W. B. 130
  Lewis M. 215
  Martha (--) 130
  Mary J. (Tripp) 182
  W. G. 141
ORVIN, H. L. 281
  Hattie L. (China) 281
OSBORN, (Cox) Larrett 175
  (Larrett) Cox 175
OSBORNE, Emma J. (McDavid) 266
OSBURN, Champion 176
OSTEEN, Joseph A. 85
  Leonora L. (Dinkins) 47
  Mary R. (Pack) 85
  Mattie (Smith) 101

N. G. 47
OTT, Fannie (Hughes) 299
  Gustavus 191
  Hampton 299
  J. P. 137
  L. M. 182
  Lizzie (Connelly) 191
  Mary E. (Connelly) 182
  S. 207
  Theodosia A. (Tyler) 137
OUTON, Jackson 97
  Mary (Knight) 97
OUTZS, Brantly 224
  George 224
  Mamie (Pickle) 272
OUZTS, J. L. 274,292,296
  Prannie (Johnson) 247
OWEN, Alice (Nail) 154
  Hattie C. (Paine) 297
OWENS, 299
  C. J. 61
  E. S. 225
  Eliza (Going) 32
  Elizabeth (Lancaster) 42
  Elvira (--) 49
  Emma (Crymes) 1
  Eugene 266
  F. M. 146
  Fannie (Cave) 111
  Fannie (McDonald) 110
  Georgia A. (Wells) 146
  J. Lenora (Boyd) 299
  J. P. 32
  J. Turner 281
  James 299
  Josephine (Coward) 111
  Lizzie (Smith) 225
  M. Adeline (Thompson) 146
  Maggie (Scott) 182
  Minnie (Harde) 266
  Perry Benjamin 61
  R. A. (--) 148,293
  Rebecca A. (--) 61
  Richard S. 1
  Sarah E. (Fowler) 281
  William 42
OWINGS, F. J. 156
  S. D. (Barksdale) 156
OXNER, Martha M. (--) 292
  Mattie (Slengrove) 58
  Mattie (Snelgrove[?]) 58
  Mattie L. (McCarley) 250
PACE, J. K. 207,263,272
PACK, B. M. 281
  Benjamin Joseph 72
  Jessie P. (Hodge) 72
  Mary E. (Hill) 281,289
  Mary R. (Osteen) 85
  Susan Parneice (Cuttino) 259
  T. A. 281
PACKER, Sarah (--) 141
PADEN, Alice (Parsons) 168
  Mark 168

PADGETT, Jennie (Goodson) 229
  Jennie (Turner) 297
  Manchester 239
  N. P. 297
PAGE, John Wesley 136
  Lewis 199
  Lizzie (Woodward) 199
  Mayo (Page) 199
  Nancy Alice (Franks) 136
  Span 199
  W. C. (Howard) 102
  Willie 102
PAINE, Hattie C. (Owen) 297
  J. D. 297
PALK, Vic (Smith) 51
PALMER, Lizzie M. (-Cudd) 151
  M. E. (Lovelace) 270
PANKEY, Lizzie J. (McFadden) 226
PARKER, Albert S. 140
  E. R. 36
  Elenora (Lipscomb) 36
  G. W. 271
  J. A. (Thomas) 225
  J. A. 52
  James A. 37
  Jane (--) 52
  John M. 52
  Laura I. (Mellichamp) 157
  Lulu (Woolly) 271
  Rosa A. (--) 140
  Rosa A. (Burn) 263
  S. P. 225
  Samuel 140,263
PARKMAN, Martha (--)-(Burnett) 267
  Sallie (Bailey) 226
PARKS, Emma (Quarles) 147
  F. G. 46
  Georgia C. (Williams) 46
  Julius C. 159
  Katie (Duckett) 148
  Lewis 159
  Martha A. (--) 159
  T. N. 147
  W. L. 205
PARLER, Annie E. (Cuttino) 263
  Brooks A. 254
  James A. 26,27,36,37,263
  Jane (Norriston) 26
  Laura E. (Hungerpiller) 84
  M. J. 72
  Mary J. (Rickenbaker) 39
  Mary R. (Wells) 97
  Nena Isadora 72
  S. Parniece (Cuttino) 254
  W. R. 38,39,72
  William Ransom 160
PARLOR, J. M. 231
  Victoria (Rast) 231

PARR, E. (--) 37
H. W. 37
Henry W. 90
James H. 233
Mamie (Smith) 233
PARROTT, B. F. 277
Jeanette (Rhodes) 248
Jesse W. 136
Matilda (Wallace) 277
PARSONS, Alice (Paden)
168
Ben L. 211
S. D. 168
Sue H. (Drummond) 211
PASS, L. D. 244
PATE, E. V. (McKay) 96
Flora (Stokes) 97
PATER, Alice (Key) 272
PATRICK, 248
C. M. 176
Charles Maxwell 157
Ella (Wannamaker) 99
Emma M. (Michaels) 247
Francis (Hutto) 100
George W. 51
J. B. 157
J. M. 13
James 99
Julia A. (Judy) 123
Kate R. (--) 176
Lavinia (--) 13
Mary A. (--) 51
Mary Louisa 51
Sarah Elizabeth (Heming-
way) 13
Silas 100
PATTERSON, Anna (Da-
vis) 5
Julia (May) 98
Nellie (Curtis) 296
Sarah (Logan) 17
Simeon 236
W. C. 283
PAUL, E. G. 197
Mary Francesca (Connors)
118
Samuel S. 118
Sarah Ann (King) 197
PAULK, Elvina (Knight)
220
PAULLING, H. C. 119
Maud (Bell) 279
Sallie A. (Carroll) 119
PAYNE, Bettie Pope (Tol-
bert) 42
E. A. (Morton) 257
Eugenia Sidney (Finley)
232
John W. 232
Thomas 42,257
PAYSEUR, G. F. 170
Mattie J. (Boyd) 170
L. C. 254
PAYSUER, Susie 254
PAYTON, Eliza (Williams)
25
PEACE, Mattie (Ross) 133

PEACH, M. E. 75
PEACOCK, 107,111
Eleanor (--) 56
L. E. (Aaron) 85
L. S. 56
Lucretia A. 91
N. W. 103
Nancy (Stansell) 103
S. L. 85
PEAGLER, (Davis) 239
Harriet (Rodgers) 63
Wm. 239
PEAK, J. W. (Jennings)
(Peake) 259
James 259
W. H. 259
PEARSON, W. A. 107,115
Wm. F. 7
PEAY, Caleb 277
E. M. (--) 167
PECK, Martha (Skelton) 34
PEDEN, Emily (Meares) 20
Thomas A. 20
PEEBLES, Jessie C. (Win-
go) 66
Lawrence A. 66
PEEL, Florence L. (Roun-
tree) 101
PEEPLES, B. F. 145,208
B. W. 174
Caledonia V. (Cunning-
ham) 136
Cattie S. (Johnston) 133
Cecil 208
Charlie L. 133
Darling 186,275
E. W. 64,71,85
Ella J. (McTeer) 85
Janette (Caruthers) 174
Jennie L. (Dunbar) 139
Kate Alexander 58
Leila (Hay) 145
Mamie (Willingham) 166
S. D. (--)(Balfour) 64
W. B. 58,166
PEGUES, James 116
Louisa S. (Bronson) 116
Sarah G. (--) 116
Sarah J. (Roberts) 116
Thomas William 116
PELHAM, George 108
Mary (--) 108
PELOT, Lilla (Ulmer) 107
PENDAR, A. (Givens) 151
Preston 151
PENDER, Annie Coor
(Eager) 124
PENDERGRASS, Adaline
(--)(Becknell) 34
Joseph 34
PENN, Fannie M. (Brun-
son) 18
PENNINGTON, B. F. 292
PENTUFF, J. R. 265
P E O C H , Rebecca
(Truesdale) 82
PEOPLES, D. 30

PEPPER, Bettie (Cason)
219
W. A. 219
PERKINS, Bonnie (Tru-
luck) 250
Sallie (Moore) 87
W. F. 87
PERRIN, Elizabeth Lee
(Cothran) 58
Fannie (--) 147
Fannie (--)(Toole) 284
Fannie (Quarles) 79
J. Elizabeth (Waldrop) 50
Mary Ann (Foster) 268
Samuel 79
Thos. C. 58
PERRY, Annie E. (--) 240
E. A. 160,240,275
E. W. 275
Ella (Roberts) 10
Governor 164
J. W. 173
Jennie E. R. (Hover) 41
Mattie (--) 275
Mike W. 160
Sallie J. (Walker) 256
W. H. 204
William 10
PERRYCLEAR, James S.
295
S. C. (--) 295
PETERSON, J. F. 158,159
Josephine S. (Floyd) 61
PETTIGREW, Alice P.
(Bostick) 140
Elizabeth Sparks (--) 214
George 140
PETTIT, Agnes (--) 212
Alice 212
Nathan 212
PETTUS, John 176
M. A. (Richardson) 44
PETTY, W. O. 248,253,-
294,296
PHILLIPS, Annie (Ray-
born) 167
Carrie (Hill) 147
Elias 147
Eliza (Weaver) 285
John 291
Laura (Hankinson) 115
Lenora A. (Kavamah) 66
Mary Elizabeth (Chap-
man) 3
Nancy (--) 169
Victoria (Lee) 185
W. H. 167
PICKET, 287
PICKETT, G. W. 16,21,-
22,30, 31
M. J. 16
PICKLE, J. 272
Mamie (Outzs) 272
PINCHARD, Alice Edg-
erton 234
Bettie (--) 234
Thomas 234

REMBERT, 176
E. T. 219
Hettie V. (Smith) 225
W. H. 225
RENFROE, J. J. D. 147
RENTS, Frank E. (Folk)
205
Holly A. 87
L. B. 87
S. E. 87
RENTZ, C. W. 294
Lizzie (Shuck) 294
S. M. (Terry) 90
REVELL, Frances M. (--)
288
James C. 288
REVILL, Alberta (Jordan)
294
J. C. 294
REY, A. M. 44
REYNOLDS, 49,135
Abram 68
Agnes W. (--) 193
Annie (Broadwater) 267
Carrie (Christian) 227
Charlotte (--) 42
E. E. (Bradley) 80
Eliza Camilla 65
Elizer (--) 65
J. L. 42,95
Julia A. (Stokes) 69
L. S. (--) 16
Ledie (Miller) 226
Lewis 193
M. H. (Bradley) 78
Martha (Scafe) 68
Mary Emma (Medlock)
245
Mollie (Vernon) 228
N. J. V. (Hancock) 97
R. A. 69
V. L. (Hall) 135
W. J. 65
William Snead 42
RHAME, Ada V. (Cloud)
244
B. F. 100
F. G. 210
L. F. (Graden) 159
Olivia (Brockington) 210
RHOADES, S. E. (Senn)
68
RHOADS, Milly Florentine
264
A. J. (Bozeman) 248
C. B. 248,292,293
Curtis (--) 232
Eliza Jane (Robert) 9
Elizabeth (Hicks) 292
Everett 243
Fannie (Bryant) 219
G. Q. S. 261
George 9
J. D. 248
Jeanette (Parrott) 248
Rosa (Lewis) 243
Sallie (--) 261

RICE, A. 3, 4, 6, 10, 13, 18,
34, 56, 156
A. E. 180
Aaron 93
Amaziah 181
B. F. 49,210
B. T. 245
Calvin 93
E. C. 50
Edwin C. 50, 56, 62, 63,
67, 70
Ella Lee (Cox) 191
Ellen (Drummonds) 80
Ellen (Reid) 49
F. U. (--) 294
Fannie Lou 275
Florie (Bryan) 295
Gussie 294
J. A. J. 66
J. B. 266
Jaunita (Hoyt) 182
John T. 295
Juanita (Hoyt) 227
Kate (Dubois) 70
Lizzie (Walker) 245
Lucy A. (Pinson) 56
Mary Elizabeth (Mobley)
195
Rebecca (--)(Nelson) 66
S. Theodosia (King) 180
Sallie A. (Roach) 266
Sally (--) 10
W. B. 294
W. D. 61, 64, 65, 68, 73,
80, 81, 89, 94, 96, 107, 120,
182, 186, 191, 199, 205, 210,
217, 227, 240, 258, 280, 284,
295, 298
William 38
William B. 275
RICH, Emma B. (Pittman)
139
M. S. (Broadway) 28
RICHARDSON, A. R. 99
Ann Letitia 132
Annie 210
Celia D. (Hatcher) 136
E. 54
E. H. (--) 99
J. B. 44
J. T. 264
James C. 99
Jane (Smith) 149
John A. 217
Julia (Brabham) 217
Lizzie (Snider) 151
M. A. (Hodge) 124
M. A. (Pettus) 44
Mamie J. (Cooner) 264
Mary (--) 210
Milton 5
Rhody V. (Andrews) 54
S. M. 22, 41, 53, 67, 68,
70, 107, 118, 136, 147, 155,
166, 223, 225, 229, 272, 274,
276
Sallie L. (Smith) 5

Samuel Richard 180
W. H. 244
RICHBOURG, M. E. (-
Burke) 89
RICHBURG, Charles W.
27
RICHER, Frank 208
Olive Rebecca 208
RICHEY, Jane (McAlister)
294
S. M. 294
RICKENBACKER, Annie
L. (Walker) 137
Cornelia E. (--) 253
Herbert James 253
Thos. E. 253
RICKENBAKER, F. T. 39
Lizzie (Galphin) 244
Mary J. (Parler) 39
Pauline (Able) 39
Thos. E. 244
RIDDEL, Pernicie (Trayn-
ham) 200
RIDDLE, Addie E. (Trayn-
ham) 286
Emma M. (Willis) 206
H. Pinkney 62
J. F. 286
James A. 206
Mary J. (Cheek) 166
Nancy S. (--)(Pulley) 62
RIDGDELL, Mary (--) 115
RIDGE, P. (--)(Agnew) 206
RIDGEWAY, Mary Jane
(Traynham) 299
William Mac 299
RIDGILL, George 173
Rosa (Bradham) 173
RIELLY, Leila (Goodwin)
233
Patrick Henry 233
RIGBY, Charles 110
Edward L. 37
Elizabeth (--) 37
Elizabeth (Hussey) (-
Grimes) 110
Emeline (--) 110
John 110
W. W. 37
William 110
RIGGAN, George W. 234
RIGHT, Sarah Ann (Muse)
140
RILEY, Allen 269
Annie E. (Antley) 269
Barbary (Utsey) 170
C. L. (Burris) 39
Frances L. (--) 61
Freeman W. 61
Henrietta (Shuler) 232
J. M. 160
Jacob 61
Jeremiah 256
Martha (Furman) 94
Mary Jane (Harper) 50
Nancy (--) 160
O. B. 61

344

(SIMPSON), Millie J. (Blackwell) 171
N. G. 31
S. E. (Evans) 46
Sallie J. (Long) 185
W. A. 185
SIMS, J. T. 170
Ross M. (Clanton) 170
SINGELTARY, Georgianna B. (--) 26
John J. 26
Mary Elizabeth 26
SINGELTON, Sarah (Golnich) 124
SINGLETARY, Cornelia (Gelzer) 182
J. H. 249
J. J. 45
James B. 94
O. M. (Hart) 249
SINGLETON, Harriet C. (Griffin) 188
W. B. 188,210
SISTRUNK, S. Oliver 52
Sophia O. (--) 52
Sue M. (Davis) 121
SIZEMORE, A. 166
Florence (Smith) 166
SIZER, Anson 19
Novella (Davidson) 19
SKELTON, Joseph 34
Martha (Peck) 34
SKINNER, James. D. 32
Joseph M. 32
William Colclough 32
SLATER, Hattie R. (Fawcette) 57
John C. 57
Julia (Gennings) 95
SLAWSON, Levi 39
Sue (Crosswell) 39
SLENGROVE, Mattie (Oxner) 58
W. 58
SLIGH, Claudia (Abney) 96
Elizabeth (--) 212
L. H. 96
P. B. 212
SLOAN, 169
Annie Maxwell (--) 139
C. H. 59
Charles 131
Curran H. 236
Dora (Dawson) 131
James M. 7
Kate T. (Hyde) 59
M. Lillian (Trowbridge) 262
R. Duff 262
Sallie J. (Lynch) 7
Septima (Gresham) 131
SMART, H. C. 118,148,-251,284
R. D. 136
SMELTZER, J. P. 197
SMITH, A. Coke 91, 125, 134

A. L. (Scarborough) 110
A. M. 282
Ada (Gorder) 284
Alice (Graham) 188
Alice (Miller) 96
Armedia (Langley) 120
Augusta (--) 102
Barbara A. (Bearden) 282
Beauregard 148
Bettie Sloan (Mauldin) 61
C. A. 206
C. M. (Carter) 147
C. T. 225
Carrie (Whitmire) 180
Carrie E. (McCreary) 218
D. B. 58
D. T. 61,137,221
D. Townsend 275
David Henry 264
Dora (Finckney) 223
E. E. 28,232
E. F. (Barnes) 187
E. F. 225
E. Julia (Mauldin) 16
E. Julia (Mauldin)(Whilden) 262
Edmond S. 281
Eliza (Duncan) 71
Elizabeth (--) 223
Elizabeth (Cuttino) 264
Ella (Holtzclaw) 148
Ellen (Shuler) 246
Elvira T. (Westmoreland) 148
Emeline (--)(Gambrell) 4
Emily (Garrison) 261
Emma (Maddox) 281
Emma C. (Stone) 132
Emma Caroline (--) 22
Ester C. (Baker) 199
F. J. 187
Fannie (Hogan) 113
Fannie E. (Boyd) 31
Fannie Lorena (Byrd) 206
Fannie S. (Kogn) 134
Fletcher 10
Florence (Sizemore) 166
Fred. 223
G. H. W. 296
Georgie 283
Hattie (Crook) 279
Henry 104,110
Henry M. 290
Henry Mason 92
Hettie V. (Rembert) 225
Hugh S. 147
Ida (Lancaster) 121
J. C. 71
J. Harvey 128,188
J. K. 149
J. McK. 96
J. Rierson 218
J. W. 55
Jack W. 284
James T. 58
Jane (Richardson) 149
Joanna (--) 89

John 63
John D. 64,223
John S. 6
Julia (--) 92
Julia E. (McKnight) 59
Julius C. 148
Kate N. (--) 128
Kohath 165
L. (Goff) 55
Landgrave Thomas 264
Laura (DeBoice) 153
Laura (Lake) 136
Lawson H. 59
Letty (Hawkins) 34
Levi 34
Lizzie (Jackson) 43
Lizzie (Kinard) 151
Lizzie (Owens) 225
Lizzie M. (Dantzler) 153
Luther 246
M. E. 199
M. J. (Long) 149
M. Lula (Tyler) 137
M. M. (Wideman) 296
M. T. 221
M. Tallulah 275
Maggie (Tucker) 58
Major 89
Mamie (Bostic) 242
Mamie (Parr) 233
Margaret Ann (Gandy) 290
Martha (Lancaster) 36
Martha A. B. (Ammons) 226
Mary A. (--) 194
Mattie (Osteen) 101
Miles 71
N. Alice E. (Morris) 129
Nancy (Miller) 223
Nannie E. (Shaw) 3
R. Sanders 4
Robert 2,180
Rosa P. (Cocke) 133
S. V. (Ulmer) 71
Sallie (Alexander) 44
Sallie (Smith) 28
Sallie C. (--) 232
Sallie L. (Richardson) 5
Samie 92
Savage 264
Shuler (Hilton) 169
Sue L. (Shirley) 6
Susan (Baker) 97
T. P. 62
T. R. 226
T. W. 51,90,124,128
Tallulah 275
Terrill 257
Thomas 149
Thomas P. 262,264
Thomas Peter 221
Thomas W. 193
Thomas Wilson 192
V. E. (Carpenter) 225
Vic (Palk) 51
Victoria (Cuming) 34

348

(TINDAL), Joseph S. 72
TINSON, Mary E.
(Crymes) 7
TISDALE, Estelle (Mc-Crea) 272
James 272
Martha B. (McCullough) 229
Samuel 229
TOBIN, (Robison) 111
Cornelius 111
TODD, Lula (Anderson) 216
TOLBERT, A. E. (Nunnery) 96
Annie (Henderson) 224
Bettie Pope (Payne) 42
J. R. 42
R. R. 224
TOLLESON, Alice (Meng) 135
John 135
Mary (--) 203
TOMPKINS, Carrie S. (Blackwell) 244
J. H. 244
Judge 297
S. James 37
TOMPSON, Martha A. (Burress) 3
TOOLE, 284
Fannie (--)(Perrin) 284
G. L. 266
Susan (--) 266
TOWILL, A. M. (Bell) 35
Angie (Bell) 81
R. J. 35
Richard Judson 81
TOWNES, A. S. 20,128
Annie L. (Harris) 241
Ella (McKellar) 128
G. F. 224
Kate F. (Corbett) 224
L. B. (Brooks) 71
Lillie B. (White) 20
Lizzie A. (Adams)(Dargan) 223
TOWNSEND, John 33
Susan M. 33
TRAIL, Hattie L. (McCarley) 207
J. B. 207
TRAPP, Elder 179
Ella (Vann) 111
J. 44,59
Mollie (Campbell) 59
Scynthia (--) 41
TRAYNHAM, Addie E. (Riddle) 286
J. A. 200
J. J. 286
James H. 78
Lee Annie (Davis) 283
Mary F. (Brown) 78
Mary Jane (Ridgeway) 299
Milton H. 283
Nimrod 299

Pernicie (Riddel) 200
TRAYWICK, J. B. 78
TRESZER, F. G. 257
Florence F. (Foster) 257
TRIBBLE, Betty (Davis) 32
C. T. 21
Emma P. (Burns) 21
James R. 260
L. W. 260
Maimee Mauldin (--) 238
R. M. 238
TRIMNAL, Mary (Hatfield) 120
TRIPP, Ellis 182
Mary J. (Orr) 182
TROWBRIDGE, M. Lillian (Sloan) 262
S. F. 262
TROWEL, Jonas 33
TRUESDALE, Eliza Ann (Westall) 84
Louis 84
Rebecca (Peoch) 82
Wm. 82
TRUITT, M. E. (Jennings) 271
TRULUCK, Bonnie (Perkins) 250
Isadore M. 192
N. C. (Hinds) 192
Sallie (Chandler) 234
Solus 237
Vermelle (Player) 237
W. D. 250
TUCKER, Clara (Jeter) 139
J. L. 124
Maggie (Smith) 58
Mattie (Carroll) 202
W. J. 21
TUPPER, James 14
TURKETT, Delilah (--) 233
TURNER, Alfred 128
Alice (Eidson) 219
Anna (Harris) 151
Della (Stallings) 54
Emma A. (Johnson) 51
G. R. 292
G. W. 258
H. Ana (Mayson) 19
J. A. 282
J. M. 51,194
J. S. 208
J. W. 13
Jennie (Crews) 240,258
Jennie (Padgett) 297
Joe 123
John 227
John M. 215
Josie (Kelly) 203
Lawrence 151
Lizzie (Rudd) 70
M. J. (--) 292
Mary (--) 88,89
P. A. (McAbee) 230
R. 199
Rachel (Lee) 123

Randolph 238
Ray F. McNeil 292
Sallie (Sharpton) 227
Sallie D. (Cornwell) 208
Toliver C. 53
W. Preston 70
William 89
Z. E. (--) 215
TUTEN, Ellen (Mixon) 103
TWIGGINS, Mary (Mc-Dougall) 260,261
Robert 260,261
TWITTY, Alice (Temple) 228
Geo. T. 228
TYLER, (Dowling) 108
C. E. 150,267
M. Lula (Smith) 137
Mary A. (Nealy)(Mason) 267
R. E. 65
S. (Lafitte) 150
Theodosia A. (Ott) 137
ULMER, Ann (Austin) 128
Eliza (--) 233
Elizabeth L. (--) 248
Ella C. (Wilson) 295
Ephraim 233
Henry 65
Janie E. (Free) 65
John C. 270
John H. 107
Lilla (Pelot) 107
Livia (Fersener) 195
Milton 195
S. V. (Smith) 71
Viola (Hydrick) 270
W. R. 295
UNDERWOOD, Peggy 23
William 23
USSURY, John W. 85
Victoria (Reddy) 85
UTSEY, Barbary (Riley) 170
VAIL, Sarah R. E. (De-Hay) 116
T. L. C. 116
VAM, Elizabeth (--) 125
VANCE, A. C. (--)(Hearst) 169
Cecilia (--) 20
J. K. 169
VANDIVER, H. 10
VANLANDINGHAM, Jennie (Caskey) 185
VANN, Charlotte W. (--) 210
Ella (Trapp) 111
R. R. 65, 96, 111-113, 148, 181, 210
Sallie (Macon) 65
T. F. 111
VARN, Frank Curtiss 297
G. Johnnie 297
Hattie (--) 297
VARNER, A. P. 203
M. E. (Murrell) 203

VASS, Annie 118
  J. L. 66
VAUGHAN, Cynthia (Clement) 50
  Francis E. (Hawkins) 148
  John 148
  K. 50
  M. T. 173
  Mary B. 173
  W. F. 173
VAUGHN, Annie (Moore) 88
  Frances M. (Woodson) 13
  Janie (Going) 273
  Joseph P. 88
  K. 13
  Lizzie (Newman) 159
  Richard H. 159
VEAZY, Hattie (Mitchell) 295
  W. B. W. 295
VENNING, R. M. 209
VERMILLION, John H. 132
  Laura L. (Shockley) 132
VERNON, A. T. 228
  Mollie (Reynolds) 228
VISAGE, Elizabeth (Rochester) 5
VOGT, A. M. 134
WACTER, J. W. 43
  Sarah R. (Welldon) 43
WADE, H. S. (--) 64
  Julia (Fairy) 254
  S. L. (Bates) 271
  W. D. 271
WAKEFIELD, Wm. M. 198
WALDEN, Lucinda (--)-(Frachuer) 5
WALDROP, E. F. 112
  Farnk E. 50
  J. Elizabeth (Perrin) 50
  Lou (Rochester) 112
  Martha (Odom) 187
  Sarah (--) 187
WALKER, (Carter) 106
  A. B. 93
  A. R. 137
  Annie L. (Rickenbacker) 137
  Bettie (Lipford) 293
  Cornelia A. (Mims) 118
  D. J. (--) 121
  Dora (Cooper) 271
  Elizabeth 263
  Ernest 286
  Esther (--) 111
  F. N. 256
  Floyd 152
  George 106
  George T. L 286
  Hattie (--) 286
  Isabella "Belle" (Hickson) 145
  J. B. 46
  J. C. (Hudson) 256
  J. N. 263

James B. 231
John B. 25
John C. 293
John H. 173
Lessie N. (Mims) 119
Lila A. (Weathersbee) 68
Lizzie (Rice) 245
Lizzie (Shaw) 155
Luella (Minus) 152
Martha (--) 46,231
Mary (--) 204
Mary A. (Courtney) 203
Mattie (Marston) (Brantly) 25
Mattie M. (Whitlock) 199
N. G. W. 79,245
N. W. 30
Nathaniel 30
Rosannah F. (Miles) 173
S. T. (Friday) 67
Sallie J. (Perry) 256
Sallie R. (Norris) 93
Silas 16
Susan (--) 155
W. S. 67
Winton T. 119
WALL, Emily (Ballenger) 296
WALLACE, Antoinette S. (--) 40
  Harriet Emma (--) 39
  J. C. 40
  Lucy C. (Spearman) 179
  Matilda (Parrott) 277
  Robert G. 179
WALLIN, Henrietta (-Metts) 299
WALLING, Aura E. (Winter) 208
  J. Burnett 104
  P. L. 208
WALLS, Mamie (Barden) 224
WALMSEY, Capt. 229
WALTER, S. S. 247
WALTERS, Anna M. (Millford) 6
  E. J. 104
  Lucia (Wheeler) 244
  S. S. 104
  W. E. 1-5,9,10,244
  William E. 6
WALTHALL, Joseph S. 24
WALTON, Alice (Spires) 63
  Ida (Cromley) 159
WANNAMAKER, Ella (Patrick) 99
WARD, Fannie (Burnett) 134
  Frances Ella (Tharp) 74
  W. M. 134
  W. W. 74
WARDLAW, Callie (-Cheatham) 131
  George 131
WARE, Henry 22

WARREN, A. M. 221
  Carson 123
  Frederick 76
  G. 76
  Lilis (Epting) 221
  Maggie (Shannon) 123
  Marcella (Thompson) 77
  R. J. 223
  Willie Bell (Douglass) 223
WASHINGTON, Mollie T. (Wright)(Reddin) 231
WATERS, C. E. 246
  Fannie M. (Backstrom) 165
  Fanny D. (Kerr) 246
  Ida (Brice) 273
  J. J. 273
  Wm. J. 165
WATKINS, Charles T. 179
  Emma C. (Hill) 179
  J. B. 207
  Lula (Dean) 207
  Minnie (Earnest) 109
  Zedekiah 255
WATKINSON, Zedekiah 200
WATLEY, E. M. 297
  Francis E. (Seigler) 297
WATSON, Addie W. (Bethea) 285
  Annie (Benson) 246
  C. E. (Kenington) 101
  D. S. 270
  E. C. (--) 293
  Edward B. 285
  Eugenia (Duckett) 102
  J. J. 246
  J. W. 43
  James 158
  Jasper 246
  John J. 144
  Kate McIver (Edwards) 283
  Lizzie (McMillan) 158
  Matthew H. 232
  Mollie (Cooper) 246
  Nannie 270
  R. B. 283
  Rosy M. (McRady) 43
WATTS, Anna B. (--) 62
  Della (Finley) 63
  Emily (Spearman) 45
  Emma 62
  J. B. 62
  James 45
  John B. 50
  Laura 109
  Lizzie (Rook) 109
  Marcus 63
  Priscilla (--) 45
  Richard 109
WAY, Willie (Zimmons) 258
WEARN, Etta (Boyd) 94
WEATHERFORD, Minnie E. (Cox) 252

WEATHERS, B. E. (Lanford) 225
  Edwin E. 114
  M. Lizzie (Harrison) 114
WEATHERSBEE, Flurnoy 268
  Hampton 106,111
  J. W. 194
  John Allen 68,243
  L. S. (Ransey) 111
  Lila A. (Walker) 68
  Martha S. 194
  ·Meta Lou 243
  Sallie (Rountree) 100
  W. F. 268
WEAVER, Eliza (Phillips) 285
  John 104
  John M. 285
  William 285
WEBB, Gertrude (Brownlee) 284
  Hammond 284
  Isabella C. (--)(Barr) 167
  J. M. 105
  Lucinda (--) 105
  Mamie E. (Keene) 110
  Sallie 105
WEBBER, Julia (Barnett) 55
WEBER, F. 124
  Ida (Newbill) 124
WEBSTER, Maggie (Wilkins) 162
  Noah 162
WEEKLEY, W. K. 120
WEEKS, Annie E. 212
  Eugenia C. (--) 212
  F. L. (--) 92
  Gula (Segler) 63
  J. M. 68,69,99,100,140
  J. S. 72
  James 63,87
  James M. 59,117
  Joseph 117
  M. (Lacky) 49
  Mary (Wells) 61
  Mary A. (--) 140
  R. P. 61
  Robert S. 212
  Z. L. (Hutto) 69
WEIR, J. W. 246
  John 127
  Laura (Castles) 127
  Maggie (Thompson) 21
  Vic (Banks) 124
  Wm. 21
WELBORN, Martin J. 235
  Annie (Price) 235
WELCH, E. V. (Shuler) 110
  James 40
  Julia (Lyrely) 86
  N. H. 265
WELDON, M. E. (Weldon) 67
  Mattie (Mathis) 102

William A. 67
WELLDON, Sarah R. (Wacter) 43
WELLER, R. H. 261
WELLS, Alice M. (Hitt) 56
  Carrie B. (Wilkes) 145
  Charles 61
  E. J. (McWatters) 44
  G. W. 97
  George 22
  Georgia A. (Owens) 146
  Henry H. 134
  Lou (Hodge) 204
  Mary (Weeks) 61
  Mary R. (Parler) 97
  Mattie (Miller) 58
  N. E. (Dunn) 44
  Peter 145
  R. N. 157
  S. P. 146
  W. B. 85
WELSH, John M. 250
  Mary A. (Harrington) 65
  Vermelle (Hicks) 250
  William E. 65
WERTS, J. Belton 152
  Susan J. (--) 152
WEST, Anna H. (Woodside) 276
  B. P. 253,276
  Betty (Aycock) 179
  Bonham (Wofford) 176
  Catherine (Brown) 81
  Dora L. (Gardner) 139
  Henry 82
  J. S. 246
  J. T. 139
  J. Toliver 171
  Joseph A. 179
  Sallie (Covington) 253
  Sallie (Munn) 81
  Samuel Jr. 81
  William J. 293
WESTALL, Eliza Ann (Truesdale) 84
WESTMORELAND, Elvira T. (Smith) 148
  George 148
WEYMAN, 137
WHALEY, R. B. (Rudd) 113
WHAM, John 152
WHATLEY, Alice (Kemp) 247
  Anna Maria (Hollingsworth) 238
  E. B. (--) 186
  Eliza (Still) 247
  H. H. (Hickman) 186
  Julia 186
  Mary Alice (Henderson) 159
  O. T. 293
  Sallie (Mims) 204
  T. B. 270
WHEELER, Lucia (Walters) 244

R. P. 244
WHELER, R. Miles 41,63
  Sallie C. (Stiles) 41
  Sallie Catherine (Stiles) 63
WHERRY, Mattie (Garrison) 163
WHETSTONE, M. B. (Brooker) 296
WHILDEN, B. W. 217
  Bayfield W. 221
  E. Julia (Mauldin) (Smith) 262
  Elias 47
  Eliza Ann (Nettles) 47
  Joseph 14
  Mary H. (--) 221
  R. Furman 151,187
  Screven Hart 151
  W. B. 105,116
  William G. 262
WHISONANT, Eliza Jane (Hardin) 21
  Joseph 22
WHIT, Adaline (Gambrell) 10
WHITAKER, Idella (Dodson) 234
WHITE, A. Judson 211
  Albert Ferguson 218
  Annie (Young) 188
  Belle (McClure) 4
  C. G. 168
  C. W. 92
  Cora A. (--)(Thomson) 199
  Corrie (Jones) 220
  Corrie J. (Jones) 211
  F. C. 263
  Florence B. (Cole) 163
  Hattie L. (Evans) 184
  J. A. 286,297
  J. T. 184
  Jane K. (Carter) 70
  Julia F. (Danner) 216
  Lillie B. (Townes) 20
  Lou (Cheatham) 244
  Luke D. 244
  M. A. (Kinard) 92
  Maggie (Christian) 247
  Matthew O. 216
  Nannie T. (Benson) 6
  Preston 197
  Robert 23
  Robert A. 163
  Sallie E. (Ferguson) 263
  Thomas M. 6
  William N. 4
WHITEFORD, Bettie (Noffz) 67
WHITEHEAD, Ben 276
  Ida M. (Sanders) 276
WHITEMON, Carrie E. (Bodie) 83
  S. W. 83
WHITEN, P. E. (Willard) 168

WHITLOCK, Franklin L.
199
  Harvey 283
  Mattie M. (Walker) 199
  S. A. (Kitchings) 282
WHITMAN, H. A. 117,207
  Hattie L. (McCants) 117
WHITMIRE, Alma M.
(McMahan) 183
  Carrie (Smith) 180
  Clayton (Reeder) 23
  D. A. (--) 263
  E. D. 187
  Edna (--) 281
  J. Brown 66
  Joseph 160
  Mary Susan (--) 160
  Metta M. (Comer) 161
  N. P. 23
  Nathan 281
  Sallie (Moon) 187
  Sallie E. (Duckett) 66
  Sallie E. (East) 281
WHITNEY, Charlotte W.
(--) 36
  Henry O. 36
  James H. 36
WICKS, Abraham 83
  Alice (Taylor) 122
  Emma (Cain) 83
WIDEMAN, Anna M. (--)
293
  Anna M. (Harrison) 153
  Annie H. (--) 228
  J. H. 251
  J. L. 153,228,293
  James 296
  James A. 282
  James Harrison 228
  James LeRoy 293
  Lucia (Harrison) 54
  M. M. (Smith) 296
  Mamie (Youngblood) 282
  Mamie W. (Youngblood)
251
WIER, Elisabeth (Castle)
59
  James 59
WIGGINS, Jane (--) 253
  Mary (McGee) 29
  Thomas 29
WILBOURN, Florence
(Mobley) 57
  G. C. 57
WILBUR, Lula M. (Thorn-
hill) 267
  T. A. 164
  Theodore A. 164,267
WILBURN, Jasper 135
  Mattie (Greer) 135
WILDER, Charles 90
  J. M. N. 33
  M. R. (Brunson) 90
  Mary J. (Brockington) 33
WILEY, M. Leroy 165
  Marietta (Atkins) 165

WILKES, Carrie B. (Wells)
145
  J. W. 215
  John E. 145
  John W. 173,287
  L. A. (--) 296
  Marian (--) 215
  Marion (Mobley) 288
  Marion Glover (Mobley)
287
  Thomas 215
  W. M. 296
WILKINS, A. C. 216, 223,
224, 228, 279
  John W. 162
  M. A. (Grant) 203
  Maggie (Webster) 162
  Martin L. 130
  S. B. 82,90
  S. G. 257
WILKINSON, H. Mack 278
  Maggie A. (Kohn) 278
WILKS, E. Alston 297
  J. R. 22
  L. (Rowell) 279
  Mattie (Byars) 297
  Regina (Carter) 22
  William 279
WILLARD, Ella Y. (Go-
ber) 179
  Ora (Mobley) 135
  P. E. (Whiten) 168
  Robert 135
WILLEFORD, A. S. 62, 64,
70, 78, 80-82, 84, 91, 97, 98,
114, 118, 129, 197, 221, 257,
259, 275
  Chas. R. 292, 294
WILLIAMS, 20, 95
  Adaline (--) 16
  Amanda (--) 287
  Angus 84
  Annie E. (Willson) 154
  Annie Lela (Strom) 245
  Antoinette (Lanneau) 214
  Arthur 231
  B. S. 39
  Belle (McCreary) 231
  C. H. B. 245
  Callie (Bates) 101
  Christiana (McDavid) 3
  Davis H. 230
  E. (--) 90
  E. (Ballard) 47
  E. (Fenters) 184
  E. M. (--) 259
  E. V. (--) 178
  E. V. (McMillan) 54
  Eliza (Payton) 25
  Elizabeth (Fenters) 184
  Elizabeth A. (--) 153
  Ella (Crouch) 82
  Emily (--) 39,44
  Emma (Thurmond) 297
  Eugene Harvey 74
  F. L. (--) 245
  Fanny (--) 58

Francis L. 246
Fred. 172
G. A. (--) 184
G. F. 172, 178, 202, 283,
293
G. K. 58
G. Newton 181
G. W. 27
Georgia C. (Parks) 46
Gilbert 290
Govan 90
H. A. 259
Henry 90
Henry R. 158
Hiller 82
J. 47
J. G. 27, 49, 54, 57, 294,
295
J. Jefferson 101
J. M. 35
J. R. 176
James A. 251
James L. 25
John 187
John Angus 99
John B. 266
John G. 44, 80, 83, 152,
178, 186, 216, 278
Jones M. 99
Jordan 153
Julia H. (Laramore) 153
K. M. (Hankinson) 54
Laura (Stallings) 103
Laura A. (Johnson) 235
Lillie M. (McMullen) 211
Lizzie (Duncan) 187
Lula (Cheatham) 202
M. A. (Carter) 87
M. W. 16
Madeline (O'Shields) 230
Manie (Gaines) 64
Martha (Freeman) 186
Mary (Knight) 176
Mary (Lee) 172
Mary (Taylor) 266
Mary Ann M. (Floyd) 87
Mary J. (James) 80
Mary V. (Compton) 181
Minnie (Hoover) 116
Mont. 87
N. B. 206,245
N. H. 87
Nannie (Beatty) 298
Nathan D. 235
R. J. 272
R. S. 54
Rasselas P. M. 39
Rebecca T. (--) 99
Robert 116
Robert L. 189
Sarah E. (--) 231
Theodore 64
Thomas 94
W. H. 100
W. J. 211
W. J. D. 187
W. K. 298

Herritage Books by Brent H. Holcomb:

*Ancestors and Descendants of Charles Humphries (d. 1837)
of Union District, South Carolina, 1677–1984*

Bute County, North Carolina, Land Grant Plats and Land Entries

*CD: Early Records of Fishing Creek Presbyterian Church,
Chester County, South Carolina, 1799–1859*

CD: Kershaw County, South Carolina, Minutes of the County Court, 1791–1799

CD: Marriage and Death Notices from The Charleston [S.C.] Observer, *1827–1845*

CD: South Carolina, Volume 1

*CD: Winton (Barnwell) County, South Carolina Minutes of
County Court and Will Book 1, 1785–1791*

*Chester County, South Carolina, Deed Abstracts,
Volume I: 1785–1799 [1768–1799] Deed Book A-F*

Chester County, South Carolina, Will Abstracts: 1787–1838 [1776–1838]

Death and Marriage Notices from the Watchman *and* Observer, *1845–1855*

*Early Records of Fishing Creek Presbyterian Church, Chester County,
South Carolina, 1799–1859, with Appendices of the Visitation List of
Rev. John Simpson, 1774–1776 and the Cemetery Roster, 1762–1979*
Brent H. Holcomb and Elmer O. Parker

Guide to South Carolina Genealogical Research and Records, Revised

Jackson of North Pacolet: Descendants of Samuel Jackson, Sr.

Kershaw County, South Carolina, Minutes of the County Court, 1791–1799

Laurens County, South Carolina, Minutes of the County Court, 1786–1789

*Lower Fairforest Baptist Church, Union County, South Carolina:
Minutes 1809–1875, Membership Lists through 1906*

*Marriage and Death Notices from Columbia, South Carolina Newspapers, 1838–1860;
Including Legal Notices from Burnt Counties*

*Marriage and Death Notices from Baptist Newspapers of South Carolina:
Volume 1: 1835–1865*

*Marriage and Death Notices from Baptist Newspapers of South Carolina:
Volume 2: 1866–1887*

Marriage and Death Notices from The Charleston Observer, *1827–1845*

*Marriage and Death Notices from the
Charleston, South Carolina,* Mercury, *1822–1832*

Marriage and Death Notices from the Southern Presbyterian:
*Volume I: 1847–1865
Volume II: 1865–1879
Volume III: 1880–1891
Volume IV: 1892–1908*

*Marriage and Death Notices from the Up-Country of South Carolina
as Taken from Greenville Newspapers, 1826–1863*

Memorialized Records of Lexington District, South Carolina, 1814–1825

*Newberry County, South Carolina Deed Abstracts,
Volume I: Deed Books A-B, 1785–1794 [1751–1794]*

www.ingramcontent.com/pod-product-compliance
Lightning Source LLC
Chambersburg PA
CBHW070239290326
41929CB00046B/1971